COMPARATIVE GOVERNMENT AND POLITICS

COMPARATIVE GOVERNMENT AND POLITICS
Series Editor: Vincent Wright

Published

Robert Elgie
Political Leadership in Liberal Democracies

Rod Hague, Martin Harrop and Shaun Breslin
Comparative Government and Politics
(3rd edition)

Neill Nugent
The Government and Politics of the European Community
(2nd edition)

Tony Saich
The Government and Politics of China

Anne Stevens
The Government and Politics of France

Stephen White, John Gardner, George Schöpflin and Tony Saich
**Communist and Post-Communist Political Systems:
An Introduction**
(3rd edition)

Forthcoming

Rudy Andeweg and Galen A. Irwin
Dutch Politics

Nigel Bowles
American Government and Politics

Paul Heywood
The Government and Politics of Spain

Robert Leonardi
Government and Politics in Italy

Douglas Webber
The Government and Politics of Germany

COMPARATIVE GOVERNMENT AND POLITICS

An Introduction

Third Edition

Rod Hague
Martin Harrop
Shaun Breslin

MACMILLAN

First edition 1982
Reprinted 1984, 1985, 1987
Second edition 1987
Reprinted 1988, 1989, 1990 (twice), 1991, 1992
Third edition 1992
Reprinted 1993, 1994

Published by
THE MACMILLAN PRESS LTD
Houndmills, Basingstoke, Hampshire RG21 2XS
and London
Companies and representatives
throughout the world

ISBN 0–333–55819–7 hardcover
ISBN 0–333–55820–0 paperback

A catalogue record for this book is available
from the British Library

Copy-edited and typeset by Povey/Edmondson
Okehampton and Rochdale, England

Printed in Great Britain by
Mackays of Chatham PLC
Chatham, Kent

Summary of Contents

Contents

PART 3 *THE SOCIAL CONTEXT OF POLITICS*

PART 4   *THE STRUCTURES OF GOVERNMENT*

PART 5 *POLICIES AND PERFORMANCE*

List of Tables, Figures, Maps, Exhibits and Exercises

■ Tables

■ Figures

■ Maps

■ Exhibits

■ Exercise

Preface

When a journalist asked British Prime Minister Harold Macmillan which aspect of the job caused him most difficulty, he replied, 'Events, dear boy, events.' We know just what he meant. Rewriting this book to take account of the dramatic events in the political world in the late 1980s and early 1990s has proved to be a challenging exercise.

In this new edition, we have given full coverage to the collapse of communism and to the emergence of postcommunist regimes in Eastern Europe. In rewriting all the sections on the second world, we aimed to give at least as much coverage to postcommunist governments as to their predecessors. In fact, limits of information and perspective mean that we have not kept completely to our own promise. But we think it has borne fruit anyway. We are delighted that Shaun Breslin, a young second-world specialist at Newcastle, agreed to join the existing authors for this edition – and we're even more pleased with his vivid coverage of the momentous developments in the second world.

On a minor note, we have used the past tense when referring to communist party states, except when discussing those states (notably China), where communist rulers still hang on to power.

The democratic revolution in the third world has been quieter, but perhaps no less important, than the changes in the second world. The retreat of the generals in Latin America has transformed the nature of regimes there. Elsewhere, international pressures have encouraged a transition towards democracy. We have sought to reflect these developments, too, in this edition.

All this raises the question: If democracy is now universal, why have we retained a three worlds approach? The answer is that we still think this is the best and simplest way to capture contrasts between countries. The political differences between Canada, Chile and Czechoslovakia remain fundamental, even if they all now share democratic forms. The political agenda in a country is set by where a country comes from, as well as where it is now. The agenda also depends on the country's relationship to the world economy. On both dimensions, the differences between the three worlds are still vast.

The world, however, continues to shrink. Traditionally, comparative politics texts, including this one, have underplayed the whole issue of interdependence between nations. We have therefore added a new chapter on 'the nation-state in one world' to this edition. Its purpose is to draw out those features of global politics which impinge most on politics within the nation-state. It reflects our belief that the dynamics of politics rest neither in national nor in global politics, but rather in the interaction between the two.

This book conforms to the law that new editions are always bigger. 'Elections and voters' and 'the military and police' now rate chapters of their own. Indeed, the section on the police is entirely new. The two opening chapters have also been strengthened, in order to provide a general introduction to political concepts (Chapter 1) and to comparative politics specifically (Chapter 2). New sections in other chapters include: majority and consensus democracy (Chapter 3); 1989 – the year of revolutions (Chapter 4); postmaterialism (chapter 6); new politics, public opinion, opinion polls and the media (Chapter 7); and the welfare state (Chapter 16).

We're pleased that this book is used in several countries where English is not the first language. We owe a special duty of clarity to such readers and we have made an effort to improve our expression throughout the book. Alison Wright, a recent politics graduate, went through the text for us, simplifying paragraphs, sentences and words. Passive sentences were also transformed by her into active ones (though she missed that one!) We are grateful to her for this careful work and to Paul Gliddon, another politics graduate, for compiling the index. Thanks also to Keith Povey, our copy editor for three editions of the book, for his painstaking work.

In these days of expanding student numbers, it's important for texts to provide students with a framework for independent study. We have tried to achieve this by including discussion points and key readings at the end of each chapter. We've also added an appendix giving detailed advice on information sources. We hope this will be useful for students' essays and projects. The appendix includes a detailed list of recent country and area studies, many (not all!) of which were used in preparing this edition. We've also included more signposting in this edition, through a more detailed contents section and by adding chapter summaries. In response to feedback from students, this edition also contains more devices to break up the text and an extensive glossary of concepts.

We want to thank all our colleagues around the world who responded to our request for advice on how best to revise the book. The replies (and reading lists) really were helpful in setting the agenda for the revisions. Comments from experts on particular countries also helped us to broaden our range of examples, and in particular to provide more coverage of Australasia, North America, the Netherlands and Scandinavia. We're especially grateful to the wise owls who advised us not to change too much!

Specific thanks to:

Peter Aimer, University of Auckland
Rudy Andeweg, University of Leiden
Hugh Berrington, University of Newcastle upon Tyne
Craig Dearden, University of Newcastle upon Tyne
George Jones, London School of Economics
Steven Kennedy, Macmillan
Jan-Erik Lane, Lund University,
Roger Leys, Institute of Political Studies, Copenhagen
Chris Rudd, University of Otago
Ulf Sundhaussen, University of Queensland
Vincent Wright, Nuffield College, Oxford

The authors and publishers are grateful to *The Observer* for permission to reproduce the article by Sir John Harvey-Jones in its edition of 25 August 1991.

What began in the 1980s as an introduction to comparative government has now broadened out in the 1990s into a comparative introduction to politics. Although the book itself has changed over the years, our underlying aim has not. We have sought to write a clear and up-to-date introduction to politics for students beginning their study of the subject. We hope this edition goes a little further towards fulfilling that objective.

ROD HAGUE
MARTIN HARROP
SHAUN BRESLIN

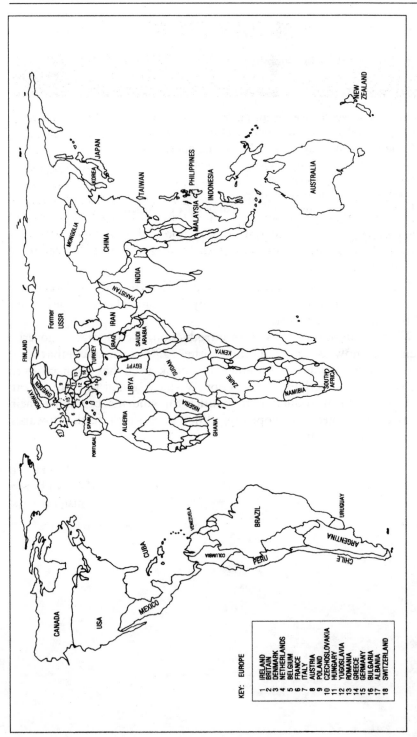

Peters' projection of the world

■ *PART 1* ■

STUDYING POLITICS

This Part provides a conceptual and comparative introduction to the study of politics. Chapter 1 considers some central concepts of the subject – politics, government, the state, sovereignty, power, authority and legitimacy. It also reviews élitist and pluralist theories of how power is distributed in modern societies. Chapter 2 discusses the pros and cons of the comparative approach, and the different conceptual frameworks and techniques that can be applied. At least in comparison with the rest of this book, this opening part is relatively conceptual; you may wish to return to it after reading the other chapters.

■ *Chapter 1* ■

Political Concepts

The main focus of this book is politics, rather than political concepts. We look at how politics is organised in nation-states and at how different countries solve the core problem of politics: determining who is to get what, when and how. But we cannot jump straight into this material. For just as what astronomers 'see' in the sky depends on the type of telescope through which they peer, so too does our interpretation of politics depend on the concepts through which we approach our subject matter. Indeed, in politics it often seems as though everyone has their own telescope – and claims that their own instrument is better than anyone else's!

This point illustrates a fundamental fact about studying politics. The basic concepts of the subject remain at the forefront of discussion in a way which does not normally apply to more scientific disciplines such as astronomy. The study of politics is always an uncertain subject in which the perspective of the observer makes a difference to the results obtained. Enlightenment comes not from ignoring differences in political approach but from confronting them and making them explicit.

Hence this chapter. In it, we set out our own interpretation of some central concepts of the discipline. Where appropriate, we also mention alternative viewpoints. These concepts provide a background against which we discuss more specialised aspects of politics in later chapters.

■ Politics and government

To start at the beginning: what is politics? In our view, politics is the process by which groups make collective decisions. The size of the group can vary from a single family at one extreme to the international community at the other. Political decisions are also arrived at in various ways: by violence, by discussion, by custom, by bargaining, even on occasion by voting. What makes them political, however, is their collective character, affecting and committing those who belong to the group.

Politics does not always involve conflict. Indeed, one reason for studying politics is to search out the conditions under which groups can achieve their goals peacefully and effectively. In this sense politics is a constructive and practical subject. However, much of the flavour of politics springs from the fact that members of a group rarely agree, at least initially, on what course of action to follow. Even if there is agreement over goals, there may still be disagreement over means.

Disagreements arise, in part, from scarcity. However big the pie, there is sure to be some haggling over the size of the slices. Limited resources mean that some goals must be given priority and that some sections within a group are likely to be treated more favourably than others. But conflict also springs from natural differences of opinion. A nomadic tribe must decide collectively when it is time to move on; a modern nation-state must decide collectively whether it should go to war. When the group as a whole is involved, there can only be one decision. Thus the content of politics involves setting goals and taking decisions for a group, as well as deciding how resources should be distributed within it.

The mere existence of a collective problem is not always enough to generate the political will needed for a collective solution. Indeed it often seems that the larger the group, the more difficult a solution becomes. Consider the issue of the environment as an example. This is a classic, and fundamental, collective concern. In this case, the entire world forms the relevant group. Whoever you are, and wherever you live, you share an interest with everyone else in preventing global warming and depletion of the ozone layer. But the countries of the world find it hard, though we hope not impossible, to overcome these problems. This is partly because heavy polluters (such as the United States) are often the slowest to adopt environmentally friendly policies. One problem of politics is to explain why such massive gaps exist between acknowledging a collective problem and agreeing a collective solution.

Our definition of politics as the process by which groups make collective decisions is relatively neutral. Other definitions are more evaluative. For example, in popular speech 'politics' is often used in a critical sense, to indicate the unscrupulous pursuit of private advantage. At the other extreme some scholars wish to reserve the term politics for the more civilised modes of decision-making. 'Why call a struggle for power "politics"' asked Crick (1982), 'when it is simply a struggle for power?' Crick preferred to define politics more positively, as the 'activity by which differing interests within a given unit of rule are conciliated by giving them a share in power in proportion to their importance to the welfare and the survival of their community.' The problem is that this defines conflict out of politics. From Crick's perspective, politics was an ideal to aim at rather than a reality to be described.

There is a political aspect to much of our everyday activity. However, as social groups and organisations grow more complex, political activity becomes recurrent, and stable patterns of collective decision-making emerge. A regular and settled pattern of decision-making is termed government. Universities, companies, clubs, churches and trade unions all possess government in so far as they have regular procedures for making and enforcing decisions. In its broadest sense, government simply indicates this condition of orderly rule.

Our concern, however, is with decisions which are inherently collective, affecting the whole society. This book is about government in the public sphere, rather than the government of private, or lower, organisations. Primarily, we are concerned with the political direction of government at national level – and indeed the term **government** is often used in just this sense, to refer to ministers in charge of major departments.

But we also need two broader terms. The first is the **state**. This covers the whole range of offices that make and enforce collective decisions for society. Ministers, judges, legislators, bureaucrats, generals and the police all form part of a single network of public offices – and that network is known by the umbrella term 'the state'. The government is the core of the state but the two terms have distinct meanings, as shown in Figure 1.1. We examine the state in the next section.

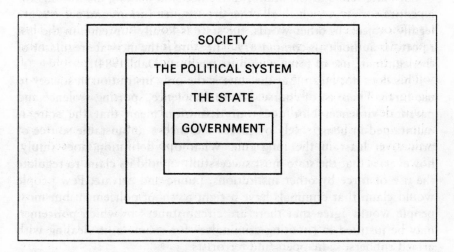

Figure 1.1 *Government, state political system and society*

The other term we need to introduce here is the **political system**. A rather elusive notion, this covers all those forces which impinge upon the state. Thus the political system is a broader term again. Parties, voters and interest groups are not formally part of the state but they are part of the political system. This is because they both affect, and are influenced by, those who govern. The political system is a concept rather than an object. It does not exist in the same direct sense as the government. Even so, the political system is the natural focus of political science (see also pp. 33–6).

■ The state

The state is an abstract idea but an extremely powerful one: 'the state benefits and it threatens. Now it is "us" and often it is "them". It is an abstraction, but in its name men are jailed, or made rich on defence contracts, or killed in wars' (Edelman 1964, p. 1).

We live in a world of states. Most of the earth's surface is now parcelled up between governments which claim an exclusive right to rule their particular territory. Uninhabited areas like the Antarctic, and nomadic tribes that wander across national boundaries, are an uncomfortable fit within this state 'system'. In reality, of course, all governments are influenced by developments outside their territory; all nations trade, many go to war, and ideas know no boundaries. No nation is an island, entire unto itself. But in theory even the smallest and weakest state is still a sovereign body. So what exactly is a 'state'?

The state refers to the authoritative decision-making institutions for an entire society, to which all other groups, institutions and persons are legally subject. In other words, the state is legally supreme: in the last resort, its authority is compulsory. The state is the ultimate regulator of the legitimate use of force within its territory (Dahl 1984).

This does not mean that the state is the only institution in society to use force. There is, of course, criminal violence, sporting violence and parental violence. Nor does our definition mean that the state is maintained in being solely by force. Violence is an unstable source of power, at least in the long run. What our definition does imply, however, is that the state must successfully uphold its claim to regulate the use of force by other institutions, public and private. Few people would claim that criminals have a right to shoot policemen, but most people would agree that there are circumstances in which policemen may be justified in shooting criminals – for example, in dealing with armed robbers, kidnappers and terrorists.

When the state's monopoly of the legitimate use of force is threatened, its continued existence is at stake. Civil wars, for example, are in essence disputes about which government should control the state in a given territory. While the conflict continues, there is no legitimate authority, perhaps indeed no state.

■ Sovereignty

The state is two-faced. The hard side, often hidden from view, is its willingness to use force to get its way. The softer side, no less important, rests on the state's ability to convince its citizens of the rightful nature of its power. The notion of sovereignty is linked to the softer of the state's two faces. Sovereignty refers to the fount of authority in society. The concept is legal (*de jure*) rather than practical (*de facto*).

Sovereignty belongs to the body which has the right to make laws for a country. In Britain, for example, this body is Parliament. With one major qualification, Britain is an example of clear, concentrated sovereignty. Parliament can make whatever laws it likes, it cannot bind its successors, judges cannot overturn its legislation and no other body can make laws applying to the country. The qualification is provided by the European Community (EC). EC regulations apply directly to Britain, as to other member states, even if the regulations have not been approved by national parliaments.

The law-making body possesses **internal** sovereignty – the right to make laws applying within its territory. But sovereignty also has an **external** dimension (Scruton 1983). External sovereignty is the recognition in international law that a state has jurisdiction (authority) over a territory. It means the state is answerable for that jurisdiction in international law. External sovereignty matters because all states claim the right to regulate the relationships between their country and the rest of the world. In fact external sovereignty grows ever more important as the world becomes more interdependent. To claim sovereignty is to put a warning sign to other states, saying 'Keep Out!' In reality, no state has full control over events within its borders but this does not annul the state's claim to sovereignty.

The traditional theory of sovereignty stressed the need for a single, sovereign body within a defined territory. In his *Commentaries on the Laws of England (1765–70)* William Blackstone observes that 'there is and must be in every state a supreme, irresistible, absolute and uncontrolled authority, in which the right of sovereignty resides.' Blackstone's view summarised an interpretation first developed by the French philosopher Jean Bodin (1529–96). Bodin defined sovereignty as the untrammelled and undivided power to make laws. Bodin's aim was to uphold the privileges of the French monarchy and his work under-pinned the later development of the absolute monarchy in France.

In today's more democratic and interdependent world, identifying the location of sovereignty is not as straightforward as the traditional theory assumes. In the United States, for example, sovereignty is shared between the Congress, the President, the Supreme Court and the fifty states which make up the federal republic. America has constitutional government, indeed more so than the United Kingdom, but it is a system which diffuses, rather than concentrates, authority. In a sense, the United States is a case of sovereignty without a sovereign.

Even in countries with parliamentary government, we would argue that the people must at least share sovereignty with parliament, since parliament's authority arises in part from its representative role. Hence in practice locating sovereignty is not quite as simple as the idea of the supremacy of parliament makes out.

Interdependence between countries also clouds the issue of sover-eignty. The expanding range of international commitments taken on by nation-states reduces the room for manoeuvre available to governments. The emergence of international organisations such as the European Community, which has the ability to bypass national parliaments in some areas, also threatens traditional ideas of sovereignty. These changes are slowly diluting the notion of sovereignty, as the gap grows between the fiction of a single source of sovereignty and the reality of interdependence. Blackstone and Bodin have had their day.

■ Power

Power is fundamental to politics. It is one of the building blocks of political science – as central to us as the concept of money is in economics. While all political scientists accept the importance of power, they differ on how it should be conceived, defined and measured.

In a broad sense, power is the production of intended effects. It is the ability to get what we want. To take an obvious example, presidents have more power than do peasants because presidents exert more influence over the course of events. Notice that the emphasis here is on power *to* rather than power *over* – on the capacity to achieve objectives, rather than to exercise control over other people. The 'power to' approach is associated with the American sociologist Talcott Parsons (1967). He regarded political power as the capacity of a government to draw on the commitments of its citizens so as to achieve collective goals – such as law and order, protection from attack and economic growth. The more powerful the government, the more effective it would be at achieving the goals of the community. For Parsons, then, power in politics was not just a matter of one social group or political party jostling with others to win control of the state. Rather, power was the tool which enabled rulers to achieve the objectives of society.

Parsons' view of power is regarded as too narrow (and too conservative) by many political scientists. They believe politics is more than a technical task of implementing a vision shared by a whole society. They see politics as an arena of conflict over what goals should be pursued. Thus they tend to define power in terms of *whose* vision wins out. What matters is whose hand is on the wheel. For example, is the government run by a conservative party whose primary concern is to protect business interests? Or by a socialist party committed to the trade union cause?

The underlying view of power here is based on the idea of **conflict** rather than **consensus**. In this perspective, power consists in the ability to get one's way, usually in the face of opposition. It is a matter of getting people to do things they would not otherwise have done (Dahl 1957). This is a question of power over others, rather than power to achieve shared objectives.

In our view, both 'power to' and 'power over' are important. It is just as important to ask, 'how much power does a government have?' as it is to ask, 'who exercises that power?' The first question concerns the quantity of power while the second asks about how it is distributed. 'How much power does a government have?' parallels the economist's question, 'How many goods does an economy produce?' On the other hand, the distributive question, 'Who exercises that power?' is the political scientist's equivalent of, 'Who is rich and who is poor?'

To amplify this distinction between 'power to' and 'power over', consider the situation of the Soviet Union in the early 1990s. At the time, many commentators concentrated on the intricate political manoeuvrings then taking place in Moscow. Was Gorbachev losing touch with the reformers and throwing his hand in with the conservative old guard? An interesting question, to be sure, but one which ignored the declining quantity of power available to Moscow. The most important development in the Soviet Union in the late 1980s and early 1990s was the collapse of central authority. The republics were ignoring, and often contradicting, directives from the central authority in Moscow. The central government had ceased to govern. The Soviet ship was sinking while the officers (and many journalists) squabbled over whose hands were on the wheel. Yet if no one governed, what did it matter who governed? Thus the Soviet Union in its death throes was an example of how the quantity of power available to a central government can decline to the point where the issue of its distribution became secondary.

Power can be exercised in a variety of ways. If we asked you to express 'power' through a symbolic gesture, you would probably raise a clenched fist. In some ways, this image is appropriate. Violence is undoubtedly one form of power. The frequency of wars, both between nations and within them, testifies to its importance in history. But, just as history is about more than warfare, so power involves more than force. Boulding (1989) provides a straightforward classification of forms of power. He says people get their way through using force, making deals, or creating obligations (see Table 1.1). To put the same point more informally, we can distinguish between the stick, the deal and the kiss.

The threat of force (the **stick**) is associated with coercive institutions such as the military and the police. It arises when A says to B, 'You do something I want – or else.' Force is a basis of state power and, although it is only a background condition in normal civilian politics, its presence still underpins many political relationships. For example, the state threatens to deprive us of our liberty if we do not pay its taxes, fight in its wars and obey its laws. Often the threat is left implicit, but that is a sign of its effectiveness, not its irrelevance. The stick which stays in the cupboard is the biggest stick of all.

Exchange power (the **deal**) is more common, and more effective, than the stick. It arises when A says to B, 'You do something I want and in return I will do something you want'. Whereas the stick is based on the threat of negative sanctions (punishment), the deal is based on the prospect of positive sanctions (reward). But both are forms of power because they are means through which one person seeks to change the behaviour of another.

Exchange is the basis of economic relationships but it is also extremely important in politics. For example, relations between the

Table 1.1   *Forms of power*

	'Use force' (the stick)	'Make deals' (the deal)	'Create obligations' (the kiss)
Nature	Coercive threats	Productive exchanges	Integrative relationships
Motive for obedience	Fear	Gain	Commitment
Institutions	Military	Economic	Social

Source: adapted from K. Boulding, *Three Faces of Power* (London: Sage, 1989).

citizen and the state are often analysed in terms of an exchange, or 'contract', between the two. The basis of the exchange is this. Citizens agree to subject themselves to the authority of the state. In return, the state provides an umbrella of protection: a police force, an education system, a welfare safety-net. Citizens pay their taxes and the state provides services. The 'contract' is imaginary but the exchange underlying it influences how citizens behave. Put simply, when people feel the state gives as well as takes, they are more likely to obey – and the regime becomes more stable.

Creating obligations (the **kiss**) refers to the capacity to inspire loyalty, respect and commitment. It arises when A says to B, 'You do something I want because you love me, respect me, or are in other ways committed to me.' When we look for examples of such obligations, we naturally think first of social institutions such as the family, churches or charities. We do not naturally turn to politics. However, of all three forms of power, the capacity to inspire is probably of greatest importance. Nationalism and religion are examples of powerful forces which have been exploited by rulers (and, even more, by their opponents) to motivate people to lay down their lives.

Some people argue that the whole idea of exerting power through commitment is a contradiction in terms. If B does what A wants voluntarily, is A really exercising power over B? If people volunteer to fight in a war, is the state exercising power over them by encouraging them to sign up? This depends on whether we want a narrow or broad definition of power. The narrower approach sees power as the ability to impose one's views against opposition. But radical political scientists would claim that this is too restrictive. They argue that 'love power' is the most insidious form of it.

For example Lukes (1974) claims that power is exercised whenever the real interests of people are ignored, even if these people are unaware of their interests. For Lukes, A exercises power over B when A affects B in a manner contrary to B's interests. So, a factory which pollutes a town may well try to hide this fact from the inhabitants. If it succeeds, then Lukes believes it has exercised power, even though the inhabitants are unaware of the pollution – and hence cannot object to it. Their interests have nonetheless been harmed.

Equally, a government that whips up patriotic fervour in order to help military recruitment is still exerting power over the recruits – for can it be in their real interest to lay down their lives in a far-off field? Whether or not we regard these as examples of power, we must accept that manipulating the knowledge, values and preferences of others is by far the most efficient way to control them.

Political power typically involves a combination of force, exchange and obligation. Consider taxation as an example. Taking money off people is an essential, but tricky, task which any state must perform with at least some efficiency. One reason people pay up is coercion: they fear the heavy hand of the state if they are caught evading payment. Another reason is exchange: people are willing to pay through taxes for such services as health, education and welfare. And the final reason is a sense of obligation: what would happen if everyone else evaded their taxes? Thus, the power of the modern state rests on its ability to draw on a variety of sources of obligation, each of which reinforces the other.

To summarise, we have reviewed three approaches to power. These are:

1. Power as the capacity to achieve collective goals;
2. Power as the ability to impose one's will against opposition;
3. Power as affecting people in a way which runs against their own interests.

The second view probably comes closest to an ordinary, common-sense interpretation of power. However, the other, less coercive modes are just as important as ways of influencing people. And, in practice, power relationships are usually based on a combination of factors.

■ Élitist theories

For students of comparative politics, a crucial question is how power is distributed in societies. This obviously varies between democracies and dictatorships. However, for one group of thinkers, known as the élitists, the similarities in the distribution of power between societies exceed the differences. Whatever the form of government, they suggest, a ruling élite is inevitable – even in so-called 'democracies'.

The concept of a ruling élite is associated with three scholars: the Italians Vilfredo Pareto (1848–1923) and Gaetano Mosca (1858–1941), and the German Robert Michels (1876–1936). This trio form the 'classical élitists' who profoundly influenced thinking about power in twentieth-century political science.

Pareto (S. Finer 1966) argued that in all societies there is a division between three groups:

1. a small governing élite;
2. a non-governing élite (e.g. the wealthy and the aristocracy);
3. the mass population or non-élite.

The composition of the élite obviously changes over time – there is a 'circulation of élites' – but an élite is always present.

Mosca (1939, 1958) argued that the rule of a governing élite is ensured by its superior organisation and calibre: 'the dominion of an organised minority, obeying a single impulse, over the unorganised majority is inevitable. Members of a ruling minority regularly have some attribute, real or apparent, which is highly esteemed.'

Michels (1949) studied power in specific organisations rather than in society as a whole. He formulated the famous 'iron law of oligarchy'. This states, 'Who says organisation, says oligarchy.' ('Oligarchy' means rule by the few.) In a path-breaking study, Michels showed that his law applied even to socialist parties, with their supposedly democratic organisation. Michels inferred from this that if even parties which set out to be democratic end up under the tight control of their leaders, then his law is likely to apply to most other parties and organisations as well. Later, McKenzie (1963) applied this analysis to Britain's Labour Party. He showed that the constitutional supremacy of the party's annual conference did not match the reality of power: increasingly the leaders dominated the party.

The élitist view of power has two implications. First it leads to scepticism about the feasibility of real democracy, in the full sense of government by (and not just for) the people. These doubts led Pareto and especially Michels to sympathise with fascism. More significantly, they also led to Schumpeter's 'realistic' restatement of democracy as a system of competing élites (see p. 50).

Secondly élite theorists do not always believe that the governing élite is the preserve of a particular social group. They were in fact reacting against Marx's notion of a ruling class – the idea that an economic group rules politically. In understanding why élites develop, the crucial point is political, not economic: the élite is organised but the mass is not. So, to use a fashionable phrase, élite theorists believed in the 'relative autonomy' of the state.

Empirical investigations of ruling élites developed in the United States from the 1920s onwards. These were studies by sociologists of the distribution of power in local communities – for example of Muncie, Indiana by Robert and Helen Lynd (1929) and of Atlanta, Georgia, by Floyd Hunter (1953). These investigations generally concluded that a small number of people, mainly from upper or upper middle class backgrounds, and/or representing business interests, were predominant in the community. In interviews, the same people would be nominated again and again as community 'influentials'. So these studies suggested that the concept of a governing élite fitted local communities, even in the supposedly democratic United States.

Wright Mills applied these findings to the national level in the United States. In his influential study of *The Power Élite* (1956), Mills argued that three interlocking groups dominated the 'command posts' of American society: political leaders (generally declining in power); corporate leaders (who joined the political directorate during the New Deal in the 1930s); and military leaders (brought to power by America's entry into the Second World War. Similar high-status backgrounds oiled the wheels of communication between all three groups, though Mills did acknowledge that their interests did not always converge. Even so it was these élite groups, most of whom are unelected, that controlled the direction of American politics. Today Wright Mills' theory can be regarded as a version of corporatism (see pp. 224–7), a thesis which maintains that elected representatives have been losing power to big institutional interests, particularly business and the military.

■ Pluralist theories

Just as élitism was a reaction to the naive expectations of early democrats, so pluralism was a reaction against the 'ultra-realism' of the élitists. Where élitism sees rule by a minority, pluralism sees rule by *minorities*. Pluralism is a doctrine of diversity. It claims that modern democracies (and, perhaps, other forms of government as well) are open and competitive arenas in which many different interests and groups compete for influence. Pluralism is a midway position between élitism and democracy. Unlike élitism, it claims there is no single, dominant élite. But unlike a 'majority rule' view of democracy, it accepts that the majority does not govern. What we have (and what we should welcome, according to the pluralists) is government by the many, rather than government by the majority (see Figure 1.2).

Pluralists are critical of the **reputational** method of studying power used in the community studies. This method consisted simply of asking people in a community to say who were the leading figures in that community. The results were regarded as valid if there was substantial overlap in the answers received – as there invariably was. Clearly this was far too crude. It meant the researchers were simply relying on people's beliefs about who was in charge of a particular town, instead of making their own direct study of the power structure. Dahl suggested that to establish the existence of a ruling élite we would have to examine a series of concrete decisions where the preferences of the 'ruling élite' run counter to those of other groups. If the 'ruling élite' consistently prevails, the élitist interpretation stands. If not, then either the 'ruling élite' has been misspecified or (more likely) there is no such group at all.

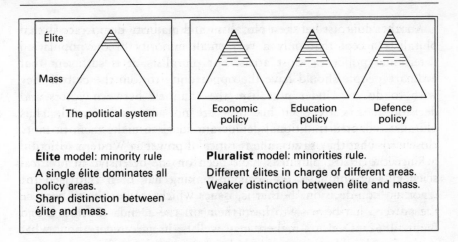

Figure 1.2 *Élitist and pluralist views of power*

Dahl adopted this **decision-making** method in his own influential study of New Haven, Connecticut (1961). He found that in this city no single group was predominant across all policy areas such as education, urban redevelopment and political nominations. 'In each issue area different actors appeared, their roles were different and the kinds of alternatives which they had to choose among were different' (Polsby 1963, p. 60). So Dahl's thesis was that whatever local 'experts' might say in interviews about the power structure of New Haven, careful scrutiny of key decisions revealed no cohesive ruling élite.

This pattern of key figures varying across different areas of public policy was then developed into a general theory of political pluralism. Many writers in the 1960s and 1970s characterised Western democracies as pluralistic in their power structure. They dismissed Wright Mills' thesis of the power élite as a sophisticated conspiracy theory which could not be sustained when the complexity and openness of real decision-making was examined. Many writers also suggested that pluralism was desirable: it was presented as an ideal as well as a description.

Perhaps the key feature of pluralism is that different minorities make, or influence, decisions in different areas. Groups with a special interest in particular areas have their say on that topic but rarely go beyond it. For example, generals express strong preferences on defence matters; teachers have their say on education policy. But neither impinges greatly on the other's territory. Thus the fragmented nature of pluralism means that intense and well-informed views receive special weight. Pluralists believe this improves on the strict democratic principle of 'one man, one vote'.

Another contrast between pluralism and majority democracy is that pluralists accept that only a very small minority of the population determines policy in most areas. For pluralists, it is sufficient that ordinary people should have the opportunity to join the club if they wish to do so. Under pluralism the channels between voters and decision-makers are open but they are not always activated. Thus pluralists adapted traditional democratic ideas to make them fit more closely to what they saw as the realities of power in Western societies.

Since the 1970s, pluralists have been on the defensive in political science. The emphasis on decision-making has been criticised for ignoring 'non-decisions' – that is, issues which are not raised because the powers-that-be wish to keep them off the agenda (Bachrach and Baratz 1962). Decision-makers may well be in agreement about what issues they should not discuss (e.g. their own positions of influence) even if they do disagree on the matters before them.

Furthermore many people who do not participate in politics, and a large number of interest groups which are not formally recognised by decision-makers, believe that the system has nothing to offer them. Given such beliefs, it becomes purely theoretical to argue that the channels of political influence are open to all citizens who wish to express a view. The fact is that a significant minority of the population is too indifferent, or too alienated, to get involved.

Finally, critics allege that the pluralists understate the independent role which politicians play in shaping policy and in deciding which interests to respond to. Even the mayor in Dahl's New Haven was influential across a wide range of policies. Where pluralists see the state as an arena of political struggle, contemporary political scientists are more likely to stress that the state is an active participant in the struggle (Skocpol 1985). So increasingly it is felt that the pluralists only captured one facet of the distribution of power in Western societies.

■ Authority

Coercive power is an inefficient form of rule. Slavery is inefficient because the slaves need to be watched over and in any case they lack commitment to their work. Coercive power is unstable as well as inefficient: those who live by the sword often die by it. So the fundamental problem confronting rulers is how to legitimise their position – how to convert power into authority. But what is authority?

Authority is the right to rule. It exists when subordinates acknowledge the right of superiors to give orders. A general may exercise power over enemy soldiers, but he does not have authority over them; this is restricted to his own forces. At the same time, authority is more than voluntary compliance. To acknowledge the authority of rulers does not mean you agree with their decisions. It means only that you accept their right to make decisions and your duty to obey them. For example, you may not agree with your teacher's request for you to read this book, but here you are, studying away. You have accepted the teacher's authority over you.

Relationships of authority are still hierarchical. Often indeed they are just a fig-leaf covering the threat of coercion. Soldiers obey generals because they face a court martial if they disobey; those who claim authority may not wait for it to be acknowledged. Equally students obey teachers because they fear the sanctions of disobedience, even though these are (we hope) far milder than a court martial. In fact political relationships typically combine elements of both power and authority.

Just as power has several sources, so does authority. The German sociologist Max Weber (1957, first published 1922) provided a path-breaking analysis of the bases of authority. He distinguished three ways of validating political power (see Table 1.2). The first type is by reference to the sanctity of **tradition**:

> In traditional authority the present order is viewed as sacred, eternal and inviolable. The dominant person or group, usually defined by heredity, is thought to have been pre-ordained to rule over the rest. The subjects are bound to the ruler by personal dependence and a tradition of loyalty, further reinforced by such cultural beliefs as the divine right of kings.

As Blau (1963) points out, nearly all systems of government before the modern state exemplify traditional claims to authority. But traditional authority is ill-suited to changing societies. In the modern world, traditional authority only provided the basis of rule in a few dynastic monarchies such as Saudi Arabia, Oman and Nepal. Even some of these have now bowed to the democratic wind which blew across the world in the late 1980s.

Charismatic authority is Weber's second type of authority. Here leaders are obeyed because they inspire their followers, who credit their heroes with exceptional and sometimes supernatural qualities. Where traditional authority is based on the past, charismatic authority spurns it. Contrary to popular use, charisma is not for Weber an intrinsic quality of a leader: rather, charisma characterises the relationship between leaders and followers. Charismatic leaders are inspiring figures who emerge in times of crisis and upheaval. Jesus Christ, Mahatma Gandhi, Martin Luther King or, indeed, Adolf Hitler are prominent examples. The role of Ayatollah Khomeini in transforming Iran after the fall of the Shah in 1979 is a more recent illustration.

Table 1.2   *Weber's classification of types of authority*

Type	*Basis*	*Example*
Traditional	Custom and the established way of doing things	Monarchy
Charismatic	Intense commitment to the leader and his message	Many revolutionary leaders
Legal rational	Rules and procedures – the office, not the person	Bureaucracy

However charismatic authority is intrinsically short lived unless the authority-figure can transfer his own authority to a permanent office or institution. This process is called the 'routinisation' of charisma. In Iran, for example, Ayatollah Khomeini established an Islamic regime which continued after his death in 1989.

The third base for authority in Weber's scheme is termed **legal-rational**. This is the exact opposite of charismatic authority. It means that obedience is owed not to an individual but to a set of principles – a government of laws, rather than men. Thus subordinates in an organisation must obey lawful commands from their superiors, irrespective of who occupies these higher offices. Weber believed legal-rational authority was becoming predominant in modern society and he was surely right.

Modern bureaucracies are the best example of organisations based on legal-rational authority. We obey laws not just from fear, nor from tradition, nor from personal allegiance to the chief of police, but because we feel law and order is necessary and desirable in a rational society. We acknowledge the authority of the law – and not just the power of those who enforce it.

Legal-rational authority can limit the abuse of power. Because it is based on the office rather than the person, we can speak of officials 'going beyond their authority'. If we are brave enough, we can then legitimately refuse to obey. The police are entitled to ask you questions but, in a well-regulated country, they do not have the authority to beat you up if you refuse to answer. In practice, people who possess the means of force often apply them, even when they are not entitled to do so. But basing power on the office rather than the individual, and spelling out the limits of that power, does help to contain abuse.

The main limit of Weber's classification is that it says little about how power is converted to authority. Suppose you have led a successful military coup in a small African country. You have sent the previous president packing, you have taken over the radio station and you have put your brother-in-law in charge of the army. What do you do next? How do you build your authority so that you do not suffer exactly the same fate as your predecessor? This is essentially a political task. The gun may have propelled you into office but it will not keep you there for ever.

Mere survival will help. Obedience which is at first coerced eventually becomes habitual. As B. Goodwin (1987, p. 215) comments, 'Today's authority is the site of yesterday's struggle for power.' Mere acquiescence may shore you up for a good while but you will do best in the long term if you can transform habitual obedience into genuine allegiance. You cannot afford to ignore the mass of the population. If they become dissatisfied with your performance, your enemies will have an excuse, or perhaps good reason, to move against you. In short, conquerors become kings by creating a stable basis of support. If they show no concern for those they rule, they will eventually confront the problems of ineffective and unstable rule which destroy nearly all tyrants.

■ Legitimacy

Legitimacy is a similar concept to authority. Legitimacy also refers to rightful power. The difference is that we normally use the term 'legitimacy' in discussing an entire system of government, whereas 'authority' often refers to specific positions within a government. Thus we tend to speak of the legitimacy of a regime but the authority of an official.

To add to the confusion, legitimacy is used in a different sense by political theorists and political scientists. Political theorists are concerned with principles. They say a government is legitimate if it conforms to some moral principle – for example, that it has been fairly elected. Political scientists, on the other hand, are concerned with politics as it is. They say a government is legitimate if its citizens regard it as such. Whether a government is democratic is only one influence on legitimacy in this second sense. For instance, no one would describe Iran under Ayatollah Khomeini as a democratic regime. Nonetheless he came to power through a popular revolution which gave his regime considerable 'legitimacy', at least to begin with. But this authority came from Islamic, rather than democratic, principles.

It is also important to distinguish between legitimacy and legality. Legitimacy refers to whether people accept the validity of a law; legality refers to whether the law was made in accordance with correct procedures, normally as laid down in the constitution. Regulations can be legal without being legitimate. For example, the majority black population rightly considered South Africa's apartheid 'laws' to be illegitimate, even though they were passed in accordance with the country's constitution.

Conversely, illegal action is sometimes seen as legitimate by at least some sections of the population, particularly when it takes the form of peaceful protest to achieve a collective goal. In the twentieth century, civil disobedience has provided a constructive force for political change around the world. It has contributed to movements for equal voting rights and for national independence from colonial rule. The success of these movements shows that legitimacy is different from, and more fundamental than, legality.

Summary

1.   Politics is the process by which groups take, or fail to make, collective decisions. The flavour of politics springs from the fact that members of a group rarely agree on what decision should be reached. Although the study of politics is not just about conflict, it often involves looking at how conflicts are resolved.

2.   Nearly all societies develop specialised institutions for reaching collective decisions. Government is the decision-making body for the society as a whole. The government forms a leading element of the state, a broader term than 'government'. The state also extends to those institutions that advise the government (e.g. the bureaucracy), and also to those that enforce its laws (e.g. the police).

3.   We can also define the state as the body which possesses sovereignty, both internal and external. 'Internal' sovereignty is the right to make laws for a country. 'External' sovereignty belongs to the body which is recognised internationally as having jurisdiction over a territory. The traditional theory of sovereignty maintained that it must be based on a single entity. However, the diffusion of power within countries, and growing interdependence between them, means that this theory is becoming less relevant.

4.   In a broad sense, power is the ability to get what we want. This is often exercised through wielding power over others. This, in turn, takes several forms: using force, making deals or creating obligations.

5.   Élitism and pluralism are two major models of how power is distributed in large societies. Élitism is the view that a small minority dominates all governments, even 'democratic' ones. Pluralism is the view that many different groups have a say in decisions, even if the majority as such does not rule. Pluralism is rule by minorities, rather than by one small élite.

6. Authority is the right to rule. Acc-ording to Weber, it can be based on tradition, charisma or law. Modern societies are characterised by lawful authority. A key task for new rulers is to convert power into authority, usually by performing services for those they rule. When rulers fail to do this, they often lose power.

7. A legitimate government is one which has authority in the eyes of the people it rules. Legitimacy is not just based on election; it too can derive from tradition, religion and from economic or military success. Legitimacy is distinct from legality. A legitimate law is one people feel obliged to obey. A legal regulation is one passed according to constitutional procedures.

Discussion points

1. Can Robinson Crusoe engage in politics on his desert island? Why (not)?

2. Why is it difficult to reach international agreements over (a) the arms trade (b) ecological problems?

3. Is politics possible without government?

4. 'Political power grows from the barrel of a gun' (Mao Zedong). Does it?

5. Who has exerted most power over you in your life – parents, teachers, advertisers, or economic policy makers?

6. Does the distribution of power in (a) local government (b) your college follow an élitist or a pluralist model? How would you go about researching that question?

7. Do the following have authority over you, or merely power: (a) your politics instructor (b) your police force (c) your national parliament?

Key reading

Dahl R. (1984) *Modern Political Analysis*, 4th edn (Englewood Cliffs, N.J.: Prentice-Hall. A perceptive introduction to political analysis by a leading American pluralist.

Goodwin, B. (1987) *Using Political Ideas*, 2nd edn (Chichester: Wiley). A wide-ranging introduction to political ideas and ideologies, written by a political theorist.

Laver M. (1983) *Invitation to Politics* (Oxford: Basil Blackwell). Deep but not impossible, this is a rewarding introduction, written by a political scientist.

Miller D. (ed.) (1987) *The Blackwell Encyclopaedia of Political Thought* (Oxford: Basil Blackwell). The 350 entries include the concepts covered in this chapter, and many more besides. A useful reference book.

Further reading

On the definition of politics, Dahl (1984) is a clear, conventional guide. On the state, Carnoy (1984) writes from an American perspective while Dunleavy and O'Leary (1987) adopt a British approach.

Boulding (1989) provides a fascinating introduction to power from a social scientist's perspective. For a more political and radical approach to power, see Lukes' accessible book (1974); his edited book (Lukes 1986) is also useful. On authority, the classic by Weber (1957, first published 1922), is the basis of modern thinking; the review by Blau (1963) helps to clarify Weber's approach. For a general introduction to authority, see Watt (1982).

On élites, see S. Finer (1966) or Parry (1969). Dahl (1961) is the classic pluralist case-study; for criticisms, see Bachrach and Baratz (1962) and Bachrach (1967). More recent criticisms of pluralism can be found in Skocpol (1985) and Alford and Friedland (1986).

■ *Chapter 2* ■

The Comparative Approach

Comparative politics has no monopoly on the comparative method. Indeed comparison is the foundation of any systematic branch of knowledge. Scientists cannot work out how quickly smoking kills people just by looking at the life expectancy of smokers. They have to compare this with the life expectancy for an otherwise similar group of non-smokers (the difference, by the way, is about four years). As the American political scientist James Coleman used to tell his students, 'You can't be scientific if you're not comparing.'

In the physical sciences these comparisons can be done in the laboratory, under carefully controlled conditions. The difficulty with comparative politics is that such precise experiments are rarely feasible. We cannot say to the government of India, 'You will change your electoral system to proportional representation (PR) because we want to see whether it will increase the number of parties in your parliament.' Instead, we have to work with variation which occurs naturally in the real world. We have to ask whether, in practice, parliaments elected by PR contain more parties than those elected by other methods.

The distinctive feature of comparative politics is its focus on comparison across nations. Most comparisons are done between countries with similar political structures: for example, analysing the party systems of the countries of Western Europe, or investigating prime ministerial power in Australia, Britain, Canada and New Zealand. But contrasting comparisons are also possible between countries with different forms of government. For example, we could compare the distribution of power in the United States and China.

In this chapter we discuss both the strengths and the dangers of the comparative approach. We then review the main frameworks and techniques available to practitioners of comparative politics.

23

■ The advantages of comparison

What is to be gained by comparing politics in different countries? Why compare across nations?

□ *Providing context*

The *first* answer is straightforward: to find out more about the places we know least about. In 1925 Munro described the purpose of his textbook on foreign governments as aiding 'the comprehension of daily news from abroad.' Background information about foreign governments not only helps to interpret new developments, it also enables one's own country to be seen in a new light. For instance, most people in Europe and the Commonwealth probably think of parliamentary systems as the natural form of government. However, directly elected presidents, on the American model, are rather more common in the world today (Derbyshire and Derbyshire 1991, p. 56). Through comparison, say Dogan and Pelassy (1990), we discover our own ethnocentrism and the means of overcoming it. 'What know they of England', asked Kipling 'who only England know?'

□ *Testing hypotheses*

Modern students of comparative politics seek to understand a variety of political systems not just for its own sake but in order to formulate and test hypotheses about the political process. This is the *second* reason for studying politics comparatively. It enables us to develop and scrutinise such questions as: Do 'first past the post' electoral systems always produce a two-party system? Are two-chambered assemblies only found under federalism? Do revolutions occur after defeat in war?

As these questions illustrate, a hypothesis suggests a relationship between two or more factors or variables, for example, between electoral and party systems, or between war and revolution. Verified hypotheses are valuable not just for their own sake but because they are essential for explaining the particular. Consider a specific question: Why is there no major socialist party in the United States? An obvious answer is: because the United States was built on, and retains, a strongly individualistic culture. This answer may seem to be particular but in fact it is quite general. It implies that other countries with similar values will also lack a strong socialist party. It also implies that countries with a more collective outlook will be more likely to have a party of the left. These comparative hypotheses would need to be confirmed before we could claim a full understanding of our original question about the United States. Thus the particular calls forth the general. Only theories can explain specific cases.

☐ *Improving classifications*

A *third* advantage of comparison is that it improves our classifications of politics. As Aristotle showed over 2000 years ago, classification is a stepping stone on the journey to explanation (see Exhibit 2.1). For instance, once constitutions have been classified into written and unwritten, we can search for the factors which predispose countries to have one type rather than the other. Similarly, once we classify executives into presidential and parliamentary types, we can look at the causes and consequences of each. But without variation, and some sort of measurement or classification of it, we have nothing to explain. In short, comparative politics turns constants into variables.

☐ *Making predictions*

Generalisations have potential for prediction. This is the *final* reason for studying politics comparatively. If we find that proportional representation (PR) is indeed associated with a multi-party system, we can reasonably predict at least one effect of introducing PR to countries such as Canada and India which still use 'first past the post'. Equally, if we know that electorates dislike high inflation more than high unemployment, we can advise governments accordingly. We can predict that an anti-inflation policy is more likely to produce their own re-election than a full employment policy.

Often, indeed, countries are selected for study precisely for their predictive value. They are, to use jargon, proto-typical. In the 1830s, de Tocqueville (1954 ed.) examined the United States because he was interested in politics in the new democratic age. America was his example but democracy was his real concern:

> I confess that in America I saw more than America; I sought there the image of democracy itself, in order to learn what we have to fear or to hope from its progress.

In the present day, we might look to Canada to see what voting patterns look like in a 'de-aligned' electorate where social groups do not

Exhibit 2.1   *The origins of comparative politics: Aristotle's classification of governments*

Aristotle (Greek philosopher, 384–322 BC), developed a classification of regimes, based on the governments of 158 Greek city-states. It is still highly instructive. Aristotle distinguished government by the one, the few and the many. In each category rulers could govern in the common interest (the genuine form) or their own interest (the perverted form). This scheme yields six types of government:

		RULE BY		
		One	*Few*	*Many*
FORM	*Genuine*	Kingship	Aristocracy	Polity
	Perverted	Tyranny	Oligarchy	Democracy

Building on this scheme, Aristotle identified the social characteristics of rulers in the four types with more than one leader. An oligarchy is ruled by the rich, an aristocracy by the virtuous. Democracy is government by the poor. The polity, Aristotle's ideal form of government, is broadly equated with middle-class rule.

Aristotle went on to use his classification in an analysis of the causes of change and disorder. He suggested, for example, that oligarchies are prone to dissension within the ruling élite. Tyrannies, he thought, are especially susceptible to external attack.

By comparison with more recent classifications, Aristotle's work is strongly deductive, working from principles to examples. Modern classification in politics, and indeed other disciplines, tends to be inductive, seeking to identify actual governments that share a number of common characteristics. These points notwithstanding, there can be no doubt that the generalising spirit behind Aristotle's work is exactly that which motivates modern students of comparative politics.

See: Aristotle (1962) bk. 3, ch.5.

determine how people vote. Thus comparative analysis provides some capacity to anticipate the future – though the control provided by this knowledge can of course be used for bad purposes as well as good.

To summarise, the advantages of studying politics comparatively are:

1. Learning about other countries casts fresh light on our own.
2. Comparison enables us to test general hypotheses about politics.
3. Comparison improves our classifications of political processes.
4. Comparison gives us some potential for prediction.

■ The problems of comparison

Several problems arise in putting the comparative approach to work. But Sartori (1970) has warned against the dangers of over-conscious thinking which leads only to the conclusion that all comparisons have overwhelming difficulties. So we will describe these problems in order to be aware of the difficulties, not to present a case against comparative politics.

Too many variables, too few countries – This is the major problem. There are between 150 and 200 sovereign states in the world today, the exact number depending on how sovereignty is measured (Derbyshire and Derbyshire 1991). Even so, it is rare to find a country which is identical to another in all respects except for that factor (say, the electoral system) whose effects we wish to detect. This means that comparison in political science can never become a full equivalent of the experiments conducted in the natural scientist's laboratory. We just do not have enough countries to go round. This is known as the 'small-N' problem ('N' is the statistician's term for 'number of cases').

To make the same point from another angle, we will never be able to test all the possible explanations of a political difference between countries. For example, several plausible reasons can be used to 'explain' why France and Italy had two of the strongest communist parties in Western Europe. Perhaps the strength of communism was a reaction against the power of the Catholic Church in these countries. Perhaps the French and Italian working classes were sympathetic to communism because the ruling élite had been slow to integrate them into democratic politics. The point is that we cannot isolate a particular factor by looking for countries where just that factor is present. The crucial comparisons are rarely possible: we just run out of countries.

Many countries, one system – In reality, far fewer than 150 'cases' are available to the student of comparative politics. This is because of relationships between states. For example it was, in principle, a straight-forward task to find out those characteristics of government which the sixteen unambiguously communist states held in common. Some were obvious to anyone who had studied or lived in a communist state. They included a dominant single party which maintained a tight control over society. From such a list, and a contrast with government in non-communist states, we could have constructed a 'model' of communist rule – a statement of those factors which identified a pure communist state.

But there is a problem with this exercise. Would it have given us the essence of communism – or just the characteristics of Soviet government which had been imposed on several other communist states by force? In other words, the idea that we had sixteen separate, independent examples of the category 'communist state' does not stand up to scrutiny.

Equally, we cannot look at the revolutions of 1989 in Eastern Europe as though they were separate cases. The 'revolutions' formed a single process, unfolding in one country after another. Once journalists had told the story of communism's collapse in one particular East European country, they would speculate on where they would meet up next: would it be Berlin, would it be Bucharest? Again, one single spark ignited these revolutions: Gorbachev's decision not to maintain communist rule in Eastern Europe by force. He was the executioner of communism. In 1989 Eastern Europe experienced an epidemic of revolutions – but epidemics cannot be understood just by conducting post-mortems on individual cases. Contagion is the essence of epidemics.

As countries become more interdependent, so this problem becomes more acute. For this reason, political scientists (and this book) now focus on world politics as well as comparative politics. We must think *globally* as well as *comparatively*. The world, as well as the state, is a crucial unit of analysis. In newspapers as well as books, we read more and more about 'the world economy' and 'the world financial system' (Wallerstein 1979). Now, however, the 'small N' problem really is acute, for there is only one world. When we take the world as our unit, we are in the position that medical researchers would be in if they had to work out the causes of measles from studying just one child with the disease. We can still describe the symptoms but we find it harder to understand the underlying causes.

Interdependence is a major theme of the modern world. However, this does not mean the nation-state can be dismissed. It is still national governments that seek solutions to problems, even if the problems are shared. It is still national policy-makers who are held accountable for problems by national electorates. Politics still happens *through* nations, even if the dynamics of politics in the late twentieth century are global.

For example, the revolutions of 1989 may have had a common origin but their development and outcomes have varied between Czechoslovakia and Bulgaria, or between Hungary and Albania. These contrasts owe much to national factors, such as the political history, economic development and ethnic composition of the countries concerned. Even when different cooks work with the same ingredients, they still deliver distinctive tastes.

Same phenomenon, different meanings – In comparing political behaviour across countries, it is important to remember that the meaning of an action depends on the conventions of the country concerned. When a British Member of Parliament (MP) votes against his party in the House of Commons, this is far more significant than when an American legislator departs from the party line in the less partisan Congress. To take another illustration, Western observers are sometimes shocked by the apparent indifference with which military coups are greeted in third world countries. They fail to recognise that coups can become a regular – and fairly peaceful – mechanism for the circulation of élites. In a sense coups may be the 'functional equivalent' of elections in the West – and should be compared accordingly.

This problem of the meaning and significance of actions is particularly important in politics. This is because politics is largely conducted in terms of signals, coded language and symbolic behaviour. At the very least practitioners of comparative politics should be aware that comparing like with like is not always straightforward: it requires some intimacy with each of the countries under scrutiny.

Bias – When does 'strong leadership' become 'dictatorship?' When is a 'terrorist' a 'freedom fighter'? Values cannot be separated from analysis by fiat; they are ingrained in the language with which we describe the world and in the concepts through which we view it. For example, people on the far left (and the far right) generally believe there is an élitist distribution of power in liberal democracies. They regard the unpopularity of their own views as a sign that real debate is being suppressed. On the other hand, people in the middle are more likely to see pluralism. They take political conflict at face value. So what one sees depends on where one looks from.

This problem of bias and competing values is particularly acute in comparative politics, where we are often seeking to understand governments and cultures with different values from our own.

The important question is whether we should even make the attempt to separate fact and value, analysis and evaluation, in comparative politics. Though complete objectivity is probably impossible, we believe that such an effort is worth while. Some aspects of politics, at least, can be treated in a relatively precise and quantifiable way (for example comparative electoral behaviour). Furthermore, debate between people of different political persuasions about such contentious matters as the distribution of power can narrow the areas of difference and force implicit assumptions to the surface.

To summarise, the main problems in comparative politics are:

1. There are not enough countries in the world to allow theories to be tested precisely.
2. Relationships between countries mean they cannot be regarded as independent of each other. This further reduces our ability to test theories.
3. The 'same' phenomenon can have different meanings in different countries. This makes it difficult to compare like with like.
4. Problems of bias and political values arise when looking at politics in contrasting countries.

■ Controlled comparisons

In comparative politics, we cannot control our comparisons completely. We are not like chemists who can manipulate their substances at will. We are more like physicians who, confronted with a patient's symptoms, have to try to identify the underlying disorder. Our 'patients' are countries and our 'symptoms' are the political characteristics we want to explain.

Let's look at an example. We can take two countries with contrasting political characteristics and we can ask: what accounts for this difference? Suppose we wanted to explain why parties in New Zealand are so strong and disciplined. We might make a comparison with Canada, another affluent liberal democracy with strong British ties. In Canada, however, national parties are notoriously weak.

So the question is: What differences between the two countries might explain the contrasting styles of their parties? One possibility is this. Canada is a vast country with a federal system of government whereas New Zealand is a small country with a centralised government. These factors certainly influence, and possibly explain, the contrasting styles of political parties in the two countries. So we have a plausible diagnosis: big country, weak parties.

In practice, there are usually many possible explanations for a political difference between two countries. Of course, doctors say the same: many disorders can produce similar symptoms. However, in contrast to doctors who can conduct tests on their patients in order to confirm a specific diagnosis, we cannot intervene in a country's politics just to test a particular theory. Thus we are rarely able to reach decisive conclusions.

To return to our example, is it the size of a country or a federal system of government which is most important in leading to weak and fragmented parties? We cannot be sure, since size and federalism go together. Federalism is, in fact, extremely rare in small countries. Here we pay the price of trying to understand what happens in the real world. We can control our comparisons only to a certain degree – but even half a comparison is far better than no comparison at all.

■ Frameworks of comparison

The practice of comparative politics is informed by a number of conceptual frameworks. These can then be used to guide specific studies. Frameworks direct attention to some aspects of a country's politics – and, by implication, distract us from others. Here we briefly review three frameworks, based on the comparison of states, societies or policies.

☐ *Comparing states*

The state-centred approach is at once the most traditional and the most fashionable approach to comparative politics. In the early part of the twentieth century, scholars concentrated their attention on the formal institutions of government – legislature, executive and judiciary – and the constitutions which governed the relationships between these institutions.

The style of these early studies was descriptive in the extreme. Constitutions and formal organisations of government were examined in legal and historical terms, reflecting the origins of political science in these two disciplines. Informal relationships between political actors went unstudied. Little attention was given to less 'official' organisations such as pressure groups or the mass media. The wider social context within which government operates was ignored. The approach was also strongly culture-bound, confined largely to the study of governments in the United States and Europe. Finally, the style was very uncritical. Perhaps the Webbs' study of Soviet government in the 1930s represented the 'summit' of this approach. This described the formal organisation of the Soviet state in minute detail, in the apparent conviction that everything worked as Stalin's propagandists alleged (S. and B. Webb 1935).

After 1945 the state-centred or institutional approach became unfashionable. The focus shifted from the state to society (see below). In the 1980s, however, attention returned to the state. 'Bringing the state back in' became a rallying-cry in comparative politics (Evans *et al.* 1985).

Partly, this reflected a belated recognition that the baby had been thrown out with the bath-water. After all, the state *is* the single central concern of political science. The institutions of government do make a difference. For example, the key contrast between the United States and the United Kingdom is institutional, indeed constitutional: the American president cannot command Congress but the British prime minister can control Parliament. Furthermore, the spread of constitutional government to parts of the second and the third world in the 1980s and 1990s meant constitutions and institutions had become a better guide to the realities of power. We cannot understand politics (and least of all political change) just by describing the operation of government institutions. But neither can we exclude such considerations. Part 4 of this book therefore adopts an institutional approach.

Despite the renewal of interest in the state, modern political scientists adopt a different approach to their forefathers. Today's focus is not so much on institutional detail but on the state as an active agent, shaping and reshaping society. The state is seen as using its administrative capacity and monopoly of legitimate force to bring about important changes in society. For example Skocpol (1985) showed how successful revolutionaries such as the Russian Bolsheviks and Iranian Mullahs used their control of the state to produce total transformations of society. Even in the Western world, the large-scale role of the state has enabled it to lead social and economic change. The state has facilitated industrialisation, led the development of mass education and helped to create modern welfare states.

Thus this new version of the state-centred approach concentrates on the impact of the state on society. In a comparative context, of course, it is clear that the power of the state is a variable rather than a constant. For example, in communist countries, the state was a paramount influence, pervading virtually all aspects of life. In liberal democracies, the state is less dominant. In much of the third world, the state is less important still: its writ may not run far beyond the capital city and a few major towns.

□ *Comparing societies*

In the 1960s and 1970s the focus of comparative politics switched to examining politics in its social context. The Second World War had stimulated new developments in social science techniques (e.g. attitude surveys) which younger scholars were keen to apply to politics. In addition de-colonisation spawned many new nations where the formal institutions of government proved to be very fragile. There was no point in studying the constitution if no one in the country abided by it.

So attention shifted away from government institutions to the **political system**. The political system refers to all the factors which influence collective decisions, even if those factors are not formally part of the government. Thus, parties, voters and social movements all form part of the system of politics, even though they are rarely mentioned in constitutions and other formal documents. The systems approach to politics was pioneered by David Easton (see Exhibit 2.2). Although few political scientists explicitly use his model today, his work still forms part of the vocabulary of politics. 'The political system' has become a widely used (probably over-used) phrase among political scientists.

The **functional** approach to comparative politics provided another important justification for the switch in emphasis from government to political system. Functionalism was a deliberate attempt to broaden the traditional institutional framework of executive, assembly and judiciary. The functional approach raised the following question: even if political systems vary greatly in their institutional arrangements, are there certain functions which any political system must perform if it is to survive and operate effectively? Almond and Powell (1978, 1988) provided the most important analysis of the functions of political systems. Their list is shown in Table 2.1. The first three functions shown there (recruitment, socialisation and communication) concern the maintenance of the system, while the last four relate to the process by which collective decisions are made and implemented.

Functionalists argued that a check-list of this kind provided an objective, standardised and culture-free approach to comparative politics. Take the first function in the table, political recruitment, as an example. All political systems have to persuade people to fill political roles, varying in scope from chief executive to humble voter. However, this function is performed by different institutions in different countries. In the first world, elections are a major recruiting agent. In communist

Exhibit 2.2   *Easton's model of the political system*

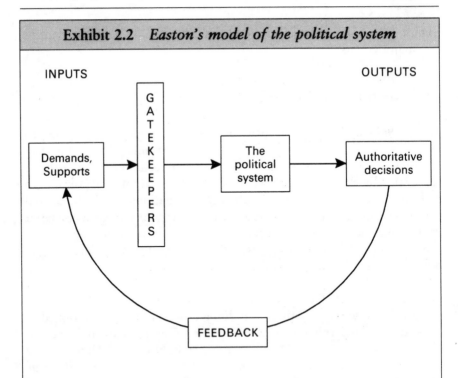

Figure 2.1   *Easton's model of the political system*

According to Easton (1957, 1965a, 1965b), the political system consists of all those institutions and processes involved in the 'authoritative allocation of values' for society. The political system takes **inputs** from society. These consist of (*a*) **demands** for particular policies and (*b*) expressions of **support**. Supports include: compliance with laws, payment of taxes and diffuse support for the regime. The political system converts these inputs into **outputs** – authoritative policies and decisions. These outputs then **feed back** to society so as to affect the next cycle of inputs. However, inputs are regulated by **gatekeepers**, such as parties and interest groups, which bias the system in favour of certain demands and against others.

Easton's model helped to move political science away from an exclusive concern with government institutions. However, he achieved this by reducing the state to nothing more than a 'black box' in an abstract diagram. Critics also alleged that Easton's model was too static, paying little attention to how political systems change.

Table 2.1 ***Almond and Powell's functions of political systems***

Political recruitment	People must be recruited to fill political roles from voters to government leaders.
Political socialisation	Their attitudes to the political system must be formed and sustained.
Political communication	Politically relevant information must be transmitted.
Interest articulation	Demands for particular policies must be expressed.
Interest aggregation	Demands must be selected and combined into a manageable number of major alternatives.
Policy-making	Demands must be converted into authoritative decisions and policies.
Policy implementation	These decisions must be put into effect.

Source: G. Almond and G. Powell, *Comparative Politics* (Boston: Little, Brown, 1978), pp. 13–16.

states, the ruling party was the key vehicle in recruitment. Once the party had approved a nomination for office, election (if indeed there was one) became a mere formality. In some third world states, personal connections are more significant in recruitment. The institutions vary but the underlying function must be performed by every political system. No recruitment, no system.

For the political scientist off on a field-trip to a distant country, functionalism provided a ready set of questions. Which political institutions performed which functions? Were any of the institutions multi-functional (that is, did they perform several functions at once)? So the central task became one of linking political structures (which vary across countries) to political functions (which do not).

Functionalism came in for some tough criticism. Can a political institution be *explained* by identifying its function in a wider system? Is a political system like a car engine, in which each component has a function in a smooth-running whole? Is the emphasis on political stability ultimately a reflection of conservative ideology? Should not political scientists be more concerned with how political systems change than with how they are maintained? This last criticism proved to be the most damaging. As with the systems model, functionalism seemed to have as little to say about the real world of political change as the narrow institutional approach it had replaced. Under the weight of these criticisms functionalism lost ground to the study of political change. Looking back, it succeeded in taking the study of politics in new directions. But the new destination was no more permanent than the old one.

☐ *Comparing policies*

All the approaches discussed so far concentrate on the process of politics rather than the substance of policy. But since the 1970s and 1980s many political scientists have become more interested in the substance of public policy – in what governments do as well as how they do it.

The policy-making perspective raises such questions as: Why do some countries distribute medical care through the market while others rely on the state? How do states go about improving the competitiveness of industry? Why do some countries give grants to students in higher education while others provide loans – and some offer precious little support at all?

A policy-centred approach has several advantages. *First*, it brings us back to the core political question of who gets what, when and how. For example, some studies of the welfare state in Western democracies suggest that the benefits which the middle classes gain from public services are at least as great as those obtained by the poorer sections of the population (Le Grand 1982).

In medical care, for instance, physicians spend more time with well-educated middle-class patients than with less articulate working-class clients. To find out who benefits from a policy, we must look at how it is carried out, and not just at how it is made.

Secondly, the policy approach is well suited to comparative analysis. Comparing health policy or industrial policy across nations is a clear, coherent brief. It can highlight cross-national differences, and their causes and consequences, in an effective fashion.

Thirdly, a policy perspective leads naturally to a concern with the implementation and effectiveness of policy. Some of the older approaches wrongly assumed that politics stopped once a policy had been adopted. In fact some policies change in the process of execution – and others are hardly put into effect at all. For instance, some Western governments have been lukewarm in enforcing legislation intended to reduce discrimination against minority groups (Neary 1992b).

Finally, comparative policy analysis offers the prospect of drawing lessons which can be used to improve the quality of public policy. A policy which succeeds in one country may be worth trying out in others; a policy which fails in one place may not be worth attempting elsewhere.

Thus the policy-centred approach is a useful addition to the frameworks available in comparative politics. It is discussed further in Chapter 16.

■ Techniques of comparison

Studying politics comparatively is a matter of technique as well as strategy. There are three main techniques, which differ by how many countries are included in the analysis. **Case studies** are based on a sample of one. **Statistical analysis** is based on many examples. **Focused comparisons** are based on two, or at most a few, countries (Lijphart 1971). We'll review each in turn.

□ *Case studies*

A case study of a specific country is not comparative in itself. Nonetheless case studies still provide most of the raw material for comparative politics. To understand how, say, political parties operate, we have to study accounts of parties in particular countries and, from them, seek general conclusions.

Often our confidence in an overall conclusion is strengthened precisely because it has been reached independently in several countries. For example, students of medical politics have noticed some decline in the power of national medical associations in liberal democracies since the 1960s (Harrop 1992). Armed with a general observation like this, we can seek a general explanation. For example, have medical associations lost ground because of some public loss of faith in orthodox medicine? Or has the emergence of a new breed of hospital manager, capable of standing up to senior physicians, been more important?

Paradoxically, unusual cases are particularly significant. **Deviant cases**, as they are known, are especially helpful in forming and testing theories. When sleep researchers discovered The Man Who Never Went To Sleep, they descended on him in droves. To work out why the rest of us go to bed each night, all they had to do was work out what else was different about this poor soul (they never did).

We have already met one example of a deviant case in politics: the absence of a socialist party in the United States. Asking why the United States never had a large socialist party is more revealing than asking why Sweden, along with most Western democracies, did. China is another example. Why did its communist rulers survive the 'year of revolution' in 1989, when most communist regimes collapsed? Is it because China was still not economically developed? Perhaps the weaknesses of a planned economy only emerge when a country reaches a certain level of development. If so, the China crisis is still waiting in the wings.

One problem with case studies is **selection bias**. This means that the cases chosen for study may not be representative of politics as a whole. For example, most political research undertaken in the world today is about the United States. The reason is simple: that's where most political scientists live! But the United States, as we have already noted, is in some ways a deviant case. Similarly, more work is done on democratic than authoritarian governments. Again, the explanation is obvious: democracies are more open and accessible to the researcher. But this should not blind us to the fact that, even in the 1990s, most people experience politics in a harsher climate than liberal democracy.

The main limitation of case studies is that they overstate distinctiveness. If you look at politics in just one country, you run the risk of ignoring similar trends in other countries. You conclude that your example is more special than it actually is. In other words, you fail to see the wood for the tree.

Case studies accumulate rather than cumulate. They only survive in the collective memory of political science discipline when they have some general significance – and many don't. As a student of comparative politics, you should not feel you must remember all the details of every study you look at. Read as much as you can but only remember the points which have value beyond the case. Comparative politics is one subject where the ability to forget is a definite virtue!

☐ *Statistical analysis*

At the opposite extreme to the single case study stand statistical projects based on all liberal democracies, all industrial societies or even all countries. Research adopting this approach deals with variables which are easily quantified. Most often, these are figures on public expenditure. Thus researchers have asked: why do some countries tax at higher rates than others? Why do some countries spend a higher proportion of public expenditure on welfare than others? (Castles 1982). The factors used to answer these questions are also numerical. They include social factors (e.g. urbanisation), economic factors (e.g. affluence) and political factors (e.g. how many years parties of the right have been in power since 1945).

This statistical research consists of complicated manipulation of simple data. Expenditure figures tell us how much is spent. They do not tell us why the money is spent, how it is spent, for whose benefit, and with what consequences. So political scientists need to look beyond the numbers at their wider significance and implications.

Furthermore the problem of selection bias exists even with statistical information. In most cases, the data available to us was originally collected by international bodies such as the World Bank or the Organisation for Economic Co-operation and Development. Their concerns are not necessarily ours. Their priorities tend to be financial, economic, social and political – in that order. Ours are just the reverse.

The meaning of a particular statistic can also vary from country to country. In particular, public programmes must be examined in conjunction with private traditions. Unemployment benefit is limited in Japan, but does this matter to a worker employed by a large company with a tradition of career-long employment? Equally, Japan appears from the statistics to be poorly equipped with nursing homes for the elderly, as indeed it is. But this is largely because Japanese families care for their parents at home. What appears as a weakness is, in some ways, a strength. For these reasons, statistical analysis based on many countries complements qualitative comparisons, but should not replace them.

Statistical relationships help to identify deviant cases – countries which diverge from the expected pattern. A special explanation can then be sought for these exceptions. Why, for example, does the United States spend far more than any other developed country on medical care? Is it because the United States is one of the few countries which relies on the private sector for health insurance? This illustration shows that statistical studies and case studies are not contradictory. Statistical research can highlight cases worthy of further study (Castles 1989).

☐ Focused comparisons

This type of study falls somewhere between case studies and statistical analysis. Done well, this approach has the strengths of both the other techniques but the weaknesses of neither.

Focused comparisons take a small number of countries, typically just two (a **paired comparison**). Most often the comparison concentrates not on all aspects of the countries' politics but just on particular aspects. To illustrate this technique, we'll take three examples from the comparative study of public policy, a growing subfield within comparative politics (see also Chapter 16).

In a classic study, Heclo (1974) examined the origins of unemployment insurance, old age pensions and earnings-related supplementary pensions in Britain and Sweden. In both countries, he concluded, the bureaucracy was the main agency of policy formulation in these areas.

More recently Kudrle and Marmor (1981) compared the growth of social security programmes in the United States and Canada. They argued that the presence of elements of left-wing and Tory paternalistic ideology in Canada explained its edge over the United States in spending and programme development.

As a third example, Grant, Paterson *et al.* (1988) examined policy-making towards the chemical industry in Britain and West Germany. They were struck by the similarity within the policy sector rather than by the difference between the nations. They suggested that national governments had to adjust to the nature of the chemical industry rather more than chemical firms had to adapt to the governments with which they had dealings.

'Small N' studies like these have proved to be the success story of comparative politics in recent decades (Collier 1991). They have been applied not just to policy studies but also to historical questions such as the origins of revolutions (see pp. 67ff. and Skocpol 1984). Focused comparisons remain sensitive to the details of particular countries and policies while retaining some ability to form, and test, explanations. They work particularly well when a few countries are compared over time, examining how countries vary in their response to common problems such as developing the welfare state.

In practice, comparison of even a small number of countries does seem to enhance understanding, whatever the purists may say about the limitations of such a small sample. Larger samples may be needed for statistical purposes, but the biggest gain in understanding comes when the sample is increased from one (a case study) to two (a paired comparison). 'Small N' comparison is therefore a useful technique, and one which is as suited to student projects as to professional monographs.

Summary

1.   Comparing politics across countries has several benefits. It casts fresh light on our own nation. It improves our classifications of political processes. It helps us to test explanations of political patterns. Finally, cross-national comparison has some potential for predicting the effects of introducing particular changes into a country's political system.

2.   But cross-national comparison also has its dangers. There are not enough countries in the world for theories to be tested precisely. Furthermore, many

countries are interdependent so that they cannot be treated as separate examples. The 'same' behaviour can mean different things in different countries. Also, the problems of bias and political values arise when comparing politics in very different countries.

3. Ideally, comparisons should be made between countries which are identical except for the one factor whose effects we wish to determine. This is known as a 'most similar systems' design. In practice, such controlled comparisons are rarely feasible.

4. Most comparative studies focus on states, societies or policies. The **state-centred** approach originally examined the institutions and constitutions of government, in isolation from society. Today, the state-centred approach emphasises the impact of the state on society.

5. The **society-centred** approach was more concerned with the impact of society on the state. It tended to adopt a static view of politics and cast little light on how political systems changed and developed.

6. The **policy-centred** approach compares a single policy sector across countries. This approach looks at how policies are put into effect, and with what effects. It rejects the assumption that politics stops once a policy is agreed.

7. The main techniques used in comparative politics are case studies (a sample of one); focused comparisons (a sample of two or three); and statistical studies (a 'sample' of many or all countries). Case studies are often too descriptive. Statistical analysis runs the danger of becoming mechanical. In practice, focused comparisons of a small number of countries are often most revealing.

Discussion points

1. If you were asked to explain the *distinctive* features of your country's politics to a visitor, what points would you emphasise? (Readers are invited to send their answers to Rod Hague, Department of Politics, The University, Newcastle upon Tyne, England NE1 7RU for use in the 4th edition.)

2. If you were to compare your country's politics with another's, which country would you choose and why?

3. Some critics allege that the comparative method is no longer relevant in an era of global politics. What is the basis of this view? Do you agree with it?

Key reading

Dogan, M. and Pelassy, G. (1984) *How to Compare Nations* (Chatham, N.J.: Chatham House). Short, stimulating but difficult.

Evans, P., Rueschemeyer, D. and Skocpol T. (eds) (1985) *Bringing The State Back In* (Cambridge: Cambridge University Press). An important and influential statement of the centrality of the state to comparative politics.

Macridis, R. and Brown, B. (eds) (1990) *Comparative Politics: Notes and Readings* (Belmont, Calif.: Brooks/Cole). An excellent selection of readings, including several on the comparative method.

Rustow, D. and Erickson, K. (eds) (1991) *Comparative Political Dynamics: Global Research Perspectives* (New York: HarperCollins). Essential reading, not least for Collier's overview of the comparative method.

Further reading

Rustow and Erickson (1991) is a 'state of the art' collection of essays on comparative and global politics. Another edited collection (Macridis and Brown 1990) contains several classic articles on comparison, and provides a good selection of material on comparative politics in general. Other influential works on method are Sartori (1985) on concepts, Lijphart (1971) on strategy and Skocpol (1985) on the comparative historical approach. Almond and Powell (1988) is a best-selling text originally written from a society-centred perspective.

■ PART 2 ■

THE NATION-STATE: EVOLUTION AND REVOLUTION

This part considers the nation-state, the central focus of this book. Chapter 3 looks at how formally equal nation-states differ greatly in power, wealth and the nature of their politics. They comprise three groupings: a first world of wealthy, industrialised liberal democracies, a second world of communist and postcommunist states of middling wealth, and a third world of poorer states. Chapter 4 turns to the question of political change, and in particular how countries are sometimes overtaken by revolutionary change. This chapter also deals with the role of ideas in political change. In Chapter 5 the focus shifts from politics within nation-states to the striking growth of interdependence between them.

■ *Chapter 3* ■

The Nation-State in Three Worlds

■ The three worlds

The traditional approach to comparative government has been to classify regimes by political factors. These include the number of rulers (one? few? many?) and how they achieved power (tradition? election? a coup?). Such distinctions are important but insufficient. It is not enough to classify governments by their formal structures alone. This is unlikely to reveal the full nature of political life in a society. For the landless peasant in Asia, it hardly matters whether the institutions of central government are controlled by a president, a parliament or a general. The daily struggles of life remain unsolved.

Equally, with the collapse of communism, people in Eastern Europe can now claim that they live in democracies just like their fellow Europeans in the West. In fact, however, the differences between East and West are, and will long remain, fundamental. A change of ruler or of the form of government does not in itself give the new regime more resources to meet its people's needs.

So governments should be classified in a way which reflects economic as well as political conditions. The level of economic development states have reached is particularly important. Nearly 200 independent nation-states in the modern world fall into three main groups. The **first world** consists of around thirty wealthy and economically advanced liberal democracies. The **second world** consists of around thirty postcommunist and communist party states. These are mainly industrialised and of middling wealth. And a large and varied number of less developed countries make up the **third world**.

Between liberal democracies and the second world, the basic contrasts have been political. In liberal democracies parties compete for power

45

and so reflect society as much as they shape it. In communist states a single party monopolised power in an attempt to reshape society. Now that communism has collapsed, economic differences between the first and second worlds are coming to the fore.

Between the industrial countries of the northern hemisphere (whether first or second world) and the less industrialised southern hemisphere, the core contrasts are economic as well as political. The vast gaps in living standards between, say, Africa and Western Europe make for very different political agendas in the two continents. Most people in Western Europe take material affluence for granted, while millions in Africa face famine and starvation. Figure 3.1 shows how dramatic are the inequalities between the three worlds. The third world has 52 per cent of the world's population but produces only 18 per cent of its output.

The figure also shows the greater affluence of the second world over the third world, reflecting its higher level of industrialisation. However, communist China (population 1.2 billion!) is a massive anomaly. China's population remains 80 per cent rural, and the country is still fairly poor. China is in the second world politically but the third world economically.

These patterns of wealth and poverty are mainly the outcome of the timing and course of industrialisation. The societies of the *first world* are capitalist. They are the product of an early transition to economies based mainly on private ownership. They are also liberal democracies.

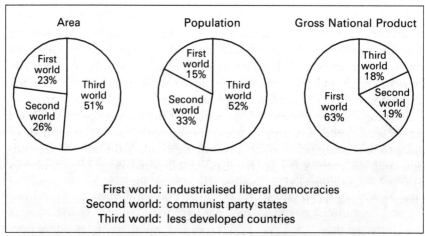

First world: industrialised liberal democracies
Second world: communist party states
Third world: less developed countries

Source: adapted from *World Bank Atlas* (1985); *The World Factbook 1985* (Washington, D.C.: US Govt, 1985).

Figure 3.1   *World divisions, circa 1983*

The creation of a liberal political order against feudal privilege and absolute monarchy was crucial in building a market society. This needed limited government, secure laws of property and contract, and basic civil liberties for individuals. Democratisation, by and large, came later. For the most part Western societies have coped well with the strains of modernisation. Capitalism and liberal democracy are dominant ideas in the first world and are now being exported to the second and third worlds.

In the *second world*, liberal political and economic doctrines undermined authoritarian rulers but did not take root well. Absolute rulers resisted reform and drove their critics to political extremes. Precommunist regimes in Russia and China finally proved unable to cope with the strains of social change and of conflicts with more modern nation-states. They fell to revolutionary communist movements. These quickened the drive towards economic modernity, again under authoritarian control. By creating planned economies and suppressing private ownership, these communist states largely took themselves out of the world capitalist economy, at least for a few decades. The planned economy was effective in the early stage of industrialisation, but later turned out to be rigid, wasteful and inefficient. Communist economic methods became more and more outmoded. This was a major factor in the dramatic collapse of the East European communist regimes in 1989 and of Soviet communism in 1991.

In the *third world*, the course of development differs again. After four hundred years of colonial expansion, the major European nations dominated the globe at the start of the twentieth century. Although Latin America had gained independence from Spain and Portugal in the nineteenth century, it remained an economic appendage of the leading capitalist countries. Most of Asia and Africa was also in European control. But empires fall more rapidly than they rise. The British, French, Dutch and other empires fell apart with amazing speed, chiefly in the great wave of decolonisation after the Second World War.

As these empires unravelled, the model of the nation-state was copied across the globe. Overnight, ex-colonies took on the trappings of independent statehood, which gave the new rulers diplomatic recognition and an entry card to the United Nations. But these countries remained economically and culturally dependent on the countries of the first world, even if they were now politically 'independent'. The postcolonial societies of the third world still rely on agriculture and extractive industries. What manufacturing industry exists is often small-scale, or consists of tariff-protected enclaves making substitutes for imported goods. The more efficient firms are likely to be foreign owned. Rapid population increase in the third world outstrips economic growth; much of the population is at or below subsistence level. The population profile of the third world contrasts sharply with an ageing first world: 80 per cent of all teenagers on the planet live in the third world. Development, then, has now turned out to be elusive while statehood has brought only small benefits; in many ways, independence is more nominal than real.

The common feature of third world politics, then, is that political rulers face huge tasks supported only by fragile and unstable political institutions.

The patterns of power and well-being in the modern world are thus largely the outcome of one overall process of transformation. The 'three worlds' of politics reflect, ironically, one increasingly interdependent world. In this chapter, we discuss the three patterns of politics in turn: the liberal democracies of the first world, the second world of postcommunist and communist party states, and finally the more varied regimes found in the third world.

■ The first world: heartland of liberal democracy

Although almost all regimes in today's world claim to be democratic, we will focus this discussion on the countries of the first world. These, after all, are the most secure and influential examples of liberal democracy.

The concept of a **liberal** democracy is in essence protective. This means that government is seen in a mixed light: necessary, certainly, but also a potential danger to individuals (Held 1987). Liberal concern to guard against the abuse of power therefore qualifies the pure democratic idea of government by the people. A liberal democracy limits government and protects individual rights.

The American constitution is by far the most well-known example of the protective approach to democracy. The founding fathers of the constitution aimed, above all else, to prevent tyranny. To this end, the constitution (see Figure 3.2) features the separation of powers, frequent elections, federalism, the Bill of Rights and judicial interpretation of the constitution. In other words, the broad diffusion of power sets one branch of government to check another. As one of the founders, James Madison, put it, 'You must first enable government to control the governed. You must next oblige the government to control itself.' In order to maintain individual freedom, public power must be restricted in scope and those who hold it must be chosen by, and accountable to, the people.

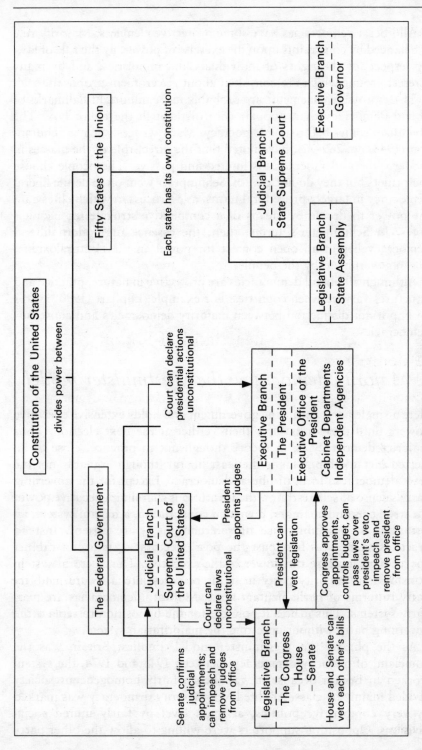

Figure 3.2 *Protective democracy: the US constitutional system*

All liberal democracies have some protective elements. Majority rule is balanced by constraints upon the exercise of power: by the rule of law; by respect for the rights of individuals and minorities; and by many interest groups which are consulted about government proposals.

These protective elements are probably more important hallmarks of liberal democracy than popular control through the ballot box. The liberalism comes before the democracy. Many writers, such as Schumpeter (1943, pp. 269–72), have noted that the direct role of the masses in modern liberal democracies is limited and passive. The people choose their rulers but they do not govern. Schumpeter went on to define liberal democracy in largely procedural terms, as a process in which élites gain the power to decide by means of a competitive struggle for people's votes. In Schumpeter's terms, then, the essence of modern liberal democracy lies in an open contest for power in the electoral arena, not in government by the people.

Although all liberal democracies are protective in nature, practice and structures vary between countries. For example, Lijphart (1990) makes an important distinction between **majority** democracies and **consensus** democracies.

☐ *Majority democracy: the Westminster model*

Here a single party forms the government and holds extensive executive powers until the voters offer their verdict at the next election. Thus majority democracy is, in theory though not in practice, close to an elected dictatorship. This is the least liberal (though arguably not the most democratic) form of liberal democracy. Except for the governing party's sense of self-restraint, the institutions that limit executive power – a strong second chamber, a written constitution, a federal system, an autonomous assembly, use of referendums – are absent. Instead practices such as a 'first past the post' electoral system and cabinet government increase the power of the executive. The electoral system transforms a minority party in terms of votes into a secure majority party in terms of parliamentary seats. Majority democracies are two-party systems. This makes it possible for the opposition to replace the governing party without upsetting the majoritarian system.

As the phrase 'the Westminster model' implies, Britain was the homeland of majority democracy. Between 1945 and 1974, the system worked in Britain because it was then a fairly homogeneous society divided mainly by class. At élite level, majority democracy was marked by very competitive politics, at mass level by fairly muted social divisions. Opposition supporters were willing to allow the other party to govern following a fair electoral contest. Defeat was accepted because the natural swing of the pendulum would return the opposition party to power in due course.

But since 1974 majority democracy in Britain has lost some effectiveness and legitimacy. The class cleavage, which underpinned the two-party system, has declined, and new divisions, especially those of nationalism, have emerged. The major parties (Conservative and Labour) were challenged by centre parties. For the two main parties, holding power has come to depend on the arbitrary working of the electoral system.

One effect has been a growing movement for constitutional reform, supported by the centre parties and even by some leading members of the Labour Party. These critics allege that majority democracy gives too much power to a single party, and that 'the swing of the pendulum' produces damaging reversals of policy as the incoming government seeks to make its mark. Majority democracy in Britain continues, but is no longer in the best of health. Similar criticisms are made about majority democracy in New Zealand (see Exhibit 3.1, p. 52), which if anything is an even 'purer' example of majority democracy than Britain.

☐ *Consensus democracy*

Lijphart uses this term to describe a model in which power is diffused throughout the government and the parties. Executive authority is shared among members of a formal or informal coalition. The executive does not dominate the legislature as it does under majority democracy. There is a multi-party, rather than a two-party, system. The party system reflects several dimensions of cleavage rather than only one. Elections are held under proportional representation rather than 'first past the post'.

Several Western European countries follow this pattern: for example, Belgium, Netherlands, Finland, (see Exhibit 3.2, p. 53) and Denmark. In its fully developed form, the consensus model also features federal and decentralised government; a strong second chamber; and a written and rigid constitution. The United States, Germany, Austria, Australia and Canada fall into this category, though these countries also have majoritarian features. Finally, devices for direct democracy (for instance, town meetings and referendums) may be used alongside representative procedures. These devices are used widely in Switzerland and in many states in the United States.

We are here, of course, contrasting theoretical models of majority and consensus democracies, not actual countries. Few countries exactly fit

Exhibit 3.1   *New Zealand: majority democracy under strain*

The Westminster model of democracy was exported to many Commonwealth countries such as Australia, Canada and New Zealand. Australia and Canada deviate from the model in that both are federal systems, but New Zealand now fits the model of majority democracy better than Britain itself.

New Zealand is a small country, traditionally isolated but now more open to external influences through modern communications and mass travel. The economy is still based on agriculture, highly dependent on overseas trade and heavily exposed to market fluctuations. With New Zealand's reduced isolation, a sense of insecurity has pervaded its politics since the 1970s. The result has been a radical shift from protectionism and welfare values in policy (in which New Zealand was a pioneer) towards freer trade and markets. The small size of its political élite (the House of Representatives has only 97 members) makes such policy changes easier to achieve.

New Zealand has a strong, disciplined two-party system. Since 1935 the Labour Party and the more conservative National Party have alternated in office under a 'first past the post' electoral system. In power, each party has firm control over its backbenchers in the unicameral assembly. Levine (1978) suggests that New Zealand's main parties approach the democratic centralism traditionally associated with communist parties.

New Zealand's politics reflect the remarkable dominance and almost unbridled power of cabinet. Government ministers, aided by a few undersecretaries, can often outvote the rest of the party in Parliament. New Zealand is also a unitary state with no written constitution, which adds to the power of the governing party. Apart from the Maori minority (9 per cent of the population), which has special political representation, New Zealand is ethnically homogeneous. Perhaps the only major respect in which New Zealand departs from the majority model is in its frequent use of local referendums – though these are usually about liquor licensing!

For how long will New Zealand's politics continue in a majoritarian form? There is clear evidence of disillusionment among voters, with low levels of stable party support. But politicians of the major parties do their best to suppress or deflect these signs of restlessness among voters. In 1986 a Royal Commission recommended changes to the electoral system, but its findings were ignored by the Labour Government.

Majority democracy is largely sustained by 'first past the post' elections, but, in New Zealand as elsewhere, the conventions underpinning adversarial politics are under strain.

Exhibit 3.2 *Consensus democracy: Finland*

Finland (population 5 million) is one of several small democracies which border the Baltic Sea in Northern Europe (see Map 5.1, p. 122) During the twentieth century, Finland evolved from a society of peasant farmers to a prosperous society based on a manufacturing and service economy. The welfare state arrived later than in the other Nordic democracies (Sweden, Norway, Denmark and Iceland), but is now well developed.

There have been several major political cleavages in the party system: among them, language (Swedish versus Finnish); communist versus noncommunist; and primary sector (forestry and agriculture) versus the non-primary (manufacturing and services) sector. The prevailing image of Finland's politics is one of extreme multi-partyism, with sizeable anti-system parties and unstable cabinets.

But how valid is this image? The transformation of Finnish society certainly involved harsh struggles, including a civil war between Whites (anti-communists) and Reds (communists). But the bitterness of these conflicts has now faded. The normal image of Finnish politics does not convey the consensual aspects of the system, the longevity in office of key political actors, and the continuity of policy. While the Red–Green coalitions (the socialist and peasant parties) of the early postwar years were beset by serious policy conflicts, in recent years centre-left coalitions have been more stable.

Policy-making in Finland resembles the consensual democracy model quite closely. As in Sweden, cabinet proceedings are a matter of public record. Regular 'evening classes' take place, in which ministers discuss matters 'off the record'. 'Sauna evenings', too, are a popular way for politicians to make deals. Despite a difficult birth as an independent state, Finland fits the pattern of a consensus democracy.

the full check-list of either model. Among those midway between the two models, according to Lijphart, are Italy, France, Norway and Sweden. The value of Lijphart's analysis is that it corrects the impression that the majoritarian 'Westminster model' is somehow the best or most genuine form of liberal democracy. In fact, strictly majoritarian democracy is becoming rare. It is only likely to work well in a fairly homogeneous society without sharp political conflict. In more pluralistic societies, consensus democracy is often more suitable. This is because it diffuses power, and ensures that all major groups and interests in society have *some* influence. Consensus democracy is in essence the politics of compromise.

■ The second world: communism and postcommunism

Between the 1917 October Revolution in Russia and the late 1970s, communist power expanded dramatically in Eastern Europe, Asia and Africa. Some sixteen communist regimes, and a dozen others of more doubtful Marxist credentials, came to power. Their routes to power were revolution, wars of national liberation, or force of Soviet arms. At their peak in the 1960s and 1970s, communist regimes accounted for more than 1.5 billion people – one-third of the world's population. China alone supplies over a billion of them.

The communist world was surprisingly diverse. It ranged from dirt poor pre-industrial societies, such as Laos and Kampuchea, to industrialised countries like Czechoslovakia and Hungary. Although all communist states subscribed to the teachings of Marx and Lenin, open splits developed between them. From the 1960s, they no longer formed a cohesive bloc.

Authoritarian rule was intrinsic to the communist system. The party could not be challenged in elections, and it played a directive role within the political system. A structure of popular representative government did exist. Communist regimes claimed to be democratic, indeed far more so than the capitalist democracies of the first world. As Cuban leader Fidel Castro told his people, 'Imperialism has a single party, it's called capitalism. There is no workers' party there, the whole social system is organised for the government of capitalists'. But popular participation in the Second World was 'guided democracy', operating under the firm hand of the party. The party ruled in the name of the ideology of Marxism-Leninism. It claimed to be building a new, equal and classless society. In practice, the party sought first and foremost to maintain its own power and privileges.

With some variations, the economy was organised along state socialist lines, with national economic planning and public ownership of the means of production.

The relationship between party and state was central to communist rule. In theory, the state in socialist society was separate from the ruling party. The party laid down the policy guidelines which the government then implemented. Again, in theory, the existence of the state was only temporary. The state was the agent of working-class dictatorship. Once class conflict was erased, so too was the need for an apparatus of control and coercion. The state would then wither away.

□ *The failure of communism*

The reality has been very different. In practice, the divide between party and state blurred through interpenetration and supervision. At higher levels of government, there is joint membership of party and state. Leading state positions are filled by party members, and leading state officials concurrently hold key party posts. For example in North Korea, one of the few surviving communist states, Kim Il Sung serves at once as Secretary General of the party, Premier of the Cabinet, President of the Republic, and as Commander in Chief of the Armed Forces. In short, he is head of the party, the state and the military.

To reinforce its control, the ruling party has always shadowed and supervised the work of state administrations through its own organisations, right down to the local level. Thus, party members acted as watchdogs in the government agencies and enterprises in which they worked. If necessary, they would intervene to ensure that party policy was firmly followed.

Why did practice diverge from theory? Basically, because the party and state bureaucracy ran the entire economy as if it were a single national firm. Rather than withering away, as Marx and Engels had forecast, the state expanded into an all-embracing network of large institutions. Lenin saw too late the danger that this bureaucracy would dominate society. In effect the *apparatchiks*, the men of the party-state apparatus, became a ruling class.

Worse than this, however, the so-called 'planned economy' was not rationally planned at all. It was a command economy, organised from above on an ideological basis. Without incentives for efficient use of resources, the economy was wastefully run and ignored people's needs. Over the long haul, it was unable to provide both guns and butter. It could not maintain heavy defence expenditures *and* improve living standards.

Communism's decline in Eastern Europe was speeded by the failure of the party-state bureaucracy to accept reform. The bureaucracy was top-heavy, politically hidebound and deeply imbued with self-interest. As Mikhail Gorbachev found, efforts at economic reform that reduced the bureaucracy's power (e.g. introducing markets) were strongly resisted. To paraphrase Marx, the ruling institutions of the Marxist-Leninist states became fetters upon the further development of the productive forces of these societies. When the chance finally came, the people threw off their communist rulers without hesitation.

☐ *The challenge of postcommunism*

A key problem facing postcommunist states in the 1990s is defining the role of the state. Because of the rapid collapse of the communist system, the transition from state to private ownership was anything but smooth. There was no gradual evolution from state planning and distribution to the market. Choices had to be made about the extent of state ownership and intervention in the economy. Some postcommunist democracies run the risk of swinging from one extreme to the other: from an over-centralised state-run economy to extreme *laissez-faire*. A population used to one system will need time to adjust to another.

This risk is increased by the tainted nature of the state after the collapse of communist control. Because of the close links between party and state, both are associated with repression, surveillance and social control. A bitter irony is that many of the new entrepreneurs will be former communist *apparatchiks* and factory directors. They are the people with the wealth, the contacts and the experience to set up new ventures and take over newly privatised businesses.

The postcommunist authorities will have no choice but to employ many officials, policemen and administrators from the old regime, in order to keep public services going. In this, history is repeating itself. After they seized power in both China and the Soviet Union, the communist parties were forced to rely on officials and experts from the old regimes. Today, in Bulgaria and Romania, many state officials from the communist era are still in place. Even in Poland, Hungary and Czechoslovakia, where the electoral revolt against communism was nearly total, many personnel from the old regime remain. Democracy may have arrived in Eastern Europe. Even so, as Lenin found after the Russian revolution, skilled and experienced personnel are still needed to run the administration.

Although individual freedom is now far greater than under commu-nist rule, the protective aspects of democracy still seem weakly rooted.

Only six months after the fall of the communist dictatorship in Romania, for example, the new government bussed thousands of miners into Bucharest. Their job, performed with gusto, was to beat up protestors and quell embarrassing criticism. Again, deep ethnic hatreds simmer in Bulgaria and Romania, and erupted into turmoil in Yugoslavia. Some observers fear that Poland, whose people struggled for decades to slough off Marxism-Leninism, could now find itself politically dominated by the Roman Catholic Church.

The transition to liberal democracy in Eastern Europe was remarkably fast, as people were united by their opposition to communism. But in societies beset by hardships, and impatient for results, the impulse towards authoritarianism and populism will be strong. Consolidating liberal democracy will be a long and uncertain business.

■ The third world: the politics of economics

Because the level of economic development is the key to their situation, it makes sense to classify third world countries in economic as well as in political terms. Among the most important factors are:

- the size and distribution of the national income,
- the extent of industrialisation and urbanisation,
- the amount of foreign debt
- the concentration of exports on a single commodity.

All these affect the options open to third world governments, whatever their form of government or political ideology. The country's relationship to international markets is vital. Third world states typically depend far more on the international economy than those in the first world, and have far less influence upon it.

□ An economic classification

There are four main clusters of third world states: oil-exporters, newly industrialising countries (NICs), less developed, least developed. We look briefly at each group.

1. **Oil-exporters** – These countries, mainly in the Middle East, supply the oil that is the lifeblood of world industry. Since they began to use the leverage this gives them, the major oil-exporting states have enjoyed vast revenues. With only small populations to support, several of these countries (Saudi Arabia, United Arab Emirates, Brunei) are enormously

rich, with average incomes exceeding $10,000 per head. These highly affluent states are ruled by traditional monarchs. The Saudi monarchy, for instance, provides its people with extensive health and education services but the regime is ultra-conservative and predemocratic. Elections and representative institutions do not exist or are of little moment. Politics is the preserve of the ruling family and its advisers.

2.   **Newly industrialising countries (NICs)** – A few countries, mainly in the Pacific rim of East Asia (South Korea, Taiwan, Singapore, Hong Kong) are striding rapidly towards the first world, economically at least. Income levels have reached $2000–$4000 per head, and are rising steadily. The political evolution of the NICs has been slower. They combine a stable (if often authoritarian) political system with a coherent development strategy. The workforce is disciplined and now fairly well educated. As a result, the NICs make goods which increasingly compete on quality, and not just price, in the world market. In theory, this then leaves room for other, lower cost countries (such as Malaysia) to enter the world's manufacturing economy and form the next generation of NICs.

3.   **Less developed countries** – In about forty other third world countries, significant economic development has taken place. However the modern sector of the economy is not internationally competitive (unlike the NICs) or else is dominated by transnational companies. Income levels in some of these countries, such as Argentina, Chile and Uruguay, can be fairly high ($1000–$3000 per head). But their economic development has come to a halt or is subject to large fluctuations. This makes for political instability.

4.   **Least developed countries** – Around seventy very poor countries, many in Africa, have incomes per head below $1000 a year. They almost entirely lack a manufacturing base. Instead, they depend on one or two commodities for export earnings. Often highly dependent on foreign aid and burdened with debt, these countries are in a very weak position from which to attempt economic development.

☐ *From oligarchy to democracy?*

The background: oligarchy

Oligarchic tendencies are most marked in third world politics because of the very uneven distribution of political resources. Oligarchy means the rule of a few. A tiny élite dominates political life and the mass of the population is inactive. Elections, if they are held, are 'made' by the men of wealth and influence. To be sure, there are quarrels and conflicts among the oligarchs: between 'old' and 'new' wealth, between land-owners and the urban bourgeoisie, for instance. But the ordinary people are not involved and neither are their interests reflected in these conflicts. They are kept at bay, by ignorance, by deference, and if necessary by repression.

Oligarchy has been a phase of political development in many countries, including most of those in the first world. But traditional élites in the third world have been more stubborn than were, say, European aristocrats in clinging to their wealth, power and privilege. When the pressure from the masses became too strong, third world oligarchs have often turned to repression rather than reform, encouraging right-wing military intervention.

There is, in fact, a long history of intervention by the army in many third world countries, especially in Latin America and more recently in Africa and Asia. But the military have been notable failures as political rulers. In the 1980s the soldiers in Latin America and Africa who seized power in the previous two decades were in retreat. The late 1980s was the twilight of state dictators.

Arguably, the final curtain has now fallen on army intervention in Latin America. Almost all the military regimes there were troubled by grave economic failure. Vicious repression to curb political opposition and industrial protest could not disguise these difficulties. As the soldiers lost confidence, so they faced growing pressure from politicians and ordinary people alike to restore civilian government. In addition, US support for right-wing military regimes came to an end. This reflected the weakening of its superpower rivalry with the Soviet Union. In recent years, the United States has supported democratic elections and the path of moderate reform.

Whether military intervention is a thing of the past in sub-Saharan Africa is more doubtful. Uncertainties arise because economic development is more limited there, and because the army is a heavyweight institution in societies where the institutions of government are weak.

But military rule is only one form of oligarchic control in the third world. The wave of de-colonisation in the postwar period soon led to **single-party regimes** in much of the third world, especially in the Middle East, North and sub-Saharan Africa. Parties of a nationalist and socialist character have ruled both Syria and Iraq since the 1960s. In North Africa, the best-known cases were the Neo-Destour party in Tunisia and the FLN in Algeria. Throughout sub-Saharan Africa, single-party regimes were common. They included Senegal, Guinea, Ghana (in the 1960s), Ivory Coast, Kenya, Tanzania and Zambia.

One-party rule was justified on various grounds. Political competition was held to be alien to Arab or African culture, or needlessly divisive and a risky luxury in societies facing great challenges. The purpose claimed for the single party was to mobilise society for development. It would focus loyalties, and integrate diverse peoples into a new nation. It would also harness their energies for a huge effort to transform society. Economic and social development was attempted under the aegis of a permanent ruling party.

Some regimes were far more repressive than others. The savagery of Saddam Hussein's regime in Iraq was of a quite different order to the bureaucratic restrictions of Julius Nyerere's Tanzania. But in neither case was open political opposition permitted. It was held down by a mixture of coercion, co-opting potential opponents into the regime, and personality cults.

Some Arab single-party regimes (for example Libya, Iraq, Syria and Algeria) had oil or other resources, which could be used to finance economic and social modernisation. But rulers like Colonel Quadafi of Libya, or Iraq's Saddam Hussein, used these resources to pursue grandiose ambitions abroad and underpin tight dictatorship at home, rather than for the benefit of the whole population.

Moreover, with only Kenya as a doubtful exception, the attempt at modernisation under single-party rule in Africa clearly failed. One-party government was barely more successful than military rule. Ruling parties became little more than businesses for the politicians. Through the party, and therefore the state, rulers acquired access to luxuries and consumer goods which the mass of the population could not obtain. Eventually, international economic pressures swamped even those states like Tanzania which tried go-it-alone economic development.

By the late 1980s, the single-party rulers of Africa faced domestic discontent, fuelled by two decades of economic setbacks. They also confronted international pressure. First world governments held the purse strings of aid but their price was more democracy and pluralism. The collapse of communist Eastern Europe also stripped away the illusion of an alternative model of development. In the 1990s the non-democratic rulers of African states faced three alternatives. First, they could stand fast and risk their own overthrow. Secondly, they could try to retain control by guiding the transition to multi-partyism. Thirdly, they could face the verdict of free elections.

Moving towards democracy

A few third world countries have been able to operate liberal democratic regimes since independence. These include India (see Exhibit 3.3), some

---

Exhibit 3.3 *India: democracy and dynasty*

A huge, poor country with over 700 million people, the Republic of India is by far the most important case of post-colonial democratic government (Ray 1989). The Congress Party has dominated Indian politics since the 1940s, having led the country to independence from British rule. The party, however, has become a coalition held together only by allegiance to the Gandhi family which has ruled India most of the time since independence.

Despite the strains imposed by India's huge diversity and poverty, parliamentary government has been maintained. This in itself is a remarkable achievement. But there are signs that Indian democracy faces a crisis of governability. It may not cope with a rising tide of discontent fuelled by expectations which politicians raise but rarely fulfil. Political democracy, imposed from above, does not transform traditional structures in a more egalitarian direction but sparks off a revivalist backlash. The growing incidence of political killings, riots, inter-communal violence and separatist conflicts are ominous signs.

India also faces severe economic problems. Its huge foreign debt gives the international community a lever with which to prise its markets open to imports from abroad. Eventually, this may increase India's growth rate but only at the cost of offending many people accustomed to a cushion of protection previously supplied by the ruling party.

At the centre of Indian politics, the ability of the parties, especially the Congress Party, to pursue effective policies has declined. Leadership has become more and more personalised, and support a matter of patron-client relations rather than of principles and policies. Also, in many areas, party organisation has passed into the hands of criminals and 'strong men'. In short, India seems to be catching up fast with how the third world used to be. (Kohli 1990)

---

small islands in the Pacific and Caribbean, and Botswana and Gambia in Africa. But these are the exceptions. Until the 1980s, military or one-party rule was far more typical.

Past conditions have not favoured liberal democracy in the third world. Political and military leaders have often been hostile to democracy; the population has not been used to it. With resources in such short supply, the state became the main point of access to them.

The struggle to gain and hold on to power was relentless. There was little restraint or tolerance, and political opposition therefore carried great risks.

However, the prospects for democracy have clearly advanced. The tide has been running towards democracy in the 1980s and 1990s. Despite an appalling economic legacy and the constant risk of further army intervention, elected governments have survived in Latin America. Some have survived the acid test of peaceful changes of leadership. The population's memory of military incompetence and widespread abuse of human rights has helped sustain civilian rule. Over the longer term, stable democracy in Latin America will be further reinforced if the economy performs well.

Ballots may replace bullets, but this does not always broaden popular influence over government. Formal democracy arrives, rather than the substance of a democratic society. Consider the Philippines as an example. Popular forces supported Mrs Cory Aquino's campaign against the corrupt regime of President Marcos. After rigging the Presidential election of 1986, Marcos was forced into exile, partly by US pressure. But most of the 'crony capitalist' élite that flourished under Marcos survives; President Aquino has been absorbed by it, according to her critics. Reforms have been shelved, while an undeclared guerilla war rages in the rural areas. Land reform programmes announced with great fanfare in Manila, the capital city, somehow peter out in the countryside where they meet stubborn resistance from landlords.

The same could be said of Mexico, India, Brazil or many other third world countries. The introduction of democratic forms does not, and cannot, solve fundamental problems of poverty and economic inequality. But this means political inequalities will continue, slightly moderated perhaps but certainly not eliminated. Even if they have the will, elected politicians lack the power to act against the interests of the economic 'haves'. Moreover, where the 'have-nots' are concerned, the real face of the state can be completely unchanged. The post-military Brazilian Government, for instance, declares its commitment to human rights, but off-duty policemen still murder street urchins, petty criminals, peasant leaders and trade union activists.

In many third world countries, the transition to democracy has taken place against the backdrop of economic deterioration. Democratically chosen politicians are picking up the pieces from years of authoritarian misrule and misspending. Prosperity is always the best handmaiden for democracy. Post-authoritarian states in the third world, just like postcommunist states in the second world, are growing up in a tough environment.

Summary

1.   The three worlds are the outcome of a single process of change, but this has led to widely divergent outcomes. There is a rich, capitalist first world of liberal democracies; a less wealthy second world in which state-controlled modernisation failed, leading to the collapse of communism; and a diverse but poorer third world, which is linked to the first world but has little influence upon it.

2.   Liberal democracy combines popular influence with controls upon government. In essence, political parties and candidates compete for the right to govern. There are two main forms. Majority democracy (e.g. New Zealand, UK) gives clear control over the levers of government to the majority party in the legislature. Consensus democracy (e.g. Finland, the Netherlands) emphasises power-sharing between parties in a number of formal and informal ways.

3.   Communist party states had state-owned economies under strict party control. Though effective for early industrialisation, the command economy could not make the transition to a modern, high-productivity economy. This was a major cause of communist collapse. Efforts at reform only worsened basic economic weaknesses and revealed the lack of popular support for the regime.

4.   The postcommunist regimes are emergent liberal democracies, but their political and economic prospects vary widely. All face the problem of erasing the residue of communism and redefining the role of the state, particularly in the economy. All face a huge task of social and economic renewal with thin resources. The resurgence of nationalism and ethnic conflict may destabilise individual countries or entire regions in the postcommunist world.

5.   Third world countries vary in their economic position. A few   wealthy oil-exporting countries enjoy considerable affluence. Another small group of newly industrialising countries supplies goods to the world market at low cost, and makes economic progress from so doing. At the bottom of the scale come the least developed countries, largely irrelevant to the international economy and highly dependent on aid.

6.   Third world politics has not   favoured stable democracy in the past. Regimes have typically been oligarchic – run by the few. Military rule or single-party government has predominated. The 1980s, however, saw a sweeping transition to democracy, at least in the sense that leaders are elected through multi-party elections. But oligarchic tendencies are deep-rooted, and renewed military intervention cannot be ruled out, particularly in Africa.

Discussion points

1.   Is liberal democracy the 'final form' of government?

2.   Has consensus democracy more of a future than majority democracy? If so, why?

3.   Are capitalism and democracy partners or enemies?

4.   Why were communist party states incapable of reforming themselves?

5.   Assess the prospects for (*a*) market-based capitalism and (*b*) liberal democracy in Eastern Europe.

6.   Is economics more fundamental to the future of third world countries than politics?

7.   Will the current moves to more democracy in the third world eventually produce stable liberal democracies?

Key reading

Diamond, L., Linz, J. and Lipset, S. (eds) (1989), *Democracy in Developing Countries*, 3 vols (Boulder, Colo.: Lynne Rienner). Comprehensive coverage of democratic trends in all major third world countries.

White, S. *et al.* (1990) *Communist and PostCommunist Political Systems: an Introduction*, 3rd edn (Basingstoke: Macmillan). Covers the end of communism in Eastern Europe but not its final demise in the Soviet Union.

Held, D. (1987) *Models of Democracy* (Oxford: Polity). This challenging book is among the most accomplished recent works on democracy.

Munck, R. (1989) *Latin America: The Transition to Democracy* (London: Zed Books) examines the development of the 'democratic discourse' in Latin America.

Wiseman, J. (1990) *Democracy in Black Africa: Survival and Revival* (New York: Paragon House) examines democratic traditions and transitions in black Africa.

Further reading

The contributions in Bebler and Seroka (1990), classifying contemporary political systems, are uneven, but the chapter by Lijphart on democracy repays reading; see also Lijphart (1984a). Powell (1982) blends empirical and theoretical approaches to democracy. Dahl's many writings (1971, 1982, 1984 among them) have been highly influential.

The nature of politics in the second world is comprehensively analysed in Holmes (1986), while Djilas (1957) remains a classic and prescient source in the light of 1989. S. White *et al.* (1990) is very good on the communist demise in Eastern Europe. For this, see also Bertsch (1990).

Third world politics are succinctly covered by Clapham (1985) and in Cammack *et al.* (1988). O'Brien and Cammack (1985) deal with the retreat of military authoritarianism in Latin America. The persistence of clientelism is the subject of Clapham (1982). Diamond, Linz and Lipset (1989, 3 vols) assess democratic trends in all major third world countries.

◼ *Chapter 4* ◼

Revolution, Ideology and Political Change

◼ Types of political change

The world of nation-states we inhabit today results from changes that have taken place over centuries. Some of these changes have been gradual. For example, developments in technology are fundamental to our world, but they tend to take place regularly and steadily. Political change, however, tends to be irregular. Long periods of calm are punctured by intense periods of change, the effects of which are felt for generations. This means we cannot just concentrate on the peaceful periods. To understand the political landscape of today, we must also analyse the political earthquakes of the past.

Political change takes several forms. At the two extremes stand **evolutionary** and **revolutionary change**. Evolutionary change is gradual but can, over time, transform the way a government works. Britain is a good example of a political system characterised by evolutionary change. The institutions of monarchy, Parliament and the Cabinet have survived, but their functions and relative importance have altered in response to changing demands. Similarly, the United States retains the institutions set up by the constitution adopted in 1789. However, the authors of the American constitution would be astonished at how government activity has developed over the last two hundred years.

Any wide-ranging change may be loosely defined as revolutionary. However, a tighter definition of political revolutions requires a fundamental change in the distribution of power in the nation concerned, and often in other nations as well. The impact of revolutions is so great that they often transcend national boundaries. The regime brought about by a revolution may not last for ever but the revolution itself is permanent and irreversible. It becomes part of the country's political culture.

Between the poles of evolution and revolution stands political change brought about by the transfer of power from one set of leaders to another within an existing political, social and economic framework. These may be **orderly** or **irregular transfers**. In the modern world orderly transfers take place through elections. Irregular transfers such as military coups are dealt with in Chapter 15. In neither case do these transfers of power reconstruct the political landscape. A single transfer of power, whether orderly or irregular, lacks the transformative drive associated with revolutions.

■ What is a revolution?

Although revolutions are associated with the modern world, they have long been a preoccupation of students of politics. However, the meaning of the term 'revolution' has changed over time. In *The Politics*, Aristotle (1962) was concerned with 'revolutions' in the city-states of Ancient Greece (see Exhibit 2.1). But when Aristotle spoke about revolution, he was merely referring to a transfer of power that involved a change in either the individuals in power, or the constitution. Such a definition of revolution would not be accepted by contemporary political scientists.

A revolution entails much broader and deeper alterations within society. Such changes may include the alteration of social values, social structures and political institutions, as well as changes in the personnel of the ruling élite or its class composition (Cohan 1975, p. 31). Whether these changes have or have not taken place within a society may take years to become apparent.

This begs another question. There is no doubt that the Soviet Union underwent dramatic political change between 1984 and 1991, but does this mean that a revolution took place? Can an aggregation of political changes over a fairly lengthy period be considered to be a revolution? If so, is there a time limit on what constitutes a revolution? The United States in 1989 was certainly very different from the United States of 1789, but to refer to a 200-year revolution is absurd. Historical judgement may be the only way to disentangle revolutionary change from other transfers of power. What the media report today as a 'revolution' may be remembered as just another coup, and what appears to be a series of radical reforms at the time may later be judged a revolution.

■ Explaining revolutionary change

In the first two decades after the Second World War, political scientists were preoccupied with the problem of political stability rather than political change. Put simply, political stability was seen as 'good' and political change was seen as potentially 'bad'. This cautious outlook was understandable. The world had just experienced the global consequences of two major liberal democracies – Germany and Italy – succumbing to fascist dictatorship. With the defeat of fascism, a new 'threat' to stability emerged in the form of communism. Political scientists also wanted to secure political stability in the newly independent nations of the third world. Soon after independence, many of these regimes had succumbed to irregular transfers of power.

The perspective of most political scientists has now shifted. The study of political stability has given way to the study of political change. Students of change claim that nation-states never reach equilibrium – they are continually adapting to their environment. Where students of stability adopted a sociological approach, the study of political change necessarily employs a historical approach.

There are (at least) four main approaches to the study of political instability and revolution. These are:

1. The Marxist approach;
2. Functionalism;
3. Social psychology;
4. Comparative history.

Although the assumptions behind these four approaches are contradictory, their interpretations also complement each other by concentrating on different aspects of political instability.

☐ *Marxism*

Marxism dominated the study of revolution for over a century. Marx viewed revolution as inescapable. The entire movement of history was inevitable – and would culminate in the creation of a communist society. For Marx, when revolution occurred, it would be much more than just a coup or uprising. It involved the transformation of society from one mode of production to another.

Marx argued that capitalism, the prevailing economic system, creates conflict in society between ruling and exploited classes. Members of the exploited class become increasingly alienated from the existing order, and are drawn together by an emerging class consciousness. Once the exploited class becomes sufficiently strong, it rises up and overthrows the ruling class. A total change in the distribution of power takes place as the exploited class takes its destiny into its own hands and begins a new historical epoch.

Marx believed that when revolution occurred, it would be workers in the most advanced industrialised nations – for example, Britain and Germany – who would revolt first. But the revolution would not stop with the overthrow of the ruling class in one nation. The international capitalist system would be unable to function if the dominant (hegemonic) economy within it was eliminated. As a result, revolution in the centre of the world economy would lead to revolutions throughout the world.

Yet the lesson of history is that the exploited workers in the most highly developed industrial nations have not risen in revolution. Nor does it appear that revolutionary class consciousness has increased; if anything, it has declined. Either the Western proletariat has failed to understand its historical mission, or the capitalist system has proved much more flexible and durable than Marx suggested.

Rather than occurring in the strongest links in the capitalist chain, communist revolutions have taken place in some of the weakest links, such as Russia and China. In the first two decades of the twentieth century, Lenin applied himself to the task of devising a revolutionary strategy that was applicable for Russia.

Lenin argued that the reactionary nature of the Tsar's (Russian Emperor's) regime could interact with peasant and worker discontent to produce a revolutionary situation. In such circumstances the proletariat, small as it was, might have the opportunity to seize power. The stage of bourgeois democracy under capitalism could thus be by-passed as Russia moved directly to a more 'advanced' socialist system – or at least the capitalist phase could be telescoped into a very short time. The crucial point for Lenin was that the proletariat should be led by a well-organised revolutionary party. In 1902 he declared: 'Give us an organization of revolutionaries and we shall overturn the whole of Russia!' In 1917, the wish was fulfilled and the deed accomplished.

Lenin's contribution to the theory of revolution lay in adapting Marxism to the purpose of achieving revolution in Russia. This process was repeated elsewhere. In China, Mao Zedong adapted Marxism to achieve revolution in a society without an established industrial proletariat of any sort. Instead, the peasants were the key to revolution in China. Long exploited by the landlords, they were spurred into revolutionary activity as their situation worsened after the arrival of Western imperialist powers such as Britain and France from 1839 onwards.

Nationalism played a major part role in the Chinese revolution. Between 1937 and 1944 with much of China occupied by Japan, the communists downplayed their policy of class war, and instead built their policies around the anti-Japanese fervour of the population. As such, the rise to power of the communists in 1949 can be seen as a victory for nationalist ideology. Communism was to come later, once the party was in power.

Marx had regarded the peasantry as a reactionary class with no role to play in the revolution. Lenin viewed peasants as at best a dispensable ally in the proletariat's quest for power. Mao rejected these views and recognised the revolutionary potential of the peasantry – at least in China.

Marx's ideas regarding revolution have not proved pertinent for political change in Western capitalist societies – the very countries that he had in mind. Marxist regimes have come to power in very different circumstances to those envisaged by Marx. In the process, the theory has been transformed. We do not just talk of Marxism, but also of Marxism-Leninism, Titoism, Maoism and so on. For Schwartz (1960) the political thought of Mao Zedong is so far divorced from the original writings of Marx, that Mao can hardly be called a Marxist at all.

□ Functionalism

The division of society into conflicting classes is the decisive factor in Marxist views of revolution. This profoundly distinguishes Marxist from functionalist theorists of revolution. If Marxism emphasises conflict in society, then the main preoccupation of functionalism is *equilibrium*. According to the functional theory, the task of government is to find an equilibrium between the political system and its environment. As long as rulers respond to new demands placed upon them, the political system is likely to remain in balance and the prospects for stability are enhanced. If rulers fail to adapt to changing conditions and demands, disequilibrium develops. If this goes unchecked for too long, a revolutionary situation develops. Thus where Marx saw revolutions as a progressive force, functionalists *see* them as a response to ineffective government.

Perhaps the best analogy is to think of a set of scales with the political system on one side, and the environment (social, economic, international) on the other. As new items are placed on the environment side of the scales, the government side has to respond by making the correct adjustments to achieve a balance. Revolution can occur when the scales are no longer in balance, but tip heavily over to one side.

The main attempt to develop a theory of revolutionary change from a functional perspective was made by Chalmers Johnson (1966). He suggested that revolutionary situations occur when the political order is no longer broadly accepted within society. This is most likely to happen when the political system is unable to cope with the pace and number of pressures for change. Leaders become swamped by the demands placed upon them, and are unable to satisfy popular expectations. As a result, legitimacy is lost, and a progressive reduction of system effectiveness – **power deflation** – follows. These pressures may come from within the society itself, from outside, or (most destructively) from both in combination. For example, in China at the end of the nineteenth century, the emperors faced both internal pressures to change, and external pressures from foreign intervention.

Initially, political élites often respond in an uncompromising way to pressures for change, resorting to force to maintain their position. However this leads to a further loss of legitimacy. Many ailing regimes attempt at the last to respond to the pressures by implementing reforms. However, the epitaph of so many reforms is 'too little, too late'. In France, Russia and China, the traditional leaders tried to defuse mounting political tensions by introducing reforms. But on all occasions they merely dealt with the symptoms, and did not treat the illness itself.

Johnson's view of what constitutes a revolution is poles apart from Marx's. Even unsuccessful attempts at overthrowing the government are taken by Johnson as instances of revolutionary change. Any behaviour that disrupts settled expectations is revolutionary violence – even if no violence is used by the 'revolutionaries'. This view seems exaggerated to say the least. The functionalists' concern with the smooth running of the system produces insensitivity to the varied forms of political change.

☐ *Social psychology*

The social psychological account seeks to identify what motivates individuals to get involved in revolutionary activity. Why do some people sometimes feel so strongly about politics that they are willing to give time, energy and ultimately their lives to achieve change? This approach focuses on the individual conditions of political instability, but says little about the differing forms of instability. It does not explain why riots sometimes become rebellions, nor why rebellions occasionally turn into revolutions.

Originally propounded by de Tocqueville (1856, 1966) in his study of the French revolution, the social psychological approach found favour in the United States in the 1960s. One of its main exponents was Gurr (1980, ed.). He argued that **relative deprivation** was the key to collective violence in politics. When there is a difference between what people perceive they are getting (value capability) and what they feel they are entitled to or should be getting (value expectations), collective violence may result. Relative deprivation does not only arise from a 'deficit' of wealth and well-being. The shortfall can also be seen in relation to social status or even political participation. The key factor is the gap between what people want and what they get.

Political instability can develop when relative deprivation is both widespread and intensely felt. If writers of politics textbooks feel that they are not getting paid enough, it is unlikely that violence will follow. Their complaint, though just, is ignored by the rest of society. However, if other larger sectors of the population also feel relatively deprived, then violence is more likely.

The dangerous situation for rulers is when expectations are rising, as with people in the third world who aspire to first world living standards, or when the ability to meet demands falls, as when the economy goes into recession. The most hazardous period of all is when a period of rising expectations is followed by a decline in the ability of the regime to meet those demands. This tension is intensified if the government has attempted to gain legitimacy by making promises of future well-being that it finds it cannot keep.

Davies (1962) sums up the implications of this approach: 'revolutions are most likely to occur when a prolonged period of economic and social development is followed by a short period of sharp reversal.' This hypothesis is known as the 'J-Curve' theory. Figure 4.1 presents the theory in a graph showing the relationship between expectations and capabilities over time.

Relative deprivation's main contribution to the study of revolutionary change lies in pointing out that how people perceive their condition is more important than the actual condition itself. Perceptions are normally based on comparisons made over time: 'Am I better off than I was last year?' This means that as long as conditions are not worsening, grinding poverty and enormous inequality will not normally yield political instability. Here, then, is an explanation of why revolutions are so rare.

As de Tocqueville noted, the most dangerous time for an oppressive ruler is to embark on reform and hold out the prospect of improvement. Grievances patiently endured become intolerable once the possibility of a brighter future crosses the population's minds. In short, reforming leaders must exercise great care if they are not to reform themselves out of power.

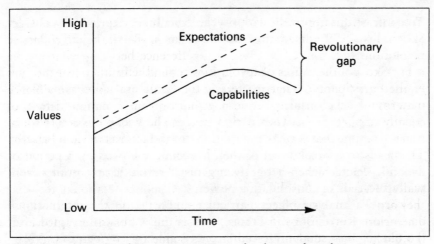

Source: An adaptation from J. Davies, 'Toward a theory of revolution', *American Sociological Review* vol. 27 (1962), pp. 5–18.

Figure 4.1 *The J-curve theory of revolutions*

Another cause of relative deprivation is when comparisons are made with other groups: 'I am better off than I was, but my position has not improved as much as theirs.' For instance, feelings among China's students that they were not getting as much out of new wealth as other groups is one reason why they took to the streets in the spring of 1989. Furthermore, the Eastern European revolutions of 1989 suggest that comparisons with other groups can play an important role in creating instability – 'I am better off than I was, but I am not as well off as people in the West.'

Although the psychological approach provides an interesting insight into the conditions of political instability, it is certainly insufficient in explaining political change. Whose discontent matters? Why does discontent sometimes lead to an uprising, but sometimes not? How and why do uprisings turn into revolutions? How is discontent channelled into organised opposition movements? Why is such opposition usually suppressed but sometimes not? Such questions are much more suited to the comparative history approach than to general psychological theories.

☐ *Comparative history*

Analysing revolutions through comparison of a small number of examples is an old trade (Brinton 1938) which has recently revived.

To contrast this approach with psychological theories we will consider Skocpol's (1979) discussion of the French, Russian and Chinese revolutions.

For Skocpol the causes of revolutions cannot be found in the motives of the participants. What matters is the 'structural conditions' – the patterns of relationships between groups within a nation-state and, equally important, between nation-states. The background to revolution is a regime that is weak internationally and ineffective domestically. This leads to a breakdown of the old regime followed by a period of dynamic change when a tightly organised revolutionary group eventually succeeds in consolidating power.

Skocpol's analysis places particular emphasis on the international dimension. Revolutions in France, Russia and China all erupted after the old regimes suddenly faced stronger military competitors. (However, this was not so with the Mexican revolution of 1910 or the Cuban revolution of 1959. The danger of proceeding by example is that selective case studies may be used to 'prove' a theory.)

On the domestic front, Skocpol suggests that revolutions occur when the capacity of the state to govern and coerce has already decayed. This collapse of domestic power is often the result of military defeat. In these circumstances, opposition leaders can draw upon previously suppressed mass hostility to the old regime to build a new order of power. The revolutionary intentions of an opposition movement are not always there at the outset but develop during the struggle itself.

So Skocpol argues that the classic revolutions occurred when well-organised revolutionaries exploited peasant frustration with the old regime in a period when the regime had already lost its effectiveness. In these circumstances the actual seizing of power can be quite straightforward. The real revolution begins as the new regime imposes its vision on opposition groups. Political revolutions do not stop with the taking of power, but often only start at this point. Thus the comparative history approach says much about how discontent is mobilised into revolutionary activity, even if it has less to say than the psychological approach on how that discontent arose in the first place.

■ Three revolutions: France, Russia and Iran

In this section, we consider three revolutions, one from each of the three worlds. Our purpose is not just to study the applicability of the theories of instability and revolution outlined above. Each of these revolutions

Exhibit 4.1   *The perfect revolutionary situation*

Suppose we took all the major theories of revolution and listed the factors that are claimed to be the causes of revolutions. We would then have the ideal revolutionary situation. This may never have existed in full, but most major revolutions share at least some of these features.

1. An authoritarian regime that has failed to build any base of popular support is in power. It uses violence and repression to hold down opposition. Neighbouring countries all have stable political systems that guarantee individual rights and popular participation in government.
2. The masses (peasantry and working class) become alienated from the existing order.
3. A well-organised group of dedicated revolutionaries forms to lead the revolution.
4. A period of rapidly rising expectations is followed by a period of sharp economic decline, while the economies of neighbouring countries continue to prosper.
5. The government becomes swamped by the pace and number of demands being placed upon it.
6. The government responds by implementing limited reforms which partially remove political repression, but refuses to give up its grip on power.
7. The reforms do nothing to allay mounting hardships for the population.
8. The regime is confronted with foreign aggression, and ends up ignominiously defeated.
9. The vanguard revolutionary leadership perceptively and skilfully mobilises the discontented groups.

It is hard to imagine any country getting into the complete mess outlined above. But the situation in Russia in 1917 perhaps comes closest to this 'ideal' revolutionary situation.

had a profound impact on the making of the modern world. Their influence was not confined to the nations concerned but spread out into the wider world. In Marx's phrase, these revolutions really were 'locomotives of history'.

☐ *France 1789*

'It is a rebellion' said Louis XVI. 'No sire,' came the blunt response, 'it is a revolution.' The verdict of history is that Louis was wrong. Perhaps his misreading of the situation was one reason for the success of the revolutionary movement. The French revolution marks a watershed in history. The revolution swept away medieval structures of power and accelerated the creation of modern nation-states which dominate the contemporary world.

Politically, the French revolution destroyed absolute monarchy based on divine right and curtailed the traditional powers of the aristocracy. Over time, the system of provincial government led by local notables was replaced by a centralised, more meritocratic bureaucracy. Thus the revolution created the tools through which modern states govern their people.

Economically, the revolution weakened aristocratic control over the peasantry and helped to create the conditions under which market relations spread and capitalism would eventually emerge. In that sense, it can be considered a bourgeois revolution. Capitalism did not emerge overnight, but the political revolution laid the ground for long-term economic change.

Ideologically, the revolution was secular and anti-clerical, hostile to religion in general and the Roman Catholic Church in particular. It fathered liberal ideas of individual rights for all citizens. Where local customs had previously shaped the nature of relations between individuals, after 1789 these rights were enforceable through codified law. The French revolution was also powerfully nationalist: the *nation* became the transcendent bond, uniting all citizens in patriotic fervour. A duty of military service to the fatherland went hand in hand with the hard-won rights and privileges of citizenship; the French revolutionary armies thus foreshadowed the vast conscript armies of the twentieth century.

The shockwaves of the French revolution reverberated throughout Europe. The ruling classes everywhere saw their very existence imperilled as the system of throne and altar (the conservative marriage between absolute monarchy and an official church) trembled. Furthermore, the subsequent revolutionary wars gave an impetus to nationalism and the nation-state which spread across Europe and throughout the world.

What does the French case reveal about the study of revolutions? Firstly, it shows how the full impact of a revolution may take decades to unfold. The initial revolutionary leadership of 1789 gave way to a period of autocratic rule by Napoleon (1799–1814) and universal male suffrage was not adopted until 1848. Yet the revolution established the future contours of liberal democracy: popular sovereignty, a professional bureaucracy, a capitalist economy and a liberal ideology.

The French case also displays the features that Skocpol believes characterises great revolutions. The international dimension can be seen in France's generally unsuccessful competition with England in the eighteenth century. The limited domestic effectiveness of the monarchy was shown by its inability to raise the revenue to pay for these foreign adventures. The ensuing fiscal crisis came to a head in the late 1780s. For the first time since 1614, the dominant classes of landowners and office-holders convened in the Estates General to demand a representative body with the right to approve the introduction of any new taxes.

Then an élite crisis gave way to a revolution. Popular disaffection was triggered by a failed grain harvest which caused peasant revolts against rents and tax demands. This combination of both élite and mass crises resulted in a nationwide collapse of authority.

Finally, the complex dynamics of revolution can certainly be seen in this case. It is one thing to overthrow a regime, but it is much more difficult (and painful) to resolve the issue of what should replace it. Opposition to a regime provides a glue that enables revolutionaries to stick together. Once the common enemy has been removed, the glue dissolves. In the 1790s, assorted attempts to build a constitutional monarchy, a republic and a parliamentary government eventually gave way to authoritarian rule by Napoleon. Creating the disorder of revolution is a much easier task than restoring order out of the chaos that has been unleashed.

Strong ingredients of class conflict were certainly present in the French revolution. However, a dogmatic Marxist approach that sees the revolution in just these terms is too simple. The functionalist interpretation does draw attention to the discordant changes taking place in the final years of the old regime. For the psychological theorists, emphasis would have to be placed on the mass peasant revolts driven by the deprivation of a failed harvest. But the dynamics of revolution in terms of causes – and above all, consequences – involved far more than just the relative deprivation of the peasantry. Marxist, functionalist and relative deprivation theories provide only limited frameworks for grasping the full significance of the French revolution.

☐ *Russia 1917*

Just as the French revolution provided the basis for liberal democracy, so the Russian revolution of 1917 signalled the origins of the communist state. It was the arrival of a totally new type of regime – a regime backed by an ideology and revolutionary movement which sought to overthrow the liberal democracies of the West. Without doubt, the Russian revolution was a decisive moment in the history of the twentieth century.

Davies suggests that his J-curve theory helps to explain the Russian revolution. Important reforms implemented between 1860 and 1904 were followed by a period of decline. By the time of the revolution, expectations were running far ahead of the Tsar's capacity to satisfy them. The main reform was the emancipation of the peasantry in 1861. Other important reforms included a modern legal system, state-sponsored industrialisation and a general liberalisation of society.

But even these reforms enhanced the feeling of relative deprivation. The peasants were legally free, but most were burdened by heavy debts. Furthermore, expectations raised by political reforms were then dashed by the Tsar's inability to push ahead with further, more radical, reforms.

Instead, reforms oscillated with repression – a perfect formula for fostering relative deprivation. Though an attempted revolution in 1905 failed, the hardships imposed by Russia's involvement in the First World War created another revolutionary opportunity in 1917. This time, the chance was not lost. The Bolsheviks exploited the opportunity and established the world's first communist party state.

The relative deprivation approach provides a framework for describing the Russian revolution but does not fully explain it. Neither does it fully explain why the 1917 revolution succeeded and the 1905 revolution failed. The historical approach offers more insight here. The international situation profoundly influenced domestic developments. Russia's defeat by the Western powers in the Crimean War of 1854–55 provided the catalyst for the Tsar's attempts to 'catch up' with the West by introducing modernising reforms. But these could not bridge the gap with the West, a failure that contributed to the Tsar's ultimate demise.

More important still, the First World War destroyed the professionalism of the army. This meant it could not be an efficient tool of domestic repression. Under the cumulative impact of military disasters, incompetent leadership, economic chaos, war weariness and mounting civil unrest, the Tsarist regime disintegrated in February 1917. The provisional government that replaced it made the fatal mistakes of continuing to fight the war and not carrying out land reform. Conditions were ripe for a seizure of power, and the communists took over with surprising ease.

As with the French revolution, overthrowing the old system proved easier than consolidating power. Confronting international and domestic opposition, the communists fought a protracted civil war that lasted until 1921. Another similarity with the French revolution was the nature of the post-revolutionary political system. A centralised, bureaucratic state created order and consolidated power.

Thus Skocpol believes that the French and Russian revolutions can both be understood in terms of peasant revolts coinciding with the failure of rulers to keep control of their populations in situations of international conflict. In the Russian case, the ideology of Marxism and the experience of industrialisation (both within and outside the Soviet Union) were used to plan the transition to an industrial society.

☐ *Iran 1979*

When the Shah of Iran fled his country to be replaced in power by Ayatollah Khomeini, nobody could doubt that a revolution was under way. A pro-Western absolute monarch committed to economic development was overthrown by a 76 year-old religious leader committed to Islamic fundamentalism. Although the new regime lost some of its revolutionary fervour in the 1980s, the Iranian revolution has, like the French and Russian revolutions before it, influenced the outside world. Encouraged by the success of their Iranian brethren, Islamic fundamentalists have challenged the authority of other regimes. Large-scale fundamentalist disturbances have put a mostly secular and socialist regime in Algeria under mounting pressure, for instance. Communist leaders in the largely Islamic southern republics of the Soviet Union donned nationalist and separatist garb, as they felt the fundamentalist wind on their necks. With the break-up of the Soviet Union, the fear that the Muslim population of western China might try to form its own independent state has gained renewed importance in Beijing.

In contrast to France and Russia, Iran's old regime had not been ravaged by war nor had it suffered economic collapse. However, development based on Iran's oil wealth had led to rapid social change. In particular it created a dislocated urban peasantry, ripe for fundamentalist mobilisation. This class saw the wealth of the Shah's élite and the merchant class, but was not allowed to share it. But the repressive capacity of the state (including an efficient and feared secret police) remained in existence right up to the revolution. The Iranian revolution does not fit in with Skocpol's theory of revolutions taking place in societies where the state has lost the capacity to govern. Indeed, Skocpol (1982) argues that the revolutionaries themselves destroyed this capacity. Khomeini himself was exiled in France, and took no active part in the revolution, although he undeniably controlled affairs from a distance. Yet in the face of mass demonstrations, the Shah's power simply and rapidly dissolved.

The Iranian revolution showed the continuing capacity of ideas to shape political behaviour. It symbolised the re-emergence of Islam as a potent political force. Islam is the predominant religion in the Middle East and North Africa. However, there are internal theological divisions within Islam, notably between Sunni and Shi'ite Muslims. In Iran, the more militant Shi'ites are in a majority. The Shi'ites believe that religion, politics and society are (and should be) inextricably linked. Religion is the foundation of all other aspects of life, and nothing can be divorced from it. Law should not be secular, but must be based on Islamic precepts. Thus traditional Islamic punishments such as stoning adulterers to death and amputating the limbs of thieves, should be enshrined in public law. Similarly, the state is legitimised by reference to Islamic principles, not by Western ideas of liberal democracy.

Another feature of Islamic fundamentalism is the rejection of foreign domination. The slogan 'neither East nor West' became a clarion call of the revolution and has played a substantial role in the revival of Islam. Encouraged by Khomeini's own development of Islamic thinking, Iranian Shi'ites also accept that the *ulama* (the clergy) should rule directly, and not simply be satisfied with advising temporal rulers. In short, the revolution established a theocracy – government by priests – in Iran.

In the late 1980s, theocratic power retreated. Faced with ineffective government, the fundamentalist clerics lost ground to the more pragmatic politicians and administrators. Khomeini's death in 1989 accelerated this process. At the beginning of the 1990s, there were two separate and competing sources of power in Iran – the theocrats and the temporalists. For example, the more secular leaders wanted to release Western prisoners held in Iran without telling religious leaders. They feared that if the news was made public in advance, the *ulama* would whip up popular opposition to the plan.

The relative deprivation approach offers more help in understanding the Iranian revolution. Iran's gas and oil reserves produced rapid economic growth in the 1960s and early 1970s. But in 1973 the economy was rocked by the oil crisis. The resulting slump in world demand for Iranian oil left the Shah unable to satisfy popular expectations that had mushroomed in the boom years.

Davies' J-curve theory establishes the background of frustration in pre-revolution Iran. Something more is needed to explain why, in the Iranian case, popular disaffection led to the overthrow of the government by a revolutionary movement. The answer seems to be that the Shah never established a social or ideological base to his regime. Instead, he chose to build his position on a combination of periodic handouts and a strategy of creating divisions among his opponents. When a well-organised opposition emerged, with deep cultural roots in the population, the foundations of his authority proved to be insubstantial.

Furthermore, the ostentatious pro-Western style of the Shah gave the *ulama* a focus around which to rally their opposition. Rapid economic change in Iran had produced massive social change. During the boom years, the urban population had grown dramatically. On the eve of the revolution, half of the Iranian population lived in cities. The urban masses proved to be key players in the overthrow of the Shah, although they were by no means the only disaffected group involved.

It took many years for the full impact of the Russian and French revolutions to emerge. It is therefore too early to assess the impact of the Iranian revolution on the world. The evidence so far suggests that rule by clerics in accordance with the Koran is unlikely to facilitate effective government in a complex modern society. Here we can see similarities with other revolutionary movements of very different complexions. Overthrowing the old regime is one thing. Knowing what to do after the revolution is another. Revolutionary agitators rarely make effective administrators.

As with the French and Russian revolutions, the impact of 1979 has not been confined to the host country. Although Iran's leaders have encouraged the establishment of strict Islamic states elsewhere, their attempts to export the revolution met with little success. True, most Muslim states experienced an Islamic revival, stimulated in part by events in Iran. This resurgence was strongest in states that had experienced (a) rapid economic growth and subsequent dislocation; (b) massive inequalities in urban areas; and a (c) period of pro-Western and relatively secular rule (Keddie 1991, p. 304). But only in Iran did these conditions lead to revolution. The events of 1979 were an Iranian as much as an Islamic revolution.

However, the upsurge in Islamic fundamentalism has had profound effects on governments, especially but not only in the third world. It has created conflict both within states (governments reacting to the rise of Islamic groups within society) and between states (for example, antagonism between Iran and the United States). The Islamic revival has provided a rallying cry behind which third world peoples can protest against the continued influence of the West on their societies. Islam is a non-Western view of the world which is always prone to become anti-Western. Whatever the future may hold for Islamic states, there is no doubt that the revolution in Iran was one of the most remarkable and surprising revolutions ever to take place in the third world.

■ 1989: the year of revolutions

The French, Russian and Iranian revolutions were all cases where an established traditional order was overthrown by a revolutionary movement. In 1989 the countries of Eastern Europe witnessed a very different kind of political change. A relatively new political order, largely imposed by the Soviet Union, was swept aside.

As with the French, Russian and Iranian revolutions, the events of 1989 marked a turning-point in world history. Furthermore, the 1989 experience provides an important insight into the causes of revolution.

□ *Documenting the revolutions*

Although the 1989 revolutions formed a single, connected series of events, the course of political change was different in each country. In Poland, Solidarity had been challenging the dominance of the ruling party throughout the 1980s. The political change was a protracted and incremental process culminating in a 'negotiated revolution'. In stark contrast, the brutal Ceaucescu regime in Romania capitulated rapidly, with little forewarning. Table 4.1 provides a comparative chronology of the key events that swept communist parties from power across Eastern Europe.

The character of the regimes that emerged after the revolutions also varied. In Hungary, Poland and Czechoslovakia, the communist party state was replaced by multi-party parliamentary democracy. In Romania and Bulgaria, the leaders have been changed, but many communists still play leading roles in politics. There has been a shift in the locus of power – in Romania the ruling Ceaucescu 'dynasty' was swept aside – but the new leaders were all major figures before the revolutions. Many noncommunist members of the Romanian National Salvation Front (NSF) resigned after its victory in the May 1990 General Election, claiming that the NSF was nothing more than 'old wine in new bottles'.

The East German population chose a different (and unique) option: reunification with West Germany. In reality, this has been less a process of unification, and more a process of absorption of East Germany by its larger and more affluent Western neighbour.

☐ *Interpreting the revolutions*

So, despite many common factors, both the course of revolution and the nature of the post-revolutionary state in each country were shaped by factors specific to each nation. However, viewing the political upheavals of 1989 as a whole does provide insights into the nature of political change.

First, the poor economic situation in Eastern Europe was extremely important. In some countries, the economic well-being of the population was declining. The 1970s and 1980s had seen a gross misuse of resources. Instead of investing in the future, the communist governments had attempted to shore up their short-term positions. Investment capital and loans from the West had been used to keep prices low and to maintain employment. The economies were becoming increasingly inefficient, and the governments lacked the means to pay their mounting debts to Western banks.

Furthermore, when people made comparisons with the lifestyle in Western Europe, feelings of relative deprivation intensified. This was most obvious in East Germany, where the population could watch West German television and see what they were missing. Even in other countries of Eastern Europe, images of Western affluence were important – and images of Western inequality were ignored.

Secondly, this deprivation was not confined to the economic sphere. Gorbachev's policies of *perestroika* and *glasnost* in the Soviet Union put the ending of authoritarian rule on the agenda of Eastern Europe for the first time in decades. It proved almost impossible for the ruling parties to satisfy the new demands placed on them. The experience of Eastern Europe confirms that limited reform is more dangerous for authoritarian regimes than no reform at all. Every new reform loosened the communist party's control over society, but only heightened expectations for further change. Every new freedom allows voices to be raised against the restrictions that remain. Authoritarian rulers faced with pressures for reform confront a dilemma. If they refuse to bow before the winds of change, they have to fall back on repression. Any support they may have had plummets. If the rulers do liberalise, they may simply be blown out of power.

In China, one of the few communist states to survive the events of 1989, conservative leaders refused to negotiate with the protesters in Tiananmen Square, and chose repression. Only with the advantage of

Table 4.1   *1989 – A year of revolution*

	Hungary	Poland	GDR *(East Germany)*
January	**11** Law of Association permitting independent political parties passed **26** Imre Nagy's body exhumed **28** Pozsgay calls 1956 revolt a 'popular uprising' and not a 'counter-revolutionary movement'.	**16** Central Committee agrees to talks with opposition **20** Lech Walesa agrees to talks	**15** Demonstrators demanding freedom of expression arrested in Leipzig
February	**11** Government accepts need to move to multiparty democracy **28** Government announces that border fences with Austria to be taken down	**6** Round table talks between government and opposition begin	
March	**29** Gorbachev reported to have pledged not to intervene in Hungary's affairs		
April	Mass protests to oppose plans to dam the Danube at Nagymcras	**5** Agreement reached on free elections	
May	Dismantling of border fences with Austria starts		Demonstrations in Berlin and Leipzig against invalidity of GDR elections
June	**24** New reformist leadership elected	**4** Solidarity crush communists in first round of elections	
July	**6** Kadar dies. Nagy formally rehabilitated		GDR leaders protest about Hungary's relaxed border controls with Austria
August		**7** Coalition parties abandon communists **17** Jaruzelski accepts offer of Solidarity government **24** Mazowiecki sworn in as prime minister	GDR refugees start to flood across border into Hungary and on into Austria

Czechoslovakia	*Bulgaria*	*Romania*	
15–21 Demonstrators marking anniversary of Jan Palach's suicide in 1968 met by police repression		19 All cultural relations with Hungary broken off	**January**
21 Vaclav Havel imprisoned for anti-state activities			**February**
		Six former party and government officials arrested after criticizing Ceaucescu	**March**
17 Hungarian TV interview with Dubcek seen throughout Czechoslovakia	60 ethnic Turks killed during demonstrations against forced assimilation		**April**
17 Havel released from jail	Huge exodus of ethnic Turks begins		**May**
			June
			July
21 300 arrested in demonstrations on the anniversary of 1968 Soviet invasion			**August**

cont.

Table 4.2 *continued*

	Hungary	*Poland*	*GDR (East Germany)*
September		12 New Solidarity-led government sworn in with only 2 communist ministers	The exodus gathers pace. Weekly demonstrations in Leipzig against the government 10 Opposition 'New Forum' established
October	12 HSWP becomes HSP and condemns its past 23 New Hungarian Republic proclaimed		2 20,000 march in protest through Leipzig 7 Gorbachev visits Berlin and urges reform 18 Honecker quits – replaced by Krenz
November	26 Presidential elections postponed to allow opposition parties to prepare		7 Entire Cabinet resigns 8 Entire Politburo resigns 8–9 Berlin Wall opened
December	21 National Assembly votes to dissolve itself to pave the way for elections	29 People's Republic abolished. Leading role of communists removed from constitution	2 Demonstrations continue. Stasi offices ransacked 4–6 Entire communist leadership resigns 6 General Election date announced

Notes: HSWP – Hungarian Socialist Workers Party (Communist Party)
HSP – Hungarian Socialist Party
Stasi – State Security Service (GDR Secret Police)
Securitate – Romanian Secret Police

Sources: The Observer. Tearing Down the Curtain (London: Hodder & Stoughton, 1990). Humphrey, S. 'A Comparative Chronology of Revolution, 1988–1990', in G. Prins (ed.) *Spring in Winter: The 1989 Revolutions* (Manchester University Press) pp. 211–40.

Czechoslovakia	Bulgaria	Romania	
			September
28 300 protestors arrested in 10 000 rally in Prague	24 Mladenov resigns – leadership thrown into turmoil	16–17 Lazlo Tokes ousted as Head of his Reformed Church in Timisoara	October
17 Police attack protestors in Prague 18–19 Mass demonstrations against use of police violence 19 Civic Forum formed 24 Politburo resigns. Dubcek addresses rally in Wenceslas Square	10 Zhivkov ousted in 'coup'. Mladenov takes power 18 Mass demonstrations for democracy in Sofia	15 Demonstrations against low pay put down in Brasov	November
3 New communist-dominated government announced – rejected in nationwide demonstrations 7 Government collapses 10 New mainly noncommunist government sworn in 28 Dubcek elected president of Federal Assembly 29 Havel elected State President	11 Communist party proposes to end its monopoly of power and move to multiparty democracy	16–17 Supporters of Lazlo Tokes gather in Timisoara. 71 killed as army move in 21 Ceaucescu shouted down as he addresses rally in Bucharest. Security forces fire on crowds 22 Army changes side. Ceaucescus try to flee. Fighting between army and Securitate forces 25 Nicolai and Elena Ceaucescu arrested, tried and executed 27 National Salvation Front seize power. Free elections promised.	December

hindsight will we know whether this was truly an effective response, or if it merely delayed the inevitable.

In Bulgaria, the ruling communists did manage to keep a grip on power through a policy of reform. After removing the ageing and unpopular party leader, Todor Zhivkov, the communists consolidated their position by announcing a series of reforms. They thus largely pre-empted reform demands from the population. Unlike Czechoslovakia, Hungary and Poland, there was no history of organised or coherent opposition to the ruling party in Bulgaria.

Thirdly, the importance of external factors can be seen. In many ways, the revolutions of 1989 were revolutions against imperialism. Rather than bracket the revolutions of 1989 with those in France, Russia and Iran, we should perhaps link them with the American War of Independence and anti-colonial civil wars in the third world. Communist party rule had been largely installed from outside by the Soviet Red Army at the end of the Second World War. The parties' support in Eastern Europe did not run very deep, and had been eroded over the years through a combination of economic mismanagement and political repression.

The external context changed dramatically, once Gorbachev abandoned the Brezhnev doctrine – the presumption by Soviet leaders that 'the gains of socialism were irreversible', and that they had a right to intervene in the internal affairs of their East European neighbours to ensure this. He replaced it by the Sinatra doctrine – the leaders of Eastern Europe were now free to do it 'my way'; Moscow would not intervene, whatever the outcome. With the Soviet bogeyman no longer threatening to call, East European leaders had lost their key weapon against reform. Unwilling to respond to the new political realities, the rulers were out of step both with Moscow *and* their own people. For the people, the disappearing threat of the Red Army encouraged them to push harder for change. This was particularly so in Hungary and Czechoslovakia, where memories of popular movements crushed by Soviet tanks were still cherished, even by those too young to have first-hand recollection.

So, in retrospect, we can see that by 1989 Eastern Europe was ripe for revolutionary political change. Regimes with little support and popular legitimacy suffered power deflation as a period of economic decline coincided with the loosening of oppression. For the first time in thirty years, the glimmer of a chance to change the 'system' appeared. Many, perhaps most, people in Eastern Europe had put up with the communist system for so long because they reckoned that they had no alternative. When the chance of an alternative did arise, it was seized without hesitation.

Unable to express their real opinions through the ballot box, the people voted with their feet. Whether by leaving the country in droves, as in East Germany and Bulgaria, or by taking to the streets in demonstrations, the popular verdict on communist party rule was decisive. Faced with such opposition, the only possible way for the communists to keep power was to put the lid back on by force. In both Czechoslovakia and East Germany, force was initially used against the protesters, but it failed. The demonstrators were not deterred: in fact the use of state violence against peaceful protests swelled the ranks of the demonstrators. The governments' bluff had been called. Once the use of firearms rather than truncheons and hoses was ruled out, the advantage clearly passed to the demonstrators.

With one exception, the revolutions of 1989 were remarkably peaceful. That exception was Romania. Initially, when demonstrations against Ceaucescu broke out, the army used great violence, and hundreds of people died. As the demonstrations continued, key sections of the military changed sides and joined the demonstrators. It could be argued that Ceaucescu's regime, in fact, fell to a coup in support of a civil uprising. Military intervention certainly changed the course of the revolution. Members of the Securitate (the secret police), fanatically loyal to Ceaucescu, spread confusion and terror by shooting indiscriminately at anyone within range. The anti-Ceaucescu soldiery had the task of flushing the snipers out of hiding in government and party buildings (linked by secret tunnels, enabling the snipers to move around).

The revolution became theatre. Crowds gathered to watch the fighting, to witness the revolution being carried forward on their behalf by the army. Some spectators got too close to the action, and were hit. Nicolai Ceaucescu tried to escape by helicopter, but was captured. Together with his wife, Elena, he faced a drumhead trial and was executed on Christmas Day 1989. Though hardly a model of legal procedure, this event was decisive. With their leader dead, Securitate resistance petered out. Thanks to teenage conscript soldiers, the Romanian people had prevailed – at least for the time being.

In France, Russia and Iran, the real political revolution came *after* the transfer of power. As yet, 'post-revolutionary revolutions' have not occurred in Eastern Europe. One explanation is that the transfer of power has not been completed. The old order has been overthrown, but the transition to a new order is still taking place. By 1991 the 'umbrella' organisations that came to power in Czechoslovakia, Hungary and Poland were finding it difficult to maintain their cohesion (see Chapter 10). In Bulgaria and Romania, the communists (under a change of label) remained the dominant political force. In these two countries, it was debatable whether a real revolution had taken place.

But the revolutions in Eastern Europe were very different from those in France, Russia and Iran. With the possible exception of Bulgaria and Romania, they clearly marked a transition from authoritarian rule to liberal democracy. The conflicts and pressures that emerge in the process of building a new political system *should* be resolved through the democratic procedures that are being put in place. Some reckoning of accounts for the injustices of the communist era is undoubtedly taking place. However, the post-revolutionary reigns of terror that were a feature of the French and Russian revolutions are unlikely to be a feature of the postcommunist political systems of Eastern Europe.

■ Ideology and revolution

The impact of ideology on social and political change has long been a matter of dispute in the study of politics. This controversy can be traced back to Marx and Weber. For Marx, technology was the real engine-room of social change. Once an economic system such as feudalism had been outdated by technological developments, it was doomed. The divisions that emerged in society would eventually revolutionise the political, as well as the economic, order. Ideology played a dependent role: its main purpose was to bolster up the ruling class with moral and political argument. But the ideology of dominant groups could at best only delay the timing of their disintegration.

Reacting against Marx's determinism, the German sociologist Max Weber (1930) sought to prove that ideas had an independent impact on political change. In his classic study, *The Protestant Ethic and the Spirit of Capitalism*, he argued that the rise of capitalism was partly attributable to the impact of Protestant religion. This was because Protestantism was an individualistic religion which encouraged people to seek their fortune, and work hard for the glory of God.

But rather than frittering wealth away in pursuit of life's pleasures, Protestantism encouraged thrift, and thus the saving or reinvestment of profits. This outlook, argued Weber, facilitated the growth of capitalism in the West – a case of ideas affecting economics, rather than the other way about. These conflicting assumptions about the impact of ideas are echoed in the analysis of revolutions. Voltaire and other writers of the eighteenth-century enlightenment ferociously attacked the injustice and absurdities of absolutist monarchy. Was the French revolution the outcome of ridicule and exposure (ideas) or did it reflect the rise of the bourgeoisie (economics)? Was the Russian revolution successful because the masses recognised the superiority of socialism, or because of the successful organisation and skilful tactics of the communist party leadership? Did the Iranian revolution stem from the resurgence of Shi'ite religious fervour, or from the impact of economic modernisation? Did the demonstrators in Eastern Europe in 1989 aspire to the values of liberal democracy, or were they driven by more materialistic desires?

☐ *What is an ideology?*

To answer such questions, the first task is to define 'ideology'. We view an ideology as a *public system of beliefs and values about human society*. 'Public' because a purely private and personal belief-system does not qualify as an ideology: it must have an identity beyond any one individual. 'System' because ideology implies an organised set of ideas. It is more articulated, more precise than, say, a political culture (see Chapter 6). 'Beliefs *and* values' because ideologies encompass the 'is' and the 'ought'. An ideology is action-related, providing both an analysis of existing society and an emotionally charged ideal to aim at (though this ideal may be presented as a reversion to the good old days). 'Human society' finally, because ideologies are inherently social and political in content.

Ideologies, as we have defined them, are distinguished from outlooks, creeds and traditions by their more coherent and intense character. However, the boundaries are hard to draw. The conservatism of Ronald Reagan might not be an ideology; that of Margaret Thatcher probably was. Ayatollah Khomeini certainly had an ideology – but what about the Archbishop of Canterbury? Marxism is an ideology – but what about social democracy? In practice ideologies are identified by the intense desire of their adherents to transform the world in accordance with their key values. This contrasts with outlooks, movements and political cultures that either favour the status quo or are just pragmatically reformist. Exhibit 4.2 gives capsule definitions of the major ideologies of contemporary politics.

☐ *How do ideologies arise?*

There are two main approaches to answering this question – the **strain** theory and the **interest** theory. For the first, ideology is a symptom and a remedy; for the second, a mask and a weapon. In the strain theory, people flee anxiety; in the interest theory, they pursue power (Geertz 1964).

Exhibit 4.2   *The 'isms of politics*

Capitalism

The economic system of 'free enterprise' based on private ownership producing for profit in the open market. In practice, market competition often needs to be sustained or modified by government intervention. All capitalist countries today have mixed economies with varying amounts of state ownership, regulation (e.g. of employment conditions) and market intervention (e.g. through subsidies or import quotas).

Communism

Karl Marx and his followers held that communist revolution was historically inevitable. With material abundance and property held in common, communism should be untainted by the exploitation and class conflict inherent in capitalism. Even if Marx's analysis is correct, the problem is how to get there. Far from creating ideal societies, communist regimes became bureaucratic dictatorships under which oppression, exploitation and alienation increased rather than disappeared.

Conservatism

Less an ideology, many conservatives would say, than a cast of mind. Conservatives reject social engineering for its own sake; they accept that people are imperfect, different and unequal. The wisdom of the past is secreted in society's traditions and institutions; these should be respected. Change is therefore justified only where it is clearly necessary. Conservative parties vary considerably, some being pragmatic, others more openly doctrinaire or reactionary.

Environmentalism

Green parties and movements have grown rapidly since the 1960s in much of the first world. Moderate environmentalists ('light greens') criticise waste and pollution, and stress the need to protect the environment. Fundamental environmentalists ('dark greens') completely reject the priority of consumerism and economic growth, and call for a different lifestyle based on conserving non-renewable resources.

Fundamentalism

Religious fundamentalists believe in the literal truth of the holy works central to their faith (the Bible, Koran, Torah) and the strict application of its teachings. Fundamentalists tend to press their political views strongly and are often intolerant of those who do not share them. The growth of the religious right has been striking in the US politics since the 1970s. Islamic fundamentalism achieved international prominence with the Iranian revolution. Rising fundamentalism generates inter-faith conflict; violence between Hindus, Muslims and Sikhs has become very marked in Indian politics.

Fascism

Classic (pre-1945) fascism was a synthesis of extreme nationalism and anti-marxist socialism. State and nation become one: as Mussolini put it, 'everything in the state: nothing against the state, nothing outside the state'. Totalitarianism is the essence of fascism. The individual is totally subordinate to the state, under an autocratic ruler (Fuhrer or Duce). Glorying in struggle and sacrifice, the fascists regarded war and conquest as the nation's supreme expression. Neo-fascist parties, centred upon hostility to immigrants and ethnic minorities, have been a feature of postwar European politics.

Feminism

Has deep roots in Western society, but its modern growth dates from the 1960s and 1970s. There are many tendencies, usually at logger-heads and sometimes aligned with other political movements (e.g. socialism). In its broadest sense, however, feminism is the demand for women's political, social, economic and sexual equality with men.

Liberalism

Associated in the eighteenth and nineteenth centuries with the elimination of feudal remnants and aristocratic privileges, liberalism was linked with the doctrine of laissez-faire: the maximum of individual liberty and the minimum of state intervention in society and the economy. However, the commitment to individual liberty drew some strands of liberalism towards more state intervention ('social liberalism'), while others cling to laissez-faire (libertarians).

Nationalism

The belief that a particular group of people is a natural community, which should live under a single political system. Nationalism is often linked to a struggle for independence and political self-determination. It can, however, also be a convenient tool for political leaders to mobilise support and overcome opposition by stressing internal or external threats to national unity. Nationalism has been a common ingredient in numerous international and civil conflicts; most recently, the collapse of communist rule has unleashed nationalist forces throughout Eastern Europe and the former Soviet Union that threaten to be uncontrollable.

Racism

The belief that races are inherently unequal, and that people should be treated according to their race of origin. Racist political movements are intrinsically intolerant (individuals do not matter, only their race), and drawn to violent and simplistic solutions. The Nazi regime of Adolf Hitler in Germany (1933–45) was racist and anti-Semitic: the (German) master race was destined to subjugate and enslave lesser races. Hitler's 'Final Solution' for what he saw as the racial struggle was to exterminate Jews and other so-called 'sub-humans' (Gypsies, homosexuals, the mentally or physically handicapped) altogether. In a less ideological form, racist attitudes remain widespread.

Socialism

A creed with many variants, but all socialists are broadly committed to the idea of equality and to policies intended to bring it about. These traditionally included the collective ownership of the economy as well as extensive welfare measures. Unlike communists, socialists have generally rejected revolution as a means of achieving socialism and have insisted on parliamentary methods. The emphasis upon collective ownership has also been de-emphasised by many socialist parties. What remains are moderately reformist parties with egalitarian intentions.

To explore further

R. Eccleshall *et al.* (1984) *Political Ideologies: An Introduction* (London: Hutchinson).
B. Goodwin (1987) *Using Political Ideas* (New York: Wiley).

The strain theory maintains that ideologies arise in response to social dislocation; they are a symptom of a malfunctioning society. For example, the rise of fascism in inter-war Germany is often attributed to the desire among Germans for a simple, all-embracing solution to the problem of mass unemployment and economic insecurity. Similarly the spread of Islamic fundamentalism in Iran's cities might be explained in terms of the need of slum-dwellers for an ideology that gave meaning and validity to their lives.

The strain theory is advocated by those authors who adopt a functional approach to revolutions. The presence of ideology is regarded as a sign that the political system is not in equilibrium with society. The virtue of the strain theory is that it does explain why ideologies often gather momentum in times of crisis and gradually lose their momentum thereafter.

The interest theory maintains that the function of ideology is to rationalise interests. It provides a gloss to self-interest, showing why the interests of a particular social group do deserve special treatment from the government. Thus for Marxists the 'dominant ideology' of capitalism uses values such as freedom and property rights to rationalise the continued exploitation of workers by employers. From this perspective, ideologies are necessarily distorted and selective (a point emphasised by Mannheim (1954), who then failed to confront the objection that this applied as much to his own interpretation of reality as to anyone else's).

In contrast to the strain theory, interest theory views the production of ideology as a normal part of politics. The interest theory is advocated by those authors who view politics as a continual struggle, rather than as a search for equilibrium within society. Marxists are the clearest but not the only advocates of the interest theory. The virtue of this approach is that much of political debate can indeed be understood, as Ambrose Bierce put it, as 'a strife of interests masquerading as a conflict of principles'. Its weakness is that the 'interests' of a particular group are not a given but are themselves defined by values and ideology. Whether people give priority to their ethnic, class or religious interests reflects the values of their society. So ideology re-enters by the back door.

Both the strain theory and the interest theory root ideology in the social structure. Neither regards ideology as an independent force. We would be inclined to give more independent weight to ideology than either theory, noting that ideologies have a natural base among intellectuals who are prominent in so many revolutions. Ideological intellectuals are responding neither to self-interest nor to social strain but to the play of ideas itself. In addition, once an ideology 'takes off' in the wider society, it gains a momentum of its own. For example, the American ethos of equal opportunity may be a rationalisation of inequality but it has been used by less privileged groups (such as blacks) to justify remedial policies (such as affirmative action).

Similarly in communist party states Marxism was an ideology that constrained rule by the communist party as well as justifying that rule. Those who start off exploiting an ideology often end up as prisoners of it.

□ The end of history?

The French revolution was an ideological factory, which generated the intellectual weapons of politics: democracy, liberalism, conservatism, nationalism, socialism. The ideological fray was joined by other contestants (communism, racism, fascism) and in our own time by other contenders again (feminism, environmentalism). Some 'isms' of politics are summarised in Table 4.2. Though the challenge of fascist and racist doctrines was acute in the first half of the twentieth century, this was overshadowed by the enduring antagonism between liberal democracy (an amalgam of ideas) and marxist communism.

With the demise of communist party control in Eastern Europe and the Soviet Union, and the crises facing the remaining ruling communist parties, it is widely held that communism is now dead. For the American policy analyst Fukuyama (1989), this means that we have witnessed 'the end of history'. Marxism, and the political systems professing allegiance to it, challenged liberal democracy as well as capitalism. The challenge has comprehensively failed. Although conflicts will continue to arise, they will not involve a fundamental alternative to liberal democracy. According to Fukuyama, the great conflict of ideology and ideas that has been going on in European and then world politics since the French revolution is now over; liberal democracy remains as the only legitimate ideology left in the world.

There has been much debate over the validity of Fukuyama's ideas. In particular, the Gulf War of 1991 was taken by many as ample proof that history was alive and kicking. He has countered by arguing that whatever the Gulf War was about (mainly oil), it was not a war over ideas or ideologies. This may be true, but to forecast an unchallenged future for the ideology of liberal democracy risks several pitfalls.

The defeat of fascism did not mark the end of history, just the end of one historical epoch. With the death of communism, another historical epoch has passed, but new conflicts over ideas will rise to dominate world affairs. The long-term future of the postcommunist societies of Eastern Europe is still far from clear. There are signs that the tolerance of minorities necessary for the effective functioning of genuine liberal democracy is not yet ingrained in the political cultures of some East European nations. Nationalism and ethnic conflict, rather than democracy, may prove to be the *leitmotifs* of the region, with profound implications for European security.

Nationalism is a powerful force throughout the world. It remains a major cause of conflict between states, and subnational ethnic conflicts are also a major cause of conflict within states. Before the communists took power, the Balkan region of South-East Europe was a byword for murderous ethnic feuds and political instability. As Yugoslavia slid into civil war between Serbs and Croats in 1991, it has become so again. As the Soviet Union breaks up, Balkan-style conflict is a real danger – but on a vastly greater scale. The world's largest democracy, India, faces severe religious, ethnic and separatist pressures, above all in Punjab and Kashmir. And now, the countervailing rise of Hindu nationalism calls into question the very conception of Indian democracy at independence as a liberal, secular and pluralist state.

Although Hinduism is a traditionally tolerant religion, rising interfaith conflict in India highlights one of the great challenges to the dominance of liberal democracy – Islam. The challenge of Hinduism may not be particularly strong outside India, but the challenge of Islam is. Despite the de-radicalisation of the Iranian revolution, the resurgence of Islamic fundamentalism has been a feature of recent history. The conflict between secularism and theism that has taken place in Iran is a pertinent example of one of the great battles for faith and belief that will face many nations in the twenty-first century. It may also intensify the emerging conflict between the developed, secular, first world and the relatively deprived, and frustrated, third world.

The conflict between liberal democracy and communism may be over, but new conflicts over political ideas are not slow to appear. Furthermore, within the developed nations of the first world, liberal democracy will be forced to make adjustments to meet the new challenges of the day. The transition from materialism to postmaterialism; the growing importance of ecological concerns; movements towards political integration between nations; such factors suggest that the death of history has been greatly exaggerated.

Summary

1. Evolutionary change is the gradual transformation of politics and society. Revolutionary change entails a fundamental change in the distribution of power in a nation and the alteration of social values, social structures and political institutions.

2.   The Marxist theory of revolution stresses the inevitability of revolution as a consequence of class conflicts in society. Marx's revolutionary theory was adapted by subsequent communist leaders, most notably Lenin in Russia and Mao Zedong in China.

3.   The functionalist theory sees revolution as a response to a failure to govern effectively. Revolutionary situations occur when the government is unable to cope with the pace and number of pressures for change. Leaders are swamped by the demands being placed upon them, and are unable to satisfy popular expectations.

4.   Relative deprivation refers to the difference between what people   perceive they are getting and what they feel they are entitled to. It forms part of the social psychological approach to understanding the origins of revolutions.

5.   Skocpol suggests that revolutions occur when the capacity of the state to govern and coerce has already decayed in the face of both internal and external crises. In these circumstances the actual seizing of power can be quite straightforward. The real revolution begins when the new regime attempts to impose its vision on opposition groups.

6.   An ideology is a public system of beliefs and values about human society. Ideologies are identified by the intense desire of their adherents to transform the world in accordance with their key values.

7.   The strain theory suggests that ideologies arise in response to social dislocation. In contrast, the interest theory suggests that the function of ideology is to rationalise interests.

8.   Nationalism and Islam present the greatest threats to liberal democracy's position as the world's dominant ideology. The collapse of communism is unlikely to represent the 'end of history'.

Discussion points

1.   Is a 'peaceful revolution' a contradiction in terms?

2.   'Overthrowing the old order without mass popular support is easy. Ruling the new order without mass popular support is impossible'. Is this true?

3.   'Far from preventing revolution, reform often accelerates it'. Why?

4.   Are the following *ideologies*?
   (*a*) feminism
   (*b*) the green movement
   (*c*) Islam
   (*d*) liberal democracy
   (*e*) capitalism

5.   Has history ended?

6.   Is liberal democracy the final form of government?

Key reading

Marx, K. and Engels, F. (first pub. 1848, many editions) *The Communist Manifesto*. One of the most influential political works of the modern era.

Cohan, A. (1975) *Theories of Revolution* (London: Nelson). A lucid analysis of Marxist, functionalist and social psychological ideas on revolution.

Skocpol, T. (1979) *States and Social Revolutions: A Comparative Analysis of France, Russia and China* (Cambridge: Cambridge University Press). A justly influential work.

Bakhash, S. (1985) *The Reign of the Ayatollahs* (London: Tauris). An accessible introduction to the Iranian revolution.

The *Observer* (1990) *Tearing Down the Curtain* (London: Hodder & Stought-on). One of several 'journalistic' guides to the collapse of communism in Eastern Europe in 1989.

Further reading

Avineri (1968) and Tucker (1970) are readable guides to Marxian ideas on revolution. The functionalist view of revolution is presented by C. Johnson (1966). On the social psychological approach, see Davies (1962) and Gurr (1972). More current work on this approach is reviewed by Gurr (1980). Cohan (1975) provides a lucid analysis of all these approaches.

On the comparative history approach, see Brinton (1938, republished 1965) or Skocpol's influential study (1979). O'Sullivan (1983) is a useful edited work in this tradition, and covers all three of the revolutions we have considered.

For accessible studies of individual revolutions, see A. Goodwin (1987) on France, Kochan (1970) on Russia and Skocpol (1982) or Keddie (1991) on Iran. Prins (1990) contains chapters by influential East European figures, many of whom played prominent roles in the overthrow of the communists. On ideologies and change, Geertz (1964) was an influential statement on strain theory; more general introductions to ideology can be found in Eccleshall *et al.* (1984) and Christensen *et al.* (1971). On whether or not 1989 marked 'the end of history', there is no better place to start than Fukuyama's (1989) controversial article.

■ Chapter 5 ■

The Nation-State in One World

■ Interdependence and the nation-state

In 1492 Christopher Columbus sailed across the Atlantic seeking a western passage to India. To his dying day, Columbus believed he had landed in India (hence the 'West Indies') but had in fact 'discovered' America. His epic voyage had momentous consequences. The conquest of the New World of the Americas by the European powers changed the nature of world politics. Great empires like those of Rome and Egypt had risen and fallen before, but the European powers, with their ships, guns and trinkets, opened up the world on an unprecedented scale.

Five hundred years later, even an explorer like Columbus would have been astonished at the world he had played a part in creating. Today, all national governments operate in an interdependent world. Information, money, weapons, technology, pollution, values, radiation, food, computers, deals, images, aid, tourists, drugs, diseases, data – all flow rapidly round the globe, giving national governments more opportunities but also posing more threats to their traditional authority.

In truth, states have always been influenced by what happens outside their borders. Key events in world history such as the French and Russian revolutions echoed round the world, even without television and fax machines. The Vatican was a powerful transnational organisation long before anyone had heard of the Ford Motor Company. We must avoid the mistake of assuming that what is important must therefore be new.

100

More generally, governments have always been the agencies through which societies deal with each other: this is one of their core functions. They have always sought to manipulate the outside world to their own advantage – and to develop 'domestic' society to further their international ambitions.

Throughout history, warfare, taxation and state-making have gone together. States have made war – and wars have made states. For instance, the origins of the modern European state lie in efforts by monarchs to raise the money and manpower needed to fight wars. Without the stimulus of competition between states, modern governments would be far slighter institutions than they are today.

What then distinguishes interdependence in today's world? How does it differ from interdependence one, two, or even five hundred years ago? We suggest three contrasts. The first is that interdependence is now global and not merely international. Automobile companies design world cars, major powers can launch missiles that cross continents, and pollution is a global problem. In the past, interdependence was restricted more to neighbouring countries and regions.

The second contrast is the sheer scale of interdependence today. There is more of it, in more areas of life, than in the past.

The third contrast lies in the variety of levels and institutions through which interdependence operates. States must confront not only other states but also *intergovernmental* actors, such as the United Nations, and *nongovernmental* actors, such as IBM and other transnational companies. States must recognise that other groups in society, such as firms, universities and regions, also have links with the outside world. Prosperous regions look across national borders as often as to the national capital. In short, the boundaries of the state have become more porous than ever before.

For students of politics *within* the nation-state, the implications are profound. We can no longer examine politics within states as though they bore no connection to politics *between* states. Instead, the two are intimately related. This does not mean global forces are replacing the role of the state. Far from withering away, states are in some ways widening their responsibilities in response to these challenges.

This chapter aims to describe those features of the global context that impinge most on national decision-makers. (For good introductions to world politics as such, see Ray 1990, or McKinlay and Little 1986). Specifically, we focus on the global economy, the global village and the global ecology. We then explore the challenges thrown out by interdependence to each of the three worlds. Thus a 'one world' perspective does not rule out a 'three worlds' perspective: rather, we have three worlds in one.

■ The global economy

The global economy is a, perhaps *the*, crucial dimension of interdependence. If Karl Marx were alive today, he would certainly place much more emphasis on international economics, and less on economic inequalities within nations, in explaining the dynamics of politics.

□ *The trading world*

The international division of labour means that goods can be made in whichever country can produce them to the combination of quality and cost demanded by customers. Thus, world trade has a natural dynamic. Between 1980 and 1989, world trade grew by about half. Over the same period, world production increased by just a quarter.

International trade is now a feature of every nation's economic activity. At the end of the First World War, only Europe depended on food imports. The rest of the world relied mainly on local food. Now, only North America and Australia are effectively independent of food imports (Segal 1991, p. 61). The *economic* dynamic of international trade springs from the fact that all participants can benefit from it. The *political* dynamic is that not all countries benefit equally.

Economic production, and in particular manufacturing, is now spread throughout the world. Manufactured goods are often the product of more than one nation. This book, for instance, was written in England, printed in Hong Kong and sells mainly outside the United Kingdom.

Manufacturers search for cheap, reliable labour and plentiful raw material supplies. Countries like South Korea and Taiwan became centres for inexpensive production in the 1960s and 1970s. More recently, Thailand and even communist states like Vietnam and China have become attractive (that is, cheaper and more reliable) options for many companies. In 1990, the main overseas manufacturing site for Japan's electronics industry was still the United States (127 plants), but other countries were catching up. Taiwan (98 sites), Malaysia (94), Korea (68), Singapore (63), Thailand (46), the UK (43) and China (31) have all become major centres of the Japanese electronics industry.

The development of a world economy means that the rhythm of economic activity is similar across the globe. Policy-makers in every country share a global context formed by the cycle of growth, recession and recovery.

The biggest players, namely Germany, Japan and the United States, help to shape the level of economic activity in the world. Hence, in their own interests, the national economic policies of these countries must take account of the international consequences of their policies. For many smaller countries, especially in the third world, the state of the global economy is simply a given factor.

Even major industrial countries cannot buck global economic trends. This was a lesson learned painfully by President Mitterrand of France. At the start of his socialist administration in 1981, he unwisely expanded the French economy. The resulting problems included a trade deficit, as export sales could not keep pace with the surge of imports. Within two years the government was forced to change direction and introduce austerity policies.

□ The competition state

International markets pit country against country in a battle for trade – and hence for investment, secure jobs and re-elected governments. This has led to the emergence of the 'competition state' (Cerny 1990, pp. 220–9). The object of the competition state is to stimulate private companies to achieve greater international competitiveness. The competition state seeks also to attract 'inward investment' from transnational companies. In the 1990s it is the transnational investor, not the national government, that calls the tune.

The competition state must look both inwards and outwards. Domestically, it must seek to provide a well-educated, well-motivated workforce as well as a stable social and political environment. Externally, it must compare its own performance with competitor countries. A country may increase the proportion of its school-leavers going onto further education but still fall behind because other countries are improving even faster. As Grant (1990) notes in a discussion of national industrial policy, 'no matter how the economy is to be guided, the process must relate more to international competitive conditions than to internal political preferences'. Thus, if a policy such as privatisation seems to work well in one country, then it is likely to be exported – though not always with the same success (Gayle and Goodrich 1990). An indirect effect of the global economy is therefore to speed the diffusion of policy across nations and to decrease the ability of governments to 'get away with' ineffective economic policies.

However not all states become competition states. Some governments just ignore the problem of declining competitiveness. Where conflicts within a country run strong, or special interests are well entrenched, it may not even be in a government's short-term political interest to attempt painful solutions to long-term problems. For example,

---

Exhibit 5.1   *Australia: sliding down the first division*

Competition states do not emerge easily, particularly in countries that achieved a high standard of living in a less demanding era. Australia is an excellent example. It is often described as a first world country with third world trading patterns. Twenty-one of its top twenty-five exports are agricultural products and minerals, commodities that have suffered a long-term decline in relative prices. A tradition of protectionism (imposing barriers against imports) meant Australian industries could survive without being internationally competitive. As a result, the economy now suffers from a persistent excess of imports over exports, rising foreign debt, and a decline in the value of its dollar.

The obvious solution is to open the economy to international competition. But in the short run this causes more problems, economic as well as political, than it solves. Australian governments must simultaneously prepare the country for competition, maintain the social fabric, and seek re-election (Emy and Hughes 1991, p. 78). Perhaps it is not surprising that until the late 1980s, many governments ducked the first of these tasks to concentrate on the last.

---

governments in Australia and Britain have more experience than most first world states of managing economic decline. In both countries, prime ministers have discovered that a short-term boom in the run-up to an election buys political popularity, even if it harms long-run economic performance (see Exhibit 5.1). This illustrates an important point. Global interdependence does not always, and certainly does not quickly, call forth an 'appropriate' response from governments. Politics within the nation-state still makes a difference, especially to the popularity of governments.

☐ *National variations*

Although all countries are touched by the international economy, they are not all affected equally. There are vast differences in the extent to which foreign trade is important for nations. The countries with the largest domestic markets (Japan, United States) have most impact on the world economy but also most insulation from it, an enviable position indeed. At the other extreme, smaller, newly industrialising countries

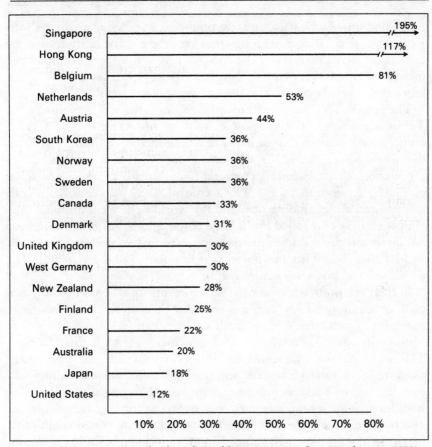

Source: The Economist Book of Vital World Statistics (London: Hutchinson, 1990).

Figure 5.1 *Trade as a percentage of gross domestic product, 1988*

(for example, Singapore and Hong Kong) live from trade and must respond rapidly to market changes (Figure 5.1).

Even the biggest countries are not exempt from international pressures. In the 1980s America's massive trade and budget deficits cost it some credibility in international financial markets. Despite Japan's undoubted economic strength, it is almost totally dependent on raw material imports – most notably energy.

☐ *Transnational corporations*

Companies that operate across national boundaries are known as multinational or transnational corporations (TNCs). Muscovites munching on MacDonald's quarterpounders and Beijingers biting into Kentucky Fried Chicken are a sign that even the historic bastions of anti-capitalism have fallen under the spell of TNCs. But these examples are merely the tip of a very large iceberg. As Clarke (1992) says, '[TNCs] are more than ever the arbiters of international investment'.

The largest TNCs are very powerful actors in the world economy. As Table 5.1 shows, the economic activity of many of the largest corporations exceeds that of many developed nations. Clarke estimates that by the year 2000, TNCs will account for 50 per cent of all industrial production. Trade in certain commodities is already firmly the preserve of TNCs. Between them, five TNCs control 80–90 per cent of all world trade in cereals (excluding rice) and the world's chemical production is almost entirely controlled by 30 large corporations. Although cartels of dominant producers do exist, they are rare in the modern world. As such, TNCs should not be viewed as manipulators of the system, but as privileged and powerful actors within it.

In their relations with national governments, the TNCs hold the ace card of mobility. They can always take their businesses elsewhere. Assembly, production and research facilities can be moved to another country if existing sites prove unsatisfactory. Through this leverage, TNCs can impose conditions on their host governments. These vary from straightforward financial incentives to set up shop in a country to a commitment by the government to improve the technical training of its workforce. This leverage applies not only to national governments but also to regional or state governments in which the proposed facility will be located. In other words, competition for inward investment is within, as well as between, countries.

But governments, especially in the first world, also have some powerful cards to play. They can influence the TNC's ease of access to the country's domestic market and they may also be a route of entry into a larger trading bloc. For example, Japanese car companies had to begin producing cars in the American and European markets if they were to become global companies and get round protectionist pressures. Furthermore, once an investment has been made in new plant, heavy costs can be incurred in closing it down. Plant is not as mobile as money, and not many countries may have the calibre of workforce needed to host a research and development facility.

Finally, TNCs are not united actors. They are organised along national or regional lines, which in a sense reconstruct national identities within the larger transnational organisation. The Hong Kong plant competes against the one in Singapore for the contract to build the company's new computer. In the twentieth century, firms competed in a world of nation-states. In the next century, nations will compete in a

Table 5.1 *The economic might of transnational corporations*

Rank		US $ billion	Rank		US $ billion
1	United States	4,235.0[a]	47	Mobil	44.9
2	Japan	2,664.0	48	Hong Kong	41.8[a]
3	USSR	2,356.7	50	BP	39.9
7	Great Britain	556.8	51	Greece	39.5
8	Canada	352.0	52	General Electric	35.2
15	Netherlands	175.3	56	Pakistan	32.0
16	Australia	159.6[a]	58	Texaco	31.6
22	Belgium	114.9	60	Toyota	31.6
23	Sweden	105.5	61	Colombia	31.0
24	General Motors	102.8	62	Daimler-Benz	30.2
25	South Korea	94.1	63	Du Pont	27.1
26	Denmark	78.7	64	Matsushita	26.5
34	Finland	70.4	65	Malaysia	25.8[a]
35	Exxon	69.9	69	Volkswagen	24.3
36	Dutch/Shell	64.8	71	New Zealand	23.5[a]
37	Ford	62.7	73	Hitachi	22.7
39	Norway	60.1	75	Chrysler	22.5
41	South Africa	58.1	76	Philips	22.5
45	Nigeria	51.6	77	Ireland	21.7
46	IBM	51.3	78	Nestlé	21.2

Notes:
A selective comparison of gross domestic product for selected nations and gross annual sales for selected corporations in 1986. All figures are in US dollars (billions). The number at the left indicates the unit's rank in the top 100.
[a] = Gross Domestic Product; other countries, Gross National Product.

Sources: James Lee Ray, *Global Politics* (Boston, Mass.: Houghton Mifflin, 1990), pp. 318–19 and CIA, *The World Factbook 1989* (Washington, D.C.: CIA, 1989).

world of transnational corporations. In practical terms, this means that a shrewd government can form alliances with the local branch of a TNC. In a joint effort, they seek to squeeze more resources from company headquarters in New York or Tokyo, where global investment decisions are reached.

Third world countries are in a weaker position in their relations with TNCs. Most TNCs have their headquarters in the developed world. The United States, Japan, Germany, Britain and France are favoured homes. Of the top 100 TNCs, only six have headquarters outside Western Europe, Japan and America. Many 'TNCs' are in fact American companies operating internationally. Profits made from local labour and resources in the third world are often 'exported' to the TNC's base in the first world. Between 1979 and 1985, about $88 billion was transferred in this way (Iba 1990, p. 105).

Despite this, many third world nations welcome TNCs with open arms. They are often more enthusiastic about inward investment than first world countries, which already have a large and diversified economic base. The attractions of TNCs to third world countries are that tax revenues are increased, local employment is created, economic efficiency is increased, access to consumer goods is expanded, and technological innovations are imported into the host country by the TNC. The host country may not get as much as it thinks it should from the TNC, but judges that something is better than nothing.

Third world nations may also benefit as the TNCs use the cheap labour of third world producers as leverage against their workers in the first world. When Pirelli workers in Milan went on strike in 1978, the management simply stepped up production of tyres in its Brazilian factories to make up lost production in Italy. By keeping wages low and enforcing strict control over the workforce, third world nations can make themselves attractive alternatives to producing in the first world.

☐ *The financial world*

The financial world has shrunk most of all. Aided by computer networks, financial information can be flashed around the world instantaneously. Capital flows across the world in seconds: it is the most mobile and liquid of all commodities. With major share-trading centres in London, New York and Tokyo, when one market shuts down, another wakes. Money never sleeps. As the world gets richer, so the stock of capital increases; as capital grows, so does the impact of the financial markets on the world economy.

In consequence, the collective power of financial markets exceeds that of any goverment. As Margaret Thatcher said, 'You can't buck the markets.' Old boy networks in London and Tokyo give governments considerable leverage over their national financial centres, but the world market is beyond the reach of any one government, even the United States.

In making financial decisions, governments must therefore consider the reaction of the markets. If the markets lose confidence in a country's economic policies, investments are withdrawn and loans to governments or individuals cost more. In extreme cases, loss of market confidence can drive a country to virtual bankruptcy. Market confidence is a fragile, uncertain affair, needing regular stroking to calm a tendency to overreact and panic. Ironically, although all markets are based on risk, financial traders seek to minimise it (even more ironically, Tokyo's stock exchange is built in an earthquake zone!). Markets look for cautious and conventional financial policies from the countries in which they invest. Not all governments deliver, but those that don't will pay an increasingly severe price.

■ The global village

In communications terms, we live in a global village. The world has been compressed into a television set. In 1776 it took fifty days for news of the English reaction to the American Declaration of Independence to get back to the United States. In 1950 British reaction to the outbreak of the Korean War was broadcast in America in twenty-four hours. With advances in satellite broadcasting, reports filmed in Britain now take a mere 25 seconds to reach American TV screens (Flammang *et al.* 1990, p. 378).

We now take for granted the almost immediate transmission of newsworthy events around the world. When the allied powers launched attacks on Iraq in the 1991 Gulf War, news reporters in Baghdad broadcast live to the world as the missiles whizzed overhead on their way (sometimes) to their programmed target. The American CNN cable news network supplied coverage of the conflict around the clock and across the globe.

The world has also been shrunk by the growth in mass travel. Tourism is now the world's largest industry. The growth of tourism exposes the host nation, and the traveller, to international standards of transport, communications and consumption. As a result, both sides develop a broader, and sometimes more critical, perspective on their own society. Tourism becomes a form of international political socialisation. For instance, in the summer of 1991, the cities of Western Europe were full of young tourists from Eastern Europe, experiencing for the first time the pleasures – and the prices – of London, Paris and Rome. Long-distance travel also opens up the possibility of mass migration from poorer to richer parts of the global 'village'. This creates new tensions of its own. By the early 1990s, support for right-wing movements was growing in several European countries, in protest at the presence of guest workers and immigrant groups. In this respect, the world is closing rather than opening. Immigration controls between the first and third worlds have grown stricter over the years.

What difference has global communication made to national governments? In essence, it has created more open societies. It is now harder than ever for governments to isolate their populations from international developments. Even communist party states found it difficult to jam foreign radio broadcasts aimed at their countries. When Gorbachev was deposed as President of the Soviet Union for sixty hours in August 1991, and imprisoned in his holiday villa, he still managed to get news from foreign radio broadcasts.

The concrete and barbed wire of the Berlin Wall were unable to prevent radio and television signals reaching the East from the West. 'Spiritual pollution', as the Chinese call it, could not be avoided. Eberle (1990, pp. 194–5) commented that 'the changes in Eastern Europe and the Soviet Union have been as much the triumph of communication as the failure of communism'. For better or worse, in the global village, all governments run the risk of being judged by the standards of the best.

First world governments also face the problem of 'foreign' penetration of their airwaves. Countries with a tradition of state regulation of the media, such as France and Britain, face a growing challenge from satellite broadcasts, over which they have no legal jurisdiction. Hence anxious governments are seeking to develop tighter international regulation of communications.

This illustrates an important general point. As interdependence develops, often driven by technology, so governments seek to collaborate to try to retain or regain their traditional authority. Functional integration (of which technological interdependence is an example) stimulates political cooperation, but the political response tends to be slow, delayed and partial. Computers talk more easily across national boundaries than governments do. In any moves towards integration, politics more often lags than leads. For example, unlike the United States with its integrated coast-to-coast system, Europe's antiquated air traffic control system is based on national centres that hand over control of the flight to the next country as the plane proceeds. An integrated European control system is technically feasible but politically complicated.

The impact of the global village depends on whether a country is a sender as well as a receiver of communication. The prime example of a 'sender' nation is the United States. Critics allege that American primacy in such fields as films and television enables it to spread American values in a form of 'cultural imperialism'. As you read this, somebody somewhere in the world will be watching Captain James T. Kirk of the Star Ship *Enterprise* boldly going where no man has gone before. A bottle of Coke or a packet of Marlboro is still a statement of high fashion in Beijing or Ouagadougou, even though such symbols are losing appeal among health-conscious Americans. The centrality of American symbols to 'world culture' eases the entry of American products into many a market; to critics, this is 'Coca-colonialism' at work.

For governments in 'receiver' countries, however, the impact of the global village is more threatening. Television is a 'window on the West', particularly for élite groups. But television and radio also affect popular aspirations. Mass communications increase awareness of inequalities within nations, between nations, and indeed, between the three worlds. In this connection, 'the revolution of rising expectations' is a useful, if glib, phrase. Governments in the third world must confront populations that are aware of higher living standards elsewhere in the world. Both rulers and ruled realise that these standards cannot be achieved quickly, if at all; but the awareness of such standards is important in itself. Emerging nation-states also find it hard to develop a national identity among their people when television (one of the few national media in most developing countries) is filled with cheap and popular American television programmes.

■ The global ecology

The final area in which the world is getting smaller is the global ecology. The nuclear cloud that crossed Europe after the Chernobyl nuclear reactor exploded in 1986 was a stark reminder that international boundaries count for nothing in the ecology. In similar vein, nuclear testing since 1945 by Britain, the United States, the Soviet Union, China and France has released large quantities of radiation into the atmosphere (and into outer space). This radiation is 40 000 times greater than the bomb dropped on Hiroshima and may kill two million people, mainly through cancer, in the centuries to come.

Furthermore, concern is growing about global warming and the depletion of the ozone layer caused by increased carbon dioxide and chlorofluorocarbon (CFC) gases. The problem has been heightened by the depletion of the rain forests, which reduces nature's ability to extract carbon dioxide from the air (Worldwatch Institute 1990). The first world has certainly played its part in releasing these gases into the atmosphere over the years, but the second and third worlds are also major contributors.

How have global ecological problems affected politics within the nation-state? In many ways, remarkably little. The response of national governments has fallen far short of what is needed to re-establish stability in the global ecology. This is a remarkable 'tribute' to the continued pre-eminence of the nation-state in modern politics. Environmental problems at the global level seem to be regarded as everyone's problem – and therefore as no one's.

A short-sighted policy, for sure, but in a sense understandable. For each individual country knows that it only makes a small contribution to the global pollution problem. However green it becomes, it cannot solve the problem by itself. If it cuts back on its own pollution, but other countries do not, the country will just have suffered pain without gain. The main exception here is the United States, which could make a difference by itself but so far has been too complacent to bother.

In political science, this problem is often described as the 'tragedy of the commons'. This refers to the tendency for common lands to be over-grazed and for oceans to be over-fished. In other words, short-term particular interests take precedence over long-term collective interests. The only solution to such problems is to establish some transnational body with the authority to enforce collective interests. Even in an interdependent world, this is hard to achieve.

It is, of course, true, that virtually all Western leaders now present themselves as 'green'. The political map of the first world has changed as the traditional red and blue rivalries become tinged with green. But how much can the first world do? Countries like China and India argue that only the West can afford the 'luxury' of ecological concern. Leaders of less-developed nations are prepared to continue polluting to increase economic development. Furthermore, it is only in the most developed nations that ecological concerns are becoming an electoral issue.

□ Population growth

One factor that influences the amount of pollution is the number of people in the world. The rate of population growth is slowing down, but world population is still increasing by three people each second. Further, the rate of change is not evenly spread. In the United States, Canada, Japan, New Zealand, Australia and much of Western Europe, the fertility rate has now dropped below the population replacement rate of 2.1 children per couple. The World Bank (1990) calculates that the population of the first world will peak in about 2020 and then begin to fall back. Fertility rates are also decreasing in Eastern Europe, and dropping towards the 2.1 point.

Population growth is also decreasing in the third world. However, it still greatly exceeds the 'population replacement' rate. If current trends continue, the population of the third world will have more than doubled by 2025 to about 8 billion. This places a great strain on third world governments which face the task of making the economy grow faster than the number of mouths.

■ The first world: the driving force

The first world is the motor force for the entire world system. Between them, the United States, Japan, Germany, Britain and France account for just under half of all world imports and exports. Add in Canada and the rest of Western Europe, and the first world's share of global trade increases to over two-thirds.

Yoked together by economic interdependence, the governments in these countries communicate regularly, both bilaterally and through numerous intergovernmental bodies. The notion of 'national sovereignty' remains a potent symbol and a card of last resort, to be played in the event of major disagreements between governments. When push comes to shove, governments can go their own way, a fact that limits the pace and extent of political integration. But people in lifeboats achieve nothing by jumping overboard. The reality is interdependence.

□ *From regulation to markets*

From the end of the Second World War, the United States played the leading role in the international economy. Its aid to European powers after 1945 helped to rebuild devastated countries. The United States also fostered economic recovery in Japan and South Korea. Ironically, Japan has now risen to challenge America's dominant position.

Until the 1970s the United States was said to 'manage' the world economy. From 1945 to the early 1970s the Bretton Woods system kept the exchange rates of the developed economies fixed – with occasional permitted adjustments – to the American dollar ('Bretton Woods' is the name of the place in New Hampshire, USA, where the conference was held in 1944 that put together this system of postwar economic management). The dollar was in turn fixed to the price of gold.

This seemingly technical scheme had deep implications. It meant, in effect, that the United States was the only country that could control its own economy with impunity. Other nations had to respond to changes in the American economy to ensure that their currencies stayed pegged to the dollar. In effect, they surrendered a degree of economic sovereignty in return for stability in the international trading system (Ray 1990, ch. 7). However, this was considered a reasonable price to pay to prevent a slide back to the 'beggar-my-neighbour' trading policies of the interwar years.

The Bretton Woods system was an attempt to *regulate* the financial system of the developed world. It ultimately failed because it placed too much of a premium on the strength of the American economy. Dollars became highly desirable. As other nations accumulated dollars, the United States began to encounter severe inflationary pressures.

Although attempts were made to find new forms of regulation, these too proved to be unsuccessful. As a result, the world has moved towards deregulation of international exchange rates. Some new formal regulations have emerged. For example, the Exchange Rate Mechanism of the European Community sets upper and lower limits for the exchange rates of member nations. But in general, the world's major currencies now float on international exchanges unencumbered by constraints of ceilings and floors. This deregulation allows capital to move relatively unhindered across the world, but nation-states probably have even less economic sovereignty now than under the Bretton Woods system. Markets have taken over where the United States left off.

□ *From markets to blocs?*

In responding to interdependence, the world's leading nations face two options. One is to continue to fine tune the operation of the world market, through such means as Group of Seven (G-7) summit meetings. These conferences bring together leaders of the United States, Japan, Germany, Britain, France, Italy and Canada (with the President of the European Commission as an occasional participant). Alternatively, countries can retreat into regional trading blocs that offer free trade within the bloc but tariffs and restrictions against outsiders.

Some countries, such as Britain, have a long tradition of free trade; they favour the first option. Others, such as France, have an equally long tradition of protectionism; they support the second option. The decisions reached on these issues in the 1990s will profoundly affect the nature of economic interdependence well into the next century.

The European Community (EC), which contains leading European powers such as France, Italy, Germany and the United Kingdom, is the most-developed bloc (for other intergovernmental organisations involving European states, see Table 5.2). The EC has already acquired the status of a weak confederation, pooling some of the sovereignty of member states. The EC is the most important single illustration of first world countries coming together to achieve together what could not be achieved separately.

However, the Americans and the Japanese claim that economic integration in the European Community is creating a 'fortress Europe' which they will be unable to penetrate. The EC's Common Agricultural Policy, which gives massive subsidies to small-scale and inefficient

Table 5.2 **Membership of major international organisations in Europe, 1991**

	EC	NATO	NC	BLUX	WEU	OECD	EFTA	ECSC	CE
Austria						+	+		
Belgium	+	+		+	+	+		+	+
Britain	+	+			+	+	#		+
Denmark	+	+	+			+	#		+
Finland			+			+			+
France	+	+			+	+		+	+
Germany	+	+			+	+		+	+
Greece	+	+				+		+	+
Iceland		+	+			+		+	+
Ireland	+					+			+
Italy	+	+			+	+			+
Luxembourg	+	+		+	+	+		+	+
Netherlands	+	+		+	+	+		+	+
Norway		+	+			+	+		+
Portugal	+	+				+	#		+
Spain	+	+				+			+
Sweden			+			+	+		+
Switzerland						+	+		+

Notes:
+ = member
# = left EFTA to join EC (EFTA and EC have now agreed to a single free trade zone)

EC = European Community
NATO = North Atlantic Treaty Organisation (includes non-European nations)
NC = Nordic Council
BLUX = Benelux customs union
WEU = Western European Union
OECD = Organisation for Economic Cooperation and Development (includes non-European nations)
EFTA = European Free Trade Association
ECSC = European Coal and Steel Community (precursor to EC)
CE = Council of Europe

farmers, is a prime example. It effectively prohibits large-scale food imports from efficient producers in the United States and from low-cost producers in the third world.

Partly in response to the emergence of the European market, moves towards another great economic bloc are taking place across the Atlantic. Canada and the United States have agreed a free trade zone. Negotiations are taking place to allow Mexico to join, with the possibility that much of Central and South America will end up inside this 'wall'. This market will be even larger than Europe and will contain a judicious mix of high-tech (USA, Canada) and low-cost (Mexico) producers.

The Pacific region could provide the third trading bloc. This is a difficult area to define. It is generally taken to mean the Asian nations of the Pacific, but can be extended to include Australia, New Zealand, the eastern coast of the Soviet Union and the western coast of the Americas. The Pacific nations have yet to mirror the process of economic integration in North America and Western Europe. The Association of South East Asian Nations (ASEAN), established in 1967 by Indonesia, Malaysia, the Philippines, Thailand and Singapore, does not include South Korea and Japan. This limits its impact on the region's affairs. The Asia-Pacific Economic Cooperation (APEC) forum, established in 1989, also needs time to develop. Its original members were the ASEAN nations plus South Korea, Japan, the United States, Canada, New Zealand and Australia.

However, as the Pacific region develops organisationally, it will undoubtedly play a major role in world economic affairs in the twenty-first century (see Figure 5.2). As early as the beginning of the 1980s, the United States was conducting more trade across the Pacific than the Atlantic – a sign of the shift in global economic power.

To date, the main conflict between blocs has been between Japan and its Western trading partners. This stems from Japan's trade surplus. Governments elsewhere in the first world face tricky problems in responding to this problem. The visibility of Japanese cars on the roads often brings the problem into the public realm. As consumers, citizens show a preference in the market for Japanese cars. But the domestic automobile industry shouts long and hard for protection – and opinion polls show that most voters are sympathetic to generous treatment for home-based companies. One solution is to try to reduce Japan's trade surplus. In 1990, Japan and the United States agreed the Structural Impediment Initiative. The Japanese agreed to increase domestic spending that would, it was hoped, increase imports from the United States.

Another way round the problem is a 'Trojan Horse' policy of direct investment by Japan's companies in Western countries. For example, Japanese car companies have set up manufacturing and assembly plants in the United States and Europe. Cars produced in these countries do not count as imports and hence avoid tariffs and quotas. As Figure 5.3 shows, the international automobile industry is linked through an intricate web of joint ventures and manufacturing and marketing agreements. In a sense it is misleading to call Nissan a Japanese firm

(a) The twentieth-century world: a Eurocentric vision

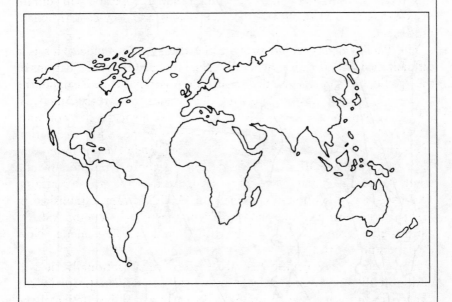

(b) The twenty-first century world: power to the Pacific?

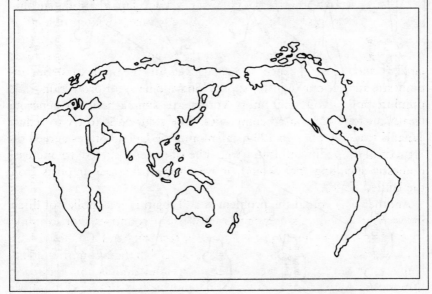

Figure 5.2 *Eurocentric and Pacific-centred views of the world*

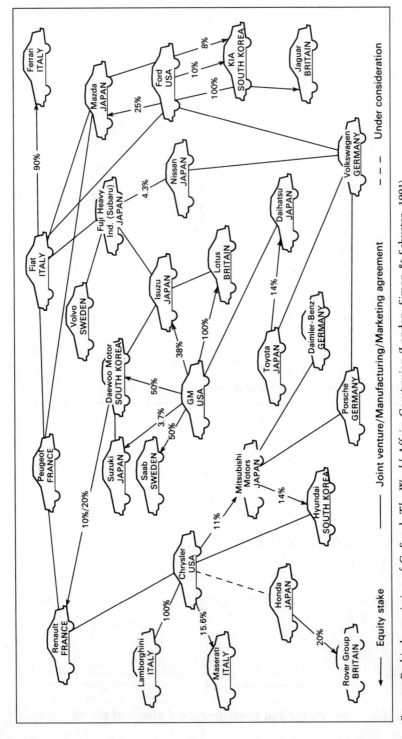

Source: By kind permission of G. Segal, *The World Affairs Companion* (London: Simon & Schuster, 1991).

Figure 5.3 *World automobile manufacturing*

– in many senses, major companies in the first world are global companies. However, strategic control (e.g. of Nissan's major investment decisions) unquestionably remains at head office in Japan.

The fears of protectionism in the first world should be allayed by the General Agreement on Tariffs and Trade (GATT). GATT was formed in 1948 to act as an international forum to encourage free trade between nations. Its aim was to remove both formal (for example, tariffs and quotas) and informal (for example, legal standards) barriers to free trade. It has around 100 member nations drawn from all three worlds.

In the 1980s GATT negotiations ran into severe problems. Foremost among these was the question of food trade. The Cairns Group of nations that export farm produce (including Australia and New Zealand), in alliance with the United States, pointed out that the EC's Common Agricultural Policy placed unfair obstacles on food trade with the EC. For a country like New Zealand that traded heavily with Britain before the UK's entrance into the community, EC agricultural policy was a devastating blow. The more integrated and protectionist the EC becomes, the more Australia and New Zealand will come to see their future linked to the Pacific region.

It is difficult to predict how strong these three trading blocs will become. It is even harder to see how they will relate to each other. Some fear that there will be intense competition between the three blocs, with internal markets developing that are difficult to penetrate from outside. However, the counter-argument is that the nations of the first world are all so integrated already that any attempt to place barriers around the blocs will lead to 'mutually assured economic destruction'. Free trade within blocs does not necessarily mean more restrictions on trade between them. In either case, a major task for all first world states is to assess how they will relate to these blocs.

▌ The second world: from isolation to integration

In this section we discuss the momentous changes that occurred in the second world's role in global politics in the 1980s. This period saw increasing contacts between communist states and the first world. In China, the post-Mao leadership opened the door to expanded economic contacts both with the west and with China's non-communist neighbours. In Europe, the demolition of the Berlin Wall and the removal of the political, economic and military barriers that previously divided Europe into East and West have fundamentally altered the political landscape of the continent. As a result, the second world is now becoming more closely integrated into the international economic system than ever before.

☐ *The old order: problems of isolation*

For many years, communist party states strove to insulate themselves from the international economy. Except for Yugoslavia, the Soviet satellites of Eastern Europe turned their backs on the West and looked East towards the Soviet Union. In East Asia, China and North Korea also became closed economies. In North Korea, radio sets are still made so that they can only receive broadcasts from the the state radio station. The Berlin Wall was the most potent symbol of barriers between the second and first worlds. Erected in 1961, and torn down by the people in 1989, the wall prevented East Germans from escaping to the West. Many of those who tried to get across were shot.

Economically, the Soviet Union built its own international trading bloc, the Council for Mutual Economic Assistance (COMECON). This was set up in 1949 largely as a response to the establishment of the Organisation for Economic Cooperation and Development in Western Europe. COMECON's stated goal was to help communist party states to develop by integrating their economies. However, it also sought to cut Eastern Europe off from its traditional European orientation, and to use the more developed economies of Eastern Europe for the benefit of the Soviet economy.

Many in Eastern Europe regarded COMECON as a kind of Soviet economic imperialism. As S. White *et al.* (1990, p. 12) note, COMECON's programme of economic integration was 'regarded with more enthusiasm in Moscow . . . than in the countries of Eastern Europe'. But it has to be said that the Soviet Union fostered the postwar economic recovery of Czechoslovakia and East Germany by providing subsidised energy and raw materials.

☐ *The collapse*

Despite all this, by the 1980s none of the major communist party states had completely avoided being pulled into the international economic order. The motive for opening up to the Western world was economic. Faced with economic stagnation, communist party states began to look to the West for advanced technology – and the loans to pay for it. China, a nation that had turned inwards and advocated self-sufficiency for many years, adopted an open-door policy in the late-1970s. Foreign companies were invited to invest in the country.

In Eastern Europe, several countries sought joint ventures with the West, and applied for loans from Western banks. However, the East European nations did not use these loans wisely. In the longer term, loans merely served to intensify economic problems. Rather than treating the disease, the ruling parties chose to deal with the symptoms. Foreign funds were not invested into projects that would generate long-term growth, but were used instead to 'buy off' the industrial working class. Thus the loans were used to keep loss-making industries going and to subsidise the price of food to maintain workers' purchasing power. As such, the capital inflow only helped to sustain inefficiency. It did not create the surplus needed to repay the debts.

Two factors then emerged. First, ruling parties found themselves caught in a vicious cycle of subsidy. Subsidies created an expectation that essential goods would always be cheap, thus making it harder to raise prices towards the true cost of provision. The greater the subsidy, the louder the complaints if they were removed. In Poland, successive party leaders tried to break out of this 'subsidy cycle'. Each time price rises were announced, the result was a rash of strikes and violence.

Secondly, huge debts mounted up. When Poland's communists handed power to Solidarity in 1989, the country's external debt stood at $40 billion – half its annual product. Similarly, in Bulgaria the national debt increased from $3.6 billion in 1984 to $10.5 billion in 1989, a threefold increase in five years. Eventually, the system cracked.

☐ *The new order: problems of integration*

For postcommunist regimes, relations with the international economic order are now a pressing concern. COMECON was dissolved in 1991 so, from a position of isolation, ex-communist states must place external relationships near the top of their agenda. The task is enormous (see Exhibit 5.2). The industrial plants of Eastern Europe and the Soviet Union are inefficient and heavily polluting. They produced goods of indifferent quality, to meet the demands of central planners rather than the market. They are managed by people for whom concepts such as market research, advertising and risk-taking are, literally, foreign. Germany illustrates the uncompetitive nature of production under communism. After reunification, the economy of East Germany contracted by a third in two years, while the West German economy grew by 7 per cent over the same period.

Western industrialists who visit factories in postcommunist countries are invariably shocked by what they find. For example, John Harvey-Jones, ex-chairman of British-based transnational ICI, wrote (1991) as follows.

> visiting factories in Eastern Europe is like taking a trip in a time machine. Investment occurred in periodic, vast, centrally-directed dollops. Thereafter the manufacturer's task was merely to maintain the planned output. There were no benchmarks for change of any sort – be it quality, cost or quantity. There were draconian punishments for failure and little reward for success, even at meeting the fossilised plans of the central bureaucrats. To keep things running at all took superhuman determination. The wonder is not that the system collapsed but that it took so long to do so.

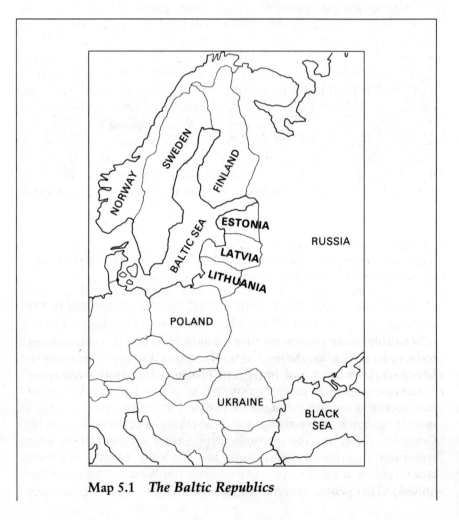

Map 5.1   *The Baltic Republics*

Exhibit 5.2   *The Baltic Republics: Joining the World League*

As the Soviet Union fell apart in 1991, the small Baltic States of Estonia, Latvia and Lithuania were the first to achieve independence. The problems they face in entering the world economy illustrate the difficulties of shifting away from the centrally planned Soviet trading bloc. They also show the enormous problems of late entry into the world trading system.

The Baltics do have some advantages over other Soviet republics. They are situated close to Western Europe: Estonia is just fifty miles from Finland. Even when it was a Soviet republic, Estonia exported chairs to IKEA, the Swedish furniture group. The three states are already more prosperous than many other Soviet republics, and with the advantage of a larger 'non-state' economic sector.

But the newcomers also face deep-seated problems. The Soviet empire was economically integrated. As a result, Latvia has no facilities to produce iron and steel, and all three states depend heavily on the East for fuel. So the links with the East cannot easily be broken. Foreign trade requires dollars and deutschmarks, the Baltic states have almost none. Moreover, unlike the rest of Eastern Europe, the Baltics have to develop their own currencies from scratch. Population transfers under communist rule also mean that they inherit substantial minority populations. About a third of Latvia's population is Russian.

With Western European countries already organised into the trading blocs of the EC and EFTA (European Free Trade Association), the Baltic republics will not find it easy to enter these markets. Even if they do, they face the root problem of uncompetitiveness. Latvia has a large bicycle industry but its products were made to Russian standards. Western mountain bikes, with their gaudy colours, index gears and high-tech tubing, were totally beyond the comprehension of any central planner in the Soviet Union. Would you buy a Latvian bike?

To be able to compete on the international market, economic reforms will have to be pushed through at home. This is the major example in today's world of how economic interdependence leads to the reshaping of domestic society. The political load borne by the new leaders of postcommunist states is therefore enormous. As these societies move towards market economies, unemployment and prices will escalate, at least in the short and medium term. Populations with expectations of instant affluence for all will discover how costly is the transition to a market economy. Even a mature market economy has losers as well as winners. Many people are reluctant to abandon the minimal guarantees provided by the planned economy: cheap and sufficient (if poor quality) food, transport and accommodation. These countries may prove vulnerable to simplistic nationalist appeals from populist leaders offering instant solutions. The political impact of paradise postponed may prove substantial.

■ The third world: dependence or interdependence?

In a sense, the countries of the third world are the most international of all. Many have vulnerable economies heavily dependent on the export of one commodity. For example, copper accounts for 88 per cent of Zambia's exports. Others are indebted to international banks. For example, over half of Argentina's exports earnings should go on paying off the interest on its massive foreign debt. Still others, particularly among the poorest countries of the 'fourth world', can barely survive without support from international bodies and assorted charities. None have even the modest insulation from the world economy provided by the large, diversified domestic markets of the United States, the European Community and Japan.

So even more than in the first and second worlds, politics in the third world must be placed in an international context. And here the big question is, why does underdevelopment persist? Two main theories exist side by side. On the one hand, the **liberal theory** argues that opening up the economies of the third world to free trade and international competition is the only way forward. This theory is severely critical of the way many ruling politicians in the third world have distorted the operation of the market in their countries. The liberal theory is popular among governments in the first world, and the intergovernmental bodies they dominate. Often simplistic, it nonetheless offers one way forward for the third world.

On the other hand, the **dependency theory** suggests that the whole international economy operates to the disadvantage of the third world. What appears as interdependence in Japan can be seen as dependence in Jakarta. The 'escape' from poverty promised by liberal advocates of economic integration is a cruel illusion. Like an addictive drug, the escape route turns into a prison of its own. According to dependency theory, the only solution is to change the entire nature of the relationship between the first and the third worlds. Popular in the third world, indeed developed largely in Latin America, this account offers a sharp analysis but unclear solutions to the problem of underdevelopment.

☐ *Liberal theory*

In its simplest form, liberal theory suggests that, if allowed to evolve naturally, unhindered by government intervention, free markets and competition will stimulate economic growth. Eventually, the developing nations will catch up. As Blake and Walters (1976, pp. 29–30) put it, 'Liberal economists feel that less-developed countries can facilitate the modernization process by exposing their domestic producers to external competition.'

The continuation, if not the causes, of underdevelopment are blamed on bad government. Trade policies of third world governments depart too far from the ideal of free trade. Thus economic underdevelopment is blamed on political mismanagement. The leaders of third world countries too often regard the state as a resource to be exploited for the benefit of themselves, their friends, their allies, or their ethnic group. Rulers are more concerned about short-term success or survival than the long-term development of their economies. In Argentina, for instance, the military regime borrowed heavily to finance arms purchases that were used in the ultimately futile attempt to wrest the Falkland/Malvinas Islands from British control in 1982. Western countries, it must be said, are always keen to supply weapons to virtually any third world country willing to buy them.

The liberal argument is propounded by some of the most influential international organisations in the modern world. Both the World Bank and the International Monetary Fund are committed to encouraging third world governments to open their economies to free trade. But they do not claim there is no role for government. Rather, the key to effective development is taken to be the interaction between markets and government.

In the 'shining examples' of Japan and Korea (see Exhibit 5.3), the governments did intervene in the economy. Both countries protected infant industries from competition during the postwar decades until they were able to stand unaided. But crucially, policy-makers sought to guide private companies towards success in the marketplace. They did not aim to create the planned economies of the second world, nor even the nationalised industries then widespread in Western Europe. International and domestic competition was encouraged by a convertible currency as soon as the economy could bear it, and so relative prices were not distorted. In the current liberal theory of development, governments 'kick-start' firms and industries that might not otherwise get moving, but once the industrial motor is running, it is expected to generate its own power.

Exhibit 5.3   *South Korea: promotion from the third division*

South Korea is one of the fastest-growing countries in the world. Since the mid-1960s, its economy has expanded at an average of around 10 per cent per year, a doubling time of just eight years. In the early 1990s, the growth rate was still about 8 per cent per year. But both domestically and internationally, South Korea now faces new challenges brought about by its own success.

Internally, South Korea has experienced an early form of the 'post-industrial revolution' (see pp. 141–2). The middle classes are no longer content with washing machines and videos. In a traditionally authoritarian society, they now demand political freedoms as well.

Internationally, South Korea, like other third world countries, is paradoxically feeling an unwelcome chill as the Cold War ends. The threat of communist domination of East Asia has now all but disappeared. So, too, has the need previously felt by the United States to foster economic development in this bulwark against communism.

Once nations reach a certain level of economic development, they hit a 'poverty gap'. This means they lose access to preferential low-interest loans from organisations such as the World Bank and the IMF. They are expected to become full players in the international community. They are also expected to shoulder the burden of protecting their own interests. South Korea was, for example, one of many countries lobbied by the West to foot the bill for the 1991 Gulf War.

In short, the transition from third to first world is painful. Just as promoted teams often change their coach, so South Korea's emergence may destroy the power of the modernising, authoritarian élite that brought the country to where it is today – on the brink of promotion to the first world.

□ *Dependency theory*

Opponents of the liberal theory argue that the very structure of the world system means that development will not take such a smooth path. Opening up domestic economies to free trade and international competition will only widen the gap between the rich and the poor. Modernisation started at different times in different countries. The ones that started earlier therefore have comparative advantages over the late starters. The market always favours the well endowed over the poor, so free trade will accentuate disparities. As N. Smith (1984, p. xi) puts it, 'uneven development is the hallmark of the geography of capitalism'.

Writers such as Frank (1981) and Amin (1977) argue that although formal colonialism is not a common phenomenon today, economic or neocolonialism persists. John Kautsky (1972, p. 60) defined economic colonialism as

> an economic relationship prevailing between an advanced industrial country and an underdeveloped one, where the underdeveloped country serves, through investment from capital principally from the advanced country, as a supplier of raw materials for the industry of the advanced country. In time, the underdeveloped country can also come to serve as a market for some of the finished goods of the advanced country.

'Neo-colonies' remain dependent on their first world patrons. This enables the ex-colonial powers to reap the economic benefits of colonialism without paying the political and financial price. Central to the theory of dependent development is the concept of a *comprador* class. This consists of local managers who take over the economy once the colonialists depart. These business people have an interest in maintaining the colonial economic relationship. Local managers derive great wealth from trading with their patrons overseas. As such, it is in their interest to maintain the relationship, even if the local workforce is heavily exploited.

Because the modernisation of the developing nation depends on the first world patron, national development is distorted. The whole pattern of the client economy is shaped by the demands of the patron. What we see is not development proper but 'the development of underdevelopment' (Frank 1969).

In particular, third world economies concentrate on commodities and minerals that the first world needs. Concentration on the development of one commodity may bring short- or even medium-term gains, but it is at the expense of more balanced development in the economy as a whole. If frost kills its coffee bushes, Colombia faces severe and immediate problems. At least a third of its legal exports come from coffee (cocaine is its largest illegal export). Many third world economies are equally dominated by the production of a small number of commodities. This makes them very sensitive to changes in the tastes and economies of the first world. Who would be a tea producer when the first world is switching to coffee?

Why don't commodity producers form a cartel to force up the price of their produce? One problem is diversification of third world suppliers – the more producers there are, the greater the alternatives for first world purchasers. If Colombia increases the price of its coffee beans, then the big coffee firms will just turn to Brazil, Costa Rica or Kenya. Another problem is that national governments must be able to control the production of that commodity in their territory. After seizing power in Libya in 1969, Colonel Qadafi threatened to take over any company that did not cut oil production and raise prices. Other nations have not possessed the same ability or desire to control commodity producers. The wave of privatisation that swept the third world (and in particular, Africa) in the 1980s and 1990s further reduced the possibility of building effective producer cartels in the future.

The only cartel of commodity producers that proved capable of exerting pressure on the developed world was the Organisation of Petroleum Exporting Countries (OPEC). Its decision to quadruple oil prices in 1973 had an enormous impact on the world economy. However, as Strange (1988) notes, the oil-dependent nations of the first world learnt quickly from their experience. Oil companies moved their prospecting and exploration efforts to non-OPEC areas, consumer states diversified their energy supplies, and countries such as Japan negotiated their own independent agreements with suppliers. By the 1990s even OPEC, the most powerful of commodity cartels, had lost its stranglehold on the first world.

Dependency theorists point to capital outflows from the third world to the first. By comparison, the amount of aid granted to third world countries pales into insignificance. In 1989 the West gave the third world £30 billion in aid, but the third world gave the West £93 billion in debt repayments. Africa's burden of debt exceeds the continent's GNP. Except for Egypt, Israel and a handful of countries in dire distress (such as Tanzania), foreign aid averages only around 2 per cent of gross national product (GNP) in third world nations – about as useful as a sticking plaster on a severed artery.

The outflow of money from the third world forms part of the debt crisis. This too shows the dependency of the third world, but in this case 'interdependency' is the more accurate term. In the 1970s Western banks found their deposits swelled by petro-dollars – the massive profits of the oil-producing nations. The banks were looking for customers, and many third world governments were looking for loans. Billions of dollars were loaned to second and third world nations. At the peak in the mid-1980s, Mexico and Brazil owed about $100 billion each. Many countries could not even afford to pay the interest on the debts. As a result, international attempts to get to grips with the debt crisis involved giving new loans to countries such as Mexico merely to allow them to pay off the interest on old loans. As Clarke (1992) says, 'If major debtor countries were declared bankrupt, as technically they were, then some major banks in the West would be ruined and international finance would be thrown into chaos. It was everyone's problem.'

In the long run, the debt crisis will help to ensure the triumph of the liberal theory of development. Many countries in the third world are turning away from commercial banks towards the International Monetary Fund (IMF). The IMF is an increasingly important actor in the management of the world economy. Contributions to the IMF come from member nations. Voting power within the organisation is based on that nation's contribution and the size of its national economy. The United States is the dominant partner in the IMF with around 20 per cent of voting power. As any change in IMF rules requires an 85 per cent majority in favour, the Americans have, in effect, veto power.

The debt crisis of the 1980s has given the liberal theories a great opportunity to be asserted in the third world. IMF loans are much more attractive than private loans in terms of repayments – but there is a catch. To qualify for an IMF (or World Bank) loan, nations must in practice surrender a degree of control over their economic policies. The IMF will stipulate certain economic policies that have to be implemented if the loan is to be granted. In particular, the IMF encourages the opening up of domestic industries to international competition, and the primacy of market forces over state planning. Many Western governments support this policy. In 1991, the British Foreign Secretary said, 'governments which persist with repressive policies, with corrupt management or with wasteful and discredited economic systems should not expect us to support their folly with scarce aid resources which could be used better elsewhere'.

Desperate to pull themselves out of the trough of debt, many third world governments have accepted first world principles of economic development. In 1991, for example, the Indian Government announced it would eliminate many subsidies, reduce tariffs on imports and exports and privatise up to a fifth of its public sector. Five weeks later, it sought loans of $15 billion from the West to help service its foreign debt of $70 billion. Ironically, the liberal theory of development is carrying all before it precisely because of the dependence of the third world on the first.

Summary

1.   The boundaries of the state have become more porous than ever before. Although contacts between nations exist at many levels, states are widening their responsibilities in response to the challenges of the interdependent world.

2.   The international division of labour means that goods can be made in whichever country can produce them to the combination of quality and cost demanded by customers. The *economic* dynamic of international trade springs from the fact that all participants can benefit from it. The *political* dynamic is that not all countries benefit equally.

3.   Until the 1970s, the United States was said to 'manage' the world economy under the Bretton Woods system. However, in the 1980s, America lost its dominant position. In the 1990s, no single nation is powerful enough to dominate the world economy.

4.   The creation of supranational trading blocs has increased fears of growing protectionism in the first world. However, the first world nations are so dependent on trade that any protectionist war would severely damage the economies of all.

5.   After a period of economic and political isolation after 1945, virtually all second world countries are now seeking to become integrated into the international economic system. However, their economies are so backward and inefficient that this transition will be a painful process.

6.   The liberal theory suggests that third world nations must open their economies to international competition if they want to develop. Dependency theorists disagree, and claim that this will only widen the gap between the developed and underdeveloped nations.

7.   Dependency theory suggests that formal colonialism has been replaced by economic colonialism. The ex-colonies of the third world are economically dependent on their first world patrons for markets and investment.

8.   One of the key concerns for third world governments is the size of its national debt. Unable to pay back loans to Western banks, some third world countries have turned to the IMF and the World Bank for loans to pay the interest. In return for these new loans, the third world countries have to agree to liberalise their economies.

Discussion points

1. Does the nature of the world economy mean that countries in the third world can never catch up with those in the first world?

2. Which transnational companies are most visible in your country? Do they strengthen or weaken the economy? What is their political role?

3. Explore the implications of the global economy for democracy within the nation-state.

4. 'As all good Marxists know, economics determines politics'. Do you agree?

5. Are postcommunist states becoming economic colonies of the first world?

Key reading

Ray, J. (1990) *Global Politics* (Boston, Mass.: Houghton Mifflin). A comprehensive introduction to world politics.

Little, R. and Smith, M. (eds) (1991) *Perspectives on World Politics*, 2nd edn, (London: Routledge). An up-to-date and well-organised reader, which examines world politics from three perspectives.

Segal, G. (1991) *The World Affairs Companion* (London: Simon and Schuster). A good and accessible introduction to international affairs.

Instituto del Tercer Mondo (1990) *Third World Guide 91/92* (Montevideo: Instituto del Tercer Mondo). A view from the third world of the problems facing the region in the 1990s. Also contains country profiles of every nation in the world.

Blake, D. and Walters, R. (1976) *The Politics of Global Economic Relations* (Englewood Cliffs, N.J.: Prentice-Hall). A good introduction to the various approaches to development and underdevelopment.

Further reading

Any student of the development and origins of the modern world system should start with Wallerstein's (1974, 1980) seminal works. Kennedy (1988) is also very influential on the rise and fall of the great powers.

More general introductions to world politics include Ray (1990), Calvocoressi (1991), Hockling and Smith (1990), and Segal (1991). Claude (1971) is a readable introduction to international organisations. Keohane and Nye (1972) and Keohane (1984) are both influential works on global interdependence. The books by Strange (1986, 1988) are both good places to start on the impact of the deregulation of the world economy. Jenkins (1987) also analyses the interaction between states and markets with specific reference to the role of TNCs.

On theories of development and underdevelopment, Kautsky (1972) and Amin (1977) are both important texts on imperialism. Hirschmann (1958) remains an influential work on liberal theories, and the World Bank (1990) is an up-to-date and highly influential vision of the importance of free trade to development. Blake and Walters (1976) and Spero (1977) both contain useful introductions to the liberal, Marxist and structuralist views.

For the specific problems facing third world development, the Third World Guide (1990) is a readable and accessible starting-point. Chan (1987) assesses the problems from African perspectives. For the impact of the debt crisis, see George (1988). Warnock (1987) is a useful introduction to the global food problem.

■ PART 3 ■

THE SOCIAL CONTEXT OF POLITICS

Government does not work in isolation, unaffected by the society of which it forms part. Much of the variation in regime types, for example, can be accounted for in terms of the characteristics of society, especially its culture and level of economic development. This part examines the central links between society and state. Chapter 6 looks at the attitudes of people towards government, while Chapter 7 discusses their participation in it. Because of their growing importance worldwide, elections and voting behaviour are separately examined in Chapter 8. Particularly in liberal democracies, interest groups form an important link between society and government; they are the subject of Chapter 9. Parties are also central to the way interests and preferences are placed on the political agenda, though parties select and combine demands where interest groups express them. Chapter 10 examines parties.

■ *Chapter 6* ■

Political Culture

'The strongest is never strong enough unless he succeeds in turning might into right and obedience into duty.' So wrote Rousseau in the eighteenth century, and rulers the world over have taken his saying to their hearts. For instance, under communist rule in the Soviet Union two- and three-year-olds were taught to sing nursery songs about Lenin; four- and five-year-olds to decorate his portrait; and six-year-olds were allowed to lay flowers at Lenin's statue. When communist power collapsed, junior school teachers were suddenly shorn of the role models which they had been presenting to Soviet children for generations. They did not know what to teach.

Attempts to foster loyalty to the regime are not of course restricted to communist states. Civics classes in American high schools, and the presentation of the monarchy to British children as a benign institution worthy of affection and allegiance, represent other ways in which rulers have tried to transform might into right, obedience into duty. Whatever the success of these attempts, a regime based on popular acceptance of its authority is likely in the long run to prove more effective and hence more durable than one based purely on force. As the Chinese proverb says, 'You can conquer a kingdom on horseback but you cannot rule from there'. It is this impact of popular opinion on the stability and effectiveness of regimes which makes the study of popular attitudes towards politics so important.

The study of a people's orientations to politics is the study of a country's political culture. The concept of political culture is essentially psychological: it refers to what people think about politics – to their beliefs, values and emotions. It does not refer to actual political behaviour. Indeed behaviour may conflict with prevailing attitudes. For example, the amount of popular participation in democracies is distinctly limited despite a participant political culture. Yet the fact that many people in liberal democracies *believe* they can influence political decisions, even though they choose not to do so, gives an important clue to the way in which liberal democracies function. In this chapter we discuss political culture in each of the three worlds. We then examine how people acquire their political attitudes. We conclude with a discussion of élite political culture.

■ The first world

There are two approaches to the analysis of political culture in the first world. The **liberal** (or behavioural) account argues that most democracies do have a national political culture. This is a product of history and is transmitted across the generations through social institutions such as the family. The alternative **radical** (or Marxist) account rejects this neutral interpretation. It suggests instead that political culture is the product of an attempt by dominant classes to impose their values on subordinate groups. This is achieved through formal mechanisms such as the mass media and the education system.

Thus, where liberals study the transmission of values across the generations, and call this socialisation, radicals study the transmission of values across the classes, and term this indoctrination. Where liberals assume that a national political culture can emerge naturally from socialisation and history, radicals argue that in capitalist society any national culture is bound to be a fragile affair. It needs constant shoring up by those who benefit from the system. We will consider these two approaches and then turn to an examination of 'postmaterialism' as an element in the political cultures of the first world.

□ The civic culture

The liberal interpretation of political culture was presented in Almond and Verba's *The Civic Culture* (1963). Based on surveys conducted during 1959–60 in the United States, Britain, West Germany, Italy and Mexico, this landmark study tried to identify the political culture within which a liberal democracy is most likely to survive and develop (see Figure 6.1).

Almond and Verba distinguished three pure types of political culture: the parochial, subject and participant. In the **parochial** political culture, people are only vaguely aware of the existence of central government – as with hill tribes whose life is largely unaffected by national decisions made by the central government. In the **subject** political culture, citizens see themselves as subjects of a government rather than as participants in the political process – as with people living under a dictatorship. In the

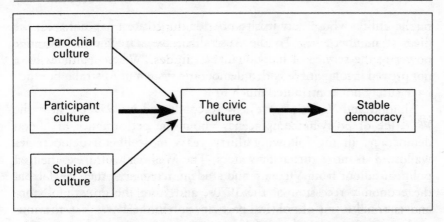

Figure 6.1 *Almond and Verba's theory of the civic culture*

participant political culture, citizens believe both that they can contribute to the system and that they are affected by it.

Almond and Verba's idea was that democracy is likely to be most stable in societies where a participant political culture is balanced by the survival of subject and parochial attitudes. This mix is termed the 'civic culture'. In this culture the citizen is active enough in politics to express his or her preferences to government but is not so involved in particular issues as to refuse to accept the decisions made by the élite. The citizen feels capable of influencing the government but often chooses not to do so, thus giving the government a measure of flexibility.

The authors concluded from their surveys that of the five countries they had studied, Britain came closest to the civic culture and was followed by the United States. In both societies respect for and trust in government was high, while the duty to participate was widely accepted. So too, was the belief that such involvement could make a difference. The main contrast between the two countries was that the subject political culture remained more important in Britain than in the United States, where participant attitudes predominated.

Though not included in Almond and Verba's study, we can look to Australia for an example of a liberal democracy which is **not** fully underpinned by its political culture. Australia's political culture has been described as 'subject participant'. Most Australians are highly conscious of the benefits they expect from government but they do not display a similar obligation to participate. Australians rely heavily on public provision but at the same time are frequently contemptuous of those who provide it (Emy and Hughes 1991, p. 121). As Hancock put it in 1930, 'Australian democracy has come to look upon the state as a vast public utility, whose duty it is to provide the greatest happiness for the greatest number . . . . To the Australian, the state means collective power at the service of individualistic "rights".' These attitudes have not proved incompatible with a democratic system in Australia but they have surely not contributed much to it.

Almond and Verba's surveys were conducted in 1959–60, near the high tide of postwar complacency about the performance of liberal democracy. In the following thirty years most liberal democracies wallowed in more turbulent waters. The Western world experienced political fallout from Vietnam and student activism in the 1960s, from the economic recession of the 1970s, and from the growth of non-conventional forms of political participation in the 1980s (e.g. the anti-nuclear movement) and the 1990s (e.g. ecology groups).

As Almond and Verba noted in their up-date (1980), these events left their mark on Western political cultures. In Britain and the United States trust in government declined. This represented a shift away from the civic culture towards a more pragmatic and instrumental attitude to politics. Yet in neither Britain nor the United States was the political culture transformed. Most Americans and many Britons still take pride in their political systems. Discontent is focused more on the performance of governing parties than on the entire political process.

More recent surveys suggest that the pattern noted by Almond and Verba still holds good. In a study of European countries, Inglehart (1988) noted that the French, Italians and Greeks ranked low on measures of political satisfaction, trust in others, life satisfaction and happiness. And these countries have been characterised by large anti-system parties. More stable democracies, suggests Inglehart, have a reservoir of support which can sustain them through bad times:

> Even when democracy has no answer to the question, 'what have you done for me lately?' it may be sustained by diffuse feelings that it is in essence, a good thing. These feelings may in turn reflect economic and other successes that one experienced long ago or learned about second hand as part of one's early socialisation (p. 1205).

Four main criticisms have been directed at the theory of the civic culture (Barry 1978; Almond and Verba 1980). First, political culture may reflect the political system rather than determine it. In a democracy people may think they can influence government because they can in fact do so; if democracy ended, then so too would the civic culture. So, far from being a *cause* of stable democracy, as Almond and Verba claimed, a civic culture might just be a *consequence* of democracy. If this is so, the initial question – what makes a stable democracy? – remains unanswered.

Secondly, Almond and Verba probably overestimated the extent to which Britain had a civic culture, even in the late 1950s. After all, there is a long tradition of unorthodox political protest in Britain, especially of urban disorder and riots against new taxes. Almond and Verba's own survey found that 58 per cent of Britons agreed that 'People like me don't have any say in what the government does'. This evidence supports Heath and Topf's claim (1987) that 'political cynicism has been a long-standing feature of British political culture'. Like many Americans of the time, Almond and Verba were prone to look at Britain through rose-tinted spectacles.

Thirdly, the importance Almond and Verba attached to democratic governments having flexibility in their decisions led some critics to doubt whether anything 'democratic' remained in the authors' concept of liberal democracy. Pateman (1980) may have gone too far in describing *The Civic Culture* as 'a celebration of political apathy' but certainly the liberalism of the book is more apparent than any commitment to participatory democracy.

Fourthly, Almond and Verba gave little attention to political subcultures. These are groups in society whose political attitudes deviate sharply from the national culture. Does it make sense to speak of American, Australian or even Dutch political culture, given the diversity of groups within these countries? In fact, is 'political culture' anything more than a fancy term for the dubious concept of 'national character'? Some critics allege that subcultures of class and race are so strong in Western societies that it makes no sense to speak of a national culture. This final point is the basis of the radical account of political culture to which we now turn.

☐ *Ideological hegemony*

For Marxists, a major task was to explain why the working class did not rebel against its exploited position under capitalism. Marx himself suggested one interpretation when he wrote that the ideas of the ruling class are in every epoch the ruling ideas. In a famous phrase, he suggested that those who control the means of material production also control the means of ideological production. Yet despite this, Marx himself believed that in the long run a crisis of capitalism would cause a working-class revolution.

Most modern radicals have abandoned this prediction. They recognise that capitalism has 'delivered the goods'. They now give more weight to the 'superstructure' (i.e. the culture) in shaping working-class attitudes. For many modern Marxists, in particular, the battle of ideas is almost as important as developments in the economy. For example, the Italian Marxist Gramsci (1971, written 1929–35) felt that dominant classes exercised power over subordinate strata as much through persuasion as through coercion. He used the term 'hegemony' to describe how one class can dominate another without resort to brute force (R. Simon 1982).

Whatever the precise position particular radicals adopt, they all agree that political culture is not a neutral product of a country's history. Rather, political culture is 'meaning in the service of domination' (Thompson 1990). It is viewed as the outcome of a more-or-less conscious effort by dominant classes to legitimise their social and economic power. To this end, the cultures of liberal democracies emphasise values which divide the working class, such as individualism, competitiveness and materialism. These cultures also offer an artificial sense of cross-class unity, through religious, nationalist and racist values. The mechanisms by which this political culture is transmitted include the mass media, the education system, business organisations and churches.

In the radical account, the hegemony of the ruling class is always superficial. Working-class people may accept dominant values in the abstract (e.g. agreeing with a pollster that trade unions are too powerful) while still being willing to take radical action in their own life (e.g. by going on strike). Thus working-class political culture is not just a passive acceptance of dominant values. It also includes ideas of solidarity drawn from the local working-class community and perhaps also some elements of left-wing ideology introduced through a trade union or a socialist party (F. Parkin 1971). These various 'value streams' compete with each other not just at the party level but also within the belief systems of individuals. Thus it would be wrong to regard the radical view of political culture as nothing more than a simple conspiracy theory. In fact it gives more weight to subcultures than the behavioural view.

The radical theory of political culture has weaknesses of its own. Above all it presumes that subordinate classes are naturally left-wing but are seduced away from the path of revolutionary righteousness by the 'dominant ideology'. But there may be more truth in viewing the working class as naturally conservative (at least with a small c). Indeed Lipset (1983, first pub. 1960) argues that features of working-class life such as limited education and economic insecurity propel manual workers to an authoritarian view of politics. This is even without the 'lift' provided by the dominant culture.

☐ *Postmaterialism*

From the late 1940s to the early 1970s, the Western world witnessed a period of unprecedented economic growth. 'You've never had it so good' became a cliché which summarised the experience of a postwar generation. This was also a period of relative international peace. A generation grew up with no experience of world war.

According to Inglehart (1971), these factors led to 'a silent revolution' in the political cultures of Western democracies. A new generation of 'postmaterialists' emerged – young, well-educated people who took their material well-being for granted and were more concerned with postmaterial values. These included lifestyle issues such as ecology, nuclear disarmament and feminism. Postmaterialists are not satisfied with a loaf of bread; they also insist that it should be wholemeal and additive-free! Postmaterialists are also more attracted to organisations giving real opportunities for individual participation. They are élite-challenging advocates of the new politics rather than élite-sustaining foot-soldiers in the old party battles.

As a rule, the more affluent a democracy, the higher the proportion of postmaterialists within its borders. In Europe postmaterialism came first to, and made deepest inroads in, the wealthiest democracies such as Denmark, the Netherlands and West Germany. With the exception of Norway, the affluent Scandinavian countries have been receptive to postmaterialist ideas (Knutsen 1990). The United States was also in the first wave of postmaterialism. In the early 1970s, American studies found a concentration of post-materialists among yuppies – young, upwardly mobile urban professionals, especially those in the wealthiest state of all, California (Miller and Levitin 1976). Postmaterialism is less common in poorer democracies with lower levels of education: Greece, Ireland, Spain and Portugal (Inglehart 1990).

Even in the richest countries, postmaterialists remain a small minority of the total population. But they are an active, opinion-leading group – and therein lies their significance.

The recession of the 1970s and early 1980s slowed down the spread of postmaterialism. At least in the Nordic countries, the younger generations became more materialistic than the generations which preceded them. Indeed in the depths of the recession some writers dismissed postmaterialism as nothing more than a fragile flower of sunshine politics. Certainly it seems likely that the 1960s generation, socialised in an era of 'flower power' and Vietnam, will remain distinctly radical as it moves into positions of power.

But as the world economy recovered towards the end of the 1980s, so too did postmaterial values. As long as the world avoids another major economic downturn, it seems likely that postmaterial values will spread further. This is partly because education (and not, contrary to Inglehart's theory, income) is the best single predictor of postmaterialism. Educational standards are continuing to rise throughout the world. But another factor also encourages the diffusion of postmaterialism. It is least popular among the oldest and least educated generations. As these are replaced, so postmaterialism will become more widespread – provided, that is, the young do not lose all their postmaterial sheen as they move through the life-cycle!

■ The second world

Communist party states provided an excellent laboratory in which to examine the impact of the state on political culture. A key aim of all communist systems was to change fundamentally the way people thought and behaved. Especially in China and Albania, the ruling parties tried to impose cultural revolutions alongside the industrial and technological revolutions. The intention was to speed up the transition from old attitudes to a new socialist political culture. The aim was a new 'Communist Man and Woman', who would live in a classless, socialist, atheist society which lacked all the poisons inhaled under capitalism. The ruling parties intended to bring about this transformation through education: both in the formal education system and through control of cultural works. The emphasis was in the first instance on persuasion, rather than on force.

□ *The failure of transformation*

This transformation of political culture never came about. Communist rule created changes in political culture but these changes were not always in the direction that the party wanted. In consequence, communist leaders altered their aims as the party recognised that the new communist personality was not emerging. Take the Soviet Union and China as examples. In both countries, the new communist rulers were committed to increasing mass participation in politics. The old feudal systems had been characterised by passive acceptance of authority – what Weber called traditional authority (see p. 17). In order to bring about a revolution in political culture, the communist citizen was to become an active participant in political life. Mass campaigns were organised to ensure that every person was involved in politics.

In China these activities ranged from participation in land reform programmes to campaigns against the 'three evils': corruption, waste and bureaucratic red tape. However, mass participation in these campaigns did not of course show that communist men and women had been created. If you did not conform by taking part in active political acts, then you faced the risk of being branded an enemy of the people. So you participated anyway. In a study of Russian political culture, S. White (1979, p. 11) referred to the concept of 'two persons in one body'. The public person repeated the phraseology of the authorities when required and took part in ritual demonstrations of unity. But the 'hidden' person retained a set of older attitudes towards politics and society. In fact, fear created citizens who outwardly conformed, but inwardly adopted strategies designed to ensure their own survival. Thus, the realities of communist rule encouraged changes in political culture that ran counter to the party's professed aims.

Furthermore, once the ruling parties realised that the new communist personality was not appearing, they relied on traditional political culture. For example, if you cannot get the people to participate actively in politics, then the next best option may be for them to accept authority passively – as they did in the precommunist era.

The continuing importance of the family in China is an example of this point. Traditionally the family, and not the state, provided welfare care for the old and the young. If this is encouraged, it removes a potentially expensive burden from the state. However, the cost is that family socialisation maintains traditional, precommunist attitudes towards society. This runs against the party's aim of creating a new political culture.

Ruling communist parties were therefore inconsistent in their attempts to modify political culture. This was nowhere more evident than in the policy towards the many nationalities of the Soviet Union. Official acceptance of non-Russian languages and the persistence of local cultures helped to maintain nationalistic feelings. Yet at the same time, resentment towards Russian 'occupation' increased, because of the central government's attempts to maintain control over the republics. Heightened hostility to an imposed political order, combined with strong local political cultures, created an irresistible force for change once Gorbachev loosened the reins of government in the 1980s.

☐ Political culture and the collapse of communism

The dramatic collapse of communist rule in Eastern Europe in 1989 was evidence of the importance of political culture in explaining whether regimes survive. It confirmed David Hume's eighteenth-century saying that all power rests ultimately on opinion. The failure of East European regimes to establish a reservoir of legitimacy among their populations was the underlying cause of their downfall.

Almost everywhere, the precommunist cultural heritage proved highly resilient in the face of official attempts to reconstruct it. Indeed, such cultural traditions were sometimes strengthened by providing a focus of opposition to communist rule. In Poland, for example, the Catholic Church became the major source of opposition to the ruling party, and a strong counterweight to communist rule. Czechoslovakia's political culture was also out of tune with strong one-party rule. Between the two world wars Czechoslovakia was the most democratic country within Central and Eastern Europe. The memory of this period, particularly among the country's large middle class, limited the acceptability of authoritarian rule.

The failure of communism to set down firm roots in Eastern Europe is due in part to its imposition, in most countries, by the Soviet Red Army after the Second World War. For the most part, communism lacked any national political characteristics. In places where communist parties came to power through indigenous revolution, the process of winning the revolution entailed adapting communism to the concrete realities of those societies. Socialism in China was socialism with Chinese characteristics, in Cuba with Cuban characteristics, and so on. In Eastern Europe, when leaders tried to take national interests to heart, as in Hungary in 1956 and Czechoslovakia in 1968, the Soviets intervened to restore the old system. Thus the political culture of the élites was out of step with the political culture of the masses, and finally this tension proved to be untenable.

The revolutions of 1989 also show the importance of élite political culture. As Schöpflin (1990) points out, 'an authoritarian élite sustains itself in power not just through force and the threat of force but, more importantly, because it has some vision of the future by which it can justify itself to itself. No regime can survive long without some concept of purposiveness.' In the initial phase of industrialisation, communist rulers could feel their planned economies were producing results. Indeed economic development gave some Eastern European regimes (such as Hungary after widespread economic decentralisation in 1968) significant 'instrumental legitimacy' among the population.

But by the late 1980s economic progress had given way to decline. The planned economies had reached a dead end while party rule prevented political reform. As even nominal support from intellectuals faded, so party officials began to lose confidence in their own right to rule. In the end, communist rule was toppled so easily because it had already been weakened from within.

Despite the persistence of traditional political cultures, the nations of Eastern Europe cannot simply pick up from the 1940s as if communist rule had never happened. Just as the political culture of the precommunist years affected the nature of communist rule in Eastern Europe, so the nature of postcommunist rule will be shaped by what preceded it.

For example, workers in the Soviet Union and Eastern Europe used to joke that they pretended to work and the state pretended to pay them. A serious point lies beneath the humour. If the economies of postcommunist states are really going to recover, then a new entrepreneurial spirit needs to be built. But this new culture has yet to emerge. Indeed, throughout Eastern Europe there is concern about what the future will bring. Despite the poor performance of communist economies, the population had become used to a measure of economic security: cheap housing, cheap food, low unemployment, and so on. Rising inequalities and mass unemployment appear to be inescapable results of the move towards more efficient market economies. The cultural legacy of communism may yet prove to be a reluctance to leave behind the equality of poverty that had become such a feature of economic life under communism.

■ The third world: local political cultures

If the political cultures of the first world have a strong participant element, and those of the second world a strong subject element, can the third world be seen in terms of parochial political cultures? Parochial cultures are those where citizens are not concerned about national government; they see themselves as neither contributing to, nor being affected by, central decisions. Undoubtedly the state is weaker in the developing than the developed world. It penetrates less deeply into society and so provides only a weak focus of public attention. But is the parochial culture a cause of the weak state, as advocates of the cultural approach claim?

The answer is yes, to an extent. Certainly the post-independence generation of third world leaders sought to nationalise the political culture in the belief that this would strengthen the authority of the state. Primary education stressed allegiance to the nation rather than the ethnic group. The mass media reported national as well as local events and often recalled memories of the heroic struggle for independence.

But just as communist party states failed to create the new man and woman, so too have attempts to transform third world political cultures met with very little success. In consequence, efforts at nation-building in the developing world have become little more than ritual in recent decades. Primary school children may be given the national flag to wave when the Education Minister comes to visit, but true nation-building can not be achieved so easily.

Besides the inherent difficulty of reshaping a culture, third world governments face the problem of the continuing authority of traditional leaders. Because the institutions of the state are underdeveloped, central governments are often forced to administer localities *through* traditional leaders, which in practice contradicts their own efforts at nation-building. For example, the Education Minister may supposedly be visiting an area to open a new modern school. But the real purpose is to cement an alliance with traditional local leaders. Nation-building without state-building is inevitably a hollow exercise.

A parochial culture implies that many people are only dimly aware of the national government. However this does not mean that citizens of third world countries are politically naive. In fact they are often well aware of the intricacies of local and ethnic politics through which resources are, in reality, distributed. For example the Hausa–Fulani emirates in Northern Nigeria, based on the unquestioned authority of the emir (the traditional religious ruler known as 'the shadow of God'), are resilient political systems which have survived successive changes of regime at national level. The emirate is at least as important a focus of attention as the national government. To describe these non-national cultures as subcultures is to understate their significance. Many third world countries are best considered as plural or poly-cultural societies rather than as countries with a weak national culture and distinct subcultures. In India, for example, where state institutions are fairly well established, the great variety of religions and the complexities of the caste system are fundamental to an understanding of the country's politics. From this perspective, then, it is better to describe political cultures in the third world as local than as parochial.

□ *Tradition and modernity*

Many authors have argued that tradition is a major quality of third world cultures. Traditional relationships are modelled on the idea of kinship. They are based on the personal qualities of the participants and embrace a wide range of activities. In politics this means that politicians and civil servants have obligations to kin, friends and supporters which conflict with a 'modern' interpretation of their role. The modern idea of a bureaucrat applying rules in an impersonal way, or of politicians seeking fairly to balance the claims of competing interests, is alien to this traditional perspective. Hence Western observers often describe as 'corrupt' activities which in the less-developed countries themselves are viewed as straightforward fulfilments of social obligations – as a matter, sometimes literally, of jobs for the boys (but less often for the girls).

This distinction between tradition and modernity is useful in understanding the politics of the third world. Often conflict between the modern and the traditional makes the tension between the capital city and the countryside more intense. But the traditional and the modern can coexist and even combine. Indeed, traditional Confucian political culture has probably contributed to economic development, not only in Japan, but also in Taiwan, Singapore and South Korea. Japan is economically successful partly because it is not a 'modern' (that is, individualistic Western) society.

In the third world, traditional loyalties, such as those to an ethnic group, can provide an effective mode of political mobilisation as well as giving people a support network as they move from the traditional countryside into the modern cities. So today most political scientists would argue that at least some elements of traditional culture provide a resource for, rather than a barrier to, economic development.

■ Political socialisation

Political socialisation is the study of what, when and how people learn about politics. Learning a political culture is very different from acquiring a formal academic skill, such as a knowledge of history, which consists largely in transmitting information from teacher to student in an educational setting. Political socialisation is a much more diffuse and indirect process. It involves the development of political emotions and identities (what is my nation? my religion? my party?) as well as the acquisition of information. Political socialisation takes place through a variety of institutions – the family, the peer group, the workplace – as well as formal education. It is as much influenced by the context of communication as its content. For example, a child's attitude towards politics will be influenced at least as much by his or her experience of authority at home and at school as by what parents and teachers say the child's attitude to politics should be.

Finally, political socialisation is a lifelong process in which basic political outlooks mature in response to events and experience; there is no point at which the skill is finally acquired and the learning finally stops. It is a process without any apparent final product.

☐ *Liberal and radical theories*

Liberal and radical theorists of political culture differ in their treatment of political socialisation (see Table 6.1). There are two key contrasts here. One concerns timing. The liberal view is that basic political loyalties are formed when young. The radical view is that adult experiences are just as important. The second contrast is over how adult socialisation takes place. The liberal view is that adult socialisation, like the child's, is the unplanned result of a variety of personal experiences. These include life-cycle events such as marriage and parenthood. The radical view, on the other hand, is that socialisation is a much more systematic process. As Miliband (1969, p. 163) puts it, socialisation 'is, in large part, the result of a permanent and pervasive *effort*, conducted through a multitude of agencies, and deliberately intended to create a "national supra-party consensus"'. We will examine both views, beginning with the liberal interpretation.

The liberal view is that core political identities are acquired in **early childhood**, when the family is the crucial influence on the child. In **late childhood**, these attachments are supplemented by a marked increase in information. The main effect of **adolescence** is to refine the child's conceptual understanding, building on information already acquired. These three stages of socialisation – early childhood, late childhood and adolescence – prepare the child for adult political life.

In adulthood, childhood learning is applied to participation in politics, though eventually participation tails off in old age (Figure 6.2).

Table 6.1   *Liberal and radical perspectives on political socialisation*

	From/to	Main agency	Timing	Style
Liberal	One generation to the next	Family	Childhood	Unplanned
Radical	Dominant class to subordinate classes	Media	Adulthood as well as childhood	Deliberate

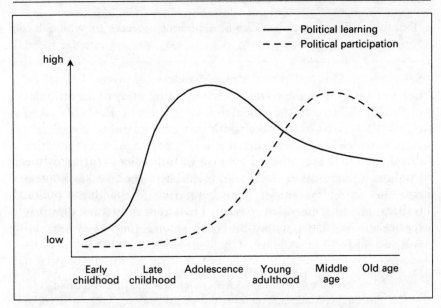

Figure 6.2 *Political learning and participation across the life-cycle: the liberal view*

Adult experiences will deepen and modify, but not usually transform, the outlook acquired when young. So the liberal view is based on the 'primacy' model of socialisation – the idea that early political learning is critical because it provides a framework within which information acquired in adulthood is interpreted (see Exhibit 6.1).

The radical interpretation of socialisation does not discount the importance of childhood. Education, in particular, can help to build loyalty to the *status quo*. Miliband (1969, p. 214) again: 'educational institutions at all levels generally fulfil an important conservative role and act, with greater or lesser effectiveness, as legitimating agencies in and for their societies.' But the radical approach also places emphasis on the 'recency' model. This is the idea that current information carries more weight just because it is contemporary. Adult reality carries at least as much socialising power as childhood myths. You may be taught as a child that Venice is a beautiful city but it is only by visiting it yourself, and smelling the stench of the canals in the summer, that you form a real opinion.

Thus the radical view stresses the importance of adult experiences. Some of these events, such as foreign travel, will be personal. But the most politically significant adult experiences will be collective events such as depression and war. Inevitably, these broad developments will be experienced, at least in part, through the media. Because the radical

Exhibit 6.1   *The benevolent monarch: how British children see the Queen*

Since 'the child is father to the man', students of political socialisation must start with the young. In a fascinating study of the attitudes of British children to the monarchy, Greenstein *et al.* (1974) asked eighty 10–13-year-olds in the south-east of England to complete a story in which the Queen, hurrying in her car to a meeting for which she is already late, is stopped by a traffic policeman. As told by the children, 53 per cent of the stories involved the policeman showing deference to the Queen; less than a quarter ended with the Queen being punished. One girl even refused to accept the assumption that the monarch could possibly be late for a meeting! Here are two typical replies:

> 'What are you doing driving so fast, my luv? I've got a good mind to fine you.' And then the Queen shows her credentials and the policeman says, 'Oh pardon me, Madam. You'd better be getting along. Otherwise you'll be late for the meeting.'

> [After stopping the car and talking with the chauffeur, the police looked in the back] and they saw the Queen, and they all went red. And they said, 'We're sorry, Your Majesty. We didn't mean to disturb you, but please don't go so fast because it might be dangerous and might cause an accident.' And the Queen said, 'I'll tell my chauffeur not to go so fast.' And the policeman said, 'We thank you,' then bowed and went away.

After noting that many children view the Prime Minister as merely a helper of the Queen, the authors conclude: 'surely no other democracy begins its political socialisation process by introducing its children to such explicitly non-democratic mythology.'

account gives more priority to adult experiences, it regards the mass media as an important socialising agent, and the family as less significant, than the liberal approach.

Further, Marxists regard the mass media as conservative in tone. This is because some media are privately owned (e.g. the national press in most countries) and others are run or at least licensed by the state (e.g. many television networks). In both cases, the argument runs, news is produced by middle-class professionals who are unsympathetic to viewpoints which fall outside a narrow range of acceptable opinion. Thus we reach a position where the radical account views socialisation as a process of class indoctrination executed through the media. In contrast, the liberal account sees socialisation as a means for transmitting values across the generations through the family.

The two processes are not incompatible. To an extent both may operate. However, we are broadly in sympathy with the liberal view of socialisation. The family is a cradle of opinion which develops core identities during a person's most formative period. Because the family and other social networks such as peer-groups are so important, no rulers anywhere are in a position to produce a political culture to order. The failure of communist regimes to reshape the political cultures of the countries they ruled, despite the ruling party's monopoly of the media, illustrated this point.

▪ Élite political culture

Élite political culture consists of the beliefs, attitudes and ideas about politics held by those who are closest to the centres of political power. In countries with a parochial or subject political culture, élite political culture is of primary importance. But even where mass attitudes to politics are well developed, as in modern liberal democracies, it is still the views of the élite which exert the most direct and profound effect on political decisions.

The values of élites are influenced by, but distinct from, the national political culture. For example even in liberal democracies, where party competition gives politicians an incentive to respond to popular concerns, studies have shown how the values of élites differ from those of the general public. Élites generally take a more liberal line on social and moral issues. Stouffer's (1966) famous survey of attitudes in the United States to freedom of speech demonstrated this. Conducted during 1954, this study showed that most community leaders maintained their belief in the right of free speech for atheists, socialists and communists at a time when the attitudes of the general public were much less tolerant. More recent surveys have shown a striking increase in the American public's support for free speech for such groups (Sullivan *et al.* 1982). None the less, it was crucial to the cause of free speech in the United States that élites remained committed at a time when the principle was under strong attack.

Élite attitudes in Britain are equally distinctive. The reason why Britain has not reintroduced capital punishment and has continued to allow a trickle of non-white immigration into the country, despite the opposition of a majority of the electorate to both these policies, is that members of the élite are more likely to approve of these policies. Implicit agreement between party leaderships on these issues has proved strong enough to survive the pressures of electoral competition.

The liberal outlook of élites owes much to their formal education. In many liberal democracies, politics has become a largely graduate profession, a trend which the second and third worlds are now following. The experience of higher education helps to build an optimistic view of human nature, strengthens humanitarian values and encourages a belief in the ability of politicians to solve social problems (Astin 1977). A degree in a social science subject (such as politics) seems to be a particularly liberating experience!

While no one can object to educated politicians, this trend does have one unfortunate result. It sharpens the division between a well-educated liberal élite and a less tolerant, more parochial underclass. In its turn, this cleavage prepares the ground for the periodic emergence of authoritarian working-class protest movements such as the Wallace movement in the United States in the 1960s, Le Pen's National Front in France in the 1980s and various right-wing movements in Europe in the early 1990s. A central aim of these movements is to recapture politics for ordinary people – to remove from office what George Wallace called the 'pointy-headed namby-pambies' who, he claimed, formed Washington's political establishment. The message is, perhaps, that élite political culture should not depart too far from the contours of the national culture.

Élites differ from the public in *how* they think about politics as well as in *what* they think. Members of political élites generally have belief systems which are more intensely held, more coherent, more stable over time and supported by more information than is the case for the mass public. In a sense, it is only the members of élites who have *systems* of political beliefs at all (Converse and Markus 1979).

The most important dimension of élite political culture is the attitudes which politicians hold towards each other. There are a range of possibilities here. Is élite competition absolute, as in countries such as Northern Ireland which are engaged in, or on the edge of, civil war? Or is strong conflict held in check by agreement on the rules of the game, as in Britain and New Zealand? Or is élite conflict subsumed beneath a shared opposition to non-élites or emerging counter-élites, as with the attitudes of some traditional ruling classes to the emergence of the working class during industrialisation?

The political consequences of these attitudes are highly significant. For example, one interpretation of America's Watergate scandal, during which President's Nixon's supporters engaged in such illegal acts as break-ins and phone-taps against their Democratic opponents, was that the President and his aides saw the political world in the frighteningly simple terms of 'us' against 'them'. Nixon was willing to dispense with the normal rules of the political game in order to ensure that his enemies got what they deserved.

By contrast, the prospects for political stability are improved when party or group leaders are willing to compromise to allow the expression of other interests or values. Lijphart (1977) argues that an accommodating attitude among group representatives in divided societies such as Austria and Holland provided a recipe for stable government in the 1950s and 1960s. At this time, religion still strongly divided these societies. However, politicians of all the major parties accepted the right of each religious grouping to a fair share of state resources. These groups – Catholic, Protestant and secular – were then free to distribute these resources more or less as their leaders wanted. This attitude of 'live and let live' successfully contained potentially explosive divisions, and showed the importance of élite values in shaping the operation of the political system.

Summary

1.   Political culture refers to the overall pattern formed by a population's political beliefs, attitudes and values. Political culture matters because, as the collapse of communism shows, the long-term prospects for a regime depend largely on its legitimacy.

2.   According to Almond and Verba, liberal democracy is likely to prove most stable when participant attitudes among most of the population are balanced by a more apolitical approach among a minority. However critics suggest that the 'civic culture' (as this mix of atttitudes is called) *results from* experience with a democratic system, rather than being a *cause of* democratic stability.

3.   In the second world, communist rulers initially tried to transform political culture so as to create the new communist man and woman. However, this experiment soon failed. Traditional cultures, based on family, nationalism and religion, proved highly resilient. Communist propaganda soon became little more than a ritual affirmation of the party's hold on power.

4.   In the third world, local or regional politics are often a more important focus of attention than the national government. This means that the national political culture is less important.

5.   Political culture is passed on through political socialisation – the process by which people acquire their understanding of politics and their place within it.

6.   The 'liberal' view of socialisation sees it as a natural process through which culture is passed on across the generations, mainly through the family. By contrast 'radicals' view socialisation as a deliberate and ongoing process of class indoctrination carried out through the media.

7.   Élite political culture has the most direct impact on public decisions. In liberal democracies, well-educated élites are often more liberal on social and moral issues than are the general public.

8.   The attitudes of sub-élites to each other bear strongly on the nature of politics in a particular country. Do the leaders of one party respect, tolerate or hate their opponents? How much respect do civilian and military leaders have for each other?

Discussion points

1.   'Any fool can govern through martial law' (Cavour). 'You can make a throne from bayonets, but you can't sit on it for long'(Boris Yeltsin, President of Russia, on the failed coup of 1991). Who's right?

2.   What does the collapse of communism in Eastern Europe indicate about the importance of political culture?

3.   'Socialisation equals indoctrination.' Does it?

4.   Will postmaterialism eventually reshape the nature of politics in the Western world?

5.   Does your country have a 'civic culture'?

6.   Describe the impact of the media on your own political socialisation.

Key reading

Almond, G. and Verba, S. (1963) *The Civic Culture* (Princeton, N.J.: Princeton University Press). A classic study which has dominated later thinking about political culture.
Almond, G. and Verba, S. (eds) (1980) *The Civic Culture Revisited* (Princeton, N.J.: Princeton University Press). Contains several commentaries on the original study together with updates on the countries covered.
Gibbins, J. (ed.) (1989) *Contemporary Political Culture: Politics in a Postmodern Age* (London: Sage). A collection of essays covering neoconserva-

tism, new politics, postmodernism and postmaterialism as well as political culture generally.

Inglehart, R. (1990) *Culture Shift in Advanced Industrial Society* (Princeton, N.J.: Princeton University Press). A series of essays about value changes in Western democracies by the inventor of the concept of postmaterialism.

Miliband, R. (1969) *The State in Capitalist Society* (London: Weidenfeld & Nicolson). A clear but powerful statement of the radical position.

Further reading

Almond and Verba's *The Civic Culture* (1963) must remain the starting-point but it needs to be supplemented by the follow-up, *The Civic Culture Revisited* (1980), edited by Almond and Verba. Barry's (1978) discussion is another good short analysis. Gibbins (1989) is a recent collection of essays on similar themes.

For the Marxist approach to political culture, Miliband (1969) can be supplemented by F. Parkin (1971) and Abercrombie, Hill and Turner (1980). Putnam (1976) provides an excellent American discussion of élite political culture.

A standard text on political socialisation is Dawson, Prewitt and Dawson (1977). On communist states, see Brown (1984), Brown and Gray (1979) and, on the Soviet Union specifically, S. White (1979) and Tucker (1987). On the third world, see Pye and Verba (1965) and Peil (1976).

■ *Chapter 7* ■

Political Participation

While political culture is the study of people's attitudes towards government, political participation is the study of actual involvement in it. Political participation is activity by individuals formally intended to influence who governs or how they do so. This chapter examines the overall patterns of citizen involvement in politics. The next chapter looks specifically at participation through the ballot box. Participation by groups rather than individuals is reserved until Chapter 9.

In all three worlds, governments now call on the public to play at least some part in the political process. Only a few regimes deny the masses any formal political role at all. These are traditional regimes, where politics remains the exclusive preserve of a tiny élite, and those military governments which do not even bother with a democratic facade.

■ Types of participation

We can distinguish between voluntary participation, regimented participation and participation as personal manipulation. In liberal democracies, **voluntary** participation is the norm. People can choose whether to get involved (e.g. by voting or abstaining) and how to get involved (e.g. by joining a party or signing petitions). The main exception to the voluntary nature of participation is compulsory voting, found in a few countries such as Australia, Belgium and until 1970 the Netherlands.

In communist states **regimented participation** was the norm. This involved the expression of support for, rather than the selection of, government personnel and policy. Its main function was to mobilise the people behind the regime in an effort to strengthen the authority of the government. Regimented participation is still characteristic of unreformed communist states such as China. However postcommunist states are seeking to move from regimented to voluntary participation.

In the third world the **patron–client relationship** is a typical form of participation. Here low-status individuals offer political support to their patrons (employers, chiefs or religious leaders) in exchange for a measure of protection. These favours might be a job or a guarantee that food will be supplied if the crops fail. The patron–client relationship is essentially a personal exchange: for example, 'You vote for me and I'll help you get a job with the government'. However the relationship is between people with vastly different resources; hence it is a form of manipulation.

■ The first world

The most striking fact about political participation in liberal democracies is how little of it there is. Voting in national elections is the only form of participation in which a majority of most populations engages (Verba, Nie and Kim 1978, pp. 58–9). In some countries, especially in Scandinavia, most people also turn out for local elections. However, throughout the democratic world anything beyond voting is the preserve of a minority of activists. Indeed the activists are outnumbered by the totally inactive – people who neither vote nor even follow politics through television.

□ *How much, by whom, so what?*

We can divide the population into three main participation groups:

1. The small number of **activists** who are mostly foot-soldiers in the party battle which rages around and above them.
2. The **voters** who are the overwhelming majority.
3. The **inactives** who ignore politics altogether.

Figure 7.1 shows how these three groups form a 'diamond' of participation, with most people in the middle category.

Few though they are, political activists tend to specialise in particular forms of participation. For example a British survey taken in 1984–85 showed that among those people who did more than vote, four subgroups could be distinguished: (1) protesters, (2) election campaigners, (3) people active in community groups and (4) people who specialised in individual contacts with officials, politicians or the media (Parry and Moyser 1991). Most legislators are familiar with constituents in this last category. It covers those who feel compelled to send in a long

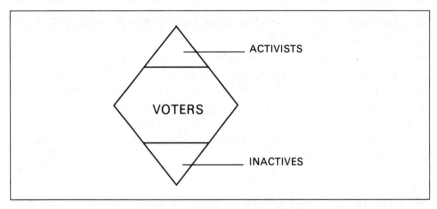

Figure 7.1   *The diamond of political participation*

letter each week about their pet topic! But it should not be forgotten that the overwhelming majority of citizens in liberal democracies – about three in four in Britain – only participate, if at all, in the electoral aspect of politics.

Political activists are far from a cross-section of society. In most liberal democracies, participation is greatest among well-educated, middle-class, middle-aged men. Furthermore the highest layers of political involvement show the greatest skew. For example, many women enter the polling booth but far fewer occupy the highest offices of state. Women leaders such as Gro Harlem Brundtland (twice Prime Minister of Norway in the 1980s), Indira Gandhi (Prime Minister of India, 1966–77) and Margaret Thatcher (Prime Minister of Britain, 1979–90) still attract extra attention because of their gender (the same cannot be said of Vigdis Finnbogadóttir, President of Iceland since 1979, even though she was the first woman in the world to be a democratically elected head of state). Similarly a degree is not a requirement for voting but in many countries it is now virtually a precondition of becoming a government minister. The message is clear: patterns of political participation reflect existing inequalities in society; those who participate most are those who already have the most.

What explains this bias in participation towards upper levels of society? Differences in participation can be explained by differences in political resources and political interest. Politically relevant resources include: education and the access it gives to information; money and the ability it gives to afford time for political activity; prestige and the advantage it provides to obtain a respectful hearing; and such interpersonal skills as the ability to speak in public and to present one's views in persuasive fashion. The advantaged have more of these resources and they also show more interest in politics. In addition, the advantaged are more likely to be brought up in a family and attend a school where an interest in current affairs is encouraged.

We can apply this framework to the question of the under-representation of women at the higher levels of politics (see Exhibit 7.1). What explains this almost universal pattern? Women generally have less formal education than men. They have child-bearing and, often, home-making responsibilities, which cut into their political time. And they sometimes lack the confidence needed to throw themselves into the hurly-burly of politics. Thus women, as a group, have fewer political resources than men.

In addition, of course, women still face the high hurdle of discrimination from sexist male politicians. These men claim that women are 'unsuited' to politics – and then use the scarcity of women in high office to prove their point!

One effect of the 'up-market' bias in participation is that those at the bottom of the pyramid of participation often feel alienated from those at the top. For example, many women feel, with justification, that politics is a male preserve. In itself this belief discourages participation by women, thus forming a vicious circle. A similar cycle applies to other under-participating groups, such as ethnic minorities. The sense of distance from the political system among non-participants is a weakness of liberal democracies.

A second consequence of the unrepresentative character of political activists is some built-in bias against radical values. Like other groups, middle-aged, middle-class men will, as a rule, seek to defend their own interests. They will not usually make waves against a system which has served them well. The political agenda naturally reflects the concerns of these middle-class activists. By definition, the inactives will only be heard if someone else speaks for them. This problem has been reduced in Europe (though not the United States) by trade unions and socialist parties. These organisations have provided an alternative channel of entry into politics for many working-class people who would otherwise have been inactive. But liberal democracies, like other forms of government, will always be biased towards the interests of the activists.

□ *New politics*

Not all middle-class participants are on the right of the political spectrum. The middle-class never was politically uniform and, with the spread of postmaterial values, has become less so. In fact, young, radical, well-educated postmaterialists were the key force behind the

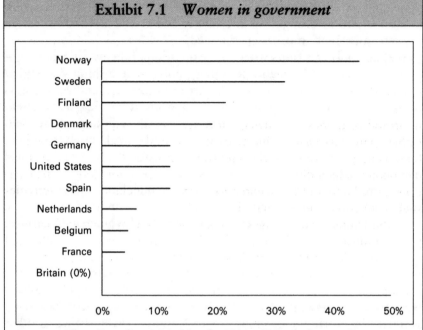

Exhibit 7.1   *Women in government*

Sources: The *Guardian*, 26 March 1991; United States Government Manual, 1990.

Figure 7.2   *Percentage of women cabinet ministers following most recent general elections*

Out of all the countries in Europe and North America, the Scandinavian countries have the highest proportion of women cabinet ministers. Norway leads, with women occupying almost half the top posts. This reflects a long tradition of female participation in Norwegian politics. Norway was the first independent country to give the vote to women, in 1913 (Australia, Finland and New Zealand came earlier but they were then dependencies). Campaigns to increase female representation have received financial support from the state. In addition, the leading parties introduced a system of quotas in 1973. The aim of the quotas is to ensure that each gender provides at least 40 per cent of elected representatives, not just candidates.

Source: B. Nicholson, 'Increasing Women's Parliamentary Representation: The Norwegian Experience' (Newcastle upon Tyne: Centre for Scandinavian Studies 1989).

'new politics' which emerged in the 1960s and has remained important since.

New politics is a style of participation which goes beyond, and sometimes even excludes, traditional participation through political parties and election campaigns. Advocates of new politics are willing to consider new (or, rather, very old) forms of participation: demonstrations, sit-ins and sit-downs, boycotts and political strikes. These unorthodox modes of participation are usually in pursuit of broad, rather than class-based, objectives: for example, nuclear disarmament, feminism, protection of the environment (see Table 7.1). In some democracies, including West Germany and Italy, unorthodox participation in the 1960s and 1970s extended further, to include violent activities such as terrorism and kidnapping.

In the United States, where unconventional activity started earliest, young radical students showed marked distaste for the middle-aged politicians who had brought them Vietnam, Cambodia and Watergate. In a few cases, such as the American civil rights movement and the French 'events' of 1968, left-wing students established a fragile alliance with less privileged but equally alienated groups – blacks in the United States, sections of the working-class in France. Such alliances, when achieved, had considerable political potential. But such partnerships were rare. The new and the old were not natural partners.

Although new and old politics are very different in style, some leaders of the new politics are making the switch to orthodox politics as they age (mature?). The protest activists of the 1960s may well become the political leaders of the 2000s. Certainly, except for their youth, the unconventional activists of the 1960s were exactly the same *type* of people who had long dominated the arena of orthodox participation: well-educated, articulate people from middle-class backgrounds. As the protesters of the 1960s move into positions of authority, not just in

Table 7.1   *Old and new politics*

	Old politics	*New politics*
Attitude to political system	Supportive	Critical
Vehicle of participation	Parties	Single-issue groups
Style of participation	Orthodox	Unconventional
Concerns	Interests	Values
Motives	Instrumental	Expressive
Typical age	Middle-aged	Younger

politics but in all the professions, so their impact on public policy will increase.

Is new politics, like postmaterialism, still a minority sport? Surveys conducted in eight Western democracies in 1974 suggested the answer was yes (the countries were Austria, Britain, West Germany, Finland, Italy, the Netherlands, Switzerland and the United States. See Marsh 1990). In each country, less than half the population said they approved of more extreme forms of protest, such as occupations, rent strikes and blockades. In this survey the most radical countries were Italy and the Netherlands; the Austrians were most cautious. Across all countries, the young were most likely to be 'protesters'.

Figure 7.3 shows the results of this study for the United States (an active but conventional population) and Finland (more inactives *and* more protesters).

■ The second world

The dramatic transition from communist to postcommunist states transformed the nature of political participation in the second world. Essentially the change was from regimented to voluntary participation. Furthermore, political involvement by the masses played an important part in the downfall of the old regimes. To understand why, we must begin by reviewing the traditional communist style of regimented participation.

□ *Regimented participation*

The quantity of mass participation in politics was always greater in communist states than in liberal democracies. This was not just because of the broader definition of the 'political' in socialist states. Citizens were drafted in to sit on comradely courts, to administer elections, to join para-police organisations, to serve on people's committees covering a range of local matters – and, in China, to kill off grain-eating sparrows (see Exhibit 7.2).

This apparatus of participation derived from the Marxist idea that all power at every level of government should be vested in soviets (councils) of workers and peasants. Whatever the real significance of this apparatus, citizens in communist party states had a wider menu of participation opportunities than their counterparts in liberal democracies.

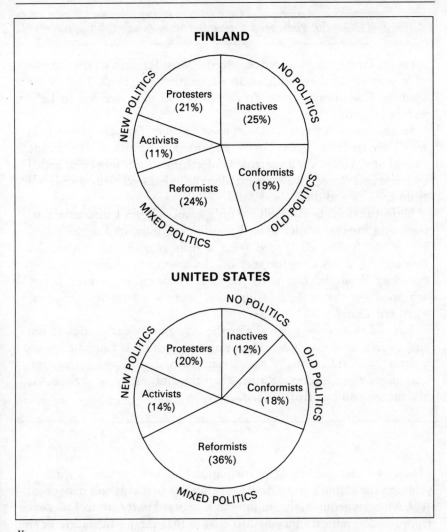

Figure 7.3   *Attitudes to participation in Finland and the United States*

Key:
Inactives   will do little more than follow politics through the media.
Conformists will discuss politics and perhaps attend meetings. But they want nothing to do with new politics.
Reformists will engage in conventional activity plus legal protests such as boycotts.
Activists   will engage in both conventional and unconventional activity, including illegal acts such as blocking traffic.
Protesters favour only unconventional participation, whether legal or illegal.

Note: this classification is based on attitudes towards participation, not actual behaviour.

Source: A. Marsh, *Political Action in Europe and the USA* (Basingstoke: Macmillan, 1990), pp. 30–2.

Exhibit 7.2　*Regimented participation: China's sparrows*

As every farmer knows, birds eat seeds. Most farmers accept the loss of a portion of their crop as an occupational hazard. Not so the Chinese Communist Party. In the early 1950s, it decided to fight nature head-on.

In an extraordinary exercise in mass participation, the population of China took up drums, pots and pans to create a nationwide cacophony. Whenever a sparrow landed for a rest, it was bombarded by noise and scared away. Eventually, the exhausted birds simply fell from the sky and died.

Unfortunately, birds don't eat only grain. They are also partial to bugs and insects. With the bird population decimated in the cities, insect life flourished. Faced with a near plague, the authorities despatched teams to wage war on the insects by digging up their breeding grounds. But with the grass now gone, winter winds whipped up the soil, creating dust storms across the cities of northern China.

But did this really matter? For the communist authorities at the time, the aim of involving the population in a mass campaign – no matter how ridiculous – had been realised. For the party, the campaign was a success. Rather than the end justifying the means, the means had justified the end.

However, the quality of participation did not match its quantity. Although the ruling party's desire for popular participation may originally have been genuine, the impulse to safeguard party control was even stronger. Communist élites had to ensure that the participation of the population always strengthened, and never weakened, the party's hold on power. Although the masses in a communist party state were seen as the source of all wisdom, Lenin argued that in the post-revolutionary society, not everybody would be politically advanced enough to make decisions on crucial points. The party was to be the vanguard of the working class – an élite group of professional revolutionaries who understood the masses' desires better than the masses themselves.

Therefore, in order to ensure that mass participation did not harm the long-term interests of the masses themselves, all participation had to be guided, directed and led by party members. The result was that communist parties channelled political participation to an extent unknown in the West.

Eventually, this overtight control of participation harmed economic development. A complex industrial society calls for technical and administrative skills, proficiently applied. But experts need discretion to perform well. So, well before the collapse of communism in 1989, a participation crisis had developed in communist states. The system required, but could not allow, genuine participation in decision-making by functionally important personnel. It also needed something more than sullen acquiescence by ordinary people.

When ruling communist parties did attempt to allow more freedom, all the submerged opposition shot to the surface. Until 1989, the result was usually another round of repression, often more intense than before. The Hundred Flowers movement in China provides a classic example. In 1956 the Chinese people were told to voice their criticisms of the first six and a half years of party rule. The criticisms were so fierce that not only was the campaign halted, but it was followed by a campaign to 'rectify' the erroneous thoughts of those who had overstepped the mark.

Eventually some ruling parties did allow more participation, but only in areas that did not threaten their monopoly of power. In particular, emphasis was placed on introducing reforms that would give a kick start to ailing economies. Managers were given more say in policy-making, and political participation became more authentic on local, specific and technical matters.

But, crucially, these reforms were not matched in the political sphere. Because no real channels existed for airing grievances, people were left with only one choice – either shut up and get on with life, or express their protests outside the system. In either case, the party had lost touch with the society it governed. Communist governments lacked feedback mechanisms which would have attuned them to dangerous, indeed total, changes taking place in their environment.

As long as repression and coercion continued, opposition could be contained. Once the lid was taken off, hidden grievances steamed out. Thus, ruling communist parties were damned if they didn't reform, but overwhelmed if they did. They had sown the seeds of their own destruction. The extent of the chasm between party and citizens became abundantly clear with the collapse of communist control in Eastern Europe and the Soviet Union.

☐ *The transition to postcommunism*

The old style of regimented participation was dismantled in the transition from communism to postcommunism. The changes introduced in the late 1980s were far more fundamental than any of the earlier tinkering. Much of the demolition work was led by Mikhail Gorbachev in the Soviet Union, the country which had previously been most insistent on restricting its population to a subject role. In the mid-1980s, Gorbachev's policy of *glasnost* (openness) allowed fuller discussion of public issues. For the first time, problems such as widespread alcoholism, prostitution and drug abuse were publically acknowledged. In Eastern Europe, the environmental damage caused by rampant industrialisation came to the fore with the liberalisation of the press. This sparked off a social revolution that preceded the political revolutions. Making information available was a fundamental condition of meaningful mass participation in politics.

In the late 1980s, *glasnost* was followed by a remarkable flowering of informal groups in the Soviet Union. The long winter of suppression of non-party groups gave way to a springtime of social development. By 1988 about 10 per cent of young people were active in informal associations. Political groups, including liberal, environmental and nationalist organisations, accounted for perhaps one in ten of these members (Lampert 1990, p. 131). In the first world, such voluntary participation would be taken for granted. In the communist world, and in the Soviet Union in particular, it was a major stage in the retreat of the party. Many people were gaining a new sense of political efficacy. Previously they had just put up with things; now they were prepared to fight for their rights.

In most of Eastern Europe, participation had never been as tightly controlled as in the Soviet Union. Consequently reform gave way to revolution at an earlier stage. Furthermore, many of the European leaders had achieved acceptability because they were a better bet than a hardliner installed by Moscow. Even so, once Gorbachev made it clear that he was not prepared to intervene to defend out-of-touch East European leaders, the regimes soon began to collapse. Mass protests confirmed the party's loss of control and triggered its final disintegration.

Street demonstrations may be almost routine in Paris and Rome but the same events carried infinitely more weight in Prague and Bucharest. In the context of a system of regimented participation, street marches were revolutionary, not just radical. For example, in October 1989, thousands of people moved through the streets of the East German cities of Leipzig and Dresden, fully aware of the lorryloads of police with live ammunition waiting in the side streets. But the troops were not used. The crowd had won.

In Romania, the crowd paid the heaviest of prices for defying a dictator. On 21 December 1989, the 71-year-old Romanian despot,

Nicolai Ceaucescu, decided to make a speech from the balcony of party headquarters in Bucharest. The audience consisted of workers bussed in from nearby factories. The authorities confidently expected that Ceaucescu's speech would be greeted by the usual cheers and prolonged applause. But, for once, things did not go according to plan. In an act of immense courage the audience booed and hissed. Faced with a vocal crowd, a confused and uncertain Ceaucescu retreated back into the building. He then ordered his security police onto the streets at dead of night to murder those who had dared oppose him.

Ceaucescu's confusion was probably genuine. His party apparatus and secret police had proved so successful in suppressing dissent that Ceaucescu was probably unaware of the true state of popular opinion. He believed his own propaganda. He could not understand why the crowd was so hostile. The emperor's nakedness had been exposed, and Eastern Europe's only violent revolution had begun. Ceaucescu and his wife were shot dead within the week.

Twenty months later, enough people found the courage to take to the streets of Moscow to discourage an assault upon the Russian parliament, symbol of resistance to the attempted coup which had sought to reimpose the supremacy of the party, the military and the KGB. In a country with a subject political culture, this display of public activism was a revolutionary episode. It sealed the fate not just of a coup but also of the Soviet communist party, an organisation which a few years earlier had been the most powerful party on earth.

Once postcommunist regimes had been created, the task was to create more structured forms of voluntary participation through parties, elections and interest groups. This was not easy. The populations of many East European states had experienced regimented participation under communist rule and seen mass participation on television during its collapse. However, they had little experience of 'ordinary' voluntary participation as understood in the first world. In the Balkan states such as Bulgaria and Romania, and in the Soviet Union, communist rule had simply continued a political tradition which had always denied the masses an effective political voice. Managing the transition from regimented to voluntary participation is a major challenge for postcommunist regimes.

■ The third world

Mass political participation in the third world is typically limited in quantity and manipulative in quality. This is not surprising. Populations are poorly educated and often illiterate. Many people are hungry or sick. The state has achieved only limited penetration of the countryside. Political leaders are preoccupied with their own survival. In these circumstances even the growing number of democratic countries in the third world can hardly be expected to achieve the participation levels of liberal democracies.

☐ *Patrons and clients*

In the third world, the **patron–client relationship** is the main instrument through which ordinary people are brought into contact with formal politics. This is a relationship of obligation and service between a high-status 'patron' and some 'clients' of lower status. Lacking resources of their own, clients provide allegiance to patrons in return for a degree of protection and security. Patrons are landlords, ethnic leaders, employers or just political entrepreneurs. They control the votes of their clients and persuade them to attend meetings, join organisations or simply follow their patron around in a deferential manner. (This explains why political motorcades are so long!)

For example, in Sri Lanka, patron–client networks, based initially on the patron's wealth and now on his access to the resources of the state, largely determine how ordinary people vote. In Sri Lanka, as in many other countries in the third world, these networks operate within a particular ethnic group (Jayanntha 1991). So the patron–client relationship is a distinctive form of participation, involving an unequal personal exchange.

One reason for the strength of patron–client networks in the third world is that formal channels of participation, such as political parties and trade unions, are weak. But poverty and inequality are more important causes. Poverty means the poor are vulnerable and need protection. Inequality means the rich have the resources to provide it, in exchange for political allegiance.

☐ *Participation and development*

The timing of independence also influences participation patterns in the third world. Countries that only escaped from political colonialism after the Second World War initially encouraged participation. They included much of sub-Saharan Africa. The struggle for independence created mass movements based on an ethos of participation, even though this was not always put into practice. The nationalist party provided a vehicle through which people could participate in politics. But this mobilising culture, and associated party structures, soon decayed after independence. In many states, participation withered. For example, only one in four voters took part in the Nigerian General Election of 1983, shortly before the military takeover. The military regimes which often replaced mobilising independence movements were inherently suspicious of popular participation.

Countries that achieved independence in the nineteenth century (mainly in Latin America) have taken a different route. Mass participation has often been demanded but, until recently, rarely achieved in anything like a stable form. Economic development, which has generally progressed further in Latin America than in Africa, produced an urban middle-class and proletariat. Both groups demanded entry into the political system. These demands encountered a haughty response from Latin America's conservative, aristocratic élites. Except in Costa Rica and Venezuela, which have functioned fairly stably through the postwar era, the result was political instability. Military governments and civilian oligarchies confronted, and occasionally gave way to, populist movements from the lower middle and working classes.

Peronism in Argentina was the classic example of a successful populist movement involving mass participation. Between 1944 and 1955, Juan Peron constructed an authoritarian regime which incorporated the workers and previously excluded sections of the middle class into the political process. But Peron himself rose to power through the army and it was by a coup that he was eventually overthrown. Until the 1980s mass participation in Latin America was limited in extent and when it did erupt, tended to be manipulated by populist demagogues.

However, in the 1980s the generals of South America went into retreat. Civilian regimes based on voluntary participation were established throughout Latin America. For example, by 1990 Bolivia had witnessed three orderly transfers of power between civilian presidents. These new regimes were based on more stable and conventional forms of popular participation than earlier waves of populism. This led George Bush to claim in 1990 that 'in Latin America the day of the dictator is over'. This remains to be seen. It is not yet clear whether the new Latin American democracies have the staying power to survive the enormous problems they confront: massive inflation, enormous debts, an impoverished underclass and the looming presence of bourgeois and military élites.

If the timing of independence is the crucial historic influence on participation in the third world, the main contemporary influence is the development strategy followed by governments. A socialist strategy of development sought economic growth through mass mobilisation of the population. It aimed to incorporate the peasants into politics so as to overcome any resistance by traditional élites to the government's development plans. Communist states in the third world, notably China and Cuba, adopted this strategy. But other noncommunist states have at one time or another also tried this approach: for example, India, Sri Lanka and Tanzania.

However, the more common modernisation strategy in the third world has been to seek economic development by deliberately reducing mass political participation. Authoritarian rulers have sought to provide transnational companies with a stable political environment and a disciplined, cheap labour force. Brazil, Taiwan, South Korea and Indonesia are examples of countries which have employed this approach, often with success. This strategy shows that the *transition* to an industrial society can reduce, rather than improve, opportunities for mass political participation.

Once this transition has been accomplished, new pressures and demands arise. As countries like South Korea and Taiwan graduate from the developing to the developed world, important sections of their populations seek an increasing role in political affairs. Students and the new middle classes are in the vanguard of these democracy movements. These groups have benefited more than most from authoritarian economic policies, but they are no longer satisfied by financial rewards alone. The challenge to authoritarianism has been thrown down.

■ Public opinion

The concept of 'public opinion' is often used in discussing electors' attitudes to current events. Especially in the first world, pollsters report on the state of public opinion, academics analyse it and politicians claim it is firmly behind them. But what exactly is 'public opinion'? Broadly, it refers to the aggregate views of the politically relevant section of the population on the parties, politicians and policies of the day.

In the first world, the politically relevant population is virtually the entire adult population. Nearly all adults have the vote, and are represented in opinion polls, so their views enter the public realm by these routes. Public opinion becomes an indirect, but significant, form of participation. In much of the third world, by contrast, far fewer people are regularly involved in national politics, even as spectators. Hence 'public opinion' shrinks and, in countries with very authoritarian governments, shrivels up entirely.

There are three reasons why public opinion is most significant in the liberal democracies of the first world. First, competitive elections give the political élite an incentive to listen to the public. Secondly, first-world countries have national media around which public opinion can crystallise. People have views on the issues of the day. By contrast, politics in many third world countries operates on a more local basis, making it difficult to speak of 'public opinion' on a national scale. Thirdly, first world countries have the infrastructure needed to conduct reliable opinion polls: lists of voters, accurate censuses and good computing facilities.

What, then, is the significance of public opinion in the first world? In a sense, public opinion pervades all policy-making. It forms part of the environment within which politicians work. Is the public willing to accept detailed advice on unsafe sexual practices? Has the education system become a national scandal which will cost us votes unless we're seen to act? If we go to war, will we be able to carry the people with us? Politicians frequently make calculations of this kind, especially but not only as an election approaches. Thus public opinion can influence decisions without any explicit mechanism. Public opinion sits in on many government meetings even though it is rarely minuted as a committee member. Its role, however, is often negative – ruling ideas out rather than bringing them in.

The influence of public opinion tends to decline as issues become more detailed. The public is concerned with goals rather than means, with objectives rather than policies. 'What policies politicians follow is their business; what they accomplish is the voters' business' (Fiorina 1981). The public is concerned with a small number of important objectives but most policies are routine, uncontroversial and special-ist. Here **organised** opinion matters more than **public** opinion. Imposing tariffs on the imports of cheap toys may be a fundamental matter for the Toy Manufacturers' Association. Yet all the children want is well-stocked shelves; and their parents are happy if the toys are safe as well as cheap. Within this broad constraint, politicians have considerable flexibility.

Even on important matters, the public is often surprisingly ill-informed. This, too, limits the impact of public opinion. In 1984 as many as 38 per cent of Americans believed that the Soviet Union was a member of NATO, the miliary alliance set up to defend Western Europe against a Soviet attack. In 1986, at the height of the debate over American aid to the Contra rebels in Nicaragua, 40 per cent of Americans supporting financial aid to the Contras did not know which side their government was on (Flammang *et al.* 1990, p. 237). Similar findings from other democracies confirm the ignorance of large sections of the public, especially on foreign policy issues where governments have traditionally had most room for manoeuvre.

Public opinion can evade trade-offs but governments cannot (though they sometimes try!) This is perhaps the most important limit on the influence of public opinion. In election campaigns, politicians can promise the earth, but in office they must learn the language of priorities. Public opinion may favour improved public services and lower taxes but the government has to emphasise one or the other. Politicians must respond to the pressures from the opposition parties, interest groups and the international community, as well as public opinion. They may find, in any case, that public opinion is itself divided. So even in the most democratic of countries, government by opinion poll remains a far-off dream – or nightmare.

■ Opinion polls

'According to a new opinion poll . . . ' is a familiar refrain in media coverage of politics in the first world. The accuracy of opinion polls in predicting election outcomes is now well established. In the United States, where modern sampling techniques were introduced by George Gallup in the 1930s, the average error in predicting the major parties' share of the vote at national elections between 1950 and 1988 was a mere 1.5 per cent. Accuracy is similar, though not always quite as good, in other democracies. But what is the broader significance of polls? Do they contribute to, or detract from, democracy?

Opinion polls contribute to the democratic process in several ways. They bring into the public realm the voices of people who would otherwise go unheard. They are the only form of participation (apart from the ballot box itself) in which all count for one and none for more than one. Polls are also based on *direct* contact by interviewers with the public; they get behind the group leaders who claim to speak 'on behalf of our members'. Polls enable politicians to keep in touch with the popular mood and polls give some insight into the reasons for election results. In short, opinion polls oil the wheels of democracy.

Yet it would be wrong to overstate the impact of opinion polls. Ordinary people answer the questions but they do not ask them. The agenda is set in the capital city – in Washington and Wellington, Oslo and Ottawa – by party officials and journalists who commission polls. The concerns of the political élite, caught up in the intricacies of day-to-day politics, differ from those of ordinary people. This reminds us of the economist who conducted an opinion poll about inflation, only to discover that many people thought, quite correctly, that it meant blowing up tyres! More seriously, people may not even have thought about the topic before answering questions on it. They may give an opinion where they have none; or agree to a statement because it's the easiest thing to do ('yea-saying'). This leads to the criticism that opinion polls construct, and even shape, public opinion at the same time as they measure it.

Perhaps it is just as well, then, that most politicians take public opinion polls with a pinch of salt. Even politicians who are sensitive to public opinion often prefer to judge it from their mailbag rather than through opinion polls.

■ The media

Communication has always been central to politics – and mass communications are a key feature of modern politics. Coup-makers are as aware of this as civilian politicians. Television centres, radio stations and newspaper offices are always priority targets in a take-over. A monopoly of the national media does not enable the conspirators to control what people *think*, but at least it allows them to limit what people *know*. And that makes it harder for the opposition to mobilise against the new rulers. Control of the media puts the coup-makers in the driving seat.

The 'mass media' refer to methods of communication which can reach large numbers of people at the same time. Television and newspapers are the most important; others are posters, radio, books, magazines and cinema.

In contrast to opinion polls, the mass media are vehicles of downward communication – from rulers to ruled – more than upward communication – from the ruled to the rulers. Through a single television broadcast, or a series of newspaper articles, presidents, generals and prime ministers can now communicate directly with the majority of their population.

□ *The first world*

The mass media are most important in the first world, where television ownership is the norm. Television is a direct, visual, credible and easily digested source of essential political information. For example, the television studio is now the main field of battle for election campaigns in liberal democracies. Local party activists, once the assault troops of the campaign, are now mere skirmishers.

Television has also transformed the skills needed to climb the 'greasy pole' of politics. Rather than needing the oratorical ability to inspire a big crowd, the trick now is to speak in clear but relaxed tones on television, delivering the apt 'sound bite' that can be recycled on later news bulletins. For masters of this art, such as Ronald Reagan in the United States, politics becomes a matter of selling policies through personality. For those who cannot adapt, such as Michael Foot (leader of Britain's Labour Party 1980–83), retirement beckons. Now that parliamentary proceedings are televised in many countries, politicans need to consider the reaction of the ordinary viewer even when addressing their fellow representatives.

Critics allege that politicians are trained to present a false image on television. Was not Margaret Thatcher taught by her PR consultants to speak lower and slower on television? Did not French President François Mitterrand have his teeth straightened so that on television he looked less like Dracula? But the critics overstate their case. In fact, nothing reveals the truth as ruthlessly as the camera's unblinking eye. Through television, modern electorates have a fuller and more accurate image of their leaders than did previous generations. The camera may not tell the whole truth, but neither does it lie.

It is, of course, true that television is at its most effective in portraying personalities. Thus, television may well have encouraged a more presidential style of politics, in which attention is focused ever more strongly on the leading actors in the political drama. But we strike a note of scepticism even here. Politics has always involved personalities. Did not Abraham Lincoln and George Washington dominate their times as much as Ronald Reagan and George Bush? Exaggerated estimates of television's impact often arise from idealised assumptions about the nature of politics BT – Before Television.

Of course, parties seek to exploit the power of television for their own purposes and, when in office, their powers of persuasion are considerable. They can invoke the big stick of the 'national interest', threaten to revoke broadcasting licences, or simply withold information from an unhelpful network. In countries with a strong state tradition (such as France), arm-twisting of the media by the government is more successful than in countries with a vigorous tradition of media independence (notably the United States). But even in the United States, the 'ins' have a head start in media manipulation over the 'outs'. Statements by the president are always more newsworthy than those made by political opponents.

Many television networks operate under a legal obligation to provide unbiased news coverage. Although impartiality is a difficult concept to define, in many democracies television now offers more neutral coverage of events than newspapers ever did.

But even in the first world, newspapers should not be forgotten. In

Britain, Japan and Scandinavia, most people still read a national daily newspaper. In response to television, the role of newspapers has changed from a source of information to a source of interpretation and opinion. Newspapers also influence the television's agenda: a story appearing on TV's evening news often begins life in the morning paper.

Where newspapers are organised on a local or regional basis (as in New Zealand and the United States), or where circulation is low (France, Italy) they tend to be less significant. Even here, however, newspapers based in the capital city may remain a significant source of communication among the political élite. In Italy, daily newspapers are quality products aimed at a small but politically sophisticated public.

How much impact do the media have on how people vote in the first world? This remains a matter of controversy. In the 1950s, before television became pre-eminent, the **reinforcement** thesis held sway (Harrop 1987). According to this, the media conserved but did not change the political attitudes and behaviour of the electorate. Party loyalties were transmitted through the family and, once developed, they acted as a political sunscreen, protecting people from the harmful effects of propaganda through the media.

This interpretation is a useful counter-weight to bland assertions of media power. But it is not an adequate guide to the role of the media in the 1990s. Party loyalties are now weaker, and television more pervasive, than in the 1950s. For this reason, the **agenda-setting** view has gained ground. According to this, the media in general, and television in particular, influence what we think about, if not what we think. Television directs our attention to the latest coup, drought or war, even if it does not determine our reaction to these events.

The impact of television on the agenda of political discussion arises from its selective coverage. If it's not among the headlines on the main evening news, many people will never get to hear of it at all. In other words, what does not appear on screen is at least as significant as what does. Walter Lippman's (1922) view of the press is applicable to the media generally: 'It is like a beam of a searchlight that moves restlessly about, bringing one episode and then another out of the darkness and into vision.' Here, perhaps, lies the real power of television.

☐ *The second world*

The media under communism

Under communism, the media played a 'top-down' role. The media provided a means through which the ruling party could express its achievements and priorities to the whole population. The communal radio blasted out the official line through a network of loudspeakers. To limit the spread of alternative perspectives, foreign stations were jammed. But very little information filtered back up the media chain, from the ruled to the rulers.

Communist theory took the media seriously. Lenin said that 'there is no other way of training strong political organisation except through the medium of an all-Russian newspaper'. More specifically, the dual role of the media in communist states was to contribute to **propaganda** and **agitation**. The purpose of propaganda was to instruct the masses in the teachings of Marx, Engels and Lenin and to explain the history and mission of the party. This was to be achieved not just through news and information but also through other cultural products, including books, films and opera. Agitation, on the other hand, was more specific. It consisted in mobilising the masses behind specific policies. 'Agitators' would work to reinforce party messages and would apply them to the local level.

To achieve both objectives, ruling communist parties developed an elaborate media network. Newspapers were pinned up for people to read at no cost. They could also be bought at subsidised prices. Even more stress was placed on the broadcast media, which provided a simpler and more direct form of communication than newspapers, especially for less-educated people. In China, most people have a radio and most villages possess a television, even in remote areas. It is much more efficient for the central party to communicate with local activists through television than it is to send teams of 'agitators' out into the countryside.

In practice, media coverage was boring and predictable. Journalists were tightly controlled by the party, a policy guaranteed to destroy their vitality. Propaganda became nothing more than the repetition of clichés. People realised that official publications gave, at best, a highly selective interpretation of events. No wonder one of the main uses for party newspapers in China was for rolling tobacco! (The other main use is easily guessed.)

The Soviet Union was an extreme example of tight control of the media by the communist party. The title of the newspaper of the Soviet communist party, *Pravda*, was ironically deceptive. Pravda means truth, yet the version of the truth presented in its pages bore little relation to life as lived by its readers. Often major disasters were not covered at all. Even the explosion at Chernobyl nuclear power station, which took place in 1986 after Gorbachev's policy of *glasnost* (openness) had begun, initially received tardy and restricted coverage in the Soviet media.

Beneath the bland pronouncements of the media in communist states, a few facts could be gleaned. If the harvest was not reported, it must have been bad. If a leading party figure was no longer mentioned, he must have been purged. Soviet specialists in the West sifted through hundreds of bland pages looking for the key word *odnako* (however), after which would come the nugget of self-criticism.

As in the West, 'letters to the editor' were also worth reading. These were often used to expose instances of petty officialdom and local inefficiency. But such incidents were always the fault of the official, not the system.

The media and postcommunism

Against this background, the political time-bomb of *glasnost* in the Soviet Union slowly ticked away. The more open the media became, the more information was released demonstrating the true scale of the Soviet Union's problems. In communist states, free media were inevitably far more damaging to the regime than in the West, where the underlying legitimacy of the regime was not in question.

As communist power waned, so the media discovered their vitality. Newspapers which had been left unsold were suddenly snapped up by eager customers. Even *Pravda* was used less often as a sunhat. Non-party publications presented alternative political choices to an intrigued, if sometimes bemused, public. The further this process went, the more irreversible it became. The media were certainly an important factor, if not a single actor, in the collapse of communism.

International images presented through the media were particularly important (see pp. 82–90). The East German government could never hide the fact that living conditions were better across the border in the Federal Republic. Even the isolated Albanians became aware through Western television of the depth of relative deprivation in their country (Glenny 1990, p. 233). Images of Western affluence were a potent stimulus for change throughout the communist world, even though they were unrealistic. Television coverage of the collapse of communism in one Eastern European country also presented a powerful stimulus to radicals in neighbouring states.

As with any change in regime, control of television and radio stations was an important stage in the final transfer of power to postcommunist leaders. This was particularly true in Romania. There, the opponents of Ceaucescu seized the television station and nervously broadcast to whoever was watching. As the army switched sides, generals came in to the studio to broadcast their conversion. In a sense, it did not matter how many Romanians were watching. The dictator's authority was being flouted, as any one could see by turning on the TV. This illustrates how, in the modern world, control of the television station has become an important symbol of power.

The media remained a vital forum of political communication in the first postcommunist elections in Eastern Europe. In many countries, the dominant players also ensured they had the lion's share of media resources. Newsprint was sometimes in short supply – and somehow opposition publications would always be the last in the queue. Channels for production and distribution of unofficial publications were often primitive in the extreme. The communists had bequeathed one system of media – and whoever controlled that system was in a strong position. Journalists also found it difficult to develop an American-style adversary relationship with politicians who had become national heroes. All this gave postcommunist umbrella organisations an incentive to hold elections quickly, before other parties could organise their own communications. The reformed Bulgarian Communist Party, which won the first 'free' elections, was particularly successful at exploiting its dominant position in the media.

In a country like the United States, such restrictions on press freedom would cause an outcry. In the exceptional conditions in Eastern Europe after 1989, the media were about as free as could be expected.

☐ The third world

In the third world, national media are less developed and day-to-day politics takes place within a smaller stratum of the population. Again, however, we can distinguish between the print media and broadcast media. Newspapers are generally élite publications, with circulation confined largely to the big cities. Editors may not operate under strict censorship but they are often fully aware that in a small country it does not do to make too many enemies. Journalists and editors are high on the hit list when repression strikes. In Argentina and Chile in the 1970s, journalists were among those who were imprisoned and tortured – or who just 'disappeared'.

Third world journalists often form part of the educated, urban élite. For many of them, the countryside is something to escape from, rather than report on. 'Everyone knows there is malaria in the countryside,' said one newspaper editor in Tanzania, 'so why write about it?' (Instituto del Tercer Mundo 1990, p. 114). Distribution problems restrict newspaper penetration in rural areas, where many people may speak a language which lacks written symbols. For example, most of Africa's 1600 languages and dialects are oral. The broadcast media are a more practical form of communication to remote areas. However, even where communist-style censorship is not practised, the broadcast media usually adopt a top-down style of communication. The voice of the capital reaches into the villages but not vice versa.

A traditional interpretation of the role of the media in the third world is that they contribute to the 'revolution of rising expectations'. Even people living in remote areas are made aware, through television, of affluent first world lifestyles. This produces impossible demands on governments to achieve rapid economic growth. When these expectations are frustrated, political instability results.

It is certainly true that television stations around the world pump out US-made programmes. Virtually all the films shown on Latin American television are from the North, mainly the United States. The same applies to many TV series, where out-of-date programmes can be picked up for a song. Even the poorest countries can afford black and white favourites like 'I Love Lucy', while middle-income countries might be able to manage early episodes of 'Dallas' and 'Dynasty'. All this forms part of the 'globalisation' (Americanisation?) of the media (see pp. 109–11) and has led to attempts by non-aligned countries to 'decolonise' information through a New International Order in Informatics and Communications.

But it is hardly credible to suppose that third world viewers aspire to Dynasty-style lifestyles. After all, the function of these programmmes is to provide escapist dreams for viewers in the first world, let alone the third world. The effects of the media are more subtle than this. They may encourage an awareness of what is happening in the next village, if not the next world. When the newspaper reports that the government has brought electricity to the next town, expectations grow that the administration should extend the supply along the valley. Conflict between regions and localities for the few resources available from the centre is a strong feature of politics in many third world countries. The media certainly strengthen this feature.

Summary

1. Political participation is activity formally intended to influence who governs or how they do so.

2. In the first world, people can choose whether and how to get involved in politics. Most are spectators, doing no more than following politics though television and voting in national elections.

3.   Orthodox political participation is greatest among middle-class, middle-aged, well-educated men. This encourages a conservative cast to first world politics. 'New politics' is a less conventional style of participation, based on broad issues rather than narrow group or party interests. It appeals most to young, well-educated radicals and fits uneasily with the 'old politics.'

4.   Participation in communist states was more regimented and extensive than in the first world. It was supervised by the ruling party which did not normally permit criticism of its own performance. This style of participation was unsuited to the effective management of complex, industrial societies.

5.   Mass demonstrations in major cities were a trigger of communism's final collapse. However, voluntary participation is an entirely new phenomenon in many postcommunist states. It may not take root in all of them, least of all in the Balkan countries with no tradition of accountable rule.

6.   In the third world, political participation is limited, local and controlled by élites. The patron–client relationship is the main means of control. Powerful people offer a little protection to the powerless in exchange for their political support. However, the extension of democracy to parts of the third world may provide opportunities for more effective participation in political decision-making to develop.

Discussion points

1.   Suppose politicians in your country were selected (*a*) by lot or (*b*) by an appointments board. What would be the effects of these methods of recruitment? Would they be beneficial or harmful?

2.   What difference would it make if most politicians were women?

3.   Could communist regimes have continued in power indefinitely if ruling parties had kept a tighter grip on mass political participation?

4.   In the first world, does public opinion affect public policy even when it's not election day? If so, how?

5.   You are given total control over the media in your country. How much power does this give you?

Key reading

Crouse, T. (1973) *The Boys on the Bus* (New York: Random House). An entertaining account of how American journalists covered the Presidential Election of 1972. Still well worth reading.

Huntington, S. and Nelson, J. (1976) *No Easy Choices: Political Participation in Developing Countries* (Cambridge, Mass.: Harvard University Press). A tough-minded but penetrating analysis.

Lampert, N. (1990) 'Patterns of Participation' in *Developments in Soviet Politics*, ed. S. White, A. Pravda and Z. Gitelman (Basingstoke: Macmillan), pp. 120–36. Reviews participation in the USSR, both before and during the era of reform.

Marsh, A. (1990) *Political Action in Europe and the USA* (Basingstoke: Macmillan). A summary of a classic comparative study of attitudes to unorthodox participation.

Milbrath, L. (1981) 'Political Participation' in *The Handbook of Political Behaviour*, vol. 4, ed. S. Long (New York: Plenum), pp. 197–240. A good review of research on political participation.

Further reading

Verba and Nie's classic American study (1972) is probably the best example of primary research on participation in the first world. For a British study in this tradition, see Parry and Moyser (1991). On unconventional participation, Barnes and Kaase (1979) is a major comparative study, based on Europe and the United States. Marsh (1990) is an abridged students' version of this influential research.

Discussions of participation in the second and third worlds are often tucked away in broader books. However, on communist states in general, see Schulz (1981). On the Soviet Union, the standard work is Freidgut (1979) while on China, Townsend (1980) is still useful. On the collapse of communism in Eastern Europe, see Gwertzman and Kaufman (1990) for a blow-by-blow account. Prins (1990) and Glenny (1990) are more interpretive. For the third world, see Clapham (1982) and Eisenstadt and Lemarchand (1981) as well as Huntington and Nelson (1976).

There are few good comparative studies of the media though Semetko *et al.* (1991) is an excellent discussion of agenda-setting in American and British election campaigns.

■ *Chapter 8* ■

Elections and Voters

The right to vote is probably the only political right exercised by a majority of the world's population. Elections are the predominant formal mechanism of orthodox participation in the modern world. But the existence of elections does not always give voters the ability to exercise a real choice. In parts of the third world, and until recently in the second world, elections were more often designed to confirm rather than select top political leaders. Even in the first world, most elections do not yield a major change in the parties in office. We therefore begin this section by looking at the significance of elections in each of the three worlds. We then turn to more detailed issues: electoral systems; the social base of parties; and, briefly, voting behaviour.

■ First world elections: bottom-up or top-down?

There are two views about the role of elections in liberal democracies: the **bottom-up** and **top-down** theories (Harrop and Miller 1987). The bottom-up theory is the more orthodox. It stresses the extent to which competitive elections render governments accountable to the governed. The last election determines who governs; the thought of the next election determines how they do so. This tradition emphasises the upward flow of communication in the electoral process from the bottom (the voters) to the top (parties and governments). Competition between parties forces them to respond to the views of the electors.

This is a conventional picture but it has not gone unchallenged. Top-down theorists such as Ginsberg (1982) are less positive about the electoral process in liberal democracies. These critics argue that 'competitive' elections are in essence a device for expanding the power of the élite over the population. Elections incorporate potential dissenters into the political system, reduce popular participation to a mere cross on a ballot and encourage people to obey the state without limiting its autonomy. Elections give a feeling of choice to voters, albeit one restricted to a few broad 'packages' of proposals. As a result of this 'choice', the authority of governments over the voters is enormously enhanced. So the top-down perspective implies that elections in democracies are as much a con-trick as were those in communist states – perhaps more so, because the con succeeds.

Bottom-up and top-down theories also offer contrasting answers to the question 'Do parties matter?' The bottom-up view is that they do – and so therefore does the electoral process which throws them in and out of office. For example, a comparison of Britain in 1979, when Margaret Thatcher came to power, and in 1990, when she left office, surely shows the difference parties (and individual politicians) can make. Had the Labour Party governed through the 1980s, trade unions, nationalised industries and public-sector housing would surely have avoided the battering they took under Conservative governments.

But the top-down view regards this as only a superficial analysis. Privatisation and deregulation were in fashion throughout the first world during the 1980s. In New Zealand, for example, a *Labour* government introduced a broadly Thatcherite economic programme (known as 'Rogernomics' after its arch-exponent Roger Douglas). Had the Labour Party also been in power in Britain, perhaps it too would have been forced to grasp the nettle of reform. From the top-down perspective, then, problems matter more than parties. Whatever parties may say before an election, they face similar problems, and seek similar solutions, after they achieve office. The idea of party 'competition' is another con.

Overall, research findings offer more support for the bottom-up view. Competitive elections do make a difference to public policy. They cannot be dismissed as just a sham. In Britain and the United States, and probably in other democracies too, parties do differ in their manifesto proposals and they generally implement their promises when elected (Pomper and Lederman 1980; Rose 1984). However, governments are less successful with their big proposals – 'peace and prosperity for all' – with which voters are most concerned.

As a result of these differences in party policy, clear contrasts exist between those democracies where the left has dominated over the postwar period (e.g. Sweden) and those where the right has been more influential (e.g. Italy). 'Left-wing' democracies have (1) more inflation but lower unemployment; (2) higher education spending but lower military spending and (3) a larger public sector (Castles 1982). So, over a period of a decade or more, parties do matter – and so therefore does the electoral process which propels them in and out of office.

Elections in the West, as elsewhere, are a forge in which rulers try to shape power into authority. The election result itself enables the government to claim a 'mandate' from the people, a claim which often succeeds in practice despite its dubious validity. For example, after Ronald Reagan's crushing victory over President Carter in the United States presidential election of 1980, opinion polls showed that the electorate interpreted the result as a simple rejection of the fumblings of Jimmy Carter. But this did not prevent the new President from claiming the election gave him a 'mandate for change'. Freshly elected governments retain the initiative in setting priorities and developing policies. The voters are, at best, back-seat drivers.

Even referendums are more often used to reinforce existing policy than to change it. By controlling the timing and wording of referendums, governments can usually secure the desired result – as with the British referendum on the Common Market in 1975 which was only held after Britain had been a member of the EEC for two years. Referendums expand élite power more than they contain it.

So our view is that competitive elections are best seen as an **exchange of influence** between élites and voters. Elites gain authority in exchange for responsiveness to voters. The voters gain influence in exchange for obedience to decisions they only partly shaped. Elections benefit both rulers and ruled.

■ Elections in the second world

An old joke in the communist Soviet Union has a television reporter coming onto the screen and announcing that the Kremlin has been broken into, and next year's election results have been stolen. Perhaps the real joke is that in the old days the theft would not even have been announced! Although elections were always part and parcel of politics in communist party states, little was left to chance, especially when it came to challenging the party's hold on power.

□ *Elections under communist rule*

Under communist rule, elections in the second world resembled the non-competitive contests still found in some developing countries. In the Soviet Union, for example, there was only one candidate – either a member of the party or a non-member who had received party approval. These 'contests' were truly elections without choice. Elsewhere, as for example in North Korea and Poland, communist rule sometimes tolerated candidates from other parties, but only as minor partners of the communists. Even then, the number of seats allocated to noncommunists was strictly limited. For instance in North Korea's Supreme People's Assembly, only ten seats are reserved for noncommunists.

In some East European countries, the electoral style became more relaxed in the 1980s. Hungary, Romania, East Germany and Poland all introduced reforms which gave voters a choice of candidates if not parties. But, again, ruling communist parties did not allow these candidate-choice elections to threaten their supremacy. It was not until communism collapsed that elections acquired real weight in the second world.

What were the functions of elections in communist states? In theory, they were supposed to mobilise the population behind the party's drive towards a communist society. The nomination process allowed the party to select candidates who had the qualities that the regime wished to emphasise – an outstanding work record, say, or active involvement in the community. The campaign itself informed citizens about party achievements and priorities. People also had some opportunity to express grievances about how their local area was run.

On election day, communist states made far greater efforts than liberal democracies to achieve a high turnout (see Exhibit 8.1). These efforts to maximise turnout generally succeeded. In 1975, for example, only 65 of the 1.5 million people in Tadzhikistan in the Soviet Union reportedly failed to vote! In North Korea the communists have claimed 100 per cent turnout and 100 per cent support for official candidates in elections to the Supreme People's Assembly. Exaggerated though the figures were, there is no doubt that most people did really turn out to vote for the official candidate. Why make trouble for yourself?

Not surprisingly, people became disillusioned with such elections. They were seen to be nothing more than a public demonstration of the power of the party. This created a problem for those communist party states that attempted to introduce limited democracy. For example, China introduced direct elections for county-level assemblies after the death of Mao Zedong. The rules required more candidates than seats and a certain proportion of non-party candidates.

The elections went badly. Although the electoral process should have been completed by the end of 1979, in 5 per cent of counties people had still not been to the polls when the campaign was brought to a halt two years later. There were three main problems. First, it proved difficult to get people to stand against party candidates. Why risk danger in the future by participating in the latest political whim? Secondly, many people did not bother to vote. However, the electoral law required a candidate to attain the support of more than half of those eligible to

Exhibit 8.1   *Getting out the vote, communist style*

Elections in communist party states did not permit any challenge to the party's supremacy but the party still made enormous efforts to maximise turnout. People in the Soviet Union found it easier to vote than people in the United States, where individuals still have to take the initiative in registering on a voters' list.

For example, in a referendum in the Soviet Union in 1990 (after the process of political reform had begun), ships at sea radioed in the results of voting among their crews; ballot stations were set up on long-distance trains; and reindeer herdsmen and women were given extra time to get to a ballot booth. Even orbiting astronauts were not forgotten; referendum officials were at ground control to register votes from the Outer Space constituency.

Ironically, turnout in many of the founding elections of the postcommunist era was lower than in elections held in the communist period.

vote, so elections had to be rerun in many areas. Thirdly, local party officials engaged in election-rigging and corruption. To its credit, the central communist party acted swiftly when electoral fraud was uncovered, but widespread corruption hardly encouraged confidence in the new electoral system. This also shows one of the key problems of all reforms in communist party states: those people charged with carrying out reform are often the people who stand to lose most from the reforms themselves.

☐ *Elections and the decay of communist rule*

Elections in a few states did play a role in the slow decay of communist power which culminated in the convulsions of 1989. In Poland and, to a lesser extent, the Soviet Union, voters used the opportunities provided by freer elections to express their hostility to communist rule.

In Poland, the elections of June 1989 proved to be the final blow in the collapse of communist power. The party did not intend these elections to challenge communist rule. Indeed only a third of the seats in the Sejm, the lower house, could be contested (though open elections were held for all one hundred seats in the Senate). Yet the fact that Solidarity, the independent movement led by Lech Walesa, won all but one of the seats they were allowed to contest created a legitimacy crisis that the Polish communists could not survive. The communist party had no popular mandate for continuing in power. The vote for Solidarity was a massive rejection of communist rule. Two months later, Poland had the first postcommunist prime minister in Eastern Europe.

In the Soviet Union, parliamentary elections held in March 1989 were also a rebuff, if a less disastrous one, to the communist party. In some seats, party and state leaders faced a genuine contest for the first time. Many were defeated. Out went the Prime Minister of Latvia, the President and Prime Minister of Lithuania and most of the party leaders in Leningrad. In came Boris Yeltsin, a leading reformer, who won 90 per cent of the vote in Moscow, despite communist harassment. With a turnout of 90 per cent, these elections certainly contributed to Gorbachev's attempt to encourage voluntary political participation in the Soviet Union. But they also weakened the position of his own party. This illustrates how hard, indeed perhaps impossible, had become the task facing reform-minded communists by the late 1980s.

□ *Postcommunism: the founding elections*

Just as 1989 had been the year of revolution in Eastern Europe, so 1990 was the year of elections (Table 8.1). The first wave of postcommunist elections basically formed a sequence of **founding elections** (Bogdanor 1990). Not all the elections were fully competitive but they did help to strengthen and confirm the postcommunist order. Indeed, Wightman has referred to the June 1990 elections in Czechoslovakia as 'a plebiscite for democracy'. As such, we can view these founding elections not as the end of the transition to democracy, but as only the beginning of a long and tortuous path. They did not give a full insight into the party systems which are likely to predominate into the twenty-first century.

In several countries, the elections were clearly transitional: the broad umbrella movements, which had demolished the crumbling structures of communism, proved to be a dominant force. For example, in Czechoslovakia, Civic Forum (led by playwright Vaclav Havel) and its Slovak equivalent, Public Against Violence, won 47 per cent of the vote and a majority of seats.

Not all of these elections met first world standards of free competition. Indeed one of the choices facing postcommunist countries is exactly which type of electoral system and democracy to adopt. As the postcommunist order strengthens, the electoral system will be

Table 8.1 *Eastern Europe and the founding elections*

Country (population)	Main religions	Main languages	Date of founding election	Dominant party
Poland (38.2m)	Roman Catholic (95%)	Polish	June 1989	Solidarity
Hungary (10.6m)	Catholic (54%) Hungarian Reformed (22%)	Magyar	March/April 1990	Hungarian Democratic Front
Romania (23m)	Orthodox (70%) Roman Uniate (10%) Roman Catholic (10%) Lutheran (5%	Romanian, Magyar, German	May 1990	National Salvation Front
Bulgaria (9m)	Orthodox (85%) Muslim (10%)	Bulgarian, Turkish (10%)	June 1990	Bulgarian Socialist Party
Czechoslovakia (15.6m)	Catholic (65%) Protestant (5%)	Czech, Slovak	June 1990	Civic Forum
Albania (3.2m)	Made illegal in 1967 (Muslim, Roman Catholic, Greek Orthodox)**	Albanian	April 1991	Albanian Party of Labour*

* Forced to resign by popular protest; then joined coalition government
** Exact figures are unreliable as religion was officially proscribed until 1990.

subject to considerable tinkering, partly to refine procedures and partly in response to attempts by postcommunist parties to adjust the system to their own interests.

The results of the founding elections of 1990 show the difficulty of generalising about Eastern Europe as a whole. However, in most cases, the electorate did give short shrift to the communists. They polled 16 per cent of the vote in East Germany, 14 per cent in Czechoslovakia, 11 per cent in Hungary and 17 per cent in Slovenia.

However, in Bulgaria and Albania, the ruling parties returned to power, at least temporarily. Like many other 'communist' parties, the Bulgarian Communist Party promised a decisive break with the past and retitled itself as a Socialist Party. Two important factors helped the Bulgarian socialists to victory. First, they had a head start through their existing control of the media. Although other parties moved quickly to start their own newspapers, they complained that their access to newsprint was blocked, and they could not overcome distribution problems in the countryside (Crampton 1990). Secondly, the opposition was severely split. Over forty opposition parties stood against the socialists, so limiting the impact of the anti-communist vote. In fresh elections in 1991, however, the Socialist Party (i.e. the ex-communists) lost ground heavily to the centre-right Union of Democratic Forces. For the first time in 46 years, the communists were out of power.

In Albania, the Party of Labour (the communist party) lost heavily in the cities but won the election thanks to strong support in rural areas. The city-dwellers supported change but poor peasants in the country-side feared it. Ironically, the communists had become the party of rural conservatism. But the election created more problems than it solved. The strength of the reform movement in the urban centres made the country virtually ungovernable while the communists remained in office.

Despite a system of one person one vote, the Albanian example shows that popular legitimacy does not always accrue to those who win elections. In a country with a strong urban–rural divide, a highly motivated minority in the cities has the capacity to override the wishes of the less-committed and less-organised majority in the remote countryside.

One swallow does not make a summer. The transition from totalitarianism to democracy is fraught with difficulties. Nationalism, in particular, may prove to be the biggest obstacle to the development of stable democracies in much of Eastern Europe. Certainly in Balkan countries like Romania and Yugoslavia, authoritarian nationalism may overpower liberal democratic governments. Competitive elections can only establish themselves when agreement is reached on the boundaries of the nation-state. In the Balkans, with its heritage of ethnic animosities, that agreement may be a long time coming.

■ Elections in the third world

Elections in the third world have taken the form of plebiscites held by dictators to 'confirm' their own rule: for example by President (ex-General) Zia of Pakistan in 1984. Or they have been notionally competitive elections where one party has used bribery and coercion to maintain its power (Mexico). Or they have taken the form of contests where competition was permitted but only between candidates standing on the same party ticket (Kenya). Only recently, in the 1980s and early 1990s, have elections offering a genuine choice between parties and policies became more widespread, especially in Latin America and parts of Africa. But the initial question about elections in the third world must remain: Why was party and policy competition so rare – and for so long?

The answer lay in the limited extent of political development. Competitive elections about policy are flesh added to the skeleton of a national political system. Where there is no skeleton, there can be no flesh. In the third world, national government is still weak. The masses remain oriented towards local rather than national politics. Elites regard the state as a profitable mine to be exploited and have little interest in competitive elections which might endanger their grip over the state's resources. Thus the state lacks the strength to sustain competitive elections.

Even in the growing number of third world countries that do hold competitive elections, the object of competition is usually specific rewards rather than ideology. Votes are exchanged for particular benefits which go to individuals, ethnic groups or communities. Whereas class-based parties in the first world used ideology to justify their promise of an improved standard of living for all their supporters, the exchange in third world countries is more practical and specific.

When life is hard, the value of a vote lies in its cash value. In extreme cases voters simply hand over signed ballots to local patrons who then negotiate the best deal they can with candidates. In other cases, where voters have acquired some independence from their patrons, they can deal directly with the candidates. For example, in the Philippines under President Marcos, 10–20 per cent of the electorate literally sold their vote, often for the equivalent of a month's wages (eventually the massive corruption in the 1986 election contributed to Marcos's downfall).

The exchange between voters and candidates can also operate on a constituency basis. In Kenya, MPs are judged by their success in winning benefits such as rural development projects for their constituencies. If they succeed, they are re-elected; if they fail, they are thrown out by the voters. In the 1983 election, for example, 57 out of 150 incumbents lost, a far higher proportion than in first world democracies such as Britain and the United States (Barkan 1987, p. 230).

Through these mechanisms, elections in the developing world can make some contribution to political integration, linking the central government to local areas. The mere fact of participating in an election, and the associated task of learning party symbols and some facts about the party's philosophy, may also facilitate national awareness among the population.

But élites drive elections in the third world. Rulers hold elections because they feel their position may be strengthened if they can tell the international community that they are an elected government. This is one reason why reasonably free elections became more common in the third world at the end of the 1980s. Western organisations made their aid more conditional on the political performance of the recipient's regime. At the same time, the Soviet Union became less willing to prop up authoritarian regimes, as the Cold War ended and the Soviet Union concentrated on its own domestic troubles. But even in many third world countries that have held free elections, politics are still not election-centred.

■ Electoral systems

An electoral system is a set of rules for conducting an election. It is far more than the procedures for translating votes into seats. One of the most important features of an electoral system is its scope. Which offices are subject to election is as fundamental as who has the right to vote. In the first world, the United States is unique in its massive number of elected offices, ranging from president to dog-catcher. At a lesser extreme, Australians engage in much more electing than New Zealanders (Crewe 1981, p. 231). Australians directly elect both chambers of parliament; New Zealand's parliament is unicameral. Federal Australia has two levels of elected subnational government: state and local; unitary New Zealand has only the one, local level. Moreover, most Australian states have two elected chambers.

The franchise (who can vote) is another important element of an electoral system. In most democracies, the vote now extends to nearly all citizens aged at least eighteen. The main exclusions are criminals, the mentally incompetent, and (perhaps least defensibly) non-citizen residents such as guest workers. However, this 'universal' franchise is relatively recent. For example, in many countries women did not get the vote until after the Second World War. Few countries can match Australia and New Zealand where women have been electors since the turn of the twentieth century. Indeed women in Switzerland, Portugal and Spain had to wait for the vote until the 1970s. Minority groups have also been discriminated against until recently. In the United States, until the mid-1960s, poll taxes and literacy tests were used to deny the vote to Southern blacks. Aborigines were unable to vote in Australia's 'whitefella' elections until 1962.

A universal suffrage does not guarantee a full turnout. In the American presidential election of 1988, only one in every two Americans of voting age cast their ballot. In part, this is because the burden of registering as a voter in the United States rests with the individual, rather than with the bureaucracy. Many people, particularly among minority groups and the young, just don't bother to register. In most other liberal democracies, turnout at national elections exceeds 80 per cent. Where voting is theoretically compulsory, as in Australia, Belgium and Greece, the rate usually tips over the 90 per cent mark.

☐ *Converting votes into seats*

Most controversy about electoral systems centres on the rules for converting votes into seats. The main types of electoral system are shown in Table 8.2. The basic distinction is between majority and proportional systems. In a majority system, the candidate(s) with the largest number of votes in a particular area wins election. The classic example is the system of 'first past the post', used in Britain, Canada, India, New Zealand and the United States. Majority systems are based on the very old idea of representing **territory**. Across the country as a whole, majority systems usually give a substantial bonus in seats to the party which leads in votes, thus encouraging government by a single party which has a clear majority in parliament.

In a proportional system, by contrast, parties acquire seats in explicit relation to the votes they receive. Proportional systems are based on the more recent notion of representation for **parties**, rather than places. Under proportional representation, majority governments are unusual and coalitions are the norm.

Although 'first past the post' is the most influential majority system, it is not the only one. Australia's lower house now uses the alternative vote (AV, see Table 8.2). This takes into account more information about voters' preferences than 'first past the post'. It was introduced in

Table 8.2 *Main types of electoral system in liberal democracies*

MAJORITY SYSTEMS – 'winner takes all'

1. Simple plurality – 'first past the post' system

Procedure: Leading candidate elected on first and only ballot.
Where used: UK, United States, Canada, India, New Zealand, South Africa.

2. Absolute majority – alternative vote ('preferential vote')

Procedure: Voters rank candidates. Bottom candidate eliminated and these votes redistributed according to second preferences. Repeat until a candidate has a majority.
Where used: Australia (House of Representatives).

3. Absolute majority – second ballot

Procedure: If no candidate has a majority on the first ballot, the two leading candidates face a run-off.
Where used: France (presidential elections).

PROPORTIONAL SYSTEMS – seats obtained by quota in multi-member constituencies

4. List system

Procedure: Vote is cast for a party's list of candidates, though in most countries the elector can also express support for individual candidates on the list.
Where used: Israel, Scandinavia, most of continental Europe, including Eastern Europe.

5. Single transferable vote (STV)

Procedure: Voters rank candidates. Any candidate over the quota (which is essentially votes cast divided by one more than the number of seats) on first preferences is elected, with the 'surplus' transferred to the voters' second choice. When no candidate has reached the quota, the bottom candidate is eliminated and these votes are also transferred. These procedures continue until all seats are filled.
Where used: Irish Republic, Malta, Tasmania, Australia (Senate, though electors can choose a party ticket if they wish).

Australia because the two major non-Labor parties wanted to gang up on the Labor Party. Under AV, they could exchange lower preferences against the Labor candidate even if they both put up candidates in the same seat. This worked because both Liberal and National Party voters disliked Labor most of all. This is an example of the extremely common practice of electoral engineering: selecting or refining a system to further the interests of the existing rulers.

The list system is the most common form of proportional representation (PR). It is used in most countries in Europe, West and East. The general principle here is that the total number of votes won by a party determines *how many* candidates are elected from that list. The number of votes gained by the individual candidates on the list determines *which* people are elected to represent that party.

List systems vary in allowing voters a choice over candidates within from a party's list. At one extreme stands the *closed party list* used in Israel, Portugal and Spain. Voters there have no choice over candidates but simply vote for the party they prefer. Candidates are elected in accordance with how far up they are placed on the party's list. For example, if party X receives 40 per cent of the votes in a 200-seat parliament, the top 80 candidates on its list would be selected. This gives the central party bureaucracy enormous control over political recruitment. At the other extreme lie the *free party* lists used in Switzerland and Luxembourg. In these countries electors can vote for candidates drawn from the lists of several parties. If 40 per cent of all the votes cast were for candidates from party X, then the party would again be entitled to 80 seats. But these 80 winners would be those on the party's list who got the most individual votes. Most countries give voters at least some choice between candidates from a party's list.

Most list systems have a threshold of representation below which a party receives no seats at all. The cut-off point is 2 per cent in Denmark and 4 per cent in Sweden. Finland has no formal threshold at all. This enabled two Green delegates to be elected in 1983, the first in the Nordic region, with just 42 045 votes (1.4 per cent of the total). Very small parties can also gain representation in the Dutch and Israeli parliaments. In the Dutch election of 1986, the Calvinist Reformed Political Federation won a seat with just 83 582 votes. The Netherlands, like Finland, has no formal threshold and parties win seats with less than 1 per cent of the vote.

To achieve a proportional outcome, PR systems must use constituencies returning several representatives. There is no way of proportionally dividing one representative between several parties. By contrast majority systems usually have single-member constituencies.

☐ *Evaluating electoral systems*

What is the relationship between electoral systems and party systems? This remains a matter of controversy in political science. In a classic work, Duverger (1954) claimed that 'first past the post' strongly favoured a two-party system while PR contributed to a multi-party system. More generally, 'first past the post' was associated with strong, decisive government. PR was found guilty by its association with unstable coalition governments.

But in the 1960s a reaction set in against attributing weight to political institutions such as electoral systems. Writers such as Rokkan (1970) adopted a more sociological approach, arguing that social cleavages had produced multi-party systems in Europe long before PR was adopted. PR did not cause a multi-party system: rather, PR was adopted because it was the only electoral system which would satisfy the numerous parties thrown up by social divisions.

Much ink is spilt on the issue of which is the 'best' electoral system. In truth, there is no such thing. Different methods work best in different circumstances. For example, in countries with intense social divisions, such as Northern Ireland and South Africa, a strong case can be made for PR on the grounds that it will provide at least some representation for parties based on minority groups. But where regular changes of government occur under a majority system, as in Great Britain, this argument for PR loses much of its force. Over a period of time, each party gets its 'crack of the whip' – **proportional tenure** without **proportional representation**.

In any case the same procedure can have different effects in different countries. 'First past the post' has reinforced Protestant supremacy in Northern Ireland but contributed to the 'swing of the pendulum' in mainland Britain. Thus the electoral system which is most appropriate for a particular country depends on the nature of its society, and especially the relative size of the major social groups within it.

Nonetheless majority systems have been losing popularity over the last few decades. Far from producing political instability, as those who observed the rise of fascism had thought, PR has contributed to continuity of policy in most of postwar Europe. The same parties often continue in government for decades, with slight variations in their coalition partners. By contrast, 'first past the post' can thrust parties in and out of office. This is because the result in seats exaggerates the result in votes. Canada is a good example. In 1984, the Conservative Party won three-quarters of the seats on just half the vote.

The bias of 'first past the post' against smaller parties with evenly spread support (including the Greens) has also become more apparent as minor parties have gained ground. In the British election of 1983, the Alliance of Liberals and Social Democrats received 7.8 million votes (26%) but only 23 out of 650 seats (3.5%). Significantly, none of the postcommunist states adopted a majority system for their founding elections.

Movements for electoral reform have emerged in most of the countries still using 'first past the post'. So far, however, little has come of these efforts. The main reason for this is that parties elected under one system have no incentive to change to another. Voices within parties of the left, such as the Canadian Liberal Party and the British and New Zealand Labour Parties, have expressed interest in reform. But specific proposals have usually remained buried inside the party's bureaucracy.

If 'first past the post' gives too little weight to smaller parties, PR arguably gives them too much. Under PR, smaller parties are often in a pivotal position in post-election coalition negotiations, able in theory to form an alliance with either major party (in practice, ideology restricts the range of feasible partners). In addition, advocates of decisive government argue that coalitions tend towards the lowest common denominator, acting in particular as a barrier against radical but necessary change. For better or worse, it is difficult to see a figure such as Margaret Thatcher emerging as a compromise coalition leader after an election fought under PR!

■ The social base of parties

Elections in liberal democracies are not fought afresh each time. They show enormous continuity in the parties which contest them and in the shares of the vote these parties obtain. To understand elections, we must focus on parties, since it is parties that structure and limit the choices available to the individual voter.

The stability of parties rests on their foundations in the social structure. Most parties have core supporters, located in one segment of society, which provide the party with a secure base of support. Most often, parties represent a particular religion, class or language group. These links between parties and social groups usually develop at crucial points in a country's history. This means that we must look at the social base of parties from a historical perspective.

Exercise 8.1   *Gulf War II: showing the effect of electoral systems*

The method used to count votes does make a difference. Here's an example which, in our experience, usually produces a different result according to how preferences are added up. The example is based on votes for a series of policy options rather than votes for a party. It also introduces some interesting ways of 'aggregating' opinions. The larger the group taking part in this exercise, the better.

Imagine that Iraq has invaded Kuwait *again*. You have to vote on what your country's response should be. Cast your vote(s) for these options:

1. No action of any kind.
2. Economic sanctions only; no military action.
3. Military action to expel Iraq from Kuwait only.
4. Military action to expel Iraq from Kuwait plus sufficient military action to make a future invasion of Kuwait unlikely.
5. As 4, plus deposing Saddam Hussein so he would no longer be a threat to the region.

Voting systems:

A. Simple plurality
You can cast one vote only. Place an X beside your most preferred option.
   The option which receives the most votes (the highest 'plurality') will win. This, of course, may be less than 50% of all the votes cast.

B. Alternative vote
Indicate your order of preference. Place 1 beside your 1st preference, 2 beside your 2nd preference, and so on.
   If no option receives more than 50% of 1st preferences, the option with the lowest number of 1st preferences will be eliminated and the 2nd preferences of those who voted for that option will be taken into account. This process will be repeated until one option achieves an absolute majority (i.e. at least 50% + 1) of the votes cast.

C. Approval voting
You express your 'approval' for as many or as few of the options as you wish. Place an X beside each of those options of which you approve.
   That option will win which receives the most votes.

cont. overleaf

D.   Borda count
Rank order your preferences. Give 4 to your 1st preference, 3 to your 2nd preference, 2 to your 3rd, 1 to your 4th, and 0 to your 5th. (Note that this is the opposite procedure to that used for the Alternative vote – you give the highest, not the lowest, figure to your first preference, and then work down.)

The numbers assigned to each option are summed. The winning option is that which achieves the highest score.

E.   Point voting
You have 50 points which you may distribute in any way you like between the options. The way that you distribute your points is intended to indicate the relative strength of your preferences as between the options. (Make sure that the points that you award add up to 50.)

The winning option will be that which receives the most points.

Now work out the results. For comparison, among first-year undergraduates at Newcastle University, England, in 1991, three different options 'won', depending on the electoral system used. To prevent biasing your own exercise, we won't say which options came out ahead!

Table 8.3 shows the main cleavages on which Western parties are based. Three main waves of change have swept through Western societies over the centuries. Even after they recede, they leave their tidemark on the party system. These waves are:

1. The national revolution
2. The industrial revolution
3. The post-industrial revolution.

□ *The national revolution*

Lipset and Rokkan (1967) called the first wave 'the national revolution'. This refers to the original construction of the state as a territory governed by a single central authority. Though fought many centuries ago, the scars of these battles can still be seen in modern party systems. One reason for this is that state-building was often a violent process. Centralising élites generally showed little mercy in imposing their

Table 8.3   *Some social bases of parties*

Wave 1 The national revolution	Wave 2 The industrial revolution	Wave 3 The post-industrial revolution
Centre vs. periphery	Class	Education
National and linguistic divisions	Trade unions	Affluence
Religion	Social mobility	Postmaterialism

Source: M. Harrop and W. Miller *Elections and Voters: A Comparative Introduction* (London: Macmillan, 1987).

authority on groups accustomed to greater autonomy, notably in peripheral areas and in the Catholic Church.

Britain is a good example of a country with a long-standing division between centre and periphery. The Conservatives have always been the party of the core regions around London and the South-East. The Labour Party's strength, by contrast, lies in the outlying, industrial areas of England, as well as in Scotland and Wales.

Parties of the periphery enjoyed a temporary recovery in the 1970s. Witness the Basques and Catalans in Spain, the French in Canada, and Scottish and Welsh nationalists in Great Britain. Though some of these groups were simply vehicles of anti-government protest, clearly the centre–periphery conflict has not been permanently solved in Western states.

The other aspect of the national revolution, conflict between state and church, proved equally influential in shaping party systems. As the modern nation-state developed, it came into conflict with the Catholic Church, which sought to defend its traditional control over 'spiritual life'. A basic issue here was: Who should control education – church or state? This battle was settled several hundred years ago in Protestant countries such as Scandinavia, the United Kingdom (except Northern Ireland) and its former colonies. These countries have therefore been largely exempt from religious parties.

In Catholic countries, such as France and Italy, and in religiously mixed countries, such as the Netherlands, the conflict continued into the twentieth century. It has had a profound effect on party systems. Anti-clerical parties (especially the communists) emerged in several Catholic countries, notably France and Italy. Their secular values were countered successfully by Christian Democratic parties, formed to defend the traditional authority of the church. Though these Catholic parties have now broadened their appeal to wider centre-right sections of the electorate, a count in the late 1960s showed that as many parties in Western Europe were still based on religion as on class (Rose and Urwin 1969).

☐ *The industrial revolution*

This also affected party systems in several ways. First, it sharpened existing divisions between urban and rural interests. Peasant hostility to the city led to the formation of agrarian parties in Norway, Sweden and Finland, though these parties too have now become broader parties of the centre. In other European countries, differences between landowners and the new industrialists fuelled the division between Conservatives and Liberals for much of the nineteenth century.

Secondly, industrialisation led later to the emergence of socialist parties, externally created, to represent the interests of the urban working class. These parties tended to be moderate in countries where working-class incorporation into the political system was easily achieved (as in Britain and Scandinavia) and more anti-system where the fight was harder (as in France and Italy). In the United States, exceptionally, mass suffrage for white males was achieved before industrialisation began, thus working against the emergence of a class-based socialist party at all.

Intimately linked with class is the growth of trade unions. As the industrial wing of the working-class movement, trade unions could be expected to increase electoral support for the left. In nearly all democracies, left-wing voting is more common among trade unionists than the non-unionised. In much of continental Europe, however, trade unions are themselves divided along party and/or religious lines, so their main effect is to reinforce the party system. For example, in France and Italy, communist and Catholic unions have fought many a battle in the workplace, with the conflict between them mirroring party divisions.

It is where trade unions *created* a party that they have had most impact on the party system. The main examples here are Australia and Britain. The Labour Parties of both countries were originally creatures of the unions, a link which served the parties well as they sought to become established. Now, however, the relationship attracts considerable criticism, and both parties are distancing themselves from their union origins.

☐ *The post-industrial revolution*

Western societies are becoming post-industrial. Increasingly, they are characterised by affluence rather than poverty; by service industries rather than manufacturing industry; and by education rather than class (Bell 1973). It remains to be seen whether the post-industrial revolution will have such profound consequences on party systems as the national and industrial revolutions. Higher education is still the preserve of a minority – but it is a vocal minority and one which is growing rapidly as countries compete with each other to produce the best-educated workforce. The post-industrial revolution is a quiet revolution but it is no less significant for that.

Affluence and education produce more confident, outward-looking people, concerned about broad social issues. This is the basis of Inglehart's theory of postmaterialism (see pp. 141–2). Postmaterialists look for a new style of politics: more participatory and single-issue based than the approach offered by traditional parties, whether of the right or the left. Even if the postindustrial revolution does not produce new parties, it challenges, and may well weaken, the existing party system.

Younger, better-educated generations have provided a reservoir of activists for new, and especially green, parties. These question the whole notion of industrial society. Green parties have emerged in most Western democracies, achieving greatest success in Europe (S. Parkin 1989). In Germany, for example, the Greens achieved representation in the national parliament as early as 1983, winning 27 seats on 5.6 per cent of the vote. Since then, green candidates have been elected to parliaments in such countries as Austria, Italy, Luxembourg, Portugal and Sweden. In the Anglo-American democracies, the high threshold for representation imposed by the 'first past the post' electoral system has held back the greens. However the Australian Democrats and the New Zealand Values Party, both based on 'new left' philosophies, have had some impact on the flavour of politics in their countries.

The 'maturing' of green parties has been restricted by their ambivalent attitude to the existing party system. Many have declined to dirty their hands through involvement with the polluted environment of mainstream politics. For example the German greens are deeply divided between the realist 'light greens', who favour collaboration with other parties, and the more fundamentalist 'dark greens', who reject conventional party politics.

□ *Parties of reaction*

The waves of social change we have reviewed produce counter-currents, which are powerful in their own right. To be more specific, social change produces tensions which can be reflected in the emergence of extreme, often short-lived, **parties of reaction**. Lipset (1983) suggests that to understand political extremism, it is necessary to identify the groups which are under threat from social change. Reactionary parties fall into three main groups:

1. Fascist parties, reacting against democracy and the decay of the old order. These had most spectacular appeal in the inter-war years, with the rise to power of Hitler's National Socialists in Germany and Mussolini's Fascist Party in Italy.
2. Parties based on the self-employed and small businessmen, reacting against large companies and powerful unions. The main example here is the Poujadists, a flash party that achieved short-term success in France in the 1950s.
3. Racist parties based on the poorly educated urban working class, reacting against immigrants and guest workers. These emerged in many West European countries in the 1960s and the 1970s, with another revival in the early 1990s. The most important illustration is again from France. The National Front (FN), led by Jacques le Pen, calls for an end to all immigration: its slogan is 'France for the French.' The FN won 35 seats on 10 per cent of the vote in the parliamentary elections of 1986. Its parliamentary presence was virtually eliminated at the next elections, due to the abolition of proportional representation. Early in 1992, however, opinion polls reported that the FN had more popular support than the ruling Socialist party.

□ *Parties in the New World*

In analysing the social base of Western parties, it is important to distinguish Europe from the New World. Countries such as Canada, Australia and the United States lack the long European tradition of church–state and urban–rural conflict; consequently, they do not have major parties based exclusively on these cleavages. Where New World democracies do diverge is in the core values of their early settlers. These values created distinctive political cultures which still exert a primary influence on party systems. In the United States, puritan and individual values, as well as the early achievement of white male suffrage, have militated against the emergence of Catholic and socialist parties. By contrast, in Australia and New Zealand, class values came with the settlers, thus facilitating strong Labour Parties.

In Canada, largely settled in the pre-class era, the crucial division between French-speakers and English-speakers can be seen throughout the country's history. In white South Africa, the even more fundamental cleavage between the Afrikaner people and English-speakers can also be traced back to settlement patterns. Within the New World democracies, the main contrast today is between the United States and Canada, where party support is only loosely linked to distinctive social bases, and Australia, New Zealand and South Africa, where social cleavages still structure party systems.

■ Voting behaviour in liberal democracies

Given that voters have a choice, how do they decide who to vote for? The prior question is *whether* voters decide. One influential theory of electoral choice, originally developed in the United States in the 1950s, argued that voting was an act of affirmation rather than choice (Campbell *et al.*, 1960; Markus and Converse, 1979). This was known as the 'socialisation' or 'Michigan' model (after the place where it was constructed).

This model developed slightly differently in Europe. In America, voting was seen as an expression of deep-seated loyalty to a **party**. This 'party identification' was acquired initially through one's family, then confirmed through membership of social groups and reinforced by lifelong electoral habit. Electors learned to think of themselves as Democrats, Republicans or (in a minority of cases) as Independents. In the United States, this theory of voting is also known as the party identification model.

In Europe, where social divisions run deeper, voting was seen as primarily an expression of loyalty to a **social group** rather than a party. The act of voting affirmed one's identification with a particular religion, class or ethnic group. Political parties then served as an expression of these group interests. Thus electors thought of themselves as Catholic or Protestant, middle class or working class. Party choices then flowed naturally from the anchor of social identity.

□ *Classifying elections*

The socialisation model emphasised electoral stability. It assumed that there was a 'natural' level of support for a party in the electorate, against which actual election results can be measured. In the United States, this idea was developed into the classification of elections shown in Table 8.4.

In a **normal** election, voting directly reflects partisanship and the party with the greatest share of party identifiers (for example the Democrats in the United States) wins the election.

In a **deviating** election, by contrast, the majority party loses the election due to short-term factors such as candidate appeal. However voters who deviate from their normal choice retain their underlying allegiance and return to it in later contests. For example, one interpretation of Ronald Reagan's victory in the 1980 presidential election in the United States was to blame the ineffectiveness of the Democratic incumbent, Jimmy Carter. The assumption was that many 'Reagan Democrats' would return to the fold next time round. However, further Republican victories in 1984 and 1988 dented the underlying theory that the Democrats are still the 'natural' majority party in the United States.

Finally a **realigning** election, or more often a realigning sequence of elections, brings about a major change in the distribution of partisanship in the electorate. It redefines the relationships between social groups and party support. The forging of the New Deal coalition by the Democrats in a series of critical elections in the United States during the 1920s and the 1930s is an example of this process. Realigning elections are rare but exciting events.

Table 8.4   *A classification of United States elections*

---

1. **Normal election** – the result expresses the balance of long-term party loyalties in the electorate as a whole.
   Example: Democratic presidential election victories from the 1930s to the 1960s.

2. **Deviating election** – the natural majority party loses the election due to short-term factors.
   Example: Republican presidential election victories in the 1950s.

3. **Realigning ('critical') election** – these change the underlying strength of parties and redefine the relationships between parties and social groups.
   Example: Presidential elections in the 1920s and 1930s which forged the Democratic 'New Deal' coalition.

☐ *Dealignment*

The socialisation approach assumed a stable rather than a volatile electorate. It explained why most people did not change their votes, not why some people did. This was a fair approach in the static and relatively apolitical 1950s but it afterwards became less appropriate. The major electoral trend in postwar democracies has been **partisan dealignment** – the weakening bonds between voters and parties.

In the United States, around 30 per cent of the electorate have described themselves as Independents since the mid-1960s, up from 20 per cent in 1954. There has also been a sharp fall in the intensity of party allegiances in Britain. Whereas 46 per cent of Conservative and Labour identifiers said their loyalty was 'very strong' in 1964, only 32 per cent did so in 1987.

Dealignment has advanced furthest in the longest-established party systems – Britain, the Netherlands and Scandinavia. However, even among the new democracies of Southern Europe (such as Spain and Portugal), voters' loyalties do not seem to be strengthening as experience with elections grows. The electorates in these countries may be partly aligned, rather than dealigned. They may behave in a similar way to electorates in the older democracies, as a result of simply missing out the stage of firm party loyalties which the older democracies went through.

What has brought about this decline in party loyalties in the 'mature' party systems? Why have voters begun to choose? One cause seems to be the weakening of traditional class and religious identities. These were fundamental to the outlook of older generations but they are less relevant to new generations of young, well-educated people living in urban, mobile and secular societies. Television has also made a difference. Its neutral style, at least compared to mass circulation newspapers, probably contributes to a less partisan outlook among voters. Also, many younger voters are more attracted to single-issue groups than to the established parties, which are seen as slow-moving and ineffective at confronting new issues.

Partisan dealignment has led to electoral volatility and the emergence of new parties (such as the greens) in several democracies. These factors in themselves cause people to question their faith in the old parties, thus contributing to further dealignment.

The decay of party loyalties has led political scientists to seek new approaches to the study of voting that are better suited to the explanation of electoral change. No longer can we locate the origins of electoral choice solely in social divisions and early socialisation.

Instead we must place more emphasis on political events and how they are reported on television.

Fiorina's theory (1981) of **retrospective voting** is particularly important here. Retrospective voting means casting one's ballot in response to government performance. It is a phrase which tells us much about the character of contemporary voting behaviour. Electors do form an overall assessment of the government's record – and, increasingly, they vote accordingly. A vote is no longer an expression of a lifelong commitment. Rather it is a piece of business like any other. The elector asks of the government, 'What have you done for me (and the country) lately?' Retrospective voting helps to explain why economic conditions, especially unemployment and inflation, have such impact on the popularity of governments (Paldam 1981). More voters now proceed on the brutal assumption that governments should be punished for bad times and perhaps also rewarded for economic advance. They judge results, not promises.

Summary

1.   Elections in liberal democracies are often seen as 'bottom up' institutions which enable the ruled to control the rulers. But they can also be viewed as 'top-down' affairs, enhancing the authority over the government over the governed. Elections are probably best seen as an exchange of influence between rulers and ruled. Voters exert some influence over government in exchange for obedience to decisions they only partly shaped.

2.   Many electors still vote according to long-term loyalties. These are acquired from the family, sustained by social groups and reinforced by electoral habit. This is the socialisation model of voting. However, 'partisan dealignment' means that party loyalties are weakening in many democracies. Electoral volatility is increasing in some countries as electors respond more to new political developments.

3.   An electoral system is a set of rules for conducting an election. These set out: the range of offices subject to election, who can vote, and the rules for converting votes into seats. Majority systems and proportional representation (PR) are the two main methods used to translate votes into seats. Majority systems are based on the idea of representing territory; they usually deliver government by a single party. Majority systems are restricted to Britain and its former colonies. PR is based on the idea of representing parties and is associated with government by coalitions.

4.   Elections under communist rule gave voters little, if any, choice. Their function was to demonstrate the party's control over the people.

5.   Postcommunist states quickly held competitive elections to help confirm their legitimacy. The umbrella movements which had overthrown communist rule won many of these 'founding' elections. Most communist parties won less than 20 per cent of the vote but they won re-election in Albania and, after internal reforms, in Bulgaria.

6.   Elections carry less weight in the third world. In the past, elections were generally uncompetitive. Any competition was restricted to individual candidates rather than parties. The transition to democracy in parts of the third world in the 1980s did raise the significance of elections. However, competition between parties over policies is still relatively unimportant. Poverty and inequality mean voters still trade their votes for a degree of protection which local patrons provide.

Discussion points

1.   How much difference do elections make to public policy in your country? What else do elections decide?

2.   Do you expect competitive elections to establish themselves in all, some or none of the countries in (*a*) the second world and (*b*) the third world?

3.   Analyse the *social* influences on your own party preference.

4.   Assess the effect of changing your country's electoral system from proportional representation to first past the post (or vice versa). Would such a change be desirable?

Key reading

Bogdanor, V. and Butler D. (eds) (1983) *Democracy and Elections: Electoral Systems and Their Consequences* (Cambridge: Cambridge University Press). Readable accounts of electoral systems in various countries, placed in their historical and social setting.

Bogdanor, V. (1990) 'Founding Elections and Regime Change', *Electoral Studies* (9) 295–302. An excellent review of the first round of postcommunist elections in East Europe.

Harrop, M. and Miller, W. (1987) *Elections and Voters: A Comparative Introduction* (Basingstoke: Macmillan). A comparative review of research on elections and voters, concentrating on the first world.

Hermet, G., Rose, R. and Rouquie, A. (eds) (1978) *Elections without Choice* (London: Macmillan). A standard work on non-competitive elections in the second and third worlds.

Further reading

On the interpretation of elections in the first world, see Butler, Penniman and Ranney (1981). Ginsberg (1982) is an effective exponent of the top-down view. Polsby and Wildavsky (1984) is the standard text on presidential elections in the United States.

On elections in communist party states, see Pravda (1986) and Zaslavsky and Brym (1978) on the Soviet Union. On elections in the third world, Hermet, Rose and Rouquie (1980) is a standard work. Diamond, Linz and Lipset (1989, volumes 2 and 3) is a useful update.

On electoral systems, Bogdanor (1984) is a clear introduction. For more detail on specific countries, see Bogdanor and Butler (1983). The classics by Duverger (1954), Rokkan (1970) and Rae (1971) are still worth reading. Lijphart (1984b) is a more recent contribution.

On voting behaviour, Campbell *et al.* (1960) is the classic statement of the socialisation model. See Markus and Converse (1979) for a more recent, but also more technical, account. Nie, Verba and Petrocik (1979) is a very influential analysis of the alleged rise of issue voting in the United States. Franklin (1985) covers similar ground for Britain, though Denver (1989) is the best simple introduction to voting and elections in Britain.

Dalton, Flanagan and Beck (1984) is a wide-ranging study of electoral trends throughout the Western world. On Europe specifically, see Crewe and Denver (1985).

■ Chapter 9 ■

Interest Groups

There is a story, possibly true, that New Zealand Premier Sid Holland was once woken by a phone call from an irate woman who could not find a plumber willing to come out in the middle of the night to fix a leak. (This being New Zealand, the premier's number was in the phone book, even if plumbers go ex-directory after hours.) A plumber soon arrived on her doorstep thanks to Holland's direct intervention (Du Fresne 1989). Another story – undeniably true – is that in 1989, the cities of Eastern Europe were filled with people demonstrating their profound dissatisfaction with communist rule, demonstrations that accelerated the collapse of communism in Europe.

Both examples show how people try to make governments listen to, and act upon, their interests. Politics and interests are, after all, inseparable. Indeed some writers have seen government as nothing more than an arena in which different groups, representing specific interests in society, jostle for special treatment. This view is too extreme because it ignores the independent role which the state plays in deciding which interests are satisfied and which are not. After all, Sid Holland *could* have slammed the phone down, ignored the loss of a vote, and gone back to sleep. Communist rulers in Berlin and Prague *could* have turned machine guns on the crowds, as they did in Beijing in 1989, and scared their people into submission for at least a short while.

Nonetheless, in all countries, interests are expressed from society to the state in some way or other. This is the process of interest articulation. In this chapter we look at patterns, channels and determinants of interest articulation; at differences between the three worlds; and at trends within them.

What is an 'interest'? Is an aggrieved housewife or an angry crowd 'articulating an interest'? One writer usefully defines interest groups as, 'organisations which have some autonomy from government or political

209

parties and . . . try to influence public policy' (Wilson 1990). Interest groups seek to influence government, but unlike political parties, they do not aspire to take control of it.

■ Classifying interest groups

Most classifications of interest groups are based on first world politics. To cover the three worlds, our classification needs to extend beyond trade unions and employers' organisations – beyond, in other words, the familiar, organised groups taken for granted in liberal democracies. At one end of the scale are groups based on communal ties. At the other end are groups based on associational ties (Figure 9.1).

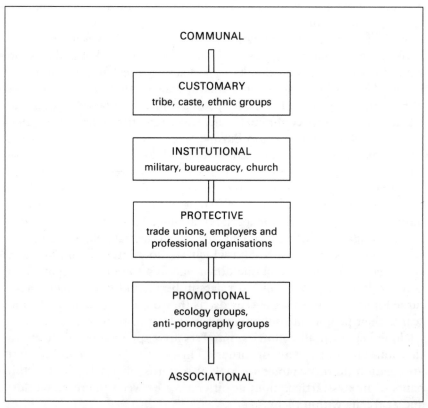

Source: adapted from J. Blondel, *Comparing Political Systems* (London: Weidenfeld) p. 77.

Figure 9.1   *A classification of interest groups*

Communal ties are based not on what people do or think but on the communal bond itself. New members are born into the group, not recruited. The clearest example of communal ties is the family, but the term also covers ethnic, linguistic and caste groups.

At the other end of the scale are associational ties, formed for specific, instrumental purposes. Here, people come together for shared but limited aims: for instance, joining a society for wildlife conservation. The interest-group system in any society largely reflects the relative weight of communal versus associational ties. Communal relations are more important in the third world, associational relations in the first world.

As Figure 9.1 shows, the distinction can also be usefully represented as a dimension along which different groups found in a society can be located. Each of the four types shown in the figure – customary, institutional, protective and promotional groups – is discussed below.

☐ *Customary groups*

These are groups such as the family which are not created for specific purposes but which are simply regarded as part of the social fabric. They are close to the communal end of the spectrum. Customary groups are still important in the politics of many societies. In much of the third world, politicians and officials are expected to use their office to benefit their family or ethnic group. Kinship or personal ties are the main basis of interest articulation. For instance, a government tax collector would be expected by his relatives to arrange favourable treatment for the family business.

Churches and sometimes social classes can have a distinctly customary character. The Roman Catholic Church, for instance, traditionally bound its members closely together, though secularisation has weakened the intensity of these links in the first world. Industrialisation in the first world produced many one-class occupational communities around industries such as mining and shipbuilding. But class loyalties have also decayed along with the industries on which they were based. Customary groups are therefore declining as a base of interest articulation in the first world.

☐ *Institutional groups*

Midway between the communal and associational extremes are public institutions such as bureaucracies and armies. These are formal organisations which seek to influence government to act on their behalf. Bureaucrats always want to extend their sphere of influence, the military always claim a new weapon is essential. Institutional groups articulate their interests and values *within* government. Because of their proximity to the decision-making process, they can have major impact upon policy-making. They are discussed in Chapters 14 and 15.

□ *Protective groups*

Sometimes called sectional or functional groups, these are formally organised groups which exist to protect the material interests of their members, be they miners, college lecturers or managing directors. Trade unions and employers' organisations are the prime examples of protective groups. Such groups often have sanctions at their disposal: workers can go on strike, for instance. For that reason, these protective organisations are sometimes called pressure groups. This term generally overstates the reliance of protective groups on pressure tactics, though governments like to have cooperation from protective groups, and sometimes depend on it.

In almost all liberal democracies, consultation between protective groups and government is extensive. Rather than using pressure tactics, the influence of protective groups mainly depends on providing governments with the information and technical advice needed to anticipate the consequences of decisions. In return groups sometimes acquire 'insider' status, and thus the potential to influence decisions.

Protective groups were less significant in communist states. The ruling ideology never fully accepted the existence of autonomous interest groups. In the Soviet Union, for example, trade unions had only a very limited role in wage-bargaining. In postcommunist states, the influence of protective groups, all seeking a better deal for their members, is increasing.

Protective groups are often grouped into conglomerate 'peak' organisations, such as the LO (Landsorganatsionen) or Swedish Federation of Labour. This represents the interests of the eight out of ten workers in Sweden who belong to a union. How far such peak organisations have the authority to make decisions for their member organisations varies between countries, with important consequences for how countries are run.

Table 9.1, based on an analysis by T. Matthews (1989) of interest groups in Australia, provides an interesting classification with wider application.

Table 9.1 *A classification of interest groups*

AIMS	
Protective groups	a group *of* – defends an interest, e.g.: trade unions
Promotional groups	a group *for* – promotes a cause, e.g.: environmental groups
SUPPORT	
Closed groups	membership is restricted, e.g.: medical associations
Open groups	anybody can join, e.g.: environmental groups
STATUS	
Insider Groups	frequently consulted by government and actively seek this role, e.g.: Canadian Bankers' Association, British National Farmers' Union
Outsider groups	not normally consulted by government – either does not seek such a role, or denied it by government, e.g.: Campaign for Nuclear Disarmament
BENEFICIARIES	
Collective	benefits go to both members and non-members, e.g.: trade unions win pay increases for all workers; cleaner environment benefits everyone
Selective	only group members benefit, e.g.: cheap insurance for union members only
ECONOMIC FUNCTION	
Corporate	promotes interests of providers of goods and services e.g.: producers' associations
Attitude	promotes attitudes and tastes etc., e.g.: consumer associations

Source: Adapted from T. Matthews (1989) 'Interest Groups' in *Politics in Australia,* ed. R. Smith and L. Watson (Sydney: Allen & Unwin).

□ *Promotional groups*

Sometimes called attitude, cause or campaign groups, these are set up to promote common ideas, values or activities. They do not protect sectional interests. Uncontroversial promotional groups simply bring together people who share similar tastes, hobbies or recreations. Such bodies are almost entirely associational, and only occasionally are they drawn into political activity. More significant are groups with contentious goals, formed specifically to influence government and public opinion. Examples include pro- and anti-abortion groups, organisations combating pornography or defending civil liberties. Contentious promotional groups tend to be single-purpose organisations, but some such as Common Cause and the Moral Majority in the United States promote their conception of the public interest on a wide range of issues.

Such groups are not primarily concerned with their members' personal welfare or material interests. They may, however, promote causes that directly affect their members. Environmentalists, for instance, believe that their policies will improve the quality of life for everybody. They are seeking collective, rather than selective, benefits.

Compared with protective organisations which often have 'insider' status, promotional groups have less easy access to government, and typically employ publicity and persuasion as their main tactic. Promotional groups are most significant in liberal democracies, with their participatory cultures and secure civil liberties. In fact, they are a more fashionable form of political engagement than joining political parties, especially among the young.

☐ Geographic groups and social movements

Some groups do not really fit any of the categories so far discussed. Geographic groups, for instance, are established to protect the interests of people living in a distinct location. Often, though not always, they are formed along negative lines. Thus, they are sometimes known as NIMBY groups (standing for 'Not In My Back Yard'). The Channel Tunnel between Britain and France produced NIMBY groups on the British side. Homeowners in the prosperous south-east of England opposed the construction of new transport links.

But geographic groups are not always negative. They are sometimes concerned with attracting investment to their area. In Northern France, the prospect of new investment and jobs generated by the Channel Tunnel was greeted eagerly in an economically declining region. In New Zealand in the mid-1970s, the population of Dunedin lobbied fiercely to persuade the national government to give the city one of the two proposed new container-port developments. The movement cut across social and political lines (Wood 1988).

Broad social movements also sit uneasily in our classification of groups. Social movements are broader, and less organised, than interest groups. They seek, and emerge from, changes in attitude and awareness across large segments of the public. The women's movement, for example, representing a broad range of feminist opinion, has become a significant political force in many first world societies. Social movements are promotional in character but they are not in themselves interest groups. Only when women's organisations are created to lobby for political change (e.g. NOW, the National Organisation for Women, in the United States) does the women's movement become an interest group.

Similarly, the ecology or 'green' movement now has a significant impact on politics throughout the first world. Many organised groups exist to focus concerns about the environment, for example Greenpeace. However, paid-up membership does not fully reflect the much broader extent of public concern about environmental issues. Too strict a concern with interest *groups*, narrowly defined, ignores the considerable impact on public policy made by social movements rather than by organised groups.

■ Channels of access

How are interests communicated to political decision-makers? What are the channels through which this process takes place? Figure 9.2 sets out three principal channels of influence. These are

1. Direct dealings with government;
2. Indirect influence through political parties;
3. Indirect influence through public opinion.

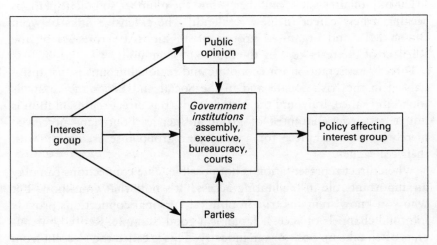

Figure 9.2   *Channels of interest group influence*

The nature of the group makes a difference to the channels employed. Protective groups normally concentrate on government institutions generally and the bureaucracy in particular. Promotional groups, on the other hand, are more likely to focus their attention on public opinion.

□ *Direct dealings with government*

This can itself take various forms. Here, we shall examine personal petition, direct representation in the government itself, élite connections, contact with the assembly, the bureaucracy and the courts.

Personal petition to the ruler was perhaps the only possibility for ordinary people with grievances in traditional political systems. In Saudi Arabia, one of a handful of traditional monarchies which remain, the king still dispenses personal justice to petitioners. Individual expression of complaints to bureaucrats and elected representatives remains important in all political systems, as the example of Sid Holland and the missing plumber shows. For organised groups, however, other modes of access are more important.

Representation in the political élite itself can be the most effective form of access. Until 1991, for instance, the Soviet Politburo contained the Minister of Defence and the Head of the KGB, conferring institutional recognition at the highest level upon the Soviet military and police. (This guaranteed favourable budgets but not, it transpired, their loyalty.) During the 1950s in the United States, President Eisenhower's Cabinet was full of business tycoons. His Cabinet was described as 'eight millionaires and a plumber' – and the plumber soon left (perhaps seeking a new career in New Zealand!) The extensive links between British MPs and organised groups of all kinds are revealed by the Register of Interests kept by the House of Commons.

Direct representation for economic and regional groups is institutionalised in the Irish Senate and in the Social and Economic Councils found in France, Italy and the Netherlands. But direct representation is not a cast-iron guarantee of group influence. Politicians perceived merely as a mouthpiece for a particular group lose credibility with their colleagues.

When direct representation is not possible, **élite connections** can play an important role in facilitating access. 'It's not what you know, but who you know' remains true in politics. Personal connections provide informal channels of access. Japan is a good example. Retired bureaucrats often take up positions in industry. This is called the 'descent from heaven'. As a result, the 'old boy network' is more important in Japan than in Britain. Similarly, in France, the *pantouflards* are civil servants who have moved across to work as representatives for business (*Pantouflard* means 'slipper-wearer' – someone who feels at home dealing with their former colleagues.) Obviously, unofficial networks of this kind are also highly selective. Only a few people can have personal access to top decision-makers.

Furthermore, many former government officials make their personal connections a saleable commodity. The increasing complexity of dealing with government has led to the emergence of specialist firms offering help for groups who want to deal with government. Such a practice has long been common in the United States. Michael Deaver, Chief of Staff to President Reagan, who put his connections in Congress and the White House to highly lucrative use within weeks of leaving office, was only the most notorious of many 'influence pedlars'. As politician turned consultant, Gerry Caplan (quoted in Rusk 1991), says of the Canadian government: 'Government has gotten so complex that a company, big or small, or an interest group cannot wheel their way through the intricacies without some advice.' He might have added that advice rarely comes cheap.

Most interest-group activity is channelled through the **bureaucracy** in liberal democracies. Even in Australia, where the federal system gives groups a variety of channels of influence,

> most interest groups that seek to influence public policy direct their activities towards the executive branch. The bureaucracy's significance is reinforced by its policy-making and policy-implementing roles. Many routine, technical and 'less important' decisions, which are nonetheless of vital concern to interest groups, are actually made by public servants. (Matthews 1989, p. 217)

There is a clear convention of government discussion with organised opinion in most countries, usually through consultative councils or committees. Indeed, the initiative for consultation often comes from government. Group organisation is sometimes government sponsored in the first place. The European Community, for instance, gives financial assistance to interest organisations provided they are European-wide. Even in France, where the higher bureaucracy prizes its autonomy, extensive consultation takes place between groups and civil servants. On the national level alone, there exist no fewer than 500 councils, 1,200 committees and 3000 commissions, all bringing together group representatives and the bureaucracy (Ehrmann 1976, p. 197).

Assemblies are another channel through which interests and demands are voiced. How much group activity is directed at the legislature depends on the assembly's role in the political system. A comparison between the United States and Canada shows this point. The United States Congress (and especially its committees) is a vital part of the policy process. Weak party discipline and strong committees make Congress an ideal habitat for lobby operations. Interest groups exert substantial influence over individual members of Congress and committee decisions. Large financial contributions by political action committees (PACs) to election campaigns make it hard for legislators to spurn group demands. In the Canadian parliament, however, party voting prevails. Lobbyists therefore concentrate much more heavily on the executive.

If interest groups feel ignored in the policy-making process, they may still be able to challenge decisions in the **courts**. This, however, tends to be an arena of last resort. Opportunities for challenging legislation vary. In the United States, business corporations routinely subject government statutes and regulations to legal challenge. Class actions, that is legal actions on behalf of a large number of people with a similar grievance, are permitted and are fairly common. These are more difficult in Australia, where litigants must prove that they have a personal and individual interest at stake. The wider interests of society or the group are not sufficient for a court to accept litigation (Matthews 1989). But in Australia, as in all federal systems, the High Court can rule on the constitutionality of legislation. Where parliament is sovereign, as in Britain and New Zealand, recourse to the courts on these grounds is impossible. In nearly all countries, legal action is expensive and time consuming.

International integration creates new patterns of interest-group activity. Among them, are appeals to international courts. For example, if an interest group in an EC country is unsuccessful at home, it can try to challenge rulings of the national government and courts in the European courts. As policy increasingly emanates from the European Commission, so more interest groups are setting up shop in Brussels, seeking to influence the administrators in the EC as well as seeking redress in European courts.

☐ *Indirect influence through parties*

Relationships between parties and interest groups are often extremely close. Some political parties are indeed the offshoot of interest groups. For example, the British and Australian Labour Parties are essentially creations of the trade union movement, though these historic ties are now weakening. Interest groups can blur into (or sometimes turn into) political parties. For example, the environmental groups have spawned green parties. In the multi-party systems of the first world, the social base of some parties is so narrow that they are little more than pressure groups aiming for a share in government to pursue highly specific objectives – for instance, the old agrarian parties in Scandinavia or the religious parties in Israel.

La Palombara (1974, pp. 333–4) uses the term *parentela* (meaning kinship) to describe relationships where parties and interest groups display a tight family-type connection in which a sharp distinction is made between insiders and outsiders. Clear examples of *parentela* relations include trade unions and parties in France and Italy. Both Catholic and communist trade unions have close relationships with their own political parties.

Looser, more pragmatic links between parties and interests are found in the United States. Business and organised labour gravitate towards the Republican and Democratic parties respectively. But these are partnerships of convenience, not indissoluble marriages. The traditional maxim of the American trade union movement has been 'to reward its friends and punish its enemies'. Business, despite its ideological affinity with the Republican Party, still contributes heavily to the election coffers of many Democratic members of Congress. Hefty donations through political action committees ensure a sympathetic hearing when a company takes a problem to a Democrat-dominated Congress.

Corporate donations to right-wing or centre-right parties are common throughout the first world. Furthermore, the ability of big business, especially transnationals, to withhold investment or transfer it abroad indirectly affects party policy, even for parties of the left.

In dominant party systems, the ruling party cannot afford to be so tightly linked to a single interest. Nonetheless the dominant party can become an umbrella under which different interests are expressed and to a degree reconciled. Examples include Mexico's PRI (Institutional Revolutionary Party) and India's Congress Party. Both parties provide loose frameworks within which more specific interests compete for the resources controlled by the party.

☐ *Indirect influence through the media*

Press, radio and television provide an additional resource available to interest groups in their efforts to voice their opinions and influence policy. By definition messages through the media are addressed to a popular audience rather than to specific decision-makers. Thus the mass media are a central focus for promotional groups, concerned to steer public opinion in a particular direction (e.g. against violence on TV).

The media are less important to protective groups, with their more specialised and sometimes secretive demands (e.g. opposing detailed nutritional labels on foods).

Because journalists serve as gatekeepers, selecting some items and excluding others in a way which certainly reflects and arguably shapes the political agenda, it is important for interest groups to provide the material that journalists want. As a general rule, employers' organisations are more adept at this than trade unions, a contrast which has led to accusations that the mass media in liberal democracies are systematically biased against workers' interests (Glasgow University Media Group, 1982, criticised in Harrison, 1985). Whatever the truth of this thesis, it is clear that interest groups seeking serious media coverage must convince journalists that they fall within the ambit of acceptable opinion.

Finally, we should note that **protest**, **direct action** and **violence** can be methods for the expression of political demands. Most commonly, this is the resort of groups which have been denied formal access to government. Until the last century in the first world, and far more recently in other societies, the masses have been excluded from political influence. Outbreaks of violence were, and may still be, the only way of expressing grievances and frustration by people who have lost hope in the future and have no trust in those who run society. Many first world countries still experience large-scale public disorder: inner-city riots remain endemic in England and the United States, for instance.

Sometimes, however, the use of coercive tactics may be carefully planned by protective groups who find legitimate methods unavailing. European farmers, especially in France and Belgium, resort to roadblocks and violent demonstrations as a means of putting pressure upon the authorities. In much of the third world, mass violence may be a widespread method of demand articulation.

■ What makes interest groups influential?

In determining the influence which interest groups can exert, individually or collectively, the key factor is the nature of the political system itself. Within the law, the expression of interests in liberal democracies is relatively unhindered, and is indeed encouraged by competition between parties. At the other pole stood communist states. There, the autonomous expression of 'unofficial' interests was tightly, if not completely, controlled.

A second factor is the degree of legitimacy achieved by a particular group. The aphorism 'What is good for General Motors is good for

America' makes an important point. Interests that enjoy high prestige and perceived importance are most likely to prevail on particular issues. Professional groups of lawyers or doctors, whose members symbolise social respectability, can be as militant on occasion, or as restrictive in their practices, as blue-collar trade unions. But lawyers and doctors escape the public hostility that trade unions attract.

Third, the effectiveness of a group relates to the sanctions it can use, and conversely depends on its usefulness to those in power. Protective groups have more impact than promotional groups because they are usually more important. With its wide-ranging responsibilities and specialised activities, modern government needs the cooperation of protective groups. It is, for example, difficult to run a system of medical care without the cooperation, indeed the commitment, of physicians and nurses. Often the government will depend on the protective group for information on how policy is working in the field – and for suggestions for improvement. By threatening a reduction in members' commitment, or just by subtle reductions in the flow of advice which the group passes on to government, pressure can be brought to bear.

A fourth determinant of influence is the resources available to an interest group. These include finance, organisation and membership. Money obviously helps. The National Rifle Association (NRA) in the United States has an annual budget of $40 million. This allows it to employ 275 full-time staff and 5 full-time lobbyists. The NRA clearly has the resources to press its opposition to gun control at every available opportunity. The coalition of gun control groups cannot match the NRA's fire power when it comes to spending. The cause of gun control depends more on winning endorsements from leading politicians, sympathetic movie stars and other public figures.

Financial capabilities are probably more important in the United States than in most other democracies. This is because more public-relations activity takes place there and legislators are subject to more (and more professional) lobbying. Even in the United States, hard-up but skilful campaigners can generate free publicity and wide public reaction. For example, Ralph Nader's Crusade for Car Safety in the 1960s stimulated wideranging product safety legislation. Since organised interests so often counteract one another, financial resources alone are unlikely to be decisive. Other political resources such as functional importance and public respectability are likely to be more vital.

The relationship between objective resources and influence is not a simple one. Size of membership, for instance, must be judged both in terms of sheer numbers and, for protective groups, in terms of coverage. What proportion of those eligible to join actually belong? Where occupations are fragmented among several organisations, influence is further weakened. For instance, American farmers are divided between three major organisations with a lower total coverage than Britain's National Farmers' Union.

Intensity of commitment is at least as important as size of membership. Commitment determines how far the members of a group will be willing to go in support of its objectives. Terrorists may be willing to kill, indeed to be killed, in pursuit of their objectives. Less extreme groups also try to increase membership commitment. Discussion groups, meetings and rallies serve to increase morale and shield members from cross-pressures, as well as propagating the group's message.

■ The first world: pluralism or corporatism?

Interest-group activity is a fundamental feature of modern liberal democracies. It creates a system of functional representation, which operates alongside electoral representation. In fact, interest groups cumulatively may have more influence upon decision-making than elections and parties. Without doubt, interest groups greatly increase the amount and quality of information available to governments. Interest groups partly redress one of the defects of democracy, because they reflect the quality or intensity of concern. If a group strongly wants or believes in something, perhaps their views should carry more weight than those of people who are not much bothered either way.

But the relationship between interest groups and democracy also poses problems. Interest groups represent sectional, and sometimes selfish interests. A small, well-organised minority may prevail over the poorly organised or indifferent majority.

The two major models of the role of interest groups in liberal democracies are pluralism and corporatism. These are best thought of as opposing ideal types.

□ Pluralism

The **pluralist** view, reflecting American experience, dominated early postwar interpretations of interest-group activity. As we showed in Chapter 1 (pp. 14–16), pluralism sees freely organised interest groups as intermediaries in a two-way flow of communication between rulers and ruled.

The pluralist model views government, in effect, as an arena for a freewheeling interplay of interests. Industrialists, trade unionists, teachers, ecology groups – all can have their say before the court of

Exhibit 9.1 *Do interest groups strangle nations?*

Students of politics have always differed in their evaluation of interest groups. Pluralists regard them as essential transmission-belts between people and government, complementing the role of political parties. Others are more suspicious, claiming that interest groups bend public policy towards their own narrow concerns. In the 1980s the American political economist Mancur Olson (1982) provided an influential version of this latter interpretation.

Olson argued that patterns of interest group activity are a major determinant in the rise and fall of nations. Fast economic growth is more likely where interests are weakly organised: contrast Hong Kong with Britain, South Korea with Australia or the State of Florida with New York State. Strong networks of interest groups will emerge over time, however, unless society is shaken by major disruptions (e.g. total defeat in war). These networks eventually cause political sclerosis and slower economic growth. They are, according to Olson, distributional coalitions of narrow, sectional interests: trade unions, business organisations, professional associations. The fundamental problem is that broader groups – consumers, say, or the unemployed – are less well-organised. Just by virtue of their size they have fewer incentives to offer to individual members. Hence needed change is blocked and nations decline.

It was a controversial argument, cogently argued. It also proved to be a a major influence on the political agenda of the 1980s. In many liberal democracies, governments sought to reduce the power of sectional interests to block change. The object was to ensure that markets became genuinely competitive, thus forcing firms to put their own house in order. Although Mrs. Thatcher's Conservative government in Britain became the leading symbol of such policies, similar changes were considered, and often implemented, in many other countries. By the 1990s Olson's thesis had received widespread acceptance, if not among all political scientists, then at least among many politicians.

government. Because many people belong to more than one interest, the temperature of inter-group conflict does not rise too high. Interest-group activity provides a more precise and helpful means of transmitting preferences to government than parties.

Pluralist interpretations of liberal democracies thus depicted a healthy process of fragmented, dispersed decision-making in which few groups and decision-makers were significant in more than one area. However, pluralism lost ground to corporatism in the 1970s as a model of the relationship between interest groups and the state in liberal democracies.

□ *Corporatism*

Where pluralism implies competition between groups, corporatism emphasises coordinated relations between groups and the state. In the corporatist model, drawing mainly on postwar European experience, public policy results from negotiation between the government and a few powerful interest groups with which the government chooses to, or has to, deal. These groups normally include 'peak' associations representing industry and the trade unions. Though formally accountable to their members, the leaders of these groups have considerable freedom of action in their contacts with governments. The leaders' main role is to carry their members with them after deals have been struck with other power-brokers. This is more important than presenting their members' views before decisions are reached. So corporatist groups are also important in implementing policy: they can secure considerable compliance from their members who may have little choice but to belong (e.g. workers having to join a union closed-shop).

Negotiations between these interest groups and the government take an administrative, technical form; policy-making is depoliticised. The significance of electoral representation is also reduced. However, dealings between the groups and the government are on a fairly equal basis. They are neither state-dominated (fascism) nor group-dominated (pluralism). The government remains an important independent force in policy-making.

So in contrast to pluralism, which emphasises an upward flow of preferences from group members to their leaders and then on to government, corporatism stresses the downward flow of influence. Also, whereas pluralism is in a sense the absence of planning, corporatism is an attempt by the state and dominant interests to develop a coordinated approach. The state controls its citizens and the groups control their members.

The Scandinavian nations, Austria (see Exhibit 9.2), Netherlands (and sometimes Belgium) have been described as corporate states. In these countries, there is a tradition of compromise and consultation between government and interest groups. As such, some commentators have referred to Scandinavia as a region of consensual democracies (Elder *et al.* 1982). It remains an open question whether they are corporatist states

| Exhibit 9.2 *Austria: a corporatist waltz?* |

Austria is undoubtedly the best example of corporatism (Fitzmaurice 1991). Many economic and social decisions in Austria are reached through a system known as 'Economic and Social Partnership'. This brings together all the major economic interests into an elaborate network of organisations which is in turn connected with the government, the parties and the bureaucracy.

At the top of this partnership stands the Party Commission. This is an entirely informal organisation (no offices, no rules) which nonetheless makes decisions affecting the whole working population. It determines price increases, decides on the timing of collective bargaining, ratifies wage increases and is an important forum for discussion of overall economic policy. Final decision-making in the Commission often ends up as a face-to-face talk between just two people. One is the President of the Chamber of Commerce, representing capital, and the other is the President of the Trade Union Federation, representing labour.

Despite cynicism about the inevitable horsetrading and some public disaffection, Austria's corporatist partnership has worked. In the 1970s and 1980s economic growth was higher, and inflation, unemployment and strikes lower, than the average for first world countries. In many ways Austria's economic performance exceeds Germany's. So why has partnership worked so well in Austria? Its success is due to the following factors:

1. The existence in Austria of statutory chambers of commerce, labour, agriculture, etc., to which all working people must belong.
2. The extensive penetration of trade unions and business organisations in Austria. For example, the League of Austrian Industrialists represents over 85 per cent of private capital.
3. The centralised character of both statutory chambers and voluntary organisations.
4. The organisation of Austrian unions on an industrial rather than on an occupational or skill basis.
5. The desire by all sides to negotiate and compromise, having experienced bitter conflict in the inter-war period.

In sum, corporatism is most likely to take root where centralised interest groups can retain both a high density of membership and extensive controls over their members.

because of a high level of social consensus, or whether corporatist relations between groups and government has created that consensus.

As Wilson (1990) points out, corporatism is in practice a relative, and not an absolute matter. In other words, no nation is fully corporate, and corporatism exists to some extent in all societies. Some questions in corporatist states may not be discussed with interest groups – such as the Norwegian government's policy on non-membership of the EC. On the other side of the coin, non-corporatist states also display some corporatist tendencies. In particular, sectors of industry may have corporatist relations with government: this has been termed meso-corporatism (Cawson 1985).

Neither Britain nor the United States could ever have been described as corporate states. In fact, anti-corporatism was a clear feature of politics in Britain and the United States in the 1980s during the Thatcher and Reagan leaderships. Corporatism was viewed as harmful to both economy and society, because it invited excessive state intervention and too much reliance on the state. Many of the formal structures that brought groups into contact with government were either abolished or marginalised. The tentative corporatism of British economic policy-making in the 1970s was abruptly ditched, as the Thatcher government undeviatingly pursued free-market ideology. Government contacts with industry continued, but with individual companies or sectoral organisations, rather than with peak organisations. The trade unions were virtually excluded from consultation.

Some large democracies show a pattern of semi-corporatism. France perhaps, and Japan certainly, are examples of this halfway house. The French state has always worked closely with big business, and in effect chooses which groups to recognise and confer with. Even under socialist governments, however, trade union influence upon public policy has been limited. In Japan, the partnership between government and business groups is closer still, though the trade unions have scarcely any role at all in policy-making, except as a subordinate partner of business.

Some political scientists argued in the 1970s that there was a long-term trend towards corporatist policy-making in (economically success-ful?) liberal democracies. From the perspective of the early 1990s, the appeal and successes of corporatism are less obvious. Economic recessions strained centralised wage-bargaining in several European countries, as highly skilled workers in expanding industries pushed for what they could get. A core weakness of corporatism is its lack of legitimacy; in many democracies (though not Austria or much of Scandinavia) corporatism runs up against deeply ingrained individualism. Finally, the election of free-market governments in the United

Kingdom, France, Norway, Germany and New Zealand has greatly weakened the notion that corporatist trends were irresistible.

The second world: from channelled to active groups?

In theory, the concept of interest groups and interest articulation was alien to ruling communist parties. The only interests to be taken into consideration in decision-making were those of the proletariat. As the party itself embodied the interests of the proletariat, other interests should be subordinated to those of the majority, as determined by the party. But as we will see, things were more complex, especially in the later periods of communist rule.

□ *Groups under communist rule*

The interpretation of interest articulation in communist party states underwent considerable change as these regimes evolved. Communist party states were initially viewed as totalitarian regimes. This means they were seen as extreme forms of ideological dictatorship, in which the regime sought to control all aspects of life. Interest articulation by freely organised groups was inconceivable under totalitarianism. The communists reconstructed all group life, destroying opposition and harnessing all organisations as 'transmission belts' for party policy. Trade unions, the media, youth groups, professional associations – all served the party in the great cause of communist construction. Thus totalitarianism and pluralism were regarded as opposed concepts.

This totalitarian interpretation gradually became less relevant. On the one hand, the use of coercion and terror declined. Conflict over policy, on the other hand, did not. Observers increasingly accepted that the struggle over power and policy was as endless in communist systems as in any other. They also recognised that this struggle involved inputs from below and was not always resolved by ruthless imposition from above.

Both Western observers and some communist theoreticians then applied some aspects of pluralism to communist societies (Skilling 1986, Hough 1983). Particularly in Poland, Hungary and Yugoslavia, and in a more limited way in the Soviet Union, writers acknowledged that distinct interests could be expressed under communist rule. Indeed they accepted that conflicts between interests could occur. However, they denied that such interests were in conflict with the party. The party's role was to arbitrate such conflicts.

But a fundamental point of contrast with liberal democracies remained. Ruling communist parties tried to restrict interest articulation to specialised, usually technical matters. Raising and resolving such issues contributed to the smooth running of the system. But communist parties continued to crack down vigorously on dissent which went beyond these confines. Thus 'socialist' pluralism was more limited than Western pluralism.

For decades, communist regimes sought to prevent interest groups from operating beyond these limits. Their efforts involved both coercion and co-option. The secret police infiltrated organisations, watching for signs of deviance. Activists were persecuted and imprisoned, and their families victimised. A more subtle approach was to divide and rule. During the 1978–79 Democracy Wall Movement in China, students and young intellectuals were not supported by older people. Those with secure jobs within the system did not want to run risks by getting caught up in calls for more intellectual freedom.

Communist parties also tried to channel interest articulation into safe areas. They set up organisations representing various social groups. These included a women's federation, trade unions, and federations of writers and artists. These bodies never enjoyed true independence from the party, and served as channels for relaying information downwards rather than for expressing group demands upwards.

□ *The emergence of active groups*

Despite the regimes' best efforts, independent groups did eventually emerge. In fact, they played an important role in challenging communist authority in Eastern Europe. Charter '77, an organisation calling for human rights in Czechoslovakia, was the forerunner of Civic Forum, which eventually replaced the communists in power. The role of New Forum in East Germany was fundamental in mobilising the popular mood against communist leadership. Similarly, the Hungarian Democratic Forum actively challenged the legitimacy of the communist hold on power. Above all, in Poland, the independent trade union organisation Solidarity (supported by the Roman Catholic Church) emerged in 1980 to assert the interests of Polish workers. Nine years later, Solidarity took over the reins of government from the communists.

Environmental groups also played a significant role in the fall of East European communism, especially in Bulgaria. Criticism by Ecoglasnost over the wanton destruction of natural resources and the appalling pollution in industrial centres became a focus for the anti-government movement in Bulgaria.

Perhaps more important, though, is the speed with which organisations have formed around nationalist, ethnic and religious bonds. These communal groups may yet prove to be the most potent force for instability in Eastern Europe. Nationalist forces brought about the disintegration of Yugoslavia and the Soviet Union. The continued health of the Czechoslovak Republic is also threatened by deep tensions between Czechs and Slovaks.

With the collapse of communist power, the expression of interests exploded, and with it the demands upon government. But political parties formed around coherent ideologies or durable coalitions of interests are still embryonic. Yet economic revival demands urgent decisions on the transition to a market economy. Under such conditions, small but well-positioned groups can have a big impact. The balance of power in Hungary, for instance, is affected by the Small Landowners Party, which opposes rapid privatisation.

This example brings into focus an important aspect of interest groups in the postcommunist second world. These groups do not fit easily into our initial definition of interest groups as organisations which seek to influence, but not to become part of, the state. In fact, postcommunist interest groups are often indistinguishable from political parties. With the nature of postcommunist politics still clarifying, there can be no 'normal' channels for interest articulation as there are no 'normal' channels for anything. With everything up for grabs, the best way of influencing policy is to form a party and seek election.

■ Groups in the third world

So far we have used the contrasting models of pluralism and corporatism to interpret developments in the study of interest articulation in the first and second worlds. This approach has some utility for the third world as well, though here the main theme is developmental. In traditional societies little interest articulation occurs. This is basically because the mass of the population falls outside the formal political process.

However, almost all societies in the third world are now transitional. Traditional ways of life are giving way to rapid urbanisation, industrialisation, cash-crop agriculture, monetary exchanges, formal education and growing penetration by the mass media. As these changes proceed, so the pattern of interest organisation alters. For instance, peasant leagues and trade unions appear, reflecting emerging political cleavages. The conditions for the organised articulation of interests are laid down.

But pluralist representation is hampered by weaknesses of organisation, finance and limited membership. Strong ethnic and tribal loyalties also inhibit the growth of formal groups. Furthermore, landowners and business operators rarely rejoice when peasants and workers begin to organise. They are far more likely to plan reprisals against 'trouble-makers', and press the government to suppress 'revolutionary' activity.

Where representative traditions are weak and civil liberties insecure, groups may not be accepted by the government as legitimate actors in the political system. Many countries, particularly those following the Roman Law tradition (e.g. in Latin America), require groups to have legal recognition. This can be used to restrict their operations.

A basic fact of third world life is that there are insufficient resources to satisfy even the most urgent priorities. Faced with woefully inadequate resources and the uncertain outcomes of pluralism, rulers are likely to veer between two strategies. On the one hand, they are tempted to repress organised group activity altogether. On the other hand, they may adopt a corporate strategy. That is, they may allow interest organisation but try to control it. By enlisting the population, particularly its more modern sectors, into officially sponsored associations, rulers hope to accelerate the push towards modernisation. Both strategies, repression and controlled representation, involve risks.

Mexico is a case in point. The ruling party (the PRI) is itself a coalition made up of the labour, agrarian and 'popular' sectors. Trade unions and peasant associations have access to the leadership of the PRI through these sectors, but in return they are expected to exercise control over their membership. With hardship and discontent endemic, workers and peasants regularly break away from their associations. These break-away movements then face continual harassment from the combined forces of the state, employers and officially favoured unions. Business is not part of the 'revolutionary family' of the PRI, but almost all large firms are organised into the chambers of commerce and industry, which have a close relationship with the government. Mexico thus exhibits both corporate techniques of policy-making and the pluralistic tensions these techniques fail to resolve.

Corporatist efforts by authoritarian modernisers can seriously back-fire. Drawing students, industrial workers, market traders and the like into front organisations can just aggravate discontent as it becomes clear that consultation with government has little impact upon the price of food or the availability of goods and jobs. Bianchi (1986) thus argues that the aversion of third world rulers to freewheeling pluralism leads them into the greater folly of 'unruly corporatism'. In a number of cases this has destabilised the regime concerned. For example, such problems fomented the discontent which led to the assassinations of Presidents Sadat in Egypt and Park in South Korea. Similar difficulties contributed to the overthrow of the Shah in Iran. The strains of modernisation in the third world mean that the underlying impetus towards interest organisation grows stronger. However, modernisation presents insecure rulers with no easy choices about how to incorporate these groups into the political process.

Summary

1.   Interest groups are organised bodies seeking to influence public policy, without trying to take over government itself. In liberal democracies, interest-group activity amounts to a system of functional, alongside electoral, representation.

2.   Interest groups of different kinds can be located along a communal–associational spectrum. A basic distinction is between protective groups and promotional groups. Protective groups defend members' interests while promotional groups express members' values.

3.   The channels of access used by interest groups include direct dealings with government, particularly through the bureaucracy. Indirect pressure can also be applied through political parties and the media.

4.   The influence of a group depends on several factors including its size and share of membership; the sanctions it can bring to bear; its prestige; and its financial resources.

5.   Analysis of interest groups in the first world has been dominated by the ideas of pluralism and corporatism. Pluralism sees a freewheeling display of groups competing for the ear of government. Corporatism stresses joint agreement between governments and a few privileged groups. These groups then sell the deal to their members.

6.   The pluralist model, deriving chiefly from American experience, lost out in the 1970s to corporatist interpretations, based on the more economically successful European nations. In the 1980s opinion shifted again towards free-market thinking in economic policy. This favoured reducing the scale of government intervention in order to 'free up' the market.

7.   In the second world under communism, all group organisation was tightly controlled by the ruling communist party. With the collapse of communism, the potential for interest articulation has exploded, but many organisations remain

embryonic. They still straddle the boundary between interest groups and political parties.

8.   Interest articulation in the third world remains dominated by communal groups. Governments often try to create corporatist arrangements, but because of scarcity and mismanagement, these can be as unstable as a pluralist pattern.

Discussion points

1.   Do interest groups have too much leverage on politics in your country?

2.   Are protective interest groups in decline, and promotional groups on the rise, in the first world? If so, why?

3.   Why should corporatist arrangements work better in some countries than in others?

4.   Should interest groups be allowed to finance political parties and election candidates?

5.   Is the power of organised groups over the economy increasing or declining in most liberal democracies? If so, why?

6.   Will ethnic and national groups be more important than economic groups in postcommunist systems?

7.   Why are formally organised interest groups unimportant in much of the third world?

Key reading

Wilson, G. (1990) *Interest Groups* (Oxford: Blackwell). A good recent treatment, dealing with liberal democracies.

Ball, A. and Millward, F. (1986) *Pressure Politics in Industrial Societies* (London: Macmillan). Covers both first and second worlds.

Cigler, C. and Loomis, B. (eds) (1985) *Interest Group Politics* (Washington, D.C.: Congressional Quarterly Press). Examines the interest group anthill in the United States.

Olson, M. (1982) *The Rise and Decline of Nations* (New Haven: Yale University Press). The most trenchant and controversial interpretation of interest-group activity in recent years.

Further reading

The classic statement of the group approach to politics is Truman (1951). For a useful survey of group theory, see Garson (1978). Wilson (1990) is a clear, concise text by a specialist on interest groups. He has also written a comparative study (1985) of business and politics.

Among the surveys of interest organisations in different countries, S. Finer (1966) remains outstanding for Britain. Richardson and Jordan (1979) reflects the shift of concern away from organisation towards the impact of groups on policy, while Rush (1990) concentrates on their parliamentary activities. Complementing Cigler and Loomis (1985), Berry (1985) is a very readable treatment of interest-group activity in American politics.

For interest articulation in the Soviet Union see Skilling and Griffiths (1973) and Skilling (1986). On concepts of corporatism, Williamson (1985) is a helpful guide; see also Schmitter and Lehmbruch (1979). For the application of corporatist ideas to particular countries and industries, see Cawson (1986) and Grant (1985).

■ *Chapter 10* ■

Political Parties

The crucial difference between the political party and other kinds of organised group lies in its relationship to the political system as a whole. Whereas the aim of interest groups is to influence the state, the political party seeks to occupy the decisive positions of authority within it. Thus the defining characteristics of a political party are:

1. A conscious aim (realistic or not) to capture decision-making power, alone or in coalition
2. The pursuit of popular support through elections
3. A permanent organisation.

Parties are creations of the modern age. They are a response to the extension of the suffrage and the need imposed on parliamentary cliques to develop extra-parliamentary organisation. 'Party', as Katz (1986) put it, 'is a strategy for cultivating public support.'

The first generation of parties were 'internally created'. This means they were formed by cliques within an assembly joining together to defend common objectives. The Conservative parties of Scandinavia and Britain are examples. These parties represented traditional élites such as the court and the aristocracy. Originally organised on a loose and informal basis, they had to reach out to a larger electorate if they were to survive the transition to universal suffrage. They succeeded – and none more triumphantly than Britain's Conservative Party, which governed Britain (alone or in coalition) for sixty years between 1900 and 1990.

Most subsequent parties were 'externally created'. They were based on demands for legislative representation by excluded, or at least unrepresented, groups. The working-class socialist parties which spread across Europe at the turn of the twentieth century are the main examples here. But these are not the only illustrations. Later in the century, communist parties and nationalist parties emerged in the second and third worlds. They demanded not merely reform but also a complete transformation of society. More recently, green parties have emerged in the first world from a growing concern with the environment, particularly among the young and well-educated.

■ The functions of parties

What is it that parties do, as opposed to what they are? What roles do parties play in the political systems of which they form part?

1. Perhaps most important, the political party provides a link between rulers and ruled. The party is a **channel of expression**, both upward and downward, which is crucial to the political management of complex societies. In competitive party systems the upward flow of communication from the ruled to the rulers is relatively strong. Even in such systems, however, the party also functions as a vehicle for informing, educating and influencing public opinion. Where there is a single ruling party, the flow of political communication is mainly downwards. In an extreme instance, such as Stalin's Russia in the 1930s, the 'democratic' expression of opinion from the grass roots of the Communist Party was negligible compared with the 'centralist' flow of directives from the top.

2. Parties also serve as important agents of **interest aggregation**. This means they transform a multitude of specific demands into more manageable packages of proposals. Where interest groups articulate interests, political parties select, reduce and combine them. They are political department stores, deciding which interests should be displayed, which should be left in the storeroom – and which should not be purchased at all. Indeed, in communist party states, many 'demands' were repressed altogether.

3. When in government, party leaders are centrally involved in **implementing collective goals** for society. Parties have been the prime movers in the revolutionary upheavals of the modern age. In the second world, the enormous transformations of Russian and Chinese society in the twentieth century were led by 'vanguard' communist parties committed to radical social change. In the third world, nationalist parties played a critical role in winning independence and in the subsequent attempt to weld new nations out of traditional societies. In the first world, parties contributed to the creation of welfare states in the third quarter of the century – and to the shift towards more competitive economies in the final quarter. In short, parties give

direction to government. A government without a party to energise it runs the risk of becoming totally becalmed.

4. Parties also function as agents of **élite recruitment and socialisation**. They serve as a major mechanism through which candidates for public office are prepared and selected at all levels, and in particular by which national political leadership is chosen. The party is an essential stepping stone on the long journey to high office. If you want to lead your country, you must first persuade a party to adopt you as its candidate. In an era of party voting, this is often much more difficult than persuading the electorate to vote for you. Thus political parties, in all three worlds, act as gatekeepers, controlling the flow of personnel into government just as they control the flow of ideas.

5. Political parties are often the objects of **powerful emotional attachment** or antagonism, exerting an important influence upon the opinions and behaviour of their supporters. In a complicated world, they act as points of reference for their followers. This was most obviously true of ruling communist parties, which made considerable demands of their members. But many electors in liberal democracies habitually vote for 'their' party, regardless of the issues or the candidates; psychologically speaking, they can do no other. As Wallas (1948, 1st pub. 1908) shrewdly observed long ago, party becomes 'an entity with an existence in the memory or the emotions of the electorate, independent of their opinion and actions'.

■ Parties in the first world

Party competition is the hallmark of liberal democracy. It is the device which makes governments responsive to electorates, providing voters with some choice while also restricting that choice to a few broad alternatives. This section examines the internal organisation of parties and patterns of competition between them.

□ *Party organisation*

Although parties are sometimes treated as unitary actors in political theories (Downs 1957), this is a massive simplification. The internal life of parties is a vital subject, acquiring special importance in those democracies such as Italy where one party has proved to be a constant element in government. Important features of party organisation are:

1. The relationship between the parliamentary party and the party organisation
2. Candidate recruitment
3. Factions.

1.   The relationship between the parliamentary party and the party outside parliament depends on the party's origin. Parties with parliamentary origins give more weight to their legislative representatives than externally created parties, particularly those on the left. However McKenzie (1955) concluded from a study of British parties that parliamentary government forces a concentration of party power in the hands of parliamentarians, whatever the formal party rules. Daalder (1987 p. 236) makes a similar point about Dutch parties: 'the parliamentary groups are in all parties autonomous organisations, on which the extra-parliamentary party can exercise no direct control. Parliamentary parties choose their own leaders and determine their own political stand'.

A contrasting account is offered by von Beyme (1985, ch.6). He suggests that party organisations are still gaining ground relative to the parliamentary party in virtually all Western democracies. Von Beyme bases his case on the provision of state financial aid to the party bureaucracy, on the inability of the parliamentary party to cope with organisational tasks such as recruiting members and fighting elections, on the strengthening of democratic norms within parties and on the emergence of professional politicians dependent on their political career (and hence their party) for their salaries.

Duverger (1964, 1st pub. 1951) was the first author to formulate a theory of party organisation. He regarded the 'basic unit' of organisation as the key to a party's character. This yielded the classification shown in Table 10.1.

The value of this classification has declined as parties have become organisationally less distinctive. It never really fitted the United States, with its originally spoils-based party organisations. Caucus parties have developed extra-parliamentary structures; branch parties have at least until very recently lost membership; and neither the French nor the Italian Communist Parties now fits the tight structure of the cell model. We would argue that other characteristics, especially the source of a party's finance and its procedures for nominating election candidates are more significant features of party organisation. Candidate selection in particular merits closer scrutiny.

2.   Given the central role of parties in political recruitment, candidate selection is a crucial aspect of party organisation. As Schattschneider

Table 10.1   *Duverger's classification of political parties*

Basic unit	Characteristics	Examples
Caucus party	Loose association of notables able to call upon localised personal followings. Weak organisation; membership by tacit co-option. Largely sustained by the desire for office.	Conservative and Liberal parties created within the legislatures of nineteenth-century Europe; France's Radical Party in the Third and Fourth Republics.
Branch party	Large-scale recruitment and socialisation of individual members a key objective. Extensive territorial network of branches. Relatively centralised, with professional leadership and strong party discipline in the legislature.	The externally created socialist parties of pre-1914 Europe.
Cell party	Members organised into small cells, based on the workplace, with an emphasis on vertical communication from leaders to members. Little horizontal communication between cells; internal factions banned. Members expected to be active. Highly centralised; legislative representatives closely supervised.	Communist parties.
Militia party	A development from the cell structure to the use of the party as, in effect, a privately controlled fighting force, reproducing the disciplined character and structure of a professional army.	Nazi Party's Storm Troopers (though the Nazi party was also a branch party); some paramilitary organisations in Northern Ireland.

Source: M. Duverger, *Political Parties* (London: Methuen, 1964), pp. 17–40.

(1942) put it, 'The nominating process has become the crucial process of the party. He who can make the nominations is the owner of the party.' One dimension here is the degree of control exercised by the central party. The most common pattern is for selection by constituency parties under supervision of the national party (e.g. the major parties in Britain, Denmark and New Zealand). The next most frequent format is national selection after consideration of suggestions from lower levels (e.g. the major parties in Japan and the Netherlands). Nomination, then, is certainly not the preserve of the party élite at the centre. Indeed in the Netherlands, as in many countries using proportional representation, candidate selection is a complex affair, based on a tug of war between national, regional and sometimes local considerations.

A second dimension of candidate recruitment is the degree to which ordinary party members can participate in the selection process. The predominant pattern here is for candidates to be selected by committees elected from the membership, rather than by members directly. However Britain's short-lived SDP (Social Democratic Party) did have a direct vote of party members (Ranney 1981) and the leading Belgian parties still do.

The United States operates the unique institution of the primary election, which in most states is open to any electors willing to declare themselves supporters of a particular party. In a primary system candidates impose themselves on parties more than they are selected by parties. This takes candidate selection away from a small group of activists, a common problem elsewhere, but distributes that control in a haphazard way to the minority of electors who bother to vote in primary contests. Primaries were introduced to eliminate corrupt party bosses. But they have had the effect of weakening parties altogether. As primary elections have become more prevalent, so political campaigning has focused ever more on candidates and ever less on parties.

3. One important factor in the internal life of parties which does not appear in the organisation charts is factionalism. Although factions are often perceived as less legitimate than parties, they are an important means for restraining the oligarchic tendencies of party leaders. A faction is an organised, self-aware group which enjoys reasonable stability of membership (Hine 1982). Factional conflict can be based principally on ideology (as in Britain's Labour Party) or on spoils (as with the Christian Democrats in Italy and the Liberal Democrats in Japan). In the 1970s and 1980s, policy-based factional conflict increased in the Social Democratic and Labour parties of Northern Europe, producing difficult management problems for party leaders (Hine 1986).

Spoils-based factions, as in Italy and Japan are encouraged by an electoral system which forces candidates from the same party into competition with each other and by the long occupancy of government by dominant parties.

□ *Party competition*

Political scientists have given considerable attention to patterns of party competition in the liberal democratic world. Traditionally a distinction was drawn between two-party and multi-party systems. Two-party systems, it was argued, showed regular alternation in office between two major parties, had an adversarial political style which yielded sharp oscillations in public policy, produced clear accountability of governments to the electorate and were found in 'first past the post' electoral systems. Britain was always regarded as the major example though New Zealand, which lacks third parties of the weight of Britain's Liberal Democrats, is a purer case.

In continental Europe, by contrast, the multi-party pattern predominates. This is characterised by proportional representation, coalition government and weak lines of accountability from rulers to the ruled. Belgium and Holland are regarded as typical examples. Many discussions of this distinction implicitly equated two-party systems with political stability and multi-party systems with instability.

But it is now clear that the distinction between two-party and multi-party systems is an inadequate guide to patterns of party competition in the first world. The number of parties indicates the **fragmentation** of a party system, but **polarisation** is at least as important. This indicates the number of, and distance between, different 'poles' such as left and right, religious and secular, pro-system and anti-system. Polarisation indicates the intensity of ideological differences between parties and influences the choice of coalition partners (Sartori 1976).

Following von Beyme (1985), we can distinguish four main patterns of party competition in the first world. The first of these is where one party is a constant element in government, either alone or in coalition with some other parties, and can only be displaced (if at all) by an unlikely coalition of virtually all the other parties in parliament. Japan is often referred to as being a one-and-a-half party state. Not since the late 1940s has the Japanese Socialist Party been able to seriously threaten the Liberal Democratic Party's hold on power. This has led to the intermeshing of state and party which characterises such systems. Such parties use state patronage to reinforce their strength, a phenomenon which can also be observed with the Christian Democrats in Italy. Until its defeat in 1977 the Israeli Mapai (now Labour Party) also occupied a dominant position in its party system. Factionalism is common in such electorally strong parties. Factions contribute to a broad ideological range and provide a mechanism for distributing spoils.

The second category is the two-party system. Now more of an ideal-type than a concrete reality, the nearest instances to two-party systems are to be found in countries with 'first past the post' electoral systems such as Britain, Canada, New Zealand and the United States. In terms of votes, if not seats, the first three of these countries are really 'two and a half' party systems. Britain's Liberal–SDP Alliance, Canada's left-wing New Democratic Party (NDP) and to a lesser extent New Zealand's Social Credit all approached or surpassed 20 per cent of the vote in elections during the 1980s. In the United States, too, independent candidates have had an impact on several presidential contests this century. However, coalitions are unusual in two-party systems.

In multi-party systems a distinction can be drawn between moderate and polarised systems, which gives us our third and fourth patterns of party competition. Moderate multi-party systems are governed by coalitions made up of parties of similar ideological persuasion. Hence they are said to be centripetal – strengthening the centre. Coalitions come and go but continuity of policy is maintained. Anti-system parties receive little support. Parties may represent distinct religious or linguistic groups but the ground rules of politics are well accepted by party leaders. Moderate multi-party systems are found throughout Scandinavia.

In polarised multi-party systems, by contrast, ideological differences between the parties are so wide and deep that they severely limit the number of feasible coalitions. Some parties, typically the communists, are excluded from government altogether, a factor which reflects the existence of, and strengthens, anti-system parties. Thus polarised systems are said to be centrifugal, tending to denude the centre.

Italy was long regarded as the major instance of 'polarised pluralism', with the communists gaining in electoral strength despite their exclusion from office. But the communists are now more integrated into the Italian system (and have briefly joined coalitions in Finland and Iceland), leading some authors to question whether the concept of a polarised party system is still useful.

■ Parties in the second world

The collapse of communist control in Eastern Europe took almost everybody by surprise. Not only foreign journalists and governments, but also the people of Eastern Europe were amazed by the speed with which ruling communist parties lost their grip on power. Political scientists, too, were caught out. In the second edition of this book published in 1987, we confidently asserted that 'In communist states, we see no convincing evidence of the party's decline' – how wrong Hague and Harrop were!

This section analyses the methods employed by ruling communist parties to extend control over all areas of society. It also offers explanations for the decline of communist party rule, and discusses the problems facing political parties in Eastern Europe today.

□ *Ruling communist parties*

In communist party states, it goes without saying that the key political institution was the communist party itself. The strength and impact of the party provided the basic point of contrast between communist states and liberal democracies. Through its control of the state sector and mass organisations, and also due to the wider definition of what is political in communist party states, the party extended its influence and outreach to an extent unknown in the first world. Virtually no sector or area of society was free from the influence of the communist party. From party domination of national-level politics down to classroom committees and young communist cells in schools, the hand of the party was everywhere to be seen.

In most communist party states (though not in the Soviet Union), other parties did and do exist. However, only parties that supported the leading role of the communist parties were allowed to continue functioning – and even then they were usually prevented from organising at grass-roots levels. They were little more than a sop to intellectual and other significant groups that the communists wanted to co-opt into the system. They never held anything other than a symbolic role in government.

The party justified its monopoly on political power by referring to its vanguard role. Only the party and party members had the 'correct' insight into the needs of the people. Only the party had the necessary foundation in socialist theory to ensure that society was being moved forwards towards socialism. In reality, the communist party began to develop a dynamic of its own – maintaining the dominant role of the party became an end in itself, rather than a means to the end of achieving communism. As such, party members became a conservative force in society, working in defence of their own interests. This is one reason why the ruling parties in Eastern Europe proved fatally resistant to change and reform during the challenges to their rule in 1989.

The Chinese Communist Party is one model of how ruling communist parties are organised. In China, inner party democracy is characterised by a system of indirect elections. Under this system, committees elect higher committees. For example, the highest level of the Communist Party is the Political Bureau. The 15 or so members of this committee, which represents China's 40 million party members, are elected by the 280 or so members of the Central Committee. Members of the Central Committee are elected by the 1500 delegates to the National Party Congress. These delegates are in turn elected by party committees in China's provinces and large cities. However, nominations for elections come from above – typically the higher organ presents the lower one with a list of names which it is asked to approve.

In the 1980s some real democracy appeared in this electoral process. More candidates stood for election than there were seats available. However, the process of indirect elections within the party has served to ensure that the voice of the individual party member is diluted as it moves up the system. Furthermore, the decisions of all higher bodies are binding on lower bodies. In other words, once the top committees decide on a policy, everybody else is expected to fall into line and dissent is not countenanced. In short, democratic centralism as practised in China enforces centralism to a much greater extent than it encourages democracy.

Communist parties invariably placed great emphasis on discipline and ideological unity. One way of ensuring this unity was through strict control of recruitment to the party. Unlike Western parties, joining the communist party was a difficult task. Prospective members did not simply sign up and send off their annual subscription, but had to prove themselves worthy of membership. The usual recruitment ground was the party's youth organisations, although the armed forces also proved to be a way into the party at times. If a prospective member proved that he or she had accepted the party's ideals, and was recognised as a loyal follower, then he or she would be allowed to join the party. This was, however, subject to a period of probation.

Even after the exalted position of party member had been achieved, nobody was allowed to rest on their laurels. Party members remained under close scrutiny to ensure that they did not step out of line. Furthermore, party members were periodically requested to renew their membership – typically after a power struggle within the party. Those who came out too strongly in support of the losing line (and had not confessed to their sins through ritual self-criticism) faced the prospect of rejection by the party.

However, it was well worth going through all the trauma of being accepted into the 'gang'. Party membership brought both psychic and

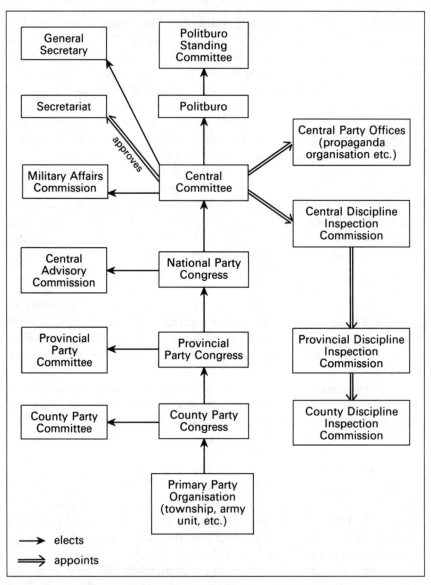

Figure 10.1   *Organisation of the Chinese Communist Party*

material benefits. As well as the feeling that you were part of the in-group – part of the vanguard – party membership brought other more tangible gains. Access to scarce goods and services, including foreign travel, were all enhanced by party membership. Furthermore, under the *nomenklatura* system, the party vetted appointments to many top jobs in society and kept a list of suitable candidates. Having 'a good class background' (being the son or daughter of a loyal party member) eased the process of joining the party. Access to higher education was also easier for those whose parents were 'politically reliable'. As a result, the benefits associated with party membership could be 'inherited', thus creating something of a self-perpetuating ruling class in communist party states.

The level of party membership in communist party states varied greatly over time and also between individual nations. For example in China, roughly 4% of the population are members of the Chinese Communist Party, while in North Korea the figure is around 10%. Although this accounts for a relatively high proportion of the total population, even these figures do not reflect the extent of party control over society.

□ *Means of control*

Ruling communist parties maintained their influence over society in several ways (see Figure 10.2).

First, and most obviously, the party held a monopoly of key decision-making élites in the government. One of the functions of parties in all political systems is to give direction and leadership to government. In communist party states, the party's grip over policy decisions was maintained by the penetration of the government and bureaucracy by party members; this occurred to an extent unknown in the first world.

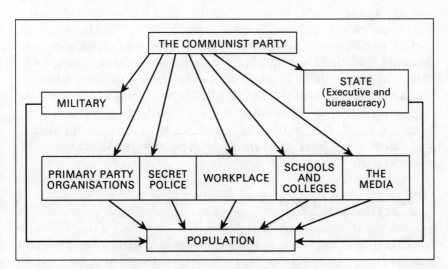

Figure 10.2 *Communist party control over society*

Secondly, the party was staffed by a secretariat of full-time officials with specialised responsibilities in all areas of society such as agriculture, heavy industry, foreign affairs, transport, and propaganda. These *apparatchiki* acted as watchdogs to ensure that party policy was followed, and if necessary as troubleshooters who stepped in to sort out problems with policy implementation.

Thirdly, the party vetted appointments to all positions of managerial and administrative responsibility in society.

Fourthly, rank and file membership was organised along functional as well as geographical lines. Thus factories, offices and farms all contained party cells. Members of these cells were required to check that party policy was indeed being executed. They also monitored the political attitudes and behaviour of their workmates, and carried out **agitprop** (agitation and propaganda) activities.

Finally, communist rule employed terror and coercion. The main instrument of repression was the secret police, such as the fearsome NKVD (later KGB) in the Soviet Union, which eliminated 'class enemies' and 'poisonous weeds' from society. A vast network of informers was recruited, some of them volunteers but many acting under duress. They reported on their families, friends, neighbours and workmates.

By all these means the ruling party effectively penetrated society at all levels, and acted to defend the interests of the ruling party élites.

Although the system was designed to ensure party dominance over society, this never implied total unity within the party. Factional conflicts were a key feature of communist party rule – most notably in China. Since the Communists took power in 1949, policy has swung radically as one or other group gained the upper hand within the party. Purges and leadership struggles have been a fact of political life in China.

In Eastern Europe, divisions within the party also arose. Challenges to the party leadership were made by communist leaders in Hungary in 1956 and Czechoslovakia in 1968. In the latter case, the reformist Alexander Dubcek used the Slovak party organisation as a power base from which to oust a Stalinist national leadership (he was soon overthrown by a Soviet-led invasion). Similarly in multinational Yugoslavia, the federal structure of the state precluded domination by a central party élite.

☐ Decline and fall

For all their multiple layers of control, communist parties failed to build genuine bases of popular support. Once they abandoned the harshest forms of Stalinist terror and repression (hoping thereby to gain goodwill), and relied mainly upon rising living standards for legitimation, they became more vulnerable. Political opposition developed slowly but steadily in several countries long before the final collapse. Solidarity sniped away at communist rule in Poland throughout the 1980s. In Czechoslovakia, Charter '77, the forerunner to Civic Forum, was active from 1977 onwards. At the end, the communist regimes **imploded**. They had become hollow, enfeebled, bereft of ideas and confidence, unable to fight for their own survival.

Where communist parties did remain in power after 1989, their positions were far weaker. In the Soviet Union, the party's condition proved fatal. Gorbachev conspicuously downgraded the Soviet Communist Party (CPSU). Millions of demoralised rank and file members quit the party. Some prominent figures, such as Boris Yeltsin, resigned and openly challenged communist rule. Yeltsin's election in May 1991 to the Presidency of the Russian Federation proved to be a turning-point. He wrested control of the Soviet Union's biggest republic from the party which had ruled it for seventy years. With the failure of the coup by communist hardliners in August 1991, the Soviet Communist Party had dug its own grave. Gorbachev and Yeltsin buried the corpse. The CPSU was dissolved, its assets and property were confiscated, its thousands of functionaries were left unemployed, and its millions of members were left to wonder what had hit them as the world they had built collapsed around them. The most powerful party on the face of the earth was blown off the face of the earth, a truly astonishing transformation. 'They say that I have come back to a different country', said Gorbachev, as he returned to Moscow after the failure of the coup, 'I agree with this'. He soon found that there was no place for him in the new world he had created.

☐ *Postcommunist parties*

The collapse of communist party rule in Eastern Europe and the Soviet Union was bound to leave a political vacuum. In a desperate attempt to hold on to power, some ruling communist parties tried to transform themselves into democratic socialist parties. Thus, the Hungarian Socialist Workers Party became the Socialist Party; the Bulgarian Communist Party did likewise. Some of these 'new' parties were the same old wine in relabelled bottles. The National Salvation Front (NSF), under President Iliescu in Romania, quickly concentrated power in the hands of ex-communists, including prominent former members of the Ceaucescu regime. As a result, many noncommunist members of the NSF resigned and joined new parties.

But the communist parties were not alone in making rapid and often uneasy transitions into new political parties. In Hungary, Czechoslovakia and Poland, broad anti-communist coalitions filled the political vacuum, but not without problems.

When the communists were in power, the opposition movement had a common enemy. Once the communists were removed, the opposition movements lost their major source of cohesion. Witness the comment of Elmer Hankiss (1990), head of Hungarian TV and Professor of Political Science at the University of Budapest:

> We have lost the devil against which we have been battling and fighting for forty years . . . this enemy has played a dirty trick on us. The enemy destroyed itself last September [1989]. We were left without an enemy, so we turned against one another.

These divisions became evident in two ways. First, umbrella organizations like Solidarity began to split into smaller components, such as the socialist left, the trade unionists and the more conservative church groupings. Secondly, small parties proliferated. By the summer of 1990, there were over 100 parties in Poland, more than 80 in Romania (including both the Romanian Social Democratic Party and the Romanian Socialist Democratic Party), and 52 in Hungary. As Hankiss has noted, this is a characteristic feature of democratic transitions. A similar explosion of small parties occurred in Spain after the long decades of authoritarian rule under General Franco. But after an initial boom, the number of parties then rapidly reduced through mergers and dissolutions as Spanish democracy found its feet.

Many of the former peasant parties from between the wars in Eastern Europe have reappeared. Moreover, the rebirth of nationalism appears to be a factor in virtually all postcommunist party systems. One result is fragmentation. Even where there is a wide umbrella movement, such as Civic Forum in Czechoslovakia, it is very difficult for any one party to gain sufficient power to push ahead with unpalatable but necessary reforms.

Communist rule suppressed both new political parties and the expression of social conflicts. With the shackles removed, the postcommunist nations of Eastern Europe are, to an extent, simultaneously experiencing the first three waves of change outlined in Table 8.3 (p. 199): the national revolution, the industrial revolution and even, to an extent, the post-industrial revolution.

Of these new divisions, the most significant are nationality conflicts and the private/public sector division. But it is often difficult to separate national tensions from centre–periphery conflict. For example, the Slovenes seceded from Yugoslavia to satisfy national aspirations (they are a 'people' demanding self-rule). Croatia followed suit. Both Croats and Slovenes feel that they have been exploited by Serbia and the more economically backward Yugoslav republics. The disintegration of Yugoslavia, long predicted, produced in 1991 the most serious civil war in Europe since the 1940s.

Economic changes also have a profound impact on party support in the second world. Several parties in Romania favoured a rapid transition from a planned to a market economy. Without question, this would have resulted in large increases in unemployment. The NSF was returned to power, however, because the working class felt that its interests lay in a reformed version of communist policies (a slow transition, guaranteed employment, fixed prices). The cost is that the economy grinds along in bottom gear and close to breakdown.

Similar trends can be seen throughout Eastern Europe. The Small-Landholders Party in Hungary opposes the move towards privatisation, because it fears an influx of competition. Communist-led unions in Poland marched to protest against Solidarity policies, which they claimed were harming the working class (reversing the roles of the previous ten years). Throughout the second world, long-term economic progress means bitter medicine has to be swallowed. As first world politicians know in their bones and as second world politicians are fast learning, the requirements of long-term economic development often conflict with the short-term imperatives for electoral success.

■ Parties in the third world

Until the dramatic transition to democratisation and multi-partyism in the late 1980s and early 1990s, political parties carried least weight in the developing world. Unlike ruling communist parties, ruling parties in third world one party states were often weak and unimportant political institutions. If politics in the second world was dominated by the party, politics in much of the third world has been dominated by the state.

□ *No-party systems*

A minority of states get by with no parties at all. These are either *pre-party* or *anti-party* states. Pre-party states are most commonly found in the Middle East: for example, Saudi Arabia, Qatar, Jordan, Bhutan, Bahrain and Kuwait. In these nations, politics is dominated by a ruling family, and parties have yet to emerge or be permitted. Restored to power in Kuwait by US and Allied forces from Iraqi occupation, the

Al-Sabah family (the ruling royal house) promised to introduce democratic reforms. As they had previously scotched a nascent but inconvenient parliamentary system, the proof of the democratic pudding will again be in the eating.

In anti-party states, parties are simply outlawed, as happens in many military regimes. Anti-party systems are not a stable form in the modern world. Parties quickly re-emerge in military regimes as the transition to civilian rule gathers pace.

One-party systems

One-party rule has been a feature of politics in the third world – and it was the weakness of these ruling parties which accounted for the relative unimportance of parties. Often the party was little more than a vehicle for the nation's leader or a device for distributing patronage.

In Liberia, the ruling National Democratic Party was virtually created by President Doe to shore up his position. (It didn't. He was captured and killed by insurgents.) Similarly, in Bangladesh, General Ershad set up the People's Party to facilitate his transition from military to civilian leader. In Zaire, President Mobutu made every citizen a member of the sole political party, an organisation built around the leader himself – The Helmsman, The Redeemer, The Messiah, The Guide and the Father of the Revolution. As such, these parties are *internally created* parties, although they are very different from the internally created parties of the first world.

Why should this be? What accounts for the weakness of parties in the third world? After all in the ex-colonies, the British ones in particular, departing rulers had erected a parliamentary system in which parties had a rightful place. Furthermore, the fight against colonialism had produced nationalist movements which in some cases, as with the Convention People's Party (CPP) in Ghana (formerly the Gold Coast), were capable of mobilising the population. But the situation changed rapidly after independence. The fragile unity of the independence movement disintegrated. Ethnic and regional identities took precedence over party loyalties. When Kwame Nkrumah, leader of the CPP, was overthrown by a coup, the CPP simply disappeared with him.

A further problem was a lack of talented replacements in the party, as the leaders of the independence movement moved into government. Once the state had been captured, it could be used to perform those functions that parties fulfil in the first world. It also had far more resources to dispense. Thus the party largely lost its purpose.

Finally, economic development called for nation-building and the concentration of political resources. A single party might help with these tasks whereas a competitive party system would fragment modernisation efforts. As President Nyerere of Tanzania once put it, rival parties were like football teams engaged in a futile game while avoiding real and serious difficulties. Economic development required technical expertise. If this existed anywhere, it was in the bureaucracy rather than the party. However, Nyerere has since had to accept more than one football team in Tanzanian politics.

Many 'one party' states in the third world became, in reality, no-party systems. They stood in sharp contrast to the disciplined party rule found in communist states. Kenya was an example of several African states (others include Tanzania and Zambia) which were one-party states only in a notional sense. The Kenyan African National Union (KANU) became the country's sole party in 1969. Yet it barely functioned outside election campaigns and lacked any meaningful central organisation. During election campaigns, competition was intra-party as rival candidates proclaim their skill at extracting resources from the central government for their constituency – a power generator, a road, a new school. This local competition suited national leaders who were left free to deal with national policy-making. It is notable that KANU was the most resistant of all African ruling parties to the wind of change sweeping the continent in the late 1980s.

In an analysis of parties in contemporary African politics, Tordoff (1984) noted a sharp decline in functional importance since independence. In some states, parties were little more than a public relations device used by the state in its quest for legitimacy. In many other countries parties became merely a channel for distributing resources to favoured local politicians. Parties may also have a weak role to play in encouraging national integration but very rarely played a central role in the policy-making process.

☐ Multi-party systems

Of course there are exceptions. One former colony which has retained a dominant party, operating in a competitive political market, is India – the world's largest democracy. There is no shortage of parties in India: over thirty parties are represented in the Indian assembly, and there are more than sixty regional parties. These range from religious-based parties, to those based on ethnic or regional groups, to ideologically based parties. However, the dominant party since independence in 1947 has been the Congress Party: a broad-based left of centre party which has emphasised secularism in a nation increasingly riven with religious tensions.

The Congress Party has been dominated by the Nehru family since 1947 – three generations of the family have led the party and consequently the nation (Jawarharlal Nehru, India's first prime minister; his daughter, Indira Gandhi; and her son, Rajiv). Though Congress has held power nationally most of the time since independence, it is now less able to dominate Indian politics. In the 1991 election (marred by great violence, including Rajiv's assassination) it emerged as the largest single party but failed to secure an overall majority.

Some other countries in the third world have seen strong parties, combined on occasion with a competitive party system. In several Latin American countries, for example, the party system around the turn of the twentieth century involved competition between liberal and conservative factions in the ruling élites. However, in contrast to Europe, these élite-level factions did not develop into mass parties seeking electoral support. Élite resistance to incorporating the masses into politics was far stronger. This produced a situation in Latin America where party competition oscillated with periods of military rule. Sustained by oil revenues Venezuela is one of the few South American countries to have had continuous party competition since the 1950s.

Mexico also has a strong party in the Institutional Revolutionary Party – so strong, indeed, that other parties are tolerated only as long as they show no signs of winning any elections that matter. Mexico is as exceptional in Latin America as India is in the newly independent countries. But systems with **dominant parties** can be found elsewhere in the third world. For example, Lee Kwan Yew's People's Action Party has similarly dominated the politics of Singapore.

Such parties rarely rely just upon the voters' gratitude. They restrict press and media freedom in order to manipulate public opinion. They run smear campaigns against opposition figures. They hint (or plainly threaten) retribution against those who vote against the party. Failing all else, and certainly in Mexico's case, the dominant party falls back on straightforward ballot-rigging.

The collapse of communism in Eastern Europe was a dramatic and rapid affair. The move away from authoritarianism and towards democracy in the third world may have been less of a media event, but has nevertheless been striking. With the resurgence of democracy, the importance of parties in the third world has also increased. Emergent democracies in the third world share many of the features of the postcommunist second world: the proliferation of small parties, soaring popular expectations followed by plummeting disappointment, inexperienced leadership and so on. They are also less sure of their future than the new democracies in Eastern Europe, which can look to the West for aid and protection. But the West will certainly not provide aid and protection throughout the world. If things do not go well in the fledgling democracies of the third world, the men in uniform may again take a hand.

■ Are parties in decline?

What is the future of party government? Will the political party remain a key link between society and state or is the era of the mass party already coming to an end? This is a suitable question to consider in this concluding section of the chapter, allowing us to extend some of the points we have already made.

The thesis of party decay is plausible, especially if one subscribes to the 'crisis' theory of parties. This theory suggests that parties will eventually outlive their usefulness. They arise in response to important problems – integrating the mass electorate into politics, say, or hastening the departure of colonial rulers. Once successful in overcoming the problem, the party loses its purpose.

The fate of communist parties in the second world clearly fits this bill. They succeeded in industrialising and modernising many of the countries they ruled. But with this mission largely accomplished, ruling communist parties lost heart and drive. Instead of leading society, they became a brake on its further development. Once the prop of support from the Soviet military was removed, they fell down dead.

A similar, if less dramatic, fate may befall some of the parties that took power from the communists in Eastern Europe. Their mission was to provide a transition from a one-party to multi-party political system. It is difficult to see a long term future for Solidarity, Civic Forum and the Hungarian Democratic Forum *in their present form*. Of course, this does not mean that parties have no role to play in the new Eastern Europe. The 'umbrella' organisations may break up, but they will fragment into – or be replaced by – more coherent parties reflecting cleavages now surfacing after decades of enforced conformity under communist party rule.

The thesis of party decline can also be applied to the first world. The conflicts of class and religion which fuelled party systems have softened, diluting the social base of parties. Voters' party loyalties have weakened, producing more pragmatic and instrumental electorates. This has encouraged what Kircheimer (1966) termed 'catch-all' parties which trawl the electoral market in search of whatever support they can find. Party decay has gone furthest in the United States. Election campaigning at every level has become candidate-centred rather than party-centred. Reasons for this include the increased use of primary elections to select candidates and changes in campaign finance laws, but fundamentally the American electorate is 'tuning out' parties, regarding them as less and less relevant to their voting decisions.

In the USA and throughout the first world, the growth of the mass media has had a profound impact on politics. Politicians have to 'perform' for the millions sitting at home watching them, and voters are increasingly mobilised by party leaders via television, not by canvassers. As a result, local party organisation has declined and parties in several democracies have had to turn to the state for financial support, starting with West Germany in 1959 and Sweden in 1965.

New generations of voters enter politics through single-issue groups rather than the broader coalitions of a political party. It is very rare for an individual to agree with *all* the policies promoted by 'catch-all' parties. As a result, it is much easier to identify with and strongly support the single issue being promoted by a *movement* as opposed to the plethora of issues being promoted by a *party*. The whole idea of party government, in which a single party is given a free rein until the next election, has come under attack, most of all in its British homeland.

Although the thesis of party decline has some strengths, we believe that the role of parties is changing rather than decaying. In the first world, British-style government by a single party is under attack, but the alternative is government by many parties rather than by none. It is also important to note that the declining effectiveness of party government does not imply any reduction in its extent (G. Smith 1989).

Parties in the West have borne the double burden of increasing demands from the voters at a time of budgetary pressures and growing social complexity. But the fact that governing parties have taken much of the popular blame indicates their continued centrality to the political process. Indeed, in the new democracies of Portugal and Spain, parties are still gaining ground. Parties will continue to play major roles in recruiting political leaders who direct and, increasingly in conjunction with interest groups, control society.

The de-radicalisation of left-wing parties provides another example of parties adapting to avoid decay. The historic mission of socialist parties, based on protecting workers' interests against those of employers, arguably has less relevance in a world where economic competition is international rather than inter-class. Certainly, the traditional socialist remedies of public ownership and entrenched rights of trade unions have less relevance in an economic system in which the market has triumphed.

The death of the Italian Communist Party (PCI), after a protracted struggle within the party, is a case in point. The collapse of communist party rule in Eastern Europe clearly had an impact on the way Western communist parties perceived their future. However, Bull (1991) argues that great changes would have taken place in the PCI even if the revolutions of 1989 had not occurred. Moves to adopt a policy platform based on electoral reform, industrial democracy and support for progressive social movements were first proposed late in 1988. The belated shift to the centre ground by Britain's Labour Party in the second half of the 1980s is another example of de-radicalisation on the left. The decision by New Zealand's Labour Party to embrace right-wing 'Rogernomics' was perhaps the most surprising switch of all.

In the third world, the future of parties is as yet uncertain. The transition to democracy is still in its early stage, and the threat of a reversion to military and/or authoritarian rule cannot be disregarded, particularly in Africa. However, in general, the remarkable wave of democratisation that has swept the third world indicates an increasingly important role in politics for parties. Rather than being in decline, parties in the third world are only just beginning to take their place in many political systems.

Summary

1   Political parties are permanent organisations that seek to capture decision-making power within the political system. They provide a channel of expression between the rulers and the ruled.

2.   Parties select, reduce and combine interests into a manageable package of proposals. They give direction to government and organise the administration. They act as agents of élite recruitment and socialisation. They act as emotional 'reference groups' for their followers.

3.   Party competition is the hallmark of liberal democracy. Communist party states, by contrast, were characterised by the dominance of government and society by the ruling party.

4.   The three main waves of charge that transformed the social bases of parties in the first world were the national revolution, the industrial revolution, and post-industrial influences.

5.   Party organisation in the first world depends on: the relationship between the parliamentary party and the party organisation; control over candidate recruitment; and the strength of factional alliances within parties.

6.   Membership of ruling communist parties was restricted to 'politically correct' applicants, and members were carefully scrutinised. Eventually ruling

communist parties became a moribund 'ruling class'. Parties in the postcommunist second world are more volatile, displaying a state of flux and transition.

7.   Parties generally played a minor role in the third world, once independence was achieved. No-party and one-party systems were the dominant form, with parties acting as a personal vehicle of the leader and as a device for distributing patronage.

8.   The crisis theory of party development suggests that parties decline after they outlive their usefulness. But democratisation in the second and third world has led to renewed importance for parties.

Discussion points

1.   Given that ruling communist parties controlled all significant levels of power, why did they collapse?

2.   Will single-issue parties like the greens ever become catch-all parties?

3.   Do members of parliament have more in common with the representatives of other parties than with their own rank and file?

4.   Compare how ruling parties in the second and third worlds attempted to control and modernise society.

Key reading

Duverger, M. (1964) *Political Parties* (London: Methuen). Despite outdated empirical data, a good introduction to the classification of parties.

Lipset, S. and Rokkan, S. (1967) *Party Systems and Voter Alignments* (New York: Free Press). The seminal work on the development of European party systems.

Mair, P. (1990) *The West European Party System* (Oxford: Oxford University Press). A wide-ranging analysis of parties and party systems in Western Europe.

Randall, V. (ed.) (1988) *Political Parties in the Third World* (London: Sage). Case studies of party systems from all areas of the third world.

White, S., Gardner, J., Schöpflin, G, and Saich, T. (1990) *Communist and Postcommunist Political Systems: An Introduction*, 3rd edn (London: Macmillan). Chapter 4 provides an excellent introduction both to the structure of ruling communist parties, and to the origins of parties in the postcommunist second world.

Further reading

A good place to start is Kircheimer's important article (1966) on the transform-ation of party systems in Western Europe which appears in the influential volume edited by LaPolombara and Weiner (1966). Wolinetz (1979) is an update of Kircheimer. The seminal work on the development of European party systems is by Lipset and Rokkan (1967); more recent discussions can be found in Daalder and Mair (1983) or, as a second choice, Merkl (1980). An authoritative work on parties is Sartori's (1976) important but difficult general book while von Beyme (1986) contains much information on Western parties. Castles and Wildemann (1986) is a careful study of the problems of party government; see also Rose (1976). On social democratic parties in particular, see Thomas and Paterson (1986). For a good general account of American parties, see Sorauf (1985), while Epstein (1980) is still an outstanding treatment of the development of parties in Western democracies.

On the Soviet Communist Party, see Hill and Frank (1983). On communist parties in general see S. White, Gardner, Schöpflin and Saich (1990) or Bertsch *et al.* (1992). On third world parties, Zolberg (1966) was an influential early work; a recent treatment is Randall (1988). Tordoff (1984, ch. 5) is a clear discussion of parties in Africa. Clapham (1985, especially ch. 4) includes perceptive comments on third world parties.

■ PART 4 ■

THE STRUCTURES OF GOVERNMENT

We examine here the key institutions of national government: executives, assemblies, bureaucracies. We also look at 'the state in uniform': the military and the police. In most societies these are the central structures through which power is exercised, and policy is shaped and implemented. However, it is the relationships between these institutions, rather than their internal workings, which are crucial. We therefore begin this part with a chapter on constitutions, federalism and the judiciary. In a growing number of countries, though by no means all, these provide a framework within which the institutions of national government operate.

■ *Chapter 11* ■

The Constitutional Framework

Most nation-states have a formal constitution. Until recently, however, the study of constitutions was only a major theme of political analysis within liberal democracies. This was because liberal democracy is partly defined as constitutional government: that is, as government in accordance with, and limited by, formal rules. In addition, several liberal democracies – including Belgium, Canada, the Netherlands, Portugal, Spain and Sweden – have adopted new constitutions since 1970. This has given new impetus to constitutional studies.

Elsewhere, constitutions received less attention from students of politics – and with good reason. Constitutions were often ignored by politicians, or were nothing more than window-dressing, or were just bland statements of national goals. For example, India's constitution contains articles about freedom; equality; exploitation; religion; property; standards of living; equal pay; the right to work; and free and compulsory education. These are important aspirations but many are not yet feasible in the Indian context. However, the dramatic spread of democracy through the second and third worlds in the 1980s and 1990s has greatly broadened the scope and importance of constitutional studies.

Constitutions are especially important in determining the territorial distribution of powers within the nation-state. Federal states invariably have a written constitution specifying the formal distribution of powers between the central and subnational governments. This contrasts with unitary states, where sovereignty is reserved to the central government. The territorial distribution of power, particularly in its federal form, is discussed on pp. 268–76.

Constitutional government requires a means of arbitrating disputes about the constitution. This task falls to the judiciary, usually in the form of a supreme constitutional court. Again, such courts are particularly important in federations. Although judges must attempt to remain aloof from the party battle, it is clear that they are important political actors in any constitutional government. The judiciary is discussed on pp. 279–84.

■ Constitutions

Described by Duchacek (1970) as 'power maps', constitutions indicate the formal distribution of authority within the state. More explicitly, a constitution is a set of rights, powers and procedures regulating the structure of, and relationships among, the public authorities, and between the public authorities and the citizens (Robertson 1985). In other words, a constitution defines the rules of the political game: it lays down the laws that govern the governors (Watson 1989). Even authoritarian and repressive regimes rarely dispense with constitutional appearances completely; constitutions are part of the tribute that vice plays to virtue. However, unless the constitution reflects dominant values within society, its prospects for stable and successful operation are poor.

□ *Classifying constitutions*

There are several types of constitution (Elazar 1985):

1. The constitution as a **loose frame of government,** in which details evolve through custom and subsequent adaptation. The US constitution is the best example: it was originally silent on many points which have had to be clarified by judicial interpretation.
2. The constitution as a **state code** in which the powers of, and relationships between, political institutions are specified in considerable detail. This is characteristic of the constitutions of West European nations such as France and Germany.
3. Some constitutions are **revolutionary manifestos,** setting forth a far-reaching programme of social transformation. The constitutions of communist party states were examples.
4. The constitutions of many third world countries **set out political ideals,** an image of the world as the regime would like it to be rather than as it is.
5. Finally, in a few cases the constitution embodies an **ancient source of authority.** Britain's 'unwritten' constitution centres upon the sovereignty of Parliament. Israel's constitution is also unformalised, though the sovereignty of the Knesset (parliament) derives from the Torah (Jewish holy book).

☐ The origins of constitutions

How do constitutions come into being? Most often, they are enacted in circumstances of a 'fresh start' after profound disruption of some kind. These disruptions include: regime change (as in France, a dozen times since the 1789 revolution); reconstruction after defeat in war (as in Germany, Italy and Japan after 1945); revolution (as in communist party states); and achieving independence (as in most of Africa in the 1950s and 1960s).

The Spanish constitution is a more recent example of a 'fresh start'. It was introduced in 1978, after nearly forty years of authoritarian rule under General Franco. Political change in Spain had lagged behind economic and social development. Support for a 'modern' political system was widespread but the transition to a new regime is never easy. Supporters of the old system had to be coaxed into accepting the new regime. Issues such as the role of the Catholic Church in society and demands for regional autonomy were deeply divisive. But with the steadfast commitment of King Juan Carlos and skilful government leadership, the constitution successfully weathered a variety of political crises. Membership of the European Community consolidated Spain's transition to liberal democracy. Given the long history of instability, political violence and authoritarianism in Spain since Napoleonic times, the construction of a stable constitutional democracy was a major political achievement.

Spain illustrates two points which are typical of constitution-making during the transition to a democratic regime (Bogdanor 1988, p. 9). First, the constitution was drawn up by people who had become influential under the old non-constitutional regime. A new constitution does not mean a new ruling élite. Secondly, to secure acceptance of the new democratic constitution, it had to be introduced in a 'top-down' fashion, using methods which were far from democratic.

Constitutions are not 'once and for all' documents. They are amended or interpreted in response to changing circumstances. The US Constitution, for instance, has been formally amended 26 times in two centuries of operation. Less formal, but probably more significant, constitutional adaptation has taken place through judicial interpretation (see pp. 282–3).

☐ Revising and replacing constitutions

Communist party states adopted a different approach to constitutional change. They regarded different constitutions as appropriate to specific stages of social development. Thus the Soviet Union's official attainment of socialism in 1936 was marked by the promulgation of the 'Stalin' constitution. Some forty years later, the 'Brezhnev' constitution consolidated intervening developments which had brought the country to what its rulers regarded as 'advanced socialism'.

Because a constitution sets out the ground rules of politics, it can become the focus of intense political conflict. As President Gorbachev's drive for *perestroika* in the Soviet Union stalled at the end of the 1980s, a 'War of the Laws' unfolded. The 15 republics sought to redefine their relationship with the All-Union government at the centre – and in some cases to secede from it. Failure of the conservative coup in August 1991 opened the way for Boris Yeltsin, President of the Russian Republic, and his reformist allies, to drive through a constitutional revolution. The Soviet Union, which had been in the grip of the Communist Party for seven decades, was dissolved in favour of a loose confederation. With the proclamation of the Commonwealth of Independent States (CIS) in November 1991, the formerly all-powerful central government was abolished.

Several liberal democracies, especially Belgium and Canada, have also experienced a resurgence of constitutional politics in response to separatist and linguistic conflicts. In 1971 Belgium adopted the principle of a near-federal constitution, with extensive autonomy for both Flemish- and French-speaking areas. But successive governments have stumbled over implementing the changes in detail (G. Smith 1989, p. 318).

Canada, a federal system with a relatively weak centre, has been under pressure since the 1960s from rising French-Canadian nationalism in Quebec. At the same time, English-speaking provinces in the West and maritime East, resentful of further concessions to Quebec, have wanted more political say. Successive attempts have been made to engineer a constitutional solution: first, official bilingualism and biculturalism; then in 1981 'patriation' of the constitution. This meant making it henceforth the sole concern of Canadians, and no longer involving the Westminster Parliament, a legacy of colonialism. More recently, the Meech Lake Accord of 1987 conceded Quebec's desire to be recognised as a separate nation, but antagonised many outside Quebec. Some provinces refused to accept the Accord and it therefore lapsed in 1990, leaving Canada with an uncertain future.

Constant constitutionalising in Canada reflects the strains on its political system. The country's identity is still uncertain. Is it a partnership of two peoples or a federation of ten provinces? As Canada's first prime minister put it, 'too much geography, not enough history'. Canada lacks a consensus about provincial–federal relationships and,

Exhibit 11.1 *The European Community: a chronology*

The European Community (EC) is the major example in the world today of countries choosing to pool sovereignty. Its members have different motives in coming together. Some are concerned to prevent a reversion to the wars which twice ravaged the continent in the twentieth century. Others, like Britain, see the EC in economic terms – as a large, affluent market which provides opportunities to those inside it – and, more to the point, a threat to those left outside. Here is a brief chronology of the major events in the continuing evolution of this major supra-national institution.

1951
European Coal and Steel Community Treaty (ECSC) signed by Belgium, France, Germany, Italy, Luxembourg and the Netherlands ('The Six'). This established supranational institutions to enforce a free trade area in some basic industrial goods.

1957
The Six sign the Treaty of Rome, establishing the European Economic Community (EEC).

1961
Ireland, Denmark and the UK request negotiations about joining the EEC.

1963
France's President de Gaulle vetoes UK entry.

1967
European Community (EC) created through merger of EEC, ECSC and Euratom.

1972
Majority vote against entry to the EC in referendum in Norway.

1973
Denmark, Ireland and the UK join the EC.

1975
A majority vote for continued membership of the EC in UK referendum.

1979
European Monetary System (EMS) comes into operation. First direct elections to the European parliament.

cont.

1981
Greece joins the EC.

1986
Spain and Portugal join the EC. Single European Act concluded, to speed up economic integration.

1990
German reunification brings the former East Germany into the EC.

1993
The internal market is supposed to be complete.

Source: N. Nugent, *The Government and Politics of the European Community* (Basingstoke: Macmillan, 1991) 2nd edn.

above all, it suffers from intractable linguistic and ethno-cultural conflicts.

A traditional distinction in constitutional analysis contrasts written with unwritten constitutions. As no constitution is wholly unwritten (even the 'unwritten' British constitution contains much statute and common law), a distinction between *codified* and *uncodified* systems is more useful. Most constitutions are codified – that is, they are set out in detail within a single document or body of laws. The constitution of Germany, for instance, is laid down in the Basic Law ratified in 1949. The constitutions of Britain, New Zealand and Israel are unusual in that they are not formalised in this way.

Procedures for amendment are important. Can the constitution be altered by a simple majority in the national legislature alone (i.e. a *flexible* constitution)? Or are special procedures required, other than those laid down for the making of ordinary laws (a *rigid* constitution)? The flexible British constitution contrasts with the apparent rigidity of the US constitution. The British constitution is subordinate to Parliament and can be altered by the ordinary process of legislation – or indeed simply by convention.

By contrast, the American constitution can be amended only by two-thirds majorities in Congress, plus ratification by three-quarters of the states. In practice, the task of adapting the constitution falls mainly to the US Supreme Court. Judicial interpretation is inherently more flexible than formal amendment. Though superior to the elected legislature, the US constitution is thus subordinate to non-elected judges.

☐ *When do constitutions succeed?*

A key question about constitutions is: When do they succeed in providing a stable framework for political activity? Essentially, it seems, when they do not attempt too much. The spirit as well as the letter of the constitution is most likely to be maintained when the provisions of the constitution accord reasonably well with dominant social interests and values. The US constitution established a limited central government, 'created' as President John Adams put it, 'out of the grinding necessity of a reluctant nation.' Had it attempted more, as some of the founders wanted, the constitution might well have sunk beneath opposition from independent-minded states and settlers.

Conversely, the liberal-democratic constitutions which departing colonialists bequeathed to the third world often failed because they did not take account of social inequalities and non-democratic cultures. 'Fresh starts' became false starts. Some constitutions were adapted to suit the political environment in which they operated, most often by strengthening executive authority. But many were suppressed by authoritarian rulers or destroyed by military takeovers. However, the widespread shift back to formal democracy and multi-party elections in both Africa and Latin America in the 1980s indicates at least a partial re-emergence of constitutions in political life.

If generals are always re-fighting the last war, constitutions are often designed to overcome the defects of the previous regime. In so doing they create new problems of their own. The hallmark of the Italian constitution, for example, is *garantismo*, meaning that all political forces are guaranteed a stake in the political system. Thus the constitution features a strong bicameral assembly, entrenched democratic rights, a constitutional court and wide regional autonomy. These multiple checks upon power were to prevent a recurrence of prewar dictatorship. *Garantismo*, however, has in practice contributed to ineffective government and so to some loss of popular legitimacy.

By contrast, the constitution of the Fifth French Republic (1958) sought not to check but to concentrate power. This was in reaction to the executive instability that beset the Fourth Republic. A curbed assembly and a strengthened executive were certainly achieved. But the hybrid nature of the constitution, straddling presidential and parliamentary forms of executive, can cause difficulites. President Mitterrand, a politician of the left, found himself saddled with Jacques Chirac, a prime minister of the right, after the parliamentary elections of May 1986. For two years, president and prime minister 'cohabited' in an uneasy situation of divided leadership.

But some 'fresh starts' have succeeded. The postwar constitutions in Japan and Germany provided frameworks within which stable and effective government proved possible, aided in both cases by a buoyant economy. Over time, these constitutions have acquired normative weight of their own, so helping to achieve that most delicate goal of regulating the exercise of political power. In Germany, the Basic Law even contained a far-sighted procedure whereby further territories could be added to the republic. This enabled postcommunist East Germany to be readmitted to the German Republic in 1990. The pre-communist *Länder* (regions) were reconstituted and then acceded to the Federal German constitution. It was no fault of the constitution that the social and economic price of re-unification turned out to be much higher than anticipated.

■ Federalism

Virtually all nation-states have more than one tier of government. Regional, state or local authorities coexist under or alongside the central power. This means that all countries must resolve the issue of the relationship between differing levels of government. The answers vary. First, there are highly centralised unitary systems (see pp. 276–9), in which authority is concentrated in the central government. Secondly, there are relatively decentralised federal systems, in which authority is shared beteen the centre and lower levels. Thirdly, there are highly decentralised confederal systems, in which the central government has little authority. This classification is shown in Figure 11.1.

□ Federations and confederations

A confederation is a relatively weak form of political union between sovereign states. In 1991 the Soviet Union moved rapidly from a nominally federal (in practice for seventy years tightly centralised) structure towards a loose confederation. Each of the 15 Soviet republics asserted its sovereign independence. Each was free to join in all, some or none of the few common functions proposed for the Commonwealth of Independent States (CIS) proclaimed in November of that year. The centre would do little more than coordinate and arbitrate. However, so strong were the centrifugal forces unleashed by the collapse of communism that complete political disintegration seemed as likely as a workable confederation.

Action in a confederation generally requires unanimity among member states. A confederal government generally lacks its own means

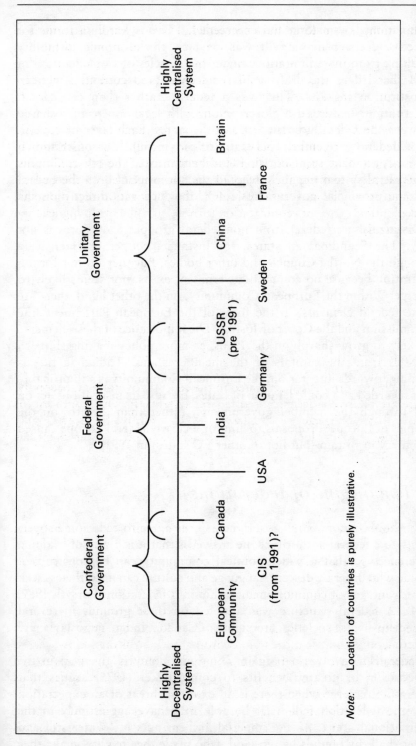

Note: Location of countries is purely illustrative.

Figure 11.1 *The territorial distribution of power*

of taxation, law-making and enforcement. This is hardly a recipe for effective decision-making. It was, in fact, the economic instability resulting from these limitations under the Articles of Confederation of 1781 that led to the drafting of the second (and current) American Constitution in 1787. This was a federal, rather than confederal, constitution. It created a closer union, with legal sovereignty shared between the federal government and the states. Each layer of government, federal (or central) and state (or provincial), has constitutional authority to make some decisions independently of the other. Citizens of a federal system remain subject to the authority of both the central and the provincial governments, each of which acts directly on the citizen.

Distinguishing federal from non-federal groupings of states is not easy. The Scandinavian states, for instance, cooperate extensively through the Nordic Council and other bodies. But they do not form a federation because no common government exists, nor seems likely to emerge. Within the European Community, on the other hand, there are some federal elements, in the form of the European Parliament, the Commission and the Court of Justice. The importance of these elements is likely to grow sharply in the 1990s, as more policy-making shifts to Brussels from the capitals of the member states. Though a tide is running towards integration, the European Community is still probably best regarded as a confederation of states, because its institutions act on and through the member governments, rather than directly on the peoples of Europe. Proposals to aim for a clearly federal Europe caused an outcry in Britain (but not in other EC states) in 1991.

□ The origins of federations

Why should autonomous governments ever agree to cede some sovereignty to a federal authority? One answer is that it is a way of bridging differences so that a wider political community can be constructed. People who differ by descent, language and culture can nevertheless seek the advantages of common membership in a federation (Forsyth 1989, p. 4). A federal structure was adopted on these grounds in several ethnically diverse societies, among them Canada, India, Yugoslavia and Nigeria.

Federalism involves a bargain: some autonomy is given up in the expectation of greater benefits to come. Riker (1975) argues that federations emerge when there is an external threat or an expectation that the federation will itself be able to behave aggressively in the international arena. As the imperial anthem puts it, 'Wider still and wider shall thy bounds be set; God, who made thee mighty, make thee mightier yet'. In Canada, for example, the constitution's framers wanted to expand their political and economic influence north-westward in the face of American competition (Hodgkins *et al*. 1978, p. 303). By the 1980s, however, the bounds of Canada's federation were becoming weaker still and weaker.

In other cases, motives for federal solutions have been as much economic as political. Australian federalists felt that a common market would promote economic expansion. Britain's reluctant entry into the EC was for similar reasons. The EC provided a large market of affluent consumers from which a middle-ranking power like Britain could not afford to be left out. But whether the motives of the framers are military or economic, federalism remains a clear example of how domestic government can be organised so as to allow rulers to compete more effectively in the international arena.

Federalism is a complex, legalistic and always conscious creation. Sometimes it emerges from a voluntary compact between previously autonomous states. This was indeed the case in the United States when the representatives of thirteen states met in Philadelphia in 1787. Similar conventions, greatly influenced by the American experience, took place in Canada in 1867 and Australia in 1897–8. But elsewhere, in Latin America and some British colonies, federalism was imposed from without rather than created from within. 'Imposed federalism' has little prospect of creating a stable devolution of power from the centre. Witness, for instance, the short-lived East African Federation, involving the former British colonies of Kenya, Tanganyika (now Tanzania) and Uganda. A similar fate befell other federations cobbled together by Britain as it shed colonial responsibilities.

☐ *Classifying federations*

Federal states have always been in the minority. There are fewer than twenty such states in the contemporary world. However these cover most of the world's land surface. Five of the six largest states by area are federal: Australia, Brazil, Canada, the United States and until 1991 the Soviet Union. (The exception, China, gives limited autonomy to its minorities.)

Federal states fall into several categories:

1. In a category by itself comes the **United States**, the inventor of modern federalism.
2. Federalism is found in some **former British colonies** (Australia, Canada, India, Nigeria) and has been abandoned in several others in the Caribbean and Africa.

3. Several **Latin American states** were influenced by the American model into adopting federalism when they achieved independence in the nineteenth century. Federal constitutions are found in the Argentine Republic, Brazil, Venezuela and Mexico, albeit in virtual abeyance during periods of authoritarian rule.

4. **European federalism** is found in Austria, Germany and Switzerland, deriving from a long tradition of associated (that is, several governments working together) rather than unitary governments in these countries.

5. **Communist federalism** was seen in Czechoslovakia, the Soviet Union and Yugoslavia.

Communist federalism was best understood as a device by which communist regimes allowed cultural, but not political, autonomy to national minorities. Ironically, this approach kept national awareness alive, while restricting its political expression. As communist power disintegrated, so long-simmering nationality problems quickly came to the boil. Communist federations have splintered under these forces. Yugoslavia descended into disorder and civil war in 1991, as Croatia and Slovenia seceded from the federation. In Czechoslovakia, Slovakia has demanded almost complete autonomy from the federal government in Prague. The break-up of the Soviet Union has been the most momentous casualty of all, with the Baltic and Caucasus republics driving for full independence and the other republics willing at most to accept only loose confederal links.

□ *The consequences of federalism*

Several institutional consequences follow from the adoption of a federal formula. First, a written constitution is needed to allocate functions to the central and provincial governments. The central government is usually responsible for external relations – defence, foreign affairs and immigration – and for some common domestic functions such as the currency. Provincial governments have responsibility for some domestic policies such as education or housing, but may share power with the central government in other policy areas.

Secondly, a constitutional court is needed to arbitrate disputes between governments by reference to the constitution. The Supreme Court in the United States is the prime example.

Thirdly, a bicameral assembly ensures representation in the national legislature for the states, provinces or republics which make up the federal union. In most federations, each state receives equal representation in the upper house, irrespective of population. Occasionally this principle of 'equal representation for unequal states' has been modified. In India, for instance, the less populous states are favoured but not to the point of equality with the heavily populated states.

Other political institutions, notably parties, must adapt to the federal framework. Crudely put, either parties control federalism, or federalism controls the parties. In communist states, a single centralised party stood at the apex of the political system, operating the federal framework and using it for its own purposes. A similar, though less extreme, form of party dominance is found in India where the Congress Party's predominance has been maintained by a federal system which makes it difficult for opposition parties to form a coherent national organisation.

The United States stands at the other extreme. There, parties are so decentralised that they are little more than weak collections of state and local interests. Decentralised parties underpin federal decentralisation. The relationship between parties and federalism is crucial to understanding how federalism works in practice.

□ *Central provincial relationships*

The balance of power and initiative between centre and province depends heavily on revenue-raising powers. Political scientists have recently focused more on the fiscal dimension of federalism. They concluded that the financial balance in federal systems has become more favourable to the centre over the twentieth century.

In the United States, for example, the national government gets four-fifths of its revenue from personal income tax, a source which has been relatively buoyant as more people join the labour force and real incomes rise. The states, by contrast, depend primarily on sales taxes, a more regressive and obtrusive tax. Until sharp cuts were introduced by President Reagan in the early 1980s, the states came to rely on revenue transfers from the federal government for a growing proportion of their resources. This was paralleled elsewhere: in Australia, about 60 per cent of the states' total revenue comes from the federal government.

Revenue sharing (Table 11.1) was introduced in the United States to reverse centralising trends which had been evident since the New Deal of the 1930s. But this did not work completely. Financial aid from the centre has been reduced and states have been forced to raise more money from local sources. But this is partly in response to new legal responsibilities which the centre has imposed on state governments. Thus centralising trends have been reversed in some ways but not others.

Table 11.1 **Financial transfers from central governments to subnational governments.**

1. **Categorical** grants for specific projects
   Example: for a new hospital.

2. **Block grants** for particular programmes
   Example: for medical care.

3. **Revenue-sharing.**
   This is general funding which places few limits on the recipient's use of the funds.

4. **Equalisation grants** are used in an effort to equalise financial conditions in some federations, e.g. Australia.

The growing authority of the centre in federal systems has been much more than a financial matter. More than anything, it reflects the emergence of a national economy which requires overall planning and regulation. To take one example, a modern economy requires an effective transport system. But individual provinces have little incentive to pay for road networks which will benefit other provinces as much as their own. So the central government must plan and fund, if not build, the national road network. Wars and economic crises have also strengthened the central authority.

Similar pressures arise in other policy areas. In Germany, for example, the federal government now coordinates higher education. It also set up an Environment Ministry after the explosion at the Chernobyl nuclear power station in the Soviet Union. The threat of radiation knows no respect for provincial boundaries.

Constitutional courts have generally acceded to central initiatives, particularly when justified on grounds of national emergency. Throughout most of this century, federal law has consistently prevailed over state law in the rulings of the US Supreme Court. In Australia, decisions of the High Court have favoured the centre to the point where some commentators regard federalism as sustained more by politics than the constitution. Of the major Western federal systems, only Canada has seen a drift away from, rather than towards, the centre.

Thus the crucial feature of most contemporary federations is the interdependence rather than the independence of the various levels of government. On domestic policies, at least, a complicated patchwork of government agencies – central, provincial and local – is involved. The centre has money and broad goals but, in contrast to unitary states, it is unable to dictate to subnational governments.

Indeed provincial governments can sometimes organise themselves into an effective pressure-group. They can then press for more resources from the centre, as with the Governors' Conference in the United States. Thus the style of intergovernmental relations is often collaborative, with distinct 'policy communities' emerging in areas such as health, education and transport. Americans use the term 'picket fence federalism' to describe the division of policy-makers at various levels of government into these policy communities. It is all a long way from the ideals of the founding fathers for separate layers of government, each of which was intended to be supreme and independent within its own spheres.

European federalism, at least in Germany and Austria (though not Switzerland), has always given a large policy-making role to the centre. German 'administrative federalism' is a constitutional style towards which many other federations have been moving in practice. In Germany, both federal government and the *Länder* (provinces) can legislate in several areas of concurrent power (for example, transport and public ownership). There is also a category of 'framework laws'. These are outline laws which are passed at the centre and then fleshed out in *Land* legislation. In addition the *Länder* are given responsibility by the constitution for executing federal law. This reduces the duplication which is characteristic of the United States and other federal systems.

Unusually, *Land* governments are directly represented in the Bundesrat, the upper chamber of parliament. The Bundesrat undoubtedly has a powerful place in the German system, but it is perhaps less a legislative organ than a meeting place of Germany's governments, with which the federal government must come to terms (G. Smith 1989, p. 35). The institutions of German federalism both necessitate and encourage intergovernmental collaboration, in which the centre's policy-making initiatives are conditioned by, the reaction of the provinces which have to implement the plans.

☐ Assessment

What overall assessment can we give of the federal experiment? What are its advantages and disadvantages? Federalism recognises the need for central authority but attempts to contain its scope. It fosters social diversity and the autonomy of minority groups. But it has also been an obstacle to the egalitarian drive of the welfare state. As Riker (1975) points out, the beneficiaries of American federalism have historically been those minorities that could use state-level government to enforce their preferred policies. What price federalism, say its critics, if it has worked for the benefit of white racists in the Southern states? Certainly federalism works to the advantage of geographically concentrated minorities.

But the general problem with federalism is that it distributes power on a territorial basis when the key conflicts in society are now social rather than geographical. Australia is typical in this respect: 'Australia is culturally and regionally heterogeneous, but these social divisions are not essentially represented by current state boundaries. Differences between the states do not equate with the fundamental cleavages in Australian society.' (Wilcox 1989, p. 152).

Where social and territorial divisions largely coincide – as in the Canadian conflicts between French and English speakers, and between the Eastern and Western provinces – adjusting federal relationships can help to manage these problems but rarely resolves them. Violence in Yugoslavia is a forcible reminder that federalism has no formula which can conjure harmony out of ethnic differences (Forsyth 1989, p. 5). It is indeed a nice question whether federalism has contributed to divisions within nation-states more than it has contained them.

Furthermore the evolution of federal states has led to complex patterns of policy-making in which the lines of accountability to the electorate are confused. Critics allege that federalism has become geographical corporatism, in which central authority is held hostage by territorially based interests. Defenders of federalism reply that this is better than the sharp oscillations of policy made possible by the unitary governments of such countries as Britain and New Zealand. As with many other political institutions, evaluations of federalism are likely to be more favourable if priority is given to diffusing, rather than concentrating, political power.

■ Unitary government

The vast majority of contemporary nation-states are unitary in character. This means that sovereignty is focused exclusively on the central government. Subnational governments, whether regional or local, may make policy as well as administer it but they do so at the pleasure of the national authority. In practice, of course, there is a balance of political resources between central and local governments in unitary systems which limits the power of the centre (Table 11.2).

□ *Dual and fused systems*

The balance between centre and locality depends on the nature of intergovernmental relations in a particular state. Central and local

Table 11.2 **The balance of power between central and local government in unitary systems**

The resources of local government typically include:

1. Control over policy implementation;
2. Responsibility for the direct provision of public services such as health, education and welfare;
3. Some revenue-raising power;
4. A local electoral mandate.

Against this must be set the resources of the centre:

1. Control over legislation, including the right to abolish or modify local government;
2. Provision of most local authority finance;
3. Setting administrative standards for service provision;
4. Popular expectations that the national government should solve problems.

governments are now closely connected in all industrial states, but historical traditions still leave their mark. In liberal democracies, the basic contrast in local government is between dual and fused systems (G. Smith, 1989).

Under a **dual** system, local government operates separately from the centre or its field executives. The English idea of the local council, responsible for all the services provided in its area, is an example of this tradition. Until the First World War, this pattern gave considerable freedom to local government, comparable in practice to many federal systems.

Under a **fused** system, by contrast, the central and local government are joined in an office such as the prefect, a central appointee who is charged with overseeing the administration of a particular community. In a fused system there is usually a Ministry of the Interior at the centre to whom the prefect reports.

France is the most influential example of a fused, centralised system of prefects. The prefect (now called Commissioner of the Republic) in each of the hundred or so departments in France is a highly influential figure. However, to be effective the Commissoner must work in conjunction with local councils rather than simply oversee them. And the councils are often headed by influential national politicians, who cherish their local power base. This offsets prefectoral power to some extent. Moreover, some traditional functions of the prefects were transferred to these councils in 1982. There is therefore a two-way flow of influence in the French prefectoral system: up from the department as well as down from Paris. Central–local relations are less top-down than earlier views suggested. The traditional French model has been influential, however. It has been adopted in many other countries, including all France's ex-colonies.

Whether dual or fused, local government systems have had to adapt to modern tasks. These are principally the delivery of welfare services and the planning of large urban areas. The delivery of welfare services tends to make local governments agents of the centre, providing services which they neither design nor fund. This trend went furthest in Scandinavia, where the principle of equal treatment for all citizens has been most fully implemented. But as the basic needs of the population for health and education were satisfied, pressures for decentralisation increased. Communes which had been amalgamated to make uniform treatment possible were taken apart again to encourage citizen participation in local government.

This dynamic – initial centralisation in the name of equality followed by attempted decentralisation in the names of participation and diversity – can also be seen in less marked form in other European countries, among them France, Spain and Italy. Britain was an exception. Central control over local government intensified throughout the 1980s. The Conservative government was more concerned with cost-control and increased efficiency than with greater citizen involvement.

□ The two-way stretch

The need for planning of large cities and regions has led to special systems of government in most unitary states. Attempts to create regional levels of government have also been made. France and Italy have both developed systems of regional authorities, though these bodies function primarily as planning units. Nonetheless they do reveal the 'two-way stretch' which applies to traditional local government in unitary states. On the one hand, contemporary socio-economic patterns call for planning units which cover larger areas than traditional local governments. It makes little sense to draw up plans for villages or small towns if major influences on those areas come from outside.

On the other hand, there is an equal, if less recognised, need to revive the very small and ancient communes and parishes so as to encourage greater citizen participation in local affairs. Outside Scandinavia, there are few signs of the radical reforms which are needed to achieve these distinct, but not incompatible, objectives.

The specialisation of local government in providing services for the general public has led some authors (e.g. Saunders 1979, 1986) to propound the **dual state** thesis. According to this, the basic function of the state in a liberal democracy is to provide the conditions under which capitalist production can continue profitably. This is the 'accumulation function'. But a second, often contradictory function of the state is to maintain its own legitimacy through the provision of services such as health and education. This is the 'legitimation function'. In unitary democracies, the argument continues, the central government gives priority to the accumulation function. Its main concern is the efficient operation of the market economy. Much of the task of legitimation – of providing services demanded by the population – falls to local government. The national government responds to the needs of capital all the more effectively because it has distanced itself from the provision of services. Democracy at local level hides capitalist power at national level. Local politicians compete for resources like hens scrabbling for the corn distributed by the farmer, and unaware of the grain supply which is hidden in the barn.

The dual state thesis has some validity. It certainly improves on the **local state** thesis which views local governments in the first world solely as agents of central government. In Britain, the idea of the dual state helps to explain the conflicts between Margaret Thatcher's Conservative government and left-wing local councils in industrial and inner-city areas with severe social problems. Neither the local state nor the dual state theories are fully adequate, however. Equating the centre with accumulation and local government with legitimation is too simple. All else aside, electoral considerations alone drive central governments into an intimate concern with the level, extent and quality of services delivered to voters.

■ The judiciary

Constitutional government must in part be judicial government. The high value placed on the independence of the courts in the first world testifies not to the irrelevance of the legal to the political realm but to their sensitive interconnection. To apply the law, judges must also interpret and create it. Indeed, the English common law was largely judge-made. Even where the law is extensively codified, as in France and Germany, unforeseen situations require the courts to fill gaps in the legal code or to decide cases by analogy. As the American jurist Oliver Wendell Homes declared, 'General propositions do not decide concrete cases.'

□ *Administrative justice*

The boundary between the creation and the application of law has been further obscured by the enormous expansion of administrative activity. This has led in turn to a growth of quasi-judicial administrative tribunals, despite lingering opposition to their use in both Britain and the United States. Such tribunals, dealing for instance with appeals involving employment law or social security regulations, are relatively informal. They are quicker, cheaper and more flexible (though often more secretive) than the courts.

France has a particularly elaborate system of administrative courts. The Conseil d'Etat (Council of State) stands at its apex. All administrative decisions taken by ministers and officials are subject to it. The Council is also consulted on all proposed legislation. Primarily motivated to protect individual liberties, the prestige of the Council and the publicity given to its rulings enable it to check executive power (Dreyfus 1990, pp. 142–3.) The Conseil Constitutionnel (Constitutional Court) has also become a significant force in French politics. Originally intended to help the executive control the legislature, it has now assumed the power to restrain the executive. It has asserted its right to invalidate unconstitutional legislation – and did so in about half of the 70 bills on which it was asked to rule between 1981 and 1986 (Kesselman *et al.* 1987, p. 184).

□ *Judicial independence and recruitment*

Liberal democracies accept judicial independence as fundamental to the rule of law. In Britain and in the American federal judiciary, judges hold office for life during 'good behaviour'. The judiciary is more closely controlled by the state in most of Western Europe than in Britain or the United States but security of judicial tenure is still well established. In fact, judges appointed during the fascist era in Italy and Germany were embarrassingly hard to remove afterwards. Similar problems are likely to be encountered in Germany with judges from the former German Democratic Republic.

The issue of judicial independence raises the problem of how judges are selected. The four main methods are shown in Table 11.3. Which method is preferred depends on the weight given to judicial independence, on the one hand, and responsiveness to social change or party balance, on the other.

An independent judiciary is not necessarily a neutral judiciary. Judges generally see it as their task to uphold the dominant values of society in order to stabilise the social order. Many observers see this as the fundamental function of law. In Britain, some writers see a conservative bias in the higher judiciary, shown by unfavourable attitudes to the trade union movement (Griffith 1977). More disturbing, perhaps, has been the record of judicial conduct in trials involving alleged Irish Republican Army (IRA) terrorists. Senior judges, supposedly guardians of the criminal justice system, seemed unable to prevent or even rectify palpably unsafe verdicts. In consequence, British justice was seriously discredited. The problem, in our view, stems more from professional arrogance than from ideological bias or the upper-class social backgrounds of judges. Basically, senior judges were loath to admit that the criminal justice system could make very serious mistakes.

Behavioural research into judicial behaviour in the United States has shown that judges' decision in court are strongly related to their political views but the effect of social background on judges' views appears to be fairly weak (Schubert 1972). Widening the recruitment base of the judiciary is intrinsically desirable but will do little to alter its fundamentally conservative role.

Table 11.3 *Methods of selecting judges*

Method	Example	Comment
Popular election	Some states in the USA	Produces responsiveness to public opinion – but at what price in impartiality and competence? May be accompanied by recall procedures
Election by the assembly	Some states in the USA; some Latin American countries	This method also formally used for senior judges in communist states but in practice the party picked suitable candidates
Appointment by the executive	Britain, Supreme Court judges in the USA (subject to Senate approval)	'Danger' (?) of political appointments, though most judges will be appointed by an earlier administration
Co-option by the judiciary	Italy, Turkey	Produces an independent but sometimes unresponsive judiciary

☐ *Interpreting the constitution*

Especially in federal democracies, the judiciary has significant constitutional jurisdiction. This, as G. Smith (1989) describes it, involves 'the power of ordinary or special courts to give authoritative interpretation of the constitution which is binding on all the parties concerned'. Constitutional jurisdiction covers three main areas:

1. Resolving conflict between the state and citizens over basic liberties;
2. Ruling on whether specific laws are constitutional;
3. Resolving conflicts between different institutions or levels of government.

These powers of constitutional review are enjoyed more fully by the Supreme Court in the United States than by any judicial tribunal elsewhere. As Chief Justice Hughes once remarked, 'We live under a constitution. But the constitution is what the judges say it is.' The Supreme Court is so important that appointments to it (nominated by the president, but subject to approval by the Senate) are key decisions. They now normally involve a set-piece battle between presidential friends and foes. The judicial experience, and the legal ability of the nominee, may matter less than ideological and partisan considerations.

Though its activities are legal in form, the Supreme Court's function is basically political. In a real sense it presides over America's constitutional system. It is responsible for protecting the rights of individuals guaranteed under the constitution. It also reviews the constitutionality of congressional statutes and the actions of the executive branch. Its judgments may be far-reaching. For example, a single ruling in 1982 (Immigration and Naturalization Service *versus* Chadha) invalidated portions of no fewer than 49 statutes. Significant checks have also been imposed on the presidency. In 1974, for example, the Court ruled that President Nixon should surrender tape-recordings of confidential discussions with his aides about the Watergate affair, a decision which effectively sealed his fate.

The Supreme Court sometimes boldly overturns its own legal precedents. This inconsistency has been a source of strength in the long run, enabling the Court to adapt the constitution to changes in national mood. For example, after its rearguard struggle against the New Deal, the Court basically conceded the right of the elected national government to regulate the social and economic life of the nation. This is just as well, for the Supreme Court, like all judiciaries, depends on other agencies for the enforcement of its decisions.

The Supreme Court has taken some striking initiatives. The most important of these, taken under the leadership of Chief Justice Warren in the 1950s and 1960s, was on the issue of black civil rights. The Supreme Court of the 1980s and 1990s is much more conservative than its predecessor but no less activist (Shapiro 1990). It seems bent on reversing much of the Warren court's liberal legacy, as it confronts cases on bitterly contentious issues such as abortion, capital punishment and affirmative action (reserved places in employment and education for minority groups). Sometimes called an unelected legislature, the Supreme Court deliberates in a calm atmosphere. In truth, judicial calm exists in the eye of the political storm.

Judicial review is an established feature of several other federal political systems. Decisions of the Canadian Supreme Court played a significant role in the constitutional crisis of 1981 and the resolution of the crisis gave the Court new responsibility for a Charter of Rights and Freedoms. The impact of the Federal Supreme Court on German politics is considerable. German policy-makers, it is said, engage in Karlsruhe astrology (Karlsruhe is where the Court sits) in order to anticipate the likely reaction of the Court to proposed legislation. In Australia and Switzerland there have been judicial efforts to resist centralising tendencies. Where parliamentary sovereignty is enshrined, there are obviously fewer opportunities for judicial review. The Dutch constitution explicitly states that 'the constitutionality of Acts of Parliament and treaties shall not be reviewed by the courts'.

□ The judiciary in the second world

The law is not always a stabilising force. In communist states, it became a major instrument for forcing through a totalitarian reconstruction of society. Under Stalin, Soviet justice showed no procedural impartiality. Vague catch-all offences – 'socially dangerous tendencies' and 'enemies of the people' – were used to ensnare those suspected of opposition to the regime. During the 1950s and 1960s in China, the police dominated the legal system, using the courts as educational devices to warn citizens against bad behaviour. There was a measure of predictability in the enforcement of party objectives but the system was certainly not legalistic.

Although judges in communist states were selected for their 'party-mindedness' and expected to put this to good effect in the courts, the situation was already altering before the sea-change of 1989. Even authoritarian regimes benefit from a consistent application of rules. A measure of 'socialist legality' was observed in the courts. Again, after the hiatus of the Cultural Revolution in China, and especially since Mao's death, laws became more precise and rules were drawn up for the investigation of crimes and prosecution of suspects.

In Eastern Europe especially, old legal traditions were revived as communist rule slackened. Following the collapse of the old order, complete reconstruction of the judiciary, police and criminal justice system is needed but will take years to accomplish.

□ *The judiciary in the third world*

The judiciary has rarely been important in the arbitration of political life in most of the third world. A general pattern of subordination to executive power becomes even more marked under military rule. The Argentine Supreme Court, for instance, routinely accepted rulings made by technically illegal military governments (Waisman 1989, p. 96). The generals, not the judges, had the means of coercion at their disposal.

But judicial weakness also reflects the greater concentration of power within the political systems of the third world. Such power as there is tends to be centred in the executive, not diffused American-style between the president, the legislature and a supreme court. Mexico has a solid record of civilian government under a US-style constitution. However, although Mexico's courts handle disputes among citizens, they have rarely sought to limit executive authority by constitutional review (Levy 1989, p. 470).

A strong and independent judiciary has developed in a few third world countries. The colonial era in India established a tradition of judicial independence which has largely held its ground since independence. In Turkey, the constitutions of 1961 and 1982 provided entrenched security of tenure for judges and prosecutors (Ozbudun 1989, p. 218).

But traditional methods for the adjudication of disputes still prevail in much of the third world, especially in rural areas. Justice continues to be dispensed by tribal elders, village courts, local chiefs or religious leaders. Indeed with the revival of Islam, priests have become more influential in the administration of justice in many Middle Eastern and African societies, enforcing the harsh penalties of the Islamic Shari'a code.

Summary

1.   Constitutions are the laws that govern the governors. Most nation-states have them and a growing number of governments abide by them. They provide the ground rules for politics and organise the formal distribution of power within the state. They often also set out the rights of individuals. Constitutions work best when they do not attempt too much. A few constitutions are unwritten, but most are codified and need special procedures for amendment.

2.   New constitutions are generally associated with fresh starts in the political life of a nation (e.g. Spain 1978). But constitutional adaptation takes place more or less continuously (e.g. the evolving interpretations of the American constitution offered by the Supreme Court).

3.   Federalism involves a constitutionally guaranteed sharing of power between levels of government. In a confederal system, the central power is weak; in a federal system, it is stronger. Fewer than twenty states are federal but these cover most of the world's land surface. Federalism is a legalistic arrangement, which almost always needs judicial arbitration.

4.   In the twentieth century, the central level of government has gained ground against the provincial level. Financial, political and policy-making relations between levels of government make for increasing interdependence. The federal theory of separate spheres of activity for each level no longer matches political and economic reality.

5.   In unitary systems, local government is subject to the legal authority of central government, which can change its functions and organisation. Local government takes two forms. In dual systems, local government is organisationally separate from the centre. In fused systems, the central and local government are joined in an office such as a prefect.

6.   Judicial independence from the executive is an established feature of liberal democracies. In many liberal democracies, especially federal ones, the judiciary plays an important role in interpreting the constitution.

Discussion points

1.   'Since judges are inevitably political, democracy requires that they should be elected.' Do you agree?

2.   'Like politics textbooks, written constitutions are out-of-date the day they are written.' Do you agree? If so, is the solution to have unwritten constitutions?

3.   Will the twenty-first century be the century of federations between nation-states? Will your country become part of a federal group and will you welcome or regret such a development?

4.   What can be done to revive local government?

Key reading

Bogdanor, V. (ed.) (1988) *Constitutions in Democratic Politics* (Aldershot: Gower). A useful volume, reviewing constitutional issues and experience in sixteen liberal democracies.

O'Brien, D. (1986) *Storm Center: The Supreme Court in American Politics* (New York: Norton). A lively account of a fascinating institution.

Forsyth, M. (ed.) (1989) *Federalism and Nationalism* (Leicester University Press). Assesses the experience of federalism around the world.

Wright, D. (1988) *Understanding Intergovernmental Relations* (Pacific Grove, Calif: Brooks Cole). An informed assessment of contemporary American federalism.

Further reading

Once neglected by modern political science, there is growing recognition of the importance of constitutions. Duchacek (1973) remains a useful introduction. Banting and Simeon (1985) is a good edited collections of essays on constitutional changes in the first world.

On federalism a comprehensive survey can be found in Duchacek (1970), though Riker (1975) is more penetrating: see also Dahl (1983). The legal approach is classically presented by Wheare (1963), but Reagan and Sanzone (1982) or D. Wright (1988) are much more realistic accounts of how contemporary federalism operates in the United States. On European federalism, G. Smith (1989) gives a useful overview while Burgess (1985) is a current but uneven collection about individual states.

For unitary states, see G. Smith (1989) on Western Europe, Nelson (1982) on communist states and Bowman and Hampton (1983) on local government in Anglo-American states.

On the judiciary, Griffith (1977) gives a challenging interpretation for Britain while Shapiro (1990) is equally astringent on the Supreme Court in the United States.

■ Chapter 12 ■

Assemblies

Elected assemblies are the very symbol of representative government. This is seen most dramatically in times of political crisis. For example, in August 1991 an eight-man junta of hard-line communist ministers and officials attempted a coup in the Soviet Union. With President Gorbachev under house arrest in his holiday home on the Black Sea, the 'White House' (the parliament building of the Russian Federation in Moscow) became the leading focus of resistance. Boris Yeltsin and his band of Russian deputies remained in the parliament building for several days, protected by a sizeable crowd and a few elderly tanks. Serious coup-makers would have flattened the place. Fortunately, these were not forceful conspirators. Their bluff was called and the coup collapsed. The 'White House' had become a powerful symbol of popular sovereignty and democracy.

An assembly is a multi-membered body which considers questions of public policy and has constitutional powers to make law. Assemblies have one core, defining function: 'They give assent, on behalf of a political community that extends beyond the executive authority, to binding measures of public policy' (Norton 1990a, p. 1).

Western political thought has traditionally stressed the law-making function of assemblies. Today, however, even in liberal democracies, most 'legislatures' have only modest law-making capabilities. As the scope of government has grown, effective control of law-making has moved to the executive and the bureaucracy. Assemblies *pass* laws without really *making* them.

The legislative role of assemblies may have declined, but in other ways their importance is undiminished, perhaps even increasing. Assemblies are versatile institutions. As in the Soviet Union in 1991, they adapt to their political environment and have great symbolic importance. Even when its impact upon policy is modest, the assembly has a capacity to legitimise those who govern. This makes it resilient. In short, assemblies help to 'mobilise consent' (Beer 1967).

This is very important in building democratic regimes. In the 1970s and 1980s, assemblies played a key role in revitalising democracy across Southern Europe in Spain, Portugal, Greece and Turkey (Liebert and Cotta 1990). A similar task of democratic consolidation is falling to assemblies in Eastern Europe in the 1990s.

Even authoritarian rulers value the appearance of public consent. Only 14 out of 164 independent states had no assembly in 1990. Of those 14, only 5 (traditional dynastic states in the Arabian Gulf) had no past experience of assemblies at all. A representative assembly of some kind throws the shadow, if not the substance, of legitimacy across authoritarian rulers.

In this chapter, we first consider questions of assembly structure and function. Then we look at how assemblies can be classified by their impact on policy. Finally we turn to a discussion of the roles played by assemblies in each of the three worlds.

■ Structure of assemblies

The two most important structural differences between assemblies lie in the number of chambers, and in the nature of the committee system. Both have a profound impact on how assemblies operate.

□ *Number of chambers*

Only two things can be said with certainty about every assembly in the world: how large it is and how many chambers it has (Blondel 1973). In terms of size, the smallest in the world is the assembly of 12 which meets from time to time in Funafuti, the capital city of the South Pacific island of Tuvalu. (As Tuvalu's population is only 8624, it has far more representatives per head than most other assemblies). The biggest in the world is the 2000 of the National Peoples' Congress in China. With some exceptions, more populous countries tend to have larger assemblies.

Chamber structure is more important than the size of an assembly's membership. Nearly all assemblies are either unicameral (single chamber) or bicameral (two chambers). Unicameral assemblies have been adopted in some liberal democracies, notably New Zealand and the Nordic countries, but are most common among newer and smaller states, particularly in Africa. Some communist and postcommunist states also have single chamber assemblies.

Despite the trend to single chambers, about half of all assemblies are still bicameral. First chambers are normally chosen by direct election. Second chambers often use some form (or combination) of indirect election, nomination or hereditary membership. In the Netherlands, for instance, members are elected by the Provincial Councils. Differences in selection procedure between the two chambers ensure that their compositions vary.

Bicameralism has two main justifications. First, it provides checks and balances within the legislature. Secondly, it enables distinct territories or interests to be represented. Modern bicameralism varies between **weaker** and **stronger** versions. In the weaker version, the second chamber is clearly subordinate to the first chamber, but retains some powers to delay legislation or force its reconsideration. The British House of Lords, which can delay non-financial legislation for a year, is an example. A bicameral assembly of the weaker variety thus provides for a revising or restraining function. However, in so doing it dilutes the principle of popular sovereignty.

Under the stronger version of bicameralism, the two chambers have broadly equal powers but embody distinct constitutional principles. The first chamber is based on popular sovereignty, the second chamber on the territories making up the political system. The Senate of the United States Congress, composed of two senators from each state, is the classic example of a strong second chamber. Its design has been copied by the Australian Senate, and by assemblies in some other federal systems. Under the stronger version of bicameralism, the dispersal of authority is substantial. Conflict, and even deadlock, between the two chambers is a real possibility. In practice, this often means that the executive lacks an assured majority in one (or, in the United States, often both) chambers. Thus a government's policy programme may face very real restraints.

☐ Committees

A powerful assembly needs a well-developed committee structure. As Kashyap (1979, p. 321) observes, 'a legislature is known by the committees it keeps'. Committees are small workgroups of members, set up in almost all assemblies to cope with the volume of business. Their functions include the detailed consideration of legislative measures and examination of financial proposals. They also scrutinise government administration and past expenditure, and investigate matters of public concern. A strong committee system can make the key difference between a 'working' and a 'talking' assembly.

Many hopes for improving parliamentary performance have been pinned on reform of assembly committees. Such hopes have not always been fulfilled. To be effective, committees need members who are not afraid of executive wrath. But governments prefer docile committees, and have jobs to offer those members of the assembly who prove to be 'reliable'. Moreover, sharing out tasks among the membership can have drawbacks for the assembly itself. Committees sometimes come to dominate the assembly they are meant to serve. They may in effect become legislatures in miniature, and substitute their own decisions for those of the full assembly.

The United States Congress is probably unique in the impact of its committees upon virtually all aspects of legislative activity. 'Congress in its committee rooms is Congress at work', wrote Woodrow Wilson a century ago. This is still true today. The expertise of congressional committees comes from specialisation. This is carried to extreme lengths in numerous subcommittees (now almost 250) with a fairly stable membership. Committees are well funded, and they have highly professional advisory staffs. Congressional committees show great autonomy, and they settle the fate and shape of most legislation.

Committees have less influence on legislation in other assemblies. In the British House of Commons, government bills are examined by **standing committees**. But these largely replicate party combat on the floor of the chamber. The standing committees of the House of Commons, unlike those of Congress, do not strongly challenge executive dominance in framing and shaping legislation. They are unspecialised and have slender resources. Because committee service is unpopular, they have grown smaller. However, the system of **select committees** of scrutiny, parallel with all the main government departments, has expanded. These assist the House of Commons in probing government policy and overseeing how it is carried out (Norton 1990b).

The Australian Parliament reveals a significant contrast between its two chambers. In the House of Representatives, interest in committee service has been weak, and efforts to strengthen the committee system have been unimpressive. By the late 1970s almost half the backbenchers in the House of Representatives had no committee assignments at all (Turner 1989, p. 78). In the Senate, by contrast, committees have grown and virtually all backbenchers served on them, averaging over two committees each. What explains this difference? The answer is that the House of Representatives is more executive-dominated: **party** committees are more important for ambitious backbenchers than **parliamentary** committees. The Senate ('The States' House') is a much stronger check on the executive than the House of Representatives. Its committees provide very good footholds for resistance. The Australian example shows that effective committees are most likely when the government does not control the relevant chamber.

The case of the German Bundestag, however, shows that influential committees can sometimes coexist with strong parties. Party discipline is firm but the committee members have more regard for objectivity than point-scoring (N. Johnson 1979, p. 124). The government gives the expertise of the committees due weight, and the impact of committee scrutiny on legislation can be considerable. In Germany, as in many countries of continental Europe, the overall political style is less adversarial than in Australia, Britain or New Zealand. This makes it easier for influential committees to coexist with strong parties.

In Canada, committees traditionally played little role in a party-dominated and generally inactive House of Commons. Franks (1971, pp. 279–80) commented that 'there are roving squads of government members whose chief ability is to sit on committees, read newspapers, sign letters and at the same time raise their right hands in approval of matters on which they had no previous experience.' But the famous bells incident in 1982 encouraged reform of parliament, including its committees. As a way of putting pressure on the government, the Conservative opposition had refused to take part in a vote. Parliament was paralysed for fifteen days as the division bells rang (W. White *et al.* 1991, p. 413). Subsequently, the membership of committees was reduced and made more stable, committees were given power to investigate matters of their own choosing, provided with more specialist support and the ability to scrutinise some government appointments.

The evidence suggests that strong committees make for a strong assembly. But what makes committees strong? The timing of committee scrutiny of bills within the legislative process makes a difference. Committees that consider bills before a general debate and vote in the assembly have more impact than those which only deal with a bill after it has received broad approval (Shaw 1979). Beyond this, the key to committee influence mainly lies in expertise, which is itself a product of four main factors: specialisation, permanence, intimacy and support facilities.

Committees with **specialised** responsibilities and a clear field of operation are most likely to develop expert knowledge. Likewise, **permanent** committees will gather knowledge in a manner which is not possible for committees created anew each session. Continuity of individual membership is no less important. **Intimacy** is a product of size. Within small committees proceedings are face to face. When meetings are held in private, a small-group setting can encourage norms of cooperation, and a search for consensus. In these conditions, committees can develop their own sense of identity. **Support**, finally, refers to the use of qualified staff to advise committees. While this may bring new problems of dependency, it does reduce reliance on the executive. It also redresses the balance somewhat against the great weight of expertise available on the government side.

■ Functions of assemblies

By 'functions', we mean the significance of assembly activities for the wider political system. Assemblies can perform a wide range of functions. Whether, and how well, an assembly performs them depends on its standing in relation to the other branches of government. Perhaps the key function of the modern assembly is representation. The other functions we examine here are making and dismissing governments; passing laws and scrutinising the executive; and recruitment and socialisation of political leaders.

□ *Representation*

Representation is at the very root of what assemblies are about. The assembly 'stands for' the people and acts for them. But assembly members can 'represent' the electorate in various ways, with differing consequences for the way the assembly works.

Styles of representation vary, most sharply between 'delegate' and 'trustee' approaches. The **delegate** is closely bound to reflect the wishes of those who elected him or her. Delegates are typically 'mandated', that is given instructions to carry out. The **trustee**, by contrast, uses independent judgement on behalf of the voters. The trustee is free to ignore the voter's views, but does so at his or her peril. Edmund Burke, the eighteenth-century statesman who classically expressed the trustee approach in an address to the electors of Bristol, England, was later rejected by them.

Today, legislators are rarely delegated to vote in a particular way by those who select or elect them, although they do work on behalf of their constituents' interests. Yet at the same time the modern assembly member is not a pure trustee. He or she can rarely use mature judgement alone in deciding how to vote on proposed legislation. Representatives are constrained by party discipline. Party loyalties cut across the traditional distinction between the delegate and the trustee.

The focus of legislators' activities varies between constituency, party, interest and policy. A **constituency** focus implies that the main aim of assembly members is to secure benefits, or provide services for the area that elected them. The 'porkbarrel' tradition in American politics epitomises this approach: see exhibit 12.1. However, it is far from unique to the United States. As voters' party loyalties weaken, so members must take more time to build a clear image in the minds of their constituents. The 'personal vote' was always significant in the United States. It can now be seen in other countries as well, including Britain (Cain, Ferejohn and Fiorina 1987).

A **party** focus implies that the legislator's main allegiance is to the party to which he or she belongs. Parties with many such members will be disciplined and cohesive, and the assembly will be party-dominated. There is a clear contrast here between Westminster-style parliaments and the US Congress. The former, found in Australia, Canada and New Zealand as well as Britain, have strong parties whose members mainly vote on party lines. The American Congress, by contrast, has weaker parties and fluid voting patterns.

Interest representation views the assembly member as a spokesperson for a particular group in society. At one extreme this may be a pragmatic relationship based on money. Many members are paid by interest groups to present their case in the assembly. This is done by asking questions of ministers, opposing 'unhelpful' legislation, and by checking on government activity that might affect the interests concerned. Such activities are common in most assemblies. The role of Political Action Committees (PACs) in the United States puts the issue of assembly members' independence in sharp focus. The PACs contribute one dollar in every four spent in Congressional elections. The money goes mostly to incumbents. At the other extreme, assembly members may identify with a particular social group, so that they feel their first duty is to support its interests. This tradition of 'social representation' is strong in many societies, particularly in Western Europe, where parties represent social, religious or regional groups.

A **policy** focus implies that the main concern of the representative is to achieve policy goals. Surprising as it may seem, many assembly members are not very active in this way. They are often more concerned with individual casework or with becoming part of the club. But for some members, policies *are* politics. Policy-oriented members may be driven by ideological commitments, or by a technocratic approach to improving public policy. Either way, they work hard and enjoy their task. They wish to influence government, and do not want to be deferential lobbyfodder. Barber (1977) calls these representatives the 'active-positive' type. The American Congress, with its strong committees and weak

Exhibit 12.1   *The legislative porkbarrel*

As the title of a classic book puts it (Lasswell 1936), politics is about who gets what, when and how. In liberal democracies, distributive issues are never far from politicians' minds – because they never are far from voters' minds. In a political system with weak parties yet so dedicated to electoral representation as the United States, the legislative porkbarrel is only to be expected. Members of Congress feel compelled to 'bring home the bacon': to demonstrate that they are serving the district in the tangible form (e.g. federally funded construction projects or subsidies for locally grown crops). The electoral imperative drives porkbarrel politics.

Congressman Robert Leggett was a prince among pork-eaters. 'We have the Mare Island Navy shipyard in my district and the only nuclear naval shipyard. I like to build lots of those nuclear subs. I've done some personal emissary work to get some of the contracts. In my district is the Travis Air Force Base (AFB), the Beale AFB, the Mather AFB, the McLelland AFB, the Sacramento Army Depot and the Aerojet General Corporation' (Sherrill 1974, p. 133).

To pass porkbarrel legislation, members of Congress exploit their committee assignments (Leggett, for example, served on the House Armed Services Committee). They employ 'logrolling' tactics, building coalitions by mutual trading of favours, regardless of party. A particular favourite is the 'Christmas-tree bill', so called because it is hung with goodies for many members' constituents. In a kind of blackmail, pork items are sometimes tacked to the end of important financial bills, which the president is virtually unable to veto.

Critics say that porkbarrel tactics lead to waste, distorted patterns of expenditure and fiscal irresponsibility. Ronald Reagan favoured a line-item veto for the president, so that he could strike out flagrant pork-barrel expenditures. This would need a constitutional amendment – which is unlikely to be passed by a Congress so addicted to pork. Similar tendencies are visible in other legislatures, but rarely so brazenly as in the United States with individualistic and highly entrepreneurial legislators.

party cohesion, favours policy-focused representation. As the educational level and professionalism of members increases throughout the world, policy-oriented representation is probably becoming more common. This may lie behind the modest re-emergence of assemblies in liberal democracies in the 1970s and 1980s (Norton 1990b).

We can look at the Netherlands as an example of how these roles work out in practice. Members of the lower house are certainly not delegated by their voters. Elected by proportional representation, they have little contact with their constituents. Neither are they representatives of particular interests. There is a cultural tradition against working for specific groups. Many members see their main role as offering serious contributions to debates on national issues. Member's views are influenced by the party group to which they belong – but even these parliamentary groupings have substantial independence from the parties outside parliament. In short, Dutch parliamentarians come closer than many to Burke's trustee model.

☐ *Making governments*

The assembly in parliamentary systems plays an important role in making, and breaking, governments. In a parliamentary system, the executive governs only so long as it retains the confidence of the assembly. Parliament remains the sovereign body. This is in contrast to presidential systems, where the chief executive is directly elected by the people and cannot normally be removed from office by the assembly.

The sovereignty of the assembly in a parliamentary system does not mean that it dominates the business of forming governments. Parliament is kept firmly under control in countries with single-party government, such as Canada, New Zealand and the United Kingdom. In these countries, the 'first past the post' electoral system usually delivers a parliamentary majority for a single party. This party then forms the government, and needs only the support of its own backbenchers to remain in office. The government is chosen *through*, but not *by*, the assembly.

Where countries employ proportional representation, the process of government formation tends to be very different. (These include nearly all European countries, West or East, except Britain.) Elections under PR rarely produce a parliamentary majority for a single party. Hence coalitions must be formed. In this situation the assembly becomes an important political arena. It sets the context for bargaining between the parties. The more seats a party has in the assembly, the bigger the punch it can throw in negotiations. Once a coalition government has been formed, the governing parties must treat backbenchers with respect lest they lose the support of some members on which their majority (now or in the future) depends.

In the Netherlands, for example, the process of legislation is executive-directed but the legislature is not executive-dominated

(Gladdish 1991). Ministers engage in extensive behind-the-scenes consultations and accept amendments on up to a half of all measures, in order to maintain the support of their party *fractie* (parliamentary group).

When a coalition government falls, the focus moves back to the assembly. A new coalition, composed of a fresh combination of parties, may emerge without any need for a general election. This explains why some European countries have had more governments than elections since the war: these include Belgium, Denmark and Italy. Finland, an extreme case, got though 33 governments in the 32 years after 1945. Even in these cases, the assembly does not itself govern; but it plays an important and recurring role in deciding who does.

☐ Law-making and scrutiny

Assemblies have authority to make law, but in practice, prime responsibility for policy-making rests with the executive. Assembly influence comes from other activities. These include formal debate on government bills and proposals; committee scrutiny of legislation; investigatory committees; questioning of ministers; and motions of censure and no confidence.

Assemblies mainly decide matters by voting. In authoritarian one-party regimes, voting is nearly always unanimous. The vote confirms the policy but does not shape it. But the contrast with liberal democracies is not clear-cut. In liberal democracies the assembly is also often under one party's control and the outcome of votes is predictable. The majority governing party is usually pitted against the minority opposition. Broadly speaking, this pattern describes legislative voting in France and Germany as well as in Westminster-style parliaments. When the government's majority is in doubt, as in periods of minority government in Canada in the 1960s and 1970s, and in Britain in the late 1970s, backbenchers have a stronger bargaining position. But these periods are still rare.

However, some cooperation between parties is vital to avoid stalemate. Much legislation, in fact, passes without division. The US Senate, for instance, processes most of its business by consent. In the British Parliament, party managers cooperate behind the scenes. In Italy tacit collaboration between the parties allows much legislation to be dealt with entirely by committees.

Oral and written questioning of ministers is a more important form of parliamentary scrutiny in many countries than votes and debates on the floor. In 1987 members of Britain's House of Commons asked 73 000 oral and written questions. The number of questions in the Dutch lower house increased sevenfold between 1960 and 1980. Questioning of administration spokespersons by Congressional committees fulfils a similar purpose in American government. In Germany, Finland, and formerly in France, 'interpellation' is used. This means that the oral questioning of a minister is followed by a snap vote of the assembly as to its satisfaction with the answers given – an instant vote of confidence. This technique brought down several governments in the French Third and Fourth Republics.

Professionalism helps the assembly to influence policy and scrutinise its implementation. When sessions of the assembly are short and its members are amateur, effective policy-making and supervision of government is unlikely. Yet this is precisely the situation in many assemblies, even in some liberal democracies. The Australian House of Representatives is, in effect, a part-time assembly. It sat for an average of 65 days a year in the 1980s. The British House of Commons, by contrast, is in session for almost nine months of the year. Yet Britain's hard-working MPs are poorly paid and many pursue outside occupations. In the past, effective performance by MPs has also been hampered by limited research and secretarial services. However, the new system of select committees in Britain does appear to have improved supervision of government.

Members of the US Congress, by contrast, are lavishly funded. They employ large personal staffs and are supported by expert research services. For the 1980 session Congress cost over $1150 million, mainly to pay its 25 000 staff. By comparison, the cost of the House of Commons in 1980–81 was a mere £12.6 million (Shaw 1983, p. 143).

□ *Recruitment and socialisation*

Assemblies play a role in recruiting and socialising political leaders. Members of the legislature form a pool of talent, experience and ambition from which leading decision-makers emerge. This is the case in most liberal democracies, and even in many authoritarian regimes. It is most true in Britain and other strong parliamentary systems, where nearly all government ministers are drawn from (and still sit) in the House of Commons. Parliament is thus the key channel of recruitment to top political office. This is less true in the United States, where recent presidents have been drawn from state governments rather than from the Congress. Constitutional rules make a differnce. In France and the Netherlands, ministers cannot be members of parliament. This may explain why so many Dutch MPs do not seek re-election. Their average tenure of office is very low at five years.

In liberal democracies, the traditions and procedures of the assembly influence national politics and shape the behaviour of politicians. Many observers have pointed to the speed with which the House of Commons absorbed and 're-educated' many of the fire-breathing socialists who entered Parliament after 1918. More recently, assemblies in Spain and Portugal served to bring together people of different ideologies and background, and reduce hostility between them. Where the commitment to parliamentary norms is strong, tensions can be managed through the assembly. They are then less likely to be ventilated on the streets – or through military coups. By integrating major political actors and power groups within society, parliamentary institutions can regulate – if not resolve – conflicts between them (Liebert and Cotta 1990 pp. 13–17). This integrative capacity of legislatives will be fully tested in Eastern Europe during the 1990s.

▌Assemblies in three worlds: a policy classification

In some countries the assembly contributes strongly to policy-making. In others it acts merely as a rubber stamp. The debating chamber of the assembly may be the focal point of national political life or nothing more than an intermittent sideshow. This variation is captured in Mezey's classification (1979) of the policy impact of legislatures (Table 12.1).

Table 12.1 *A policy classification of assemblies*

Type	Nature	Example
Active	Assembly makes policy actively and autonomously	US Congress
Reactive	Assembly reacts to and influences government policy	Westminster-style parliaments
Marginal	Assembly is a minor partner in executive policy-making	Polish Sejm (pre-1989)
Minimal	Assembly is a rubber stamp under executive domination	Malawi

Source: Adapted from: M. Mezey, *Comparative Legislatures* (Durham, N. Carolina: Duke University Press, 1979).

Mezey distinguishes between active, reactive, marginal and minimal assemblies. **Active** assemblies, such as the United States Congress, make policy actively and autonomously. **Reactive** assemblies, such as Britain's House of Commons, mainly respond to executive initiatives. The reactive assembly influences policy more than it makes it. **Marginal** assemblies are executive-controlled to the extent that they influence executive behaviour and contribute to policy-making only slightly. In the communist states of Eastern Europe, assemblies were at most marginal participants in the policy process. Finally, **minimal** assemblies, common in the third world, are largely irrelevant to policy-making. They are retained to provide some legitimacy for the regime.

These variations in the policy-making role of assemblies are the product of several factors. First, history makes a big difference. A few countries such as Britain have a long history of parliamentary development. Parliament is a stable, entrenched institution. For many other countries, representative institutions are a recent creation. Therefore they are more vulnerable to executive domination or outright suppression.

Secondly, the party system also influences the assembly's role. Assemblies generally have more impact in multi-party systems than in two-party systems. They are also more significant in competitive party systems than in one-party states.

Thirdly, constitutional rules on executive-legislative relations are a major factor, at least in liberal democracies. Here, the main contrast is between presidential and parliamentary systems, though some countries have hybrid arrangements.

Fourthly, the capabilities of assemblies are related to their internal structures and procedures. Committee systems and support facilities enhance the impact of assemblies on policy.

But the major contrast in the role of assemblies is between the three worlds. We will consider assemblies in each of the three worlds in turn.

▌ First world assemblies: policy-making and ▌ influencing

The United States Congress is the best example of an active policy-making assembly. In law-making, it displays strong autonomy from the executive. Presidents may seek to influence what Congress decides, but they cannot dictate to it: 'The President proposes but Congress disposes.' The president must mostly accept what Congress offers or, if he employs his power of veto, do without. Legislature and executive share power in relative balance. Cooperation is possible, but so too are conflict and stalemate. The autonomy of Congress from presidential control is underpinned by the separation of powers, by limited party cohesion, and by the authority of its committees.

However, Congressional power is often used in negative and obstructive ways, to benefit narrow but well-connected interests in American society. From the New Deal onwards, the American public looked to the White House rather than Congress for political leadership. This was reflected by the way in which presidents took legislative initiatives. But the 1970s saw a resurgence of Congressional power in reaction to the so-called 'imperial' presidency. Within Congress major changes took place in the committee and seniority systems. These made the legislature more egalitarian where power had previously been the preserve of a few senior Congressmen.

As a result, the 1980s saw deadlock within the Congress. Struggles took place between president and Congress over nominations and the budget. Thus, managing relations with Congress has become even harder and more complex for the president. In effect, he has to deal with numerous independent assembly members, each with good resources, rather than with the legislature as a whole (Bailey 1989, p. 164).

The American Congress is an exceptional, perhaps even unique, institution. Most assemblies in liberal democracies are policy-influencing rather than policy-making bodies. Their role is reactive, responding to policy-making initiatives from the executive. The reactive assembly ratifies more than it makes legislation, but may often modify it. This pattern is best seen in Westminster-style parliaments, found in countries with close historical ties with Britain.

Reactive assemblies often function along adversary lines. In New Zealand, for example, 'opposition MPs see their task as discrediting the government. They seek to extend the range of perceived problems. They search out and exploit all grievances which they can appropriate, within limits set by their own biases and commitments' (Wood 1988, p. 52).

The British House of Commons, similarly, is an arena in which a ritualised confrontation takes place between government and opposition. Behind its often arcane proceedings, a continuous election campaign goes on. It is a form of theatre, now aimed at the television audience. Sustained by a disciplined party majority, the cabinet commands the Commons and can expect to see almost all its proposed legislation enacted. As in New Zealand, the task of the opposition is to oppose: to force the government to account and to question, debate and criticise its policy. Parliamentary debate and committee scrutiny may not have much direct impact upon legislation, but it affects the government's morale – and its prospects of re-election.

In a reactive assembly, the key relationship for the government lies with its own backbenchers. As Margaret Thatcher found to her cost in November 1990, even a dominant leader must address the concerns of backbenchers. If she is deaf to growing criticism, in the end she forfeits their loyalty and her own position. Commanders who lose the confidence of their troops do not last long. Such exceptional episodes aside, the direct impact of reactive assemblies upon legislation is modest. Their real importance is that the government is forced to account for itself. In theory, this process helps voters to decide whether the government should continue, or be thrown from office, at the next election.

The parliament of the Fifth French Republic is another example of a reactive assembly. It is policy-influencing, but only to a mild extent. The French parliament has been described as a loyal workhorse but a poor watchdog (Frears 1990, p. 32). It does not initiate legislation, is not the main channel for ministerial recruitment, and does not function well as an arena of national debate. However, it does examine, improve and legitimise legislation.

Where assemblies do gain greater significance, this is often a reflection of deeper political instability. For instance, the National Assembly of the Third (1870–1940) and Fourth (1945–58) French Republics over-shadowed political life generally and the executive in particular. The assembly often used its constitutional power to overthrow the executive. In the twelve years of the Fourth Republic, 25 governments came and went. The life of many cabinets was measured in weeks rather than months. The influence of the assembly was strong but negative. Governments could not muster stable support for a variety of reasons. Deputies engineered their downfall in the hope of gaining office for themselves. The many parties in the Assembly were sorely at odds with one another. The Communists on the left and the Gaullists on the right rejected the regime itself.

Italy provides the nearest modern case of 'assembly government'. It experienced 48 governments between 1945 and 1990. Government crises are such a recurring feature of Italian politics that the word 'crisis' inaccurately describes what is usually a routine reshuffle of ministerial faces. Again, these 'crises' are more rooted in the party system than in the procedures of parliament itself. However, the policy impact of the Italian parliament remains considerable. Government legislation is often amended and many private bills are passed (Furlong 1990, p. 52).

The Swedish Riksdag is a more stable case of an assembly which exerts strong policy influence (Arter 1990, p. 139). The impact of the

Riksdag was enhanced by organisational changes linked with the transition to a unicameral assembly in 1971, in particular the strengthening of the committee system. The Riksdag's impact also reflects the exceptionally strong norms of consultation in Swedish politics. Policy is arrived at through discussion and compromise between representatives of interested groups. Backbench initiatives and legislative committees are both significant features of the policy-making process.

■ Second world: the assembly as theatre

In the second world, assemblies have always been a form of theatre rather than a decision-making arena. However, the nature of their performance changed greatly as communist rule fell apart. Under communism, the legislative actors performed without gusto, merely reading out a dull script outlined for them by the ruling party. In the move to postcommunism, the drama came alive. The script became more impromptu, the outcome less certain and the acting more passionate. As postcommunist rule matures, the quality of the legislative performance may fall back – but not, surely, to the banal level of the communist era.

□ *Assemblies under communist rule*

Under communism, the ruling party dominated the assembly. In theory, the assembly was sovereign but in practice its main functions were ritual and propaganda. Assemblies symbolised both the unity within the ruling party and the links between the leaders and the led. Government officials used assemblies to outline past successes and future targets. There was little real debate and even less dissent. The assembly formally elected the prime minister and other ministers but invariably rubber-stamped the party's choices. Standing ovations for the leaders were a major feature of the script; free debate was not. The lack of time devoted to sessions further limited the impact of assemblies. Plenary sessions were brief and infrequent – about ten days per year. Thus the policy-making role of assemblies in communist party states was, for most of their history, minimal.

This remains the situation in the People's Republic of China (PRC). Some reforms have taken place, but criticism of the party is still confined to local and minor matters. After the death of Mao, real efforts were made to strengthen the role of the National People's Congress (NPC) which did not meet during the last twelve years of Mao's life. However, the NPC still meets in very short plenary sessions, so the real debate takes place in the assembly's preparatory groups and committees. Here specific policies can meet opposition and local and national minority interests can be aired. For example, after the Chinese leadership announced an economic retrenchment policy in 1988, representatives of the poorer areas complained that their districts would be hit hardest by the new policy.

There is also another assembly in China, the Chinese People's Political Consultative Conference. However, this is nothing more than a talking shop, which brings non-party members into the political process. A safe and sanitised forum for debate, it rewards those who have toed the line over the years – a Chinese counterpart to Britain's House of Lords. Although assemblies have recovered some power and influence in the PRC since the death of Mao, they remain clearly subordinate to the ruling communist party.

☐ *Assemblies in postcommunist states*

Far-reaching changes took place in the role of assemblies in the second world during the late 1980s, not least in the Soviet Union. In the Supreme Soviet (the USSR's assembly), real and often heated debates over key issues replaced the contrived proceedings of the past. For the first time in Soviet history, the great questions of the time were played out in public rather than behind closed doors. The problems posed by disintegration of the Soviet Union itself made the situation even more tense. Many old-style deputies remained, behaving compliantly towards the leadership on the platform, and aggressively towards the reformers. But the radical minority seized the new opportunities now open to it. The television cameras were their main weapon. The leaders could no longer impose an artificial consensus; instead, they had to seek genuine agreement. Party leaders could no longer be certain that their proposals would be accepted without demur by the assembly.

These developments were radical and rapid, but they speeded up changes already under way in the role of communist assemblies. Even under Brezhnev's rule, S. White (1982) argued that the Supreme Soviet was playing a real, if still marginal, role in influencing policy. As in China after the death of Mao, criticism of specific policies had increased, as had special pleading for local interests. Permanent standing commissions of the assembly had become more significant in making policy and in influencing the budget.

Before the late 1980s, however, legislative criticism posed no real threat to party leaders. With the introduction of semi-free elections in

1989, President Gorbachev sought mass support for *perestroika* to overcome bureaucratic resistance. But the legislative outcome was paradoxical. The Supreme Soviet rapidly became a significant arena of conflict and decision-making, in which Gorbachev's policies and specific decisions came under fire from both radicals and conservatives. Approval by docile, hand-picked deputies was no longer guaranteed. Turbulent and unpredictable sessions became compulsive viewing on television for the Soviet public. But the revitalised Supreme Soviet also contributed to the decline of Gorbachev's authority. It revealed a political leader who was no longer in control of his own programme of reform. The assembly ended up biting its reformer's hand.

In Eastern Europe, assemblies also became important arenas in the fall from power of ruling communist parties. Poland is the best example. Minor parties have always been represented in Poland's parliament, the Sejm. Committees frequently amended government policy and committee members often introduced major legislation. However, the real drama came in April 1989, when the government made a desperate move to improve its legitimacy. It decided to put up a third of the seats in the Sejm for free election, plus all 100 seats in a new upper house (Senate). Amazingly, Solidarity won all but one of the seats open to it. Although the communists kept their majority in the Sejm (because they had 'won' the seats where Solidarity was not permitted to stand), the Communist Party could no longer even pretend to have a popular mandate. Its days in power were numbered. President Jaruszelski opened negotiations with Solidarity, and Poland's first non-communist government since 1945 took office three months later.

Assemblies are now undoubtedly stronger in relation to governments in postcommunist Eastern Europe, but their role is still evolving. The strength of parliamentary norms and democratic traditions varies greatly from one country to another. These are stronger, for example, in Czechoslovakia and Poland than in Romania and Bulgaria. The future of the assembly is likely to hinge upon developments in the wider political system. Assemblies will be critical agencies for democratic consolidation, as in southern Europe two decades earlier. There is a clear danger in several countries, however, that assemblies may degenerate into sounding-boards for intensely felt but intractable questions of national minorities and ethnic relations. These issues were suppressed (but not resolved) during decades of communist control. The politics of authoritarian collectivism may be replaced by the politics of authoritarian nationalism.

One difficulty facing the new rulers of several postcommunist states is that they lack the special legislative majorities needed to push through radical economic and constitutional reforms. The Polish Sejm, for instance, continued to be dominated by communists chosen under the semi-free elections in 1989. This meant it quickly became a site of resistance to postcommunist reforms. By mid-1991 a crisis unfolded as the Sejm blocked emergency measures which the government said were needed to revive the economy. When the Prime Minister offered the government's resignation, the Sejm refused it. Assembly–executive relations had become locked in an unproductive stalemate, which continued after the elections of October 1991 produced extremely fragmented party representation in the Sejm.

Several of the new regimes have executive presidents, and real power is likely to be tilted toward presidents rather than assemblies. In both Poland and Czechoslovakia, the president has the right to dissolve the national assembly, name a new government and rule by decree. As postcommunist regimes stabilise, so assemblies will probably settle into a policy-influencing but mainly reactive role. The drama of communist collapse is over; but so too is the era when second world assemblies were nothing but a rubber stamp for the policy of the ruling communist party.

■ Third world assemblies: minimal and vulnerable

Assemblies in the third world differ from the policy-making and policy-influencing assemblies of the first world. The decline of the assembly as a decision-making body in liberal democracies is usually discussed in terms of the legislature losing ground to the executive and the bureaucracy. However, assemblies in most third world countries never exercised this authority in the first place. Executive leaders intent on monopolising power did not look kindly on autonomous assemblies. Assemblies lacked élite support. When the temperature of conflict rose, executive rulers were tempted to dispense with the assembly altogether. At one time or another, many assemblies have been suspended or abolished. Examples from the 1970s include Chile, Pakistan and the Philippines; in the 1980s assemblies were suspended in Nigeria and Turkey, after military intervention.

As democratic governments became more widespread in the third world in the late 1980s and early 1990s, there were grounds for believing that assemblies would gain political weight. When elections are taken seriously, then so too are the institutions they produce. In many third world democracies, and especially in Latin America, presidential elections are a stronger focus of public attention than elections to the assembly. However, assemblies still have a symbolic role to perform in any democracy. As the epitome of representative institutions, they will surely benefit from the current wave of democratisation in the third world.

☐ *Problems of third world assemblies*

In the past (and still today in many countries), the underlying problem has been that representative political institutions were not strong enough to handle the sharp cleavages experienced in developing societies. Conflicts of class, religion, ethnicity, region or language are reflected, but rarely transcended, by organisations such as assemblies. Under fairly free elections, deep social cleavages are likely to be reflected only too clearly in the legislature. Norms of parliamentary behaviour are not well enough established to contain such conflicts. A lack of professionalism worsens this condition: assembly sessions are short, support facilities are scarce, the turnover of members is high and many deputies are inexperienced. Rather than 'councils of consent', assemblies in third world countries easily degenerate into disorderly 'councils of conflict' (Opello 1986).

From the point of view of the executive, therefore, the priority is to keep the assembly on a short leash. For instance, the members of the National Assembly of South Korea have been under constant government scrutiny. Opposition parties are tolerated but only just. The permissible limits of political argument have extended but remain very narrow (Kim *et al.* 1984, p. 8).

In Latin America, assemblies modelled on the US Congress have sometimes had a strong (though often obstructive) impact. In the context of social tensions, economic instability, and multi-party systems, the presidential system, which is common in Latin America, can result in ungovernability. Directly elected presidents confront assemblies which may not support them. In fact, an assertive assembly may become deadlocked with the executive. This, in turn, has led to several breakdowns of democratic governments (Diamond and Linz 1989, p. 26). For example in Chile between 1970 and 1973, conflicts over policy between executive and assembly helped bring about a military coup. The assembly was then itself suppressed. The wave of democratisation which swept over Latin America in the 1980s will take time to revitalise assemblies, given the popular appeal which the political or military 'strong man' has had in the past.

Neither did the leaders of many emergent nations in Africa and Asia see a policy-making role for the assembly in the decades after independence. The assembly's main role was integrative – to assist in nation-building. It was one of the few institutions which drew together representatives from different groups and areas within the country. Though largely symbolic, this integrative role was seen as a reason or excuse to rule out party competition and punish criticism. Debates on broad questions of policy were not encouraged. As in Latin America, the 1980s saw some moves back to multi-party systems in Africa. Even so, policy-making remained an executive preserve; the impact of assemblies on policy has remained slight. In much of the third world, therefore, assemblies have had a broken history even when they have not been irrelevant sideshows.

☐ *Functions of third world assemblies*

If they do not function as a check on executive power and contribute little to broad policy debate, what do third world assemblies do? They have their uses, both for those in power and for those aspiring to it. First, they provide a fig-leaf of legitimacy. Authoritarian rulers are keen to have a showcase of support, providing it is well-orchestrated. Secondly, even in undemocratic regimes, assemblies provide useful sources of recruitment to the political élite. As Packenham (1970, pp. 267–8) said of the Brazilian Congress during the years of military rule:

> Some politicians gain experience in the legislature which enables them to go on to other posts like governorships, national ministries, state ministries and the like. They learn the norms of the élites, they acquire political skills, and they acquire visibility and prestige resources . . . . [The] activities of the Brazilian Congress constitute training ground for Brazilian politicians.

Thirdly, assembly members may well press constituency interests and raise individual cases. They are likely to stress, however, that the individual grievance does not imply general criticism of the government, whereas in policy-influencing assemblies the broader political implications are often discussed. Energetic activities on behalf of constituencies have been documented in such varied settings as the Philippines, Kenya and Korea (Kim *et al.* 1984). Before it was suspended by President Marcos, the Philippine Congress received so many 'local' bills that Fridays were set aside solely for their consideration (Mezey 1979, pp. 160–1). Members of the Kenyan National Assembly keenly press constituency claims, but would be unwise to criticise the government and especially the president.

Sometimes activity on behalf of constituents becomes such a habit that assembly members find it difficult to consider broader issues even when the chance is there. Writing about the Brazilian Congress elected in 1982, Wynia (1990 p. 241) comments that 'the new legislature was weak, its members still more accustomed to involving themselves in petty disputes and playing ombudsmen for constituents who sought favours from the national bureaucracy than with writing major pieces of legislation.'

So assemblies in many third world countries have had a chequered existence. The level of support for the assembly within society is low, military and bureaucratic élites have been hostile, and on the whole the policy significance of assemblies has been limited. But they have been persistent institutions, for several reasons. They confer some legitimacy upon rulers; they serve as a linking mechanism in weakly integrated societies; and they provide a training ground for recruits to the political leadership. For these reasons, assemblies in third world countries have survived through hard times. If democracy in the third world continues to recover, then so too should assemblies.

■ The fall and rise of assemblies?

Legislatures rarely make laws. Bills pass through the assembly on their way to the statute book and receive some legitimation *en route*. But their origins lie elsewhere: in the executive, the bureaucracy and the interest groups. 'You draft the bills and we work them over', said a member of the US Congress to a member of the administration. In less professional and active assemblies than the US Congress, this process of working over can be rather cursory.

But to speak of the decline of assemblies in an era of big government and growing executive power is too simple. In several ways, assemblies are growing in importance: as arenas of debate, as intermediaries in transitions from one political order to another, as raisers of grievances, and as agencies of oversight. The televising of proceedings in many countries is making assemblies more, not less, central to political life. Moreover, where the US Congress led the way in equipping assembly members with the staff and resources to do their jobs professionally, other legislatures are following. In the assemblies of Western Europe, backbench members are now more assertive: party leaders can no longer expect well-educated and well-resourced backbenchers to be loyally deferential (Norton 1990b).

Law-making is but one aspect of the assembly's role. Indeed, it can be argued that the main responsibility for policy should not rest in the assembly, given the instability to which assembly-dominated regimes have been prone. What could be more odd, asked the nineteenth-century writer, Walter Bagehot, than government by public meeting? What assemblies can do is to oversee the executive, forcing politicians and civil servants to account for their actions before a body which still in some sense represents the nation.

In performing this supervisory role, assemblies will need to adapt to the emergence of international organisations. For example, as European integration gathers pace in the 1990s, national parliaments must better equip themselves to maintain supervision of government. If they do not do this, then by default they will yield power and influence to the European Community's policy-making institutions.

This shift in function from legislation to supervision is paralleled by a shift in assemblies away from floor debate to specialised committee work. Assemblies could probably do more to influence policy, particularly by greater professionalism. Members can also involve themselves, as in Sweden, in the first analysis of policy problems before drafting of bills has begun. Japan is a useful model here. In Japan many members of the Diet form part of a *zoku* (an informal policy 'tribe') on the basis of a common interest in a particular area of policy. In this capacity they gain the expertise needed to influence the policy process.

Critics argue that a stronger policy role for the assembly is a mixed blessing. They suggest that supervision of the executive can be too effective, creating problems which are not found in a reactive assembly. They cite the US Congress as a negative example of a powerful, decentralised legislature which produces a stalemate in policy-making and gives too much weight to partial interests. At least in a reactive assembly, it is argued, the executive is directly accountable to voters for its success or failure. Whether these problems linked with legislative supervision outweigh the gains from thorough scrutiny of the executive, comes down to a question about the proper balance between diffusion and concentration of power in government.

Summary

1.   An assembly is a multi-membered body with powers to make law, but in most countries the executive now initiates proposals for new laws. Assemblies remain major symbols of representative government, however.

2.   Nearly all countries have an assembly of some description. About half of all assemblies have two chambers. These provide checks and balances within the legislature and represent different territories or interests in society.

3.   Assemblies may perform various functions, including law-making, forming governments, executive scrutiny and political recruitment. The key function of assemblies is to represent the nation and act on its behalf.

4.   In parliamentary systems, the assembly makes (and sometimes unmakes) governments, which remain accountable to the assembly. But where a single party has a majority, as in Westminster-type parliaments, a government, once formed, can usually rely on the support of its members of parliament.

5.   Assemblies are training grounds for political leaders. In authoritarian regimes, as well as in liberal democracies, assemblies provide a channel of recruitment and socialisation into the political élite.

6.   Even in liberal democracies, assemblies mainly react to government initiatives; they influence policy rather than making it. However, scrutiny of government activity by assemblies through questions, debate and committee investigation is growing in importance.

7.   The strength of an assembly (including its ability to scrutinise) depends strongly on its committee system and the resources and incentives available to individual members. The United States Congress has an exceptionally well-developed committee structure, but many other assemblies in the first world strengthened their committee systems in the 1970s and 1980s.

8.   In communist states, assemblies were of marginal significance. However, they became lively arenas of debate in the transition to postcommunism. Their significance will probably decline again – but not back to past levels.

9.   Assemblies have also been of little importance in most of the third world. Rulers found them too 'divisive'. However, they will probably acquire more political weight as democracy strengthens.

Discussion points

1. Are assemblies important because they legitimate, rather than legislate?

2. 'If the upper chamber agrees with the lower it is superfluous. If it disagrees, it is pernicious' (Abbé Sieyes, 1789). Do you agree with this critique of bicameralism?

3. Are 'working' assemblies really preferable to 'talking' assemblies?

4. What could be done to increase the policy influence of the assembly in your country? Should it be done?

Key reading

Mezey, M. (1979) *Comparative Legislatures* (Durham, N.C.: Duke University Press). Remains the best comparative treatment of assemblies.

Norton, P. (ed.) (1990a) *Legislatures* (Oxford: Oxford University Press). A helpful volume, drawing together the most influential writings on the subject.

Norton, P. (ed.) (1990b) *Parliaments in Western Europe* (London: Frank Cass). Well-informed specialist assessments of assemblies in Western Europe.

Bailey, C. (1989) *The US Congress* (Oxford: Basil Blackwell) A good accessible account of an exceptionally powerful assembly.

Further reading

Until a few years ago there were few good comparative treatments of legislatures. Pioneering efforts were Wheare (1968) and Blondel (1973) but the best treatment is Mezey (1979), which is very wide-ranging but well integrated. Lees and Shaw (1979) provide detailed studies of legislative committees.

The comparative approach is carried forward by Arter (1984) on the Nordic parliaments. Loewenburg and Patterson (1979) cover Kenya, West Germany, Britain and the United States, while Kim *et al.* (1984) also cover Kenya plus Korea and Turkey. Olsen and Mezey (1990) focus on the legislative role in economic policy. Liebert and Cotta (1990) address the important topic of the assembly's role in democratic consolidation. Many misconceptions about second world legislatures are dispelled in Nelson and White (1982).

The most intensively studied legislature is the US Congress. Good books are legion but Mayhew (1974) remains an outstanding work of synthesis and interpretation. Norton (1985) and Walkland (1968) are valuable for the British House of Commons.

■ *Chapter 13* ■

The Political Executive

■ What does the political executive do?

The political executive is the historic core of government. Its history is the development of government authority itself, from absolute monarchs to modern forms of executive. The executive predates the emergence of separate legislatures, judiciaries and bureaucracies. These developed as bodies to aid, advise and later constrain executive rulers. In the modern era executives have tended to acquire powers not specifically lodged elsewhere. The executive is where the buck stops.

Our concern here is with *core* executives, defined as the 'commanding heights' of the state apparatus. At the core is the top leader and his or her ministers and key officials. In parliamentary systems, for instance, the core executive is a complex of institutions and actors, including the prime minister, the cabinet, cabinet committees, and the coordinating departments, such as the finance ministry (Dunleavy 1990, p. 102).

The task of the political executive is leadership. The executive is the seat of authoritative power in society, entrusted with managing the country's affairs. But this involves several functions. The first of these is to provide broad direction of national policy. 'To govern,' as the French politician Pierre Mendes-France declared, 'is to choose.' Second, executive leadership involves supervising the implementation of policy. Given the scale and complexity of modern government, this is in itself a great challenge. Third, the executive must mobilise support for its policies. Since implementation in practice needs the compliance or even cooperation of those affected, policy goals will not be achieved without some degree of political support. Fourth, the executive is charged with ceremonial leadership, symbolising the unity – real or alleged – of the nation-state.

313

The final function of the executive is crisis leadership – the exercise of wide, formally unlimited powers in emergencies. When swift and decisive action is called for, power must be concentrated to be effective. In two world wars, legislatures granted American presidents and British cabinets such sweeping authority that they became, in effect, constitutional dictatorships. Necessity, however, is always the tyrant's plea. The Stroessner regime in Paraguay, for instance, maintained a 'state of siege' for three decades, enabling it to suppress opposition almost at will.

Identifying the executive is not always easy. In communist party states the party rather than the government was the ultimate source of authority and the boundary between the two was often unclear. Party and administration were deeply intertwined, with both institutions nominally committed to the transformative goals of the regime. Thus the bureaucracy was highly politicised.

In liberal democracies the formal distinction between the politician, responsible to parliament or people, and the permanent civil servant, responsible to his or her political overlords, is more easily drawn. However, senior civil servants in liberal democracies are in reality centrally involved in forming as well as implementing policy. Yet the politicians still take primary responsibility for certain aspects of executive leadership, such as mobilising political support and providing ceremonial leadership.

A distinction is often drawn between constitutional and authoritarian executives. Constitutional executives have effective restraints on the exercise of power and succession to executive offices. Both in theory and in practice, political leaders are accountable for their conduct. Constitutional executives are of two main types: presidential and parliamentary, with some intermediate cases. In presidential systems, of which the United States is the main example, the chief executive is elected independently of the assembly. In the parliamentary type, found in most of Western Europe as well as Australia, Canada and New Zealand, the chief executive is chosen by the assembly. Both types are accountable, though presidents are directly responsible to the electorate rather than indirectly through the assembly.

With authoritarian executives, by contrast, constitutional and electoral controls are either unacknowledged or ineffective. The outward forms of elected government may be adopted but they do not constrain the exercise of power. In practice, authoritarian executives are responsible to no one. Human rights are neither recognised nor respected. Savage violence may be inflicted on political opponents. According to Amnesty International, torture remains commonplace in at least one hundred states of the modern world.

Though inherently coercive, authoritarian rulers nonetheless lack total power. For one thing, they rely on their henchmen and those who control the apparatus of repression. For another, like the absolute monarchs of old, authoritarian executives are not accountable for what they do, but still lack the ability to achieve whatever they want. In the modern era, communist party states formed the main institutionalised example of authoritarian rule. Government in the third world has also often been authoritarian, though power there has tended to be more personal and hence unstable.

The first part of this chapter examines constitutional executives, looking in turn at first world presidential and parliamentary forms. We then examine the executive in the second world of communist and postcommunist states. Finally, we consider the executive rulers of the third world.

■ First world: presidential executives

The essence of the presidential executive is that the responsibilities of leadership are vested in a chief executive, elected for a fixed term and independent of the legislature, but counterbalanced by other political institutions. (See Figure 13.1 for the general structure of the presidential executive.) In the United States, for example, the chief executive is chosen by popular election. As President Carter found in 1980, he is also sometimes rejected by it. Where electoral, legislative or constitutional constraints are weaker than in the United States, as in much of the third world, executive rule by 'Presidents' often approaches the authoritarian model.

□ *The United States*

The United States is the prime example of the constitutional presidential executive. The constitution states rather tersely; 'the Executive Power shall be vested in a President of the United States'. It also provides that the president shall be commander-in-chief of the armed forces. Subject to confirmation by the Senate, the president can make treaties and nominate ambassadors, ministers and judges of the Supreme Court. The president may not dissolve the legislature, but can propose measures to it. He may veto legislation, but his veto can be overridden by a two-thirds majority in Congress. Conversely, Congress can only remove the

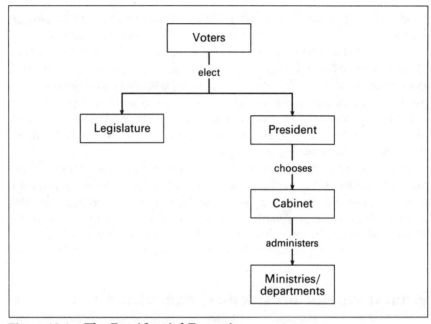

Figure 13.1   *The Presidential Executive*

president from office by using the constitutional blunderbuss of impeachment for high crimes and treason.

To describe the relationship between the US president and Congress as the 'separation of powers' is misleading. In reality, there is a separation of institutions rather than of legislative and executive powers. This means president and Congress share the powers of government in the United States: the president seeks to influence Congress but cannot dictate to it. Presidential power is in essence the power to persuade.

In this, the president has three main strategies: 'going Washington'; 'going public'; and 'going international' (Rose 1987). 'Going Washington' involves the president in wheeling and dealing with Congress – to assemble majorities for the legislative measures he wants. Nowadays this means dealing with individual members of the House and Senate. 'Going public' means the president uses his unrivalled access to the mass media to influence public opinion and persuade Washington indirectly. 'Going international' reflects increased US involvement in world affairs. Every president now spends more time on foreign relations and national security issues than on anything else.

Only one person can be president. But the presidency is not a one-person job. To meet presidential needs for information and advice, a variety of supporting bodies has evolved. Together they are known as the Executive Office of the Presidency, and they provide far more direct support than is available to the chief executive in parliamentary systems. These bodies include the Cabinet; the White House Office (which itself has a staff of about 400); the Office of Management and Budget; the National Security Council; and the Council of Economic Advisors.

Yet the apparatus of presidential advisers has been a critical source of weakness. Despite extensive facilities for advice and support, and a much larger number of political appointments to administrative positions than in most parliamentary systems, the American president has weak control over much of what is done in his name. The Watergate scandal in the 1970s destroyed the presidency of Richard Nixon: the Iran–Contra scandal in the 1980s undermined the reputation of Ronald Reagan. Though the president bore primary responsibility in each case for what happened, presidential advisers were also deeply implicated in serious wrongdoing.

One problem is that advisers are recruited because of their personal loyalties, rather than because of their proven ability and experience in public affairs. In addition, the cabinet does not offer a counterbalance. This is in sharp contrast to the parliamentary executive, in which the cabinet is the formal apex of the decision-making process.

Some presidents are more successful than others. A major factor in success is skill in the arts of communication and personal persuasion. Ronald Reagan was the 'Great Communicator', who restored prestige to the presidency after almost two decades of failure. In comparison with the hard-working but unsuccessful Jimmy Carter, Reagan concentrated his efforts where these were likely to be most effective: in responding to, and amplifying, an optimistic national mood. His successor, George Bush, benefitted from the sudden collapse of communist power in Eastern Europe. With the Soviet Union on the sidelines, Bush went on to assert US military power confidently against Iraq, temporarily boosting his reputation.

However, no matter how high the president stands in the opinion polls, we should remember that power remains widely dispersed within the American political system. Invested with the moral authority of the nation and entrusted with responsibility for its well-being, the president often lacks the stable political support needed to fulfil the demands placed upon the office. Within the federal government, power is spread among legislative, bureaucratic, judicial and executive institutions – and state and local governments themselves retain much independence from Washington. 'He'll sit here,' said President Truman, discussing the problems which his successor General Eisenhower would face in office, 'and he'll say "Do this! Do that!" and nothing will happen.

Poor Ike – it won't be a bit like the Army.' Since the time of Truman and Eisenhower, American government has become even less manageable. Not surprisingly, the extensive dispersal of power which characterises American politics is rarely seen as a good idea elsewhere.

☐ *France*

Constitutional dispersal of power is less apparent in France, the other major Western example of the presidential executive. French Presidents operate under fewer constraints than their American counterparts. France is, in fact, a constitutional hybrid, falling between the presidential and parliamentary executives (see Figure 13.2). A dual leadership is shared between president and prime minister. Formally speaking, the prime minister directs the government which is itself accountable to parliament. However, the president is the leading figure in the political system. Since 1962 he has been chosen by direct popular election for a seven-year term. The president chooses the prime minister, chairs the meetings of the Council of Ministers and often deals with individual ministers rather than through the prime minister.

There have been repeated trials of strength between president and prime minister. Certain areas of policy (notably defence and foreign relations) are regarded as presidential domains. But successive presidents have intervened without hesitation in whatever areas of policy were of interest to them (V. Wright 1989). French presidents have also exerted some direct control over the mass media, especially television.

Although presidents of the Fifth Republic have overshadowed parliament, their power has in part depended on an acquiescent majority in the assembly. The parliamentary elections of May 1986 dramatically confirmed this. The left-wing President Mitterrand faced a right-wing majority in the Assembly. He chose to 'cohabit' with a right-wing government, headed by Jacques Chirac, and accepted a reduction in his own authority. However, Mitterrand skilfully took advantage of the falling popularity of Chirac's government in 1988 in using his constitutional prerogative to dissolve the Assembly. At the ensuing elections, Chirac lost his majority. Mitterrand then promptly asked the socialist politician Michel Rocard to form a new government of the left.

Even though the French president cannot ignore the need for the government to have parliamentary backing for its legislative programme, he does have substantial powers of manoeuvre. Since 1958, the French presidency has provided a strong focus for national aspirations, with fewer constraints than in the United States on the president's ability to achieve these aims.

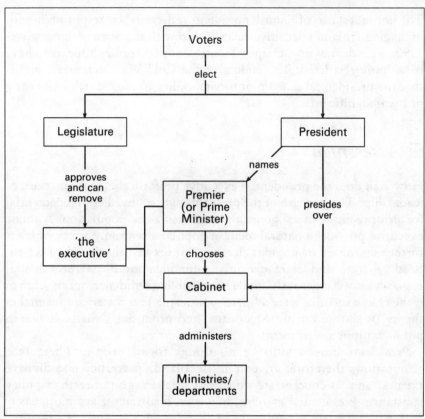

Figure 13.2 The Semi-Presidential Executive

☐ *Finland*

The semi-presidential system of Finland resembles the French pattern. The Finnish president has a degree of influence over the political process which is unique in Scandinavia. Finnish presidents are constitutionally responsible for foreign affairs, dissolving the assembly and appointing leading civil servants. They can reject proposed legislation and veto bills approved by the parliament, powers beyond even those of the French president. In practice presidents play an important role in delivering cabinets (which the constitution requires to consist of 'honest and capable' citizens) out of the complexities of Finnish multi-party politics. Since a new government is formed almost every year, this gives the president considerable opportunity to influence public affairs.

The unusual status of Finnish presidents reflected their responsibility for managing Finland's sensitive relationship with the Soviet Union (Arter 1990). Presidential impact upon Finnish domestic policy appears to have been more restricted. The ending of the Cold War, moreover, means that the presidential domain of foreign policy has lost much of its early postwar significance.

□ Assessment

How well does the presidential executive perform the vital functions of leadership? The strength of the presidential executive lies in its potential for prioritising political goals and mobilising the population. A single executive provides a natural focus of popular attention, a focus which is further sharpened by popular election. But because the president is both head of state and chief executive, unethical or illegal presidential conduct may dangerously undermine public confidence, more so than if the chief executive were a 'mere' politician. The Watergate scandal in the 1970s shocked many Americans, and produced a sharp decline in public faith in government.

Presidents must try to be all things to all people. There is a temptation, therefore, to emphasise bland, patriotic, non-divisive themes, and to concentrate on presidential image rather than policy substance. Presidential systems, however, lend themselves more easily than parliamentary governments to crisis leadership. Authority invested in a single figure allows a faster response to emergencies than does shared authority. Unfortunately, presidents tend to govern by crisis: 'rally round the President' can become a routine political ploy, and constitutional executives slide into authoritarian habits. Where policy implementation is concerned, it is doubtful whether presidents are more successful than parliamentary executives in controlling the bureaucracy. Despite the array of advisers around the American president, for instance, the federal bureaucracy is often strikingly unresponsive to his objectives.

■ The first world: parliamentary systems

Whereas the presidential executive is separate from the assembly and independently elected, the parliamentary executive is organically linked to it (Figure 13.3). Parliamentary executives are, in effect, a special kind of committee, whose members come entirely, or mostly, from the assembly and are accountable to it. The distribution of power in

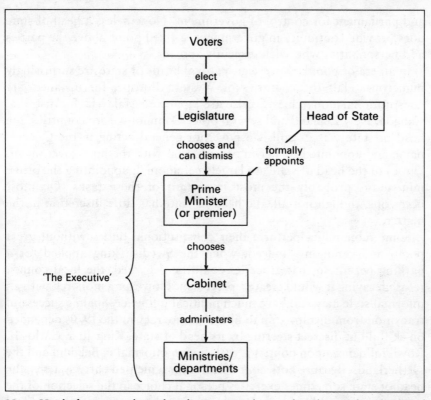

Note: Head of state may be an hereditary monarch, or a directly or indirectly elected president. The post, however, is essentially ceremonial and without executive authority.

Figure 13.3   *The Parliamentary Executive*

parliamentary executives is affected by three main factors: the role of the head of state; the relationship between executive and assembly; and the relationship between prime minister and cabinet. We shall consider each of these areas in turn.

☐ *Heads of state in parliamentary systems*

One of the hallmarks of a parliamentary system is, in Bagehot's classic analysis, the distinction between the 'dignified' and 'efficient' aspects of government (Bagehot 1963, p. 63). Dignified or ceremonial leadership centres upon the head of state, either a titular president or a constitutional monarch. 'Efficient' leadership rests with a team of ministers, headed by a prime minister and accountable to parliament. This arrangement is mainly an outcome of past struggles between crown

322 The Structures of Government

and parliament for control of government. Nonetheless a head of state does provide continuity in government, a fixed point above the parties and personalities who wield executive power.

In an era of popular sovereignty, royal heads of state are surprisingly numerous. Half the countries of Western Europe, for instance, are constitutional monarchies. So also are Japan and Malaysia. In Australia, Canada, New Zealand and several other Commonwealth countries, the head of state was or still is a governor-general acting in the Queen's name and appointed by her in consultation with the host government. Duties of the head of state are largely ceremonial; appointing the prime minister is probably the most important of these tasks. On most occasions, though not all, the head of state has little discretion in the matter.

Some monarchies perform their constitutional duties without great pomp and ceremony. Indeed, when the Swedish king applied for a parking permit so that groceries could be delivered, the local council refused, saying it would create a precedent. However a monarch with an informal style may still have much political influence. Spain's successful transition from dictatorship to liberal democracy in the 1970s depended on skilful but discreet steering by its head of state, King Juan Carlos II. Royal influence upon politics is real though informal in Belgium and the Netherlands. Because both countries have fragmented party systems, the head of state sometimes exercises personal choice in the selection of the prime minister. Moreover, Dutch cabinets have sometimes modified policy positions in order to take the royal view into account.

The British monarchy, on the other hand, though still conducted in grand style, probably has very little influence on policy. Only in the formation of a government might there be some scope for direct royal initiative, and then only if no party had an overall majority after an election or if the majority party had become hopelessly split. Perhaps the most controversial intervention by a parliamentary head of state of recent years was the dismissal in 1975 of the Whitlam Government and the dissolution of the Australian Parliament by the Governor-General, after the Senate had rejected the Government's budget. But this was an exceptional episode. In general, heads of state in parliamentary systems stay above the political battle, a position which allows more effective intervention in the rare circumstances when it is deemed necessary.

Where parliamentary systems take a republican form, they usually provide for an elective or appointed president to act as titular head of state. Sometimes the president is directly elected by the population, as in Austria, Ireland and Portugal. In other cases the chief of state is elected by parliament or by an electoral college. This usually comprises the national legislature plus representatives of regional or local government, as in Germany, Greece, India, Italy and Israel. The duties of the president in most of these countries are largely ceremonial. Politically sensitive decisions such as the dissolution of the legislature would normally be taken on the advice of the prime minister and government.

But the boundaries of the role are not always tightly drawn and the chief of state may be more than a figurehead. Mary Robinson, Ireland's first woman president, has not been reluctant to declare her views on controversial issues. Italian presidents also sometimes state their positions on contentious matters such as divorce and abortion. More-over, the Italian president has considerable importance in the frequent and delicate task of forming governments. By the early 1990s, the role of the Italian president was coming under fire, with several parties of the left demanding direct election to the office in view of its increasingly bitter relations with parliament.

☐ *Government and parliament*

The basis of the parliamentary executive is its interdependence with the assembly. A cabinet or council of ministers emerges from the assembly and is ultimately responsible to it. The government holds office just as long as it retains the confidence of the assembly. If that confidence is withdrawn, as for example by a vote of censure, the government is expected to resign. If no new government can be found which commands the assembly's support, the normal course is the dissolution of the assembly and a general election.

But the relationship between assembly and executive is two-way. Various procedural devices are available to the government in its dealings with the assembly. In some parliamentary systems, the government controls the parliamentary agenda and timetable; in most, the premier (that is, prime minister) can request the dissolution of the assembly before it has run its full course. This, however, is a double-edged weapon since the premier's own party might well be the chief casualty of its use. But in practice the major influence on the stability of parliamentary executives is the legislative party system. Two contrast-ing versions can be identified: cabinet-dominated and assembly-domi-nated executives.

The **cabinet-dominated** version is where the executive can count upon disciplined majority support in the assembly, as in Britain, Australia and New Zealand. The cabinet fuses control of executive and legislature. As long as leaders retain the support of their parliamentary party, the cabinet-dominated system enables coherent direction of government, both in terms of legislation and implementation of policy. Cabinet government based on disciplined legislative support provides a direct chain of accountability running from the government to the assembly and from the assembly to the electorate. In choosing their representatives in the assembly, the people indirectly choose their rulers in the executive. This form of the parliamentary executive is mainly associated with adversarial (or Westminster-style) assemblies.

In **assembly-dominated** systems, by contrast, the relationship between elections and government formation is less direct. Where the party system is fragmented, the formation and survival of governments depends more on inter-party bargaining in the assembly than on election results. In the Netherlands, for example, the average length of time taken to form a new cabinet after an election or resignation is 86 days – with a record, in 1977, of 208 days! (Gladdish 1991, p. 128.) This would seem to be a recipe for precarious government, as indeed it is in Italy and was in France during the Third Republic (1870–1940) and the Fourth Republic (1946–1958). True, few cabinets in the Netherlands since the war have seen out their four year term. But the distinction here is not simply between stable majority-party and unstable coalition governments. Coalition government in Germany has been as stable and durable as majority-party rule. Even where the party system is highly fragmented, as in the Netherlands and nowadays in the Scandinavian countries, Italian-style instability of the political executive is not seen.

☐ Prime ministers and cabinets

The parliamentary executive involves a tension between collegiality and hierarchy, between a ministerial college of political equals and a pre-eminent chief executive. How strong are prime ministers in relation to other members of the executive? One extreme is India during the 1975-77 'Emergency'. Indira Gandhi became a virtual dictator. At the other extreme is the French Third Republic, where the prime ministers produced by the game of ministerial musical-chairs were once described · as 'transient and embarrassed phantoms'. Prime ministerial power results from a complex interaction between personalities, parties and constitutions. The powers of prime ministers *vis-à-vis* their ministerial colleagues have tended to increase, though the distinction between a prime minister in a parliamentary system and a directly elected president remains fundamental.

Control of appointments is a major source of power in any setting. How free in practice are prime ministers to choose their ministerial teams? The powers of appointment of the British prime minister are without doubt substantial. Moreover, what prime ministers give they may also remove. Subject to some constraints of party balance, British prime ministers may form a government of their choosing from the talent available in the parliamentary party. Only a handful of senior figures possess such stature or experience as to be too important – or too dangerous – to be excluded. A British prime minister has even more scope with lesser appointments. As former Labour Minister Gerald Kaufman (1980, p. 13) advises, 'If the Prime Minister makes you an offer and you are not in an exceptionally powerful position, take what you are offered or be ready to return to the back benches; dozens will be ready to accept what you have rejected.'

In other countries which adopted the British parliamentary model, prime ministers generally have less freedom of appointment (see Exhibit 13.1). In Canada, prime ministers have to ensure adequate representation in cabinet for the various provinces; ministers speak for their province as well as their department. In New Zealand, the small size of the parliament means that nearly half of the MPs from the governing party are likely to find themselves in an executive post (Weller 1985, p.86). Party practice may also curtail the prime minister's choice, as in the case of the Australian Labor Party. In government, as well as in opposition, elections within the parliamentary party decide the composition of Labor's front-bench team. A Labor prime minister distributes the portfolios among the cabinet team but does not himself decide its membership. The New Zealand Labour Party follows the same practice, though there a Labour prime minister retains the right to dismiss, if not appoint, ministers.

The Basic Law (Constitution) of the German Republic also leaves no doubt that the chancellor enjoys the right to name his own ministerial team, though in practice party and especially coalition considerations restrict his freedom of choice (Mayntz 1980, p. 145). However, compared with their British counterparts, ministers in the Federal Republic tend to be appointed to posts suited to their professional training and experience. This is also the case in other West European countries such as the Netherlands and Belgium: party standing is of less account in qualifying individuals for cabinet office than specialist expertise, though the cabinet needs to be carefully balanced by party (Gladdish 1991).

Where no party commands an overall majority in parliament, the business of forming a cabinet is more complex and the autonomy of the prime minister can be much reduced. In Belgium and the Netherlands, for instance, the distribution of ministerial posts is the result of bargaining between the coalition partners, with each party filling its share from its own nominees. Ministers serve *with* the prime minister, not *under* him. (See Exhibit 13.2.) The position of the Italian prime minister is similarly constrained by the factions in the Christian

Exhibit 13.1 *How powerful are prime ministers?*

Although Australia, Britain, Canada and New Zealand all have parliamentary systems, Weller's study (1985) reveals considerable differences in prime ministerial power between the four countries:

	Australia	Britain	Canada (Liberal governments)	New Zealand
Control over party	low	variable	medium	variable
Control over cabinet committees	variable	high	medium	medium
Hiring/firing ministers	variable	high	medium	variable
Control over parliament	variable	medium	low	high

Indeed, even within countries the power of prime ministers depends on the party in government, as the frequency of the variable category suggests. Overall Weller concludes that Conservative prime ministers in Britain have fewest constraints, followed by National Party leaders in New Zealand. In all four countries, left-wing parties attempt firmer controls over their leader than parties of the right; in Australia and New Zealand they partly succeed.

What explains the cross-national differences in the table? The major factor is tradition. Each country evolves its own conventions about what prime ministers can and cannot do. For example, cabinet committees are permanent and regulated in Australia and New Zealand; they are far easier to manipulate in Britain, which strengthens the prime minister's hand. British prime ministers can also sack ministers with relative impunity; in Canada, Australia and New Zealand, this is an unusual event.

Democrat Party and by the need for bargaining between parties to maintain a governing coalition. Since there may be several ex-prime-ministers in the cabinet, the prime minister may not even be the undisputed leader. The premier's acceptability to the various coalition

---

Exhibit 13.2   *The Dutch Prime Minister: not yet a chief*

In the comparative study of Prime Minister/Cabinet relations, the Netherlands is an interesting 'deviant case'. In a variety of ways, and for a variety of reasons, Dutch Prime Ministers have not become such commanding figures as they are in many other countries with parliamentary government.

In the Netherlands, Ministers serves *with* Prime Ministers rather than *under* them. The Prime Minister (or, to use the correct title, Minister-President) can neither appoint Ministers, nor dismiss them. PMs cannot give direct orders to Ministers, nor would they consider attempting to reshuffle the composition of the Cabinet. Furthermore, the PM is involved in only a handful of other appointments to executive office.

One reason for the weakness of the PM lies in the variety of parties represented in parliament, which is elected by pure proportional representation. As a result, the allocation of Cabinet posts is determined by lengthy inter-party negotiations which precede the formation of a new coalition. Once a new government has formed, no PM wants to upset the apple-cart by attempting an untactful reshuffle. Dutch politics brings forth skilful conciliators, not dashing heroes.

In addition, Dutch government departments guard their independence. They are staffed by specialists, recruit their own staff and would not take kindly to orders from the PM.

Finally, the Dutch cabinet has only 14 or so members, smaller than elsewhere. This reinforces a collegial culture, which has its roots in an era when the Dutch political élite had to reconcile the conflicting interests of religious subcultures in society.

Andeweg (1991) notes that the position of the Dutch PM is slowly increasing in importance. Media visibility grows apace, the PM's international role is expanding, and the PM is now called on to attempt more co-ordination of policy across departments. But these are changes at the margin. The Dutch Prime Minister has become more than a chairperson, but remains far less than a chieftain.

---

parties or faction leaders may be more critical than their acceptability to him (Hine and Finocchi 1991, pp. 79–81). A similar situation prevails within the dominant but highly factionalised Liberal Democratic Party in Japan.

☐ *Collective responsibility*

How cohesive is the parliamentary executive? Are its members bound to common policies and a common fate? 'Collective responsibility' means that ministers share responsibility for the decisions agreed by the cabinet. Where collective responsibility is firmly entrenched, it strengthens the authority of the executive. Collective responsibility increases the executive's powers of co-ordination over the bureaucracy since ministers are pledged to the same set of policies. It also presents the assembly with a clear-cut choice: either to accept or reject the government as a whole.

Collective responsibility does not of course remove conflict among government ministers. It merely conceals it by requiring that ministers publicly support – or at least refrain from attacking – the settled policy of the cabinet. As a nineteenth-century British Prime Minister, Lord Melbourne, once remarked, 'It matters not much which we say, but mind, we must all say the same.' British parliamentary norms strongly emphasise this doctrine and it has been transplanted to other Westminster-type parliamentary systems in Canada, Australia and New Zealand. However, the norm has not always been 'internalised' there to the same extent.

In several parliamentary systems, the sense of collective responsibility within the executive is distinctly limited. The Italian constitution enjoins collective responsibility of the Council of Ministers to parliament but in practice this is notably lacking. Italy has 'government by ministry'. Inter-departmental co-ordination of policy is notoriously weak and conflict notoriously common. The underlying problem is that the parties are extremely factionalised. These factions tend to 'colonise' (i.e. take into their own possession) different ministries.

The convention of collective responsibility remains fairly weak in the Netherlands, where there is a semi-separation of the executive from the legislature. Ministers may not sit in parliament; indeed, many have no parliamentary experience and are brought into government from the universities, the professions and the civil service. Rather than achieving collective solidarity, Dutch cabinets are multi-party coalitions which produce accommodations between ministers with accepted areas of expertise.

The constitution of Germany emphasises hierarchy rather than collegiality among government ministers. Accountability to the Bundestag is mainly channelled through the chancellor. He answers to parliament; ministers answer to him. The strong position of the chief executive derives from the Basic Law of the Federal Republic which makes the chancellor removable only by a 'constructive vote of no confidence' – to dismiss the chancellor, the Bundestag must elect his successor. Yet the Federal cabinet has a fairly weak collective character. Ministers tend not to question the decisions of other departments and many matters are despatched without discussion. Ministers conduct the affairs of their departments within the chancellor's guidelines, though in practice chancellors have shown regard for the expertise of ministers. It is an exaggeration to speak of 'Chancellor democracy' in Germany, but its cabinet is certainly more hierarchical, and somewhat less cohesive, than its British counterpart.

The doctrine of collective responsibility conceals the extent to which decision-making in most cabinet-style executives has become fragmented into numerous decision-arenas. As government has grown, so too has the number of ministers. In Canada, the cabinet reached the unwieldy size of 40 in 1987, partly due to pressures for representation from the various regions and linguistic groups of this divided nation. Elsewhere, cabinets have been kept to a more manageable size of 20–25 members. However this has meant excluding some ministers from cabinet and making more use of cabinet committees. Australia, for example, has nine committees, three coordinating and six functional. In most countries, most decisions are now made in these committees, and are merely reported to the full cabinet for ratification. Indeed, in Australia, decisions made by cabinet committees can only be reopened in full cabinet with the approval of the prime minister. Cabinet government has become government by the cabinet **system** of which committees are the decisive part.

However, although the doctrine of collective cabinet responsibility does not accurately reflect executive decision-making, regular cabinet meetings do have an important solidifying function within government. Cabinet can act as a final court of appeal for disputes between departments. Legislative accountability is also a spur to cabinet cohesion in Westminster-style assemblies. Compared with the American president, parliamentary systems with cabinet structures are better able to coordinate policies (Mackie and Hogwood 1985, p. 35).

■ The second world: the communist and executive

The record of leadership in communist systems is rich in both tragedy and irony. Communist revolution was supposed to liberate the workers from oppression and exploitation. Instead, it produced dictatorships of unprecedented depth and ferocity. Communist rule was supposed everywhere to create classless, egalitarian societies of plenty. Instead, it produced shortage economies and alienated peoples, ruled by corrupt and ideologically bankrupt bureaucracies.

☐ Personality cults

Communist rule was also supposed to be collective. Instead, one-man rule and grotesque leadership cults were striking features. The objects of adulation included Lenin and Stalin in the Soviet Union, Mao Zedong and Deng Xiaoping in China, Castro in Cuba, Ho Chi Minh in Vietnam, Enver Hoxha in Albania, Tito in Yugoslavia, Ceaucescu in Romania and Kim Il Sung in North Korea. Although Marxism was supposed to be a doctrine of impersonal forces, individual leaders can rarely have had so great an impact as in communist party states.

It is true that Janos Kadar, the Hungarian Party leader (1958–88), rode the tramcar to work every day, unrecognised by most people. But from Stalin onwards, most Marxist rulers sought to bolster their position by fostering a cult of personality. The leader's name and face were everywhere: huge photographs on buildings, statues in public squares and a bust in every bureaucrat's office, glorified in speech and song, endlessly publicised in newsprint, and on radio, film and television. The supreme leader was promoted as the revolution perso-nified. Any criticism was equated with opposition to the party and the revolution as a whole, and invited harsh repression.

The ideological foundations of the communist system were linked with the supreme leader. He alone fully understood the truths of Marxism, and how to apply them to the concrete situation in the country. Thus Marxism was redefined in the 1920s as Marxism-Leninism by Stalin; other *isms* were then proclaimed, including Stalinism, Titoism and Maoism (personality cults and -isms are not confined to communist states, as any one who lived in Britain during the era of Thatcherism will know).

In North Korea, the political thought of Kim Il Sung virtually replaced Marxism as the ideological cornerstone. The cult of personality in North Korea runs deeper than elsewhere even in the communist world. Korean history has been recast in terms of the heroic revolutionary activities of Kim Il Sung's family. The Soviet Red Army, which actually installed Kim and his party at the end of the Second World War, goes unmentioned. Loudspeakers throughout the land incessantly extol the virtues of Kim Il Sung. Although the domestic electricity supply is on for only a few hours a day, huge statues of the 'Great Leader' are brightly lit for all to admire.

Such cults of personality acted as a brake on innovation and political change. New policies were risky if they departed from those identified with the dominant leader; politicians who crossed the supreme leader, or threatened his position, were purged.

However, the existence of a cult of personality did not mean that the leader was all-powerful. Supreme leaders have more often been the final arbiter in the decision-making process than the sole source of initiative. Sometimes events or pressures from colleagues have forced them to change policies. In China, Mao was forced into a political back-seat in the early 1960s by the failure of the Great Leap Forward, his radical attempt to make a swift transition to communism. To get back in command, he had to unleash the Cultural Revolution in 1966 over the heads of his party colleagues.

☐ Succession crises

Communist party states have lacked an orderly process for succession. As a result, they have suffered crises of succession. These obviously occur after the death of the leader, but there have also been 'pre-mortal' succession crises. For example, in Albania in 1981, long-time Prime Minister Mehmet Shehu, a close associate of party leader Enver Hoxha, supposedly committed suicide after bizarre accusations that he had simultaneously spied for Yugoslavia, the United States, the Soviet Union and Britain.

Men like Lenin, Mao, Hoxha, Castro and Tito were perceived as hero-founders. They were leaders who had brought a revolutionary party to power. However, maintaining legitimacy is difficult for the post-revolutionary generation. The successor may claim the mantle of the founder's authority for himself but this severely limits his ability to embark on new policies. Consider the situation which threatens to engulf Kim Jong Il, son of Kim Il Sung and heir-apparent in North Korea. He has been promoted as the only person truly able to understand his father's political philosophy. But the North Korean economy desperately needs fundamental reform. If Kim Jong Il embarks on reforms, he loses the main source of legitimacy for his rule. Yet if he does not reform the economy, its collapse will probably take him with it.

Alternatively, new leaders can distance themselves from their predecessors, blaming current ills on past failings. The new leader promotes himself as the person who will rectify old evils and move the nation forward. Pushed to extremes, this strategy can undermine the ideological foundations of the state. Under Gorbachev's policy of *glasnost* in the Soviet Union, virtually all aspects of the Soviet past were assailed. If nearly everything that went before was wrong, how could the party have any mandate to continue in power? This was indeed the outcome of the coup attempt by hardline communists in 1991. Stripped bare of any remaining vestige of legitimacy, the communist system was simply swept away in the reaction to the coup. Gorbachev's initial efforts to salvage the communist party after the failed coup prompted the memorable description (by one of his closest advisers) as 'Discussing how to offer tea to a corpse'.

□ *Formal structures: state and party*

The **formal** executive structure of communist states followed a standard pattern, though this was hardly an accurate guide to the realities of power. The model is shown in Figure 13.4. Before *perestroika*, the Soviet Union exemplified the model. According to the 1977 constitution of the Soviet Union, 'the Supreme Soviet [the federal assembly] is the supreme body of state power.' The Supreme Soviet 'elected' a Council of Ministers, under the stage-management of the party, of course. Constitutionally the Council of Ministers was the 'highest executive and administrative body of the USSR'; it was the formal government. Its real task, however, was to supervise the implementation of party policy. The Council of Ministers, however, was a large and unwieldy body, over one hundred strong. Much of its work was therefore delegated to its Presidium, an inner steering body, whose chairman was in effect the Soviet prime minister. The Soviet head of state, however, was the president, officially styled the Chairman of the Presidium of the Supreme Soviet.

Traditionally, though, the key to supreme power was the post of the General Secretary of the CPSU. Once his hold over the party was secured, the General Secretary took on a major state office, either prime minister or presidency. Stalin and Khrushchev became 'prime minister'; Brezhnev, Andropov, Chernenko and Gorbachev chose the presidency. The multiple hats worn by communist leaders illustrate the central feature of the political executive in communist states: the penetration of the state by the party. The communist party permeated, guided and controlled the entire apparatus of government (on party organisation, see Chapter 8). Broadly speaking, the party determined overall policy while the state apparatus, under the direction of the Council of Ministers, implemented it. But of the highest levels it was more accurate to say that the party governed through the state, rather than merely

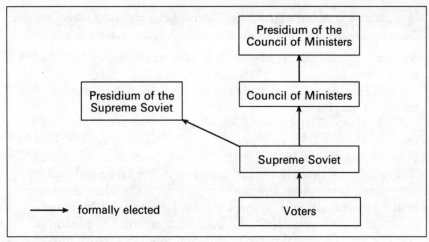

Figure 13.4   *Soviet executive structure, 1936–91*

controlling it through supervision. This was because of overlapping membership between party and state institutions at the top.

This pattern of distinct yet interlocked party and state organisation was copied in other communist regimes, particularly in Eastern Europe (Yugoslavia excepted). In China, party and state have been intertwined even more closely. Throughout their history, party, state and army have been closely fused.

The high command of the communist party-state was never accountable. Neither the assembly, nor the electoral process, nor the courts provided an independent power-base from which to challenge the record or authority of party leaders, or to secure redress for individuals. The communist party dominated society and party leaders were dominant within the party. The non-accountable character of the communist executive explains two of the weaknesses that contributed to its collapse: slow turnover at the top and the lack of an agreed succession procedure. In liberal democracies, changes of personnel and policy result either from elections or from rules restricting length of tenure – US presidents, for instance, can serve no more than two four-year terms. In communist states, by contrast, 'biology [was] the midwife of change' (McCauley and Carter 1985, p. 2). Biology works slowly, but also irregularly – Stalin's rule lasted for thirty years, that of Andropov for less than two. Until the emergence of Gorbachev in 1985, slow turnover at the top restricted policy innovation, reflecting cautious, unimaginative leadership that was really intent only on preserving its own privileges. The paradox of the political executive in communist party states is that strong, authoritarian leadership was insecure in tenure and uncertain in succession.

Exhibit 13.3   *Mikhail Gorbachev: communism's undertaker*

Vladimir Ilyich Lenin is known to history as the man who founded the communist system, Mikhail Sergeivich Gorbachev will be remembered as the man who set out to reform communism, but ended up burying it.

Little about Gorbachev's early background marked him out for destiny. He was born to a peasant family in Privolnoe, a village in Southern Russia, in 1931, during the worst years of collectivisation. The teenage Gorbachev worked on the collective farm, and became a committed communist. Unusually for a peasant lad, he gained entry to the Law Faculty of Lomonosov State University in Moscow. On graduating with distinction, he became a communist functionary: soon he was a regional party boss in Stavropol, his native province. So far, so orthodox.

Gorbachev's big break came when senior party leaders noticed his drive and initiative, and brought him to Moscow. In 1978, he became the youngest member (age 47) of an ageing CPSU Politburo. By 1985, signs of political and economic stagnation were everywhere. The old guard finally ran out of options. Gorbachev became General Secretary of the CPSU, and later President of the USSR. He launched the series of reforms which the world came to know as *perestroika* (restructuring).

Abroad, he aimed to end the Cold War. This was achieved – but at the price of communist collapse throughout Eastern Europe. At home, Gorbachev's aim was to revive and reconstruct the Soviet system. Instead, by mid-1991 *perestroika* had turned into *katastroika*, with the reforms stalled and the economy collapsing.

Then came the coup of August 1991: Gorbachev's closest comrades tried to depose him and reimpose centralised authoritarian rule. The coup failed. In the week following, communism was swept away. After initial qualms, Gorbachev dissolved the communist party. Pushed on by Boris Yeltsin, who had led resistance to the coup, Gorbachev bullied the Congress of People's Deputies into swallowing a midnight deal in which the central government turned over most of its former functions to the republics. Gorbachev survived in office for a few more months. He was now an isolated figure without a power base, and was brushed aside by Yeltsin and the leaders of the other republics.

Why did *perestroika* go off track? Gorbachev was a master tactician, manoeuvring brilliantly between reformist and conservative forces, but a bad strategist. The effect was policy confusion, which undermined the central planning system and pushed the economy downhill. Though keen for others to face the electoral music, he did not do so himself. Thus he lacked the democratic legitimacy which alone might have enabled him to face down the hardliners in the bureaucracy, military and the KGB. Instead, as living standards fell, Gorbachev's popular standing reached rock bottom and *perestroika* lost credibility.

His policies of democratisation and *glasnost*, however, did bear fruit. They accelerated the transition to pluralism and encouraged people to defy the coup successfully. With this, Gorbachev's work was essentially done, though not as he had planned. He had accomplished the fairly peaceful dismantling of a totalitarian empire. He had also transformed the postwar international world. Not bad for a country boy from Privolnoe.

▌ The second world: the postcommunist executive

Whereas communist regimes strove to manufacture 'charismatic' leaders through cults of personality, leaders of genuine charisma played an important role in the overthrow of communism in Eastern Europe. Exceptional individuals like Lech Walesa in Poland and Vaclav Havel in Czechoslovakia provided focal points for opposition to rally round. They also provided resolute leadership in the anti-communist struggle, their characters steel hardened by years of harassment and repression.

Once the revolution was won, dissidents suddenly became presidents. Shelley declared that poets were the unacknowledged legislators of the world. In Eastern Europe, their authority is now recognised. For a playwright who was a reluctant politician, President Vaclav Havel wields considerable power in Czechoslovakia. He is commander of the armed forces; he can dissolve the national assembly and nominate a new government. Also in Czechoslovakia, Jan Czarnogursky was installed as Deputy Prime Minister the day after he was released from prison, hardly the best training for the job. The skills required to run a government, and undertake an immense task of social and economic reforms, are very different from those needed to lead a revolution. One problem facing the new societies of Eastern Europe is similar to that which plagued many communist party systems in their early years – good political agitators do not necessarily make good administrators.

Czechoslovakia, like Poland and several other postcommunist republics, has adopted an elected presidential head of state, operating in tandem with parliamentary government. This means that trials of strength are inevitable in postcommunist states between the president, government and assembly. In Poland, for example, the reforming President Walesa faced first a communist-dominated and then a highly fragmented assembly. Postcommunist regimes must confront divisive questions of economic reform and harsh budgetary choices. Their 'semi-presidential' systems provide arenas in which different views can be expressed and in which support can be mobilised behind much-needed change. But it is far from clear whether the executive structures now in place provide sufficient concentration of authority for the hard decisions of office to be both made and implemented.

■ The third world executive

Until recently, the pattern of rule in the third world rarely favoured constitutional and democratic rule. In the Gulf, some states (Saudi Arabia, Kuwait and the United Arab Emirates) are still traditional monarchies, governed by ruling families. In Latin America, most states have oscillated between periods of unstable civilian government and military rule. In Africa, single party-regimes and military rule have been the dominant forms of executive authority.

Genuinely constitutional rule has been rare. Especially in Africa, the state itself is weak and may hardly exist outside the major cities. At the same time, the state's coercive and financial resources are used in uncontrolled and unaccountable ways. Civilian government has been either unstable or authoritarian. Either way, it lay beyond effective constitutional restraints. The incentives of patronage, and the risks of non-cooperation with the government, have ensured that assemblies are docile, elections are uncompetitive, and the courts rarely independent. In the least complex political systems of the third world, these alternative sources of institutional power only exist in nominal form: the executive is the government.

□ Personal and unaccountable rule

Political leadership in the third world is frequently personal and unaccountable. One reason for this is that political power is the shortest route to wealth in very poor societies. The lack of accountability in third world governments has, not surprisingly, often led to corruption. Presidents Marcos of the Philippines and Mobutu Sese Seto of Zaire are not the only leaders who shipped vast sums of money abroad. Such regimes are basically kleptocracies – governments of thieves. The same lack of accountability often also produces appalling repression, as in the regimes of Saddam Hussein in Iraq or General Pinochet in Chile. Tyranny is inherently likely when executive power is both personal and non-accountable.

Although third world leaders are rarely accountable in a constitutional sense, they can be tightly constrained by other *political* actors. These can include: the military (and all the factions within it), leaders of ethnic groups, landowners, the bourgeoisie, the bureaucracy, students, multinational companies, foreign governments, ex-presidents, the factions in the leader's own court, and the mobs in the streets of the capital city. The problem of the political executive in many third world states is its lack of autonomy from powerful elements in society. Insufficiently accountable in a constitutional sense, executive leaders of the third world are highly dependent in other ways.

To survive, leaders have had to maintain a viable coalition of support. This has been a difficult and full-time job, leaving little room for concern over broader issues of national development. When enemies come to outnumber friends, a change of leader is as predictable as the transfer of power following an election defeat for a governing party in a liberal democracy. The mechanism is often a military coup but the underlying cause is a 'shrinking' of the governing coalition. Following Machiavelli, who sought to advise Renaissance princes in Italy, Clapham (1985) suggests two styles by which leaders attempt to maintain their position: the fox and the lion.

The fox is a manipulator. He plays off one political group against the other. He tries to keep groups dependent on him through the careful use of state largesse, and avoids committing himself to any irreversible course. It was the strategy, suggests Clapham, of Haile Selassie in Ethiopia, Kenyatta in Kenya and Senghor in Senegal. Lions, by contrast, seek to dominate rather than manipulate. They drive out their enemies rather than form alliances with them. They are strongly committed to policy goals – economic development, say, or national prestige. Lions seek popular support whereas foxes rest content with acquiescence. Examples included Banda in Malawi and Nkrumah in Ghana. The struggle for independence in the third world brought forth lions but in the post-independence era the foxes gained ground.

Some individuals may be both lions and foxes. For instance, Iraq's Saddam Hussein was brutally oppressive when strong, but conciliatory when his position weakened. The value of this distinction between lions and foxes is that it points to what has been the key feature of the third world executive: its personal nature.

□ *Towards accountable executives*

A sea-change occurred, however, in third world executives during the 1980s and early 1990s. The pattern began to change with the retreat from military rule in Latin America. The soldiers gradually gave ground in Brazil after 1975, though the pivotal moment was the legislative elections in 1982. Brazil's first civilian president for twenty-one years, Tancredo Neves, was elected in January 1985. In Argentina, the transition was more abrupt as the ruling junta collapsed. Military defeat by Britain in the Falklands (Malvinas) war triggered off pent-up social protest which swept a demoralised military regime away. The military also returned to barracks in Uruguay, Peru, Ecuador, Bolivia, and Paraguay (in the latter, after three decades of dictatorship by General Stroessner!). Finally in 1990, the hardline and now isolated Chilean dictatorship of General Pinochet gave way to a civilian president (though Pinochet remained commander-in-chief of the armed forces).

Democratic resurgence began in Africa after the spectacular collapse of communism in Eastern Europe in 1989. This showed what could happen to illegitimate rulers. It also robbed the one-party systems of Africa of an alternative model of development and a source of support which could be played against the Western capitalist nations. The economic failure of almost all African countries in the 1980s resulted in widespread discontent. This led to demands for democratic rule.

Some rulers, for instance President Moi in Kenya, forcibly resisted democratic pressure. But most sensed that the democratic tide was flowing strongly and turned to swim with it. By 1991 multi-party elections were as much in favour with African rulers as they had been the previous year in Eastern Europe. Some governments were voted out (Sao Tome, Cape Verde, Benin and Zambia). Others were re-elected (Gabon, Ivory Coast, Comoros). Many other regimes have accepted the idea of multi-partyism and competitive elections in principle, but have not yet implemented it.

Why this democratic revival in the third world? The basic reason is the failure of authoritarian rule, whether by military or civilian dictators. Restrictions on freedom were normally justified in terms of political stability and economic development. With few exceptions, they delivered neither. Even authoritarian rulers need some support; the circle of support shrank as hardship increased and failure became apparent.

External pressures were also crucial. First, American foreign policy towards the third world began to shift in the mid-1980s. From supporting anti-communists of even the most extreme kind, the United States warmed to moderate reform and free elections. Secondly, the International Monetary Fund, the World Bank and first world governments put pressure on third world governments to adopt market-oriented policies and to reduce the role of the state. They also encouraged direct moves to democracy. Thirdly, by 1990, Britain and France explicitly linked much of their aid to 'good government' and multi-party democracy. The vulnerability of many third world countries to international economic forces, and their need for aid or debt rescheduling, left their rulers with few options but to endorse policies favoured by major donor nations and international organisations.

However, the form and content of democracy may diverge. Underlying conditions in most third world societies are still unconducive to stable, functioning democracy. The commitment of the governing élites is suspect or uncertain. Voting turnout is often low, vote rigging and intimidation often considerable. Electoral competition may be 'Mobutu multi-partyism', so-called after President Mobutu, authoritarian ruler of Zaire. This means that token parties are set up but with no real intention of broadening popular influence. The depth of democratisation in the third world is uncertain; so too is the prospect of stable constitutional government.

Summary

1. The major function of the political executive is leadership. This involves deciding, directing and implementing policy, and mobilising support for it.

2. Constitutional executives differ from authoritarian executives in that they have effective restraints on how power is gained and exercised. The two main forms of constitutional executive are the presidential and the parliamentary.

3. Presidential executives combine ceremonial with effective political leadership. Presidents are popularly elected for a fixed term, independent of the assembly. The United States is the most influential model. The American president shares power with Congress, in a system of checks and balances. Presidents in other countries are often stronger, relative to the assembly and subnational governments, than American presidents.

4. Parliamentary executives separate ceremonial leadership (head of state) from effective leadership (head of government). The head of government is the prime minister, chosen by and accountable to the assembly. In practice, the

prime minister is usually the leader of the majority party, or of a coalition of parties, in the assembly.

5.   In communist party states, executive leadership involved a fusion of party and state at the top and an extreme concentration of power. The lack of accepted ground rules contributed to personality cults, succession crises and severe power struggles.

6.   Several postcommunist executives have a dual leadership. This combines a prime minister accountable to parliament with a president directly elected by the people. The president's role was strengthened by the crisis conditions obtaining in the early years of postcommunist regimes.

7.   Constitutional executives in the third world have been the exception rather than the rule. Leaders have survived by maintaining a coalition of personal support, which often involved bribes and pay-offs.

8.   Recently, however, there has been a strong resurgence of elected leadership across the third world. Pressure from the first world, the collapse of communism in the second world, and the economic failure of authoritarian rule in the third world have all contributed to this trend.

Discussion points

1.   You have been asked to report on the advantages and disadvantages of changing the system of government in your country from parliamentary to presidential (or vice versa). What's your conclusion – and why?

2.   Why is the presidential executive becoming more common?

3.   Are 'personality cults' as strong a feature of leadership in the first world as in communist party states? Have even prime ministers become presidential in style?

4.   Should political advisers to presidents and prime ministers be accountable in public for their advice?

5.   Can democratically elected leaders cope better with major social and economic problems than authoritarian rulers?

Key reading

Rose, R. (1987) *The Postmodern Presidency: The White House Meets the World* (New York: Chatham House). An illuminating interpretation of the contemporary American presidency.

Weller, P. (1985) *First Among Equals: Prime Ministers in Westminster Systems* (Sydney: Allen & Unwin). An instructive comparative analysis of executive leaders in Australia, Britain, Canada and New Zealand.

Jones, G. (ed.) (1991) *West European Prime Ministers* (London: Cass). Specialists deal with individual countries, but within a comparative framework.

McCauley, M. and Carter, S. (eds) (1985) *Leadership and Succession in the Soviet Union, Eastern Europe and China* (London: Macmillan). Looks at leadership patterns in communist systems before the deluge. A scholarly literature on postcommunist executives has still to emerge.

Further reading

There are many works of distinction on the political executive yet few are genuinely comparative. The literature review by King (1975) remains a good starting-place. Rose and Suleiman (1980) is valuable, covering executive leaders in eight major Western nations.

Neustadt (1980) remains a classic source on the American presidency and a seminal analysis of political power. Barber (1977) offers a fascinating study and provocative theory of presidential character. Rose (1987) provides new insights on the presidency in an age of interdependence. Shaw (1987) offers the views of UK scholars on the American presidency.

In Britain, much of the debate about the political executive has centred upon the issue of prime ministerial power. The reader by King (1985) on the British prime minister is also useful. For a biography of Margaret Thatcher, the dominant politician of her era, see H. Young (1989).

On executives in communist systems, see Holmes (1986) as well as McCauley and Carter (1985). G. Smith (1992) is a good account of Soviet *perestroika*.

On the executive in the third world generally, see Clapham (1985, ch. 4). On Africa in particular, see Jackson and Rosberg (1982) or alternatively Cartwright (1983).

■ *Chapter 14* ■

The Bureaucracy

Organising and administering modern states is a massive process that requires skill, experience and expertise. For centuries, bureaucracies have played an important role in politics, and rulers have wrestled with the problem of keeping effective control over their civil servants. However, the impact of the bureaucracy on policy-making has grown with the expansion of government. In communist party states, centralised party control over society placed great power in the hands of the bureaucrats. Civil servants also play a major role in many liberal democracies. For example, Metternich's description of Austria in the last century as 'not governed but administered' still fits. Similarly, C. Johnson (1982) has argued that in Japan, although elected politicians have formal positions of power, bureaucrats are the major influence on decision-making.

■ The functions of bureaucracies

The bureaucracy is the institution that carries out the functions and responsibilities of the state. It is the engine-room of the state. Although the word 'bureaucracy' conjures up images of inefficiency and red tape, the term is used here in the more technical sense developed by the German sociologist, Max Weber (Gerth and Mills, 1948). His analysis of bureaucracy can be summarised in the following points:

1. Bureaucracy involves a carefully defined division of tasks.
2. Authority is impersonal, vested in the rules that govern official business. Decisions are reached by the methodical application of the rules to particular cases and are not based on any private motive.
3. People are recruited to serve in the bureaucracy based on proven or at least potential competence.

4. Officials who perform their duties competently have secure jobs and salaries. Competent officials can expect promotion according to seniority or merit.
5. The bureaucracy is a disciplined hierarchy in which officials are subject to the authority of their superior.

Weber argued that the development of bureaucracy did for social organisation exactly what the introduction of mechanical power did for economic production – it made the process of administration more efficient and rapid. In his view the emergence of the reformed, merit-based bureaucracies of nineteenth-century Europe signalled, in effect, the arrival of administrative machinery.

There are two main problems in applying Weber's ideal-type. Firstly, it can lead to an understatement of differences between countries in their bureaucratic styles. For example Heady (1991, pp. 170–94, 198–212) separates *classic* from *political* bureaucracies. Classic bureaucracies derive from the administrative instruments created by the absolute rulers of Europe. As in France and Germany, they are often profess-ional and efficient though they tend towards rigidity and an aloof, even suspicious, attitude towards party politics. Political bureaucracies, as found in Britain and the United States, are more amenable to political control, accepting their constitutional role of carrying out the will of elected governments.

Secondly, Weber's ideal-type draws too sharp a distinction between politics and administration. Politicians, it implies, make policy while civil servants administer it; politicians make choices while civil servants present options. At senior levels in a bureaucracy this distinction breaks down – most notably in the communist world, but also in the first world. It would be more accurate to say that civil servants are as involved in politics as politicians, but in different ways. Civil servants work quietly behind the scenes; for example, negotiating with relevant interest groups. However, elected politicians must publicly promote both themselves and their party's image to the populace. Yet there is no doubt that the tasks of both groups are political in that they shape collective decisions.

In thinking about bureaucracy, it is important to distinguish between the small number of top-level civil servants, and the vast number of routine staff at the base of the pyramid. Senior public servants work at the centre, have policy-advising responsibilities and day-to-day contact with politicians. They are often recruited into a 'fast stream' which guarantees rapid promotion to positions of influence. As they inhabit a broadly political world, much of the discussion of the power of *bureaucrats* concentrates on this élite group.

However, the vast majority of public officials do not work at this rarefied level. They work on routine tasks away from the capital city. Much discussion on the power of *bureaucracy* concentrates on the total organisation, including lower-level staff.

This distinction between higher and lower levels, or between policy-advisers and managers, is becoming more important as governments seek to delegate the tasks of management and implementation to at least semi-independent agencies. This has been a familiar pattern in Sweden, where

> most Swedish civil servants do not work directly for ministries, which are mostly just small planning staffs; instead, boards and agencies handle most of the daily work, and they have considerable autonomy. Although the several dozen boards and agencies have standardized salary scales and regulations, they by and large recruit their own people. (Roskin 1977, p. 31)

It is likely to become a familiar pattern in other countries, too.

■ Sources of bureaucratic power

A modern government department is a large, multi-tiered organisation, containing enormous knowledge and experience in its specialist area. Departments, like all other organisations, develop their own ways of proceeding, their own priorities, and their own 'house view'. They have a network of links with other departments and interest groups, to which they are bound by ties of tradition, agreements, and personal relationships. All this complicates the task of political control. It means that steering a department in a new direction is a slow and complicated business which needs sustained effort from the minister. Without that effort, the department will tend to 'bounce back' into its original shape.

Bureaucrats implement political decisions. Ministers cannot be everywhere at once; their 'span of control' is limited. In any case, civil servants need discretion if they are to carry out policies effectively. But this means that in applying policy, civil servants can 'bend' it, not just to fit conditions in the field, but also to suit their own concerns and interests. Control over implementation is a key source of bureaucratic power.

Power gravitates to the bureaucracy if there is a vacuum elsewhere in the political system. This is particularly important in much of the third world. If politicians are unwilling or unable to govern, then civil servants will and can.

Another source of bureaucratic power is found in a comparison between the career structures of civil servants and elected politicians. Civil servants' security of tenure is much stronger than that of the politicians who head departments and ministries. Particularly in parliamentary governments, ministers are moved, promoted, demoted and removed as the balance of power within the leadership changes. This gives bureaucrats an incentive to resist change – they just have to hang on until the minister is moved elsewhere.

Politicians have less technical knowledge of the area under their control than civil servants. Civil servants at the top levels of the bureaucracy will have had decades of experience in that field, whereas cabinet ministers will be newer to the job. Ministers therefore become dependent on the advice and information presented to them by their civil servants. Thus the bureaucracy possesses considerable potential power through deciding what information should be presented to politicians, and what should be suppressed. This power can affect decision-making functions in two ways.

First, civil servants and advisers may choose not to pass on information that they know the decision-makers will not like.

Secondly, bureaucrats affect decisions through the realities of *bureaucratic politics*. Civil servants' futures are linked with the fate of their department. They want to see their department (and their jobs) grow in stature. Bureaucrats will act to defend the interest of their particular organisation when resources are being allocated or fundamental reform is being considered. As Dunleavy (1991, p. 147) points out in his discussion of the literature on bureaucracy, officials and public servants are basically portrayed as wanting to maximise their budgets, within external political constraints. Bureaucracies are often characterised as expansionist organisations, seeking to increase their size, staff, financing and scope of operations.

Communist party states abounded with examples of bureaucratic politics. For example, in the late 1970s China took important decisions about its future economic policy. One possibility was to decentralise power from central departments to provinces, and to place more emphasis on light industry. The bureaucracies representing heavy industry and central planning opposed this move as it would lead to a loss of both political power and finance allocated to their ministries. Bureaucratic resistance to economic reform in the Soviet Union was a major factor in the failure of Gorbachev's *perestroika*, contributing heavily to the ultimate collapse of the system.

■ How are bureaucracies organised?

The bases on which bureaucracies are arranged vary from country to country. The four main principles of organisation are shown in Table 14.1 on p. 348.

Exhibit 14.1   *The Minister's tale*

When Flora MacDonald became Secretary of State for External Affairs in the Canadian Government in 1980, she found that bureaucrats impaired the power of ministers. MacDonald felt particularly vulnerable – she was a new Minister in a new government, representing the Conservative Party that had been out of power for sixteen years. While she lacked experience of the 'labyrinth of bureaucracy', her civil servants were well trained in the art of getting ministers to approve their favoured policies.

Macdonald claimed that bureaucrats used several 'entrapment devices' in an attempt to limit her decision-making power. First, civil servants would demand an immediate decision, thus eliminating the minister's ability to seek independent advice. Secondly, they would delay the delivery of reports that MacDonald had to make to Cabinet until as late as possible before the meeting. Thirdly, bureaucrats would give 'one dimensional' opinions. They presented recommendations as the unanimous decision of her advisers, and did not offer alternatives.

At times, bureaucratic attempts to influence decision-making took on more sinister forms. For example, private and confidential reports were copied and distributed without MacDonald's knowledge.

Cynics suggest that this shows that MacDonald was not on top of her job. A better manager would have got her staff working for her rather than against her. But the civil servants did not have it all their own way. MacDonald's aides would 'bootleg' copies of documents that were grinding their way through the slow and complex process of gaining bureaucratic approval.

For MacDonald, life as a Cabinet Minister was almost one long battle – not with the opposition parties, but with the senior bureaucrats who staffed her ministry.

Source: Flora MacDonald, 'Who is on Top? The Minister or the Mandarins?' in *Politics: Canada*, 7th edn, ed. P. Fox and G. White (Toronto: McGraw-Hill Ryerson, 1991, pp. 395–400)

The most common yet also the most ambiguous form of organisation is by **purpose** or **function**. Most ministries exist to pursue distinct objectives, such as tax collecting, transport, education, health, defence and so on. The ambiguity arises from defining the real objectives of a functional bureaucracy. Are they the objectives of the ministry's

Exhibit 14.2 *Bureaucratic power in Japan*

Japan is a classic example of a country where bureaucrats wield great political power. A key task for the Japanese premier is to ensure a balance between various factions in the ruling Liberal Democratic Party (LDP). One result is that ministers are frequently rotated (or replaced) in government departments. Ministers rarely serve in any one department long enough to learn about their jobs, and so depend on their civil servants. This has created a situation in Japan where politicians reign, but bureaucrats rule.

The Japanese bureaucracy has close links with both party politicians and big business. Bureaucrats must retire at the age of 55, and many then go on to start second careers – either as politicians or on the boards of companies. Thus, the LDP, the bureaucracy and big business are entwined through a process of interlocking connections. They form a single, cohesive ruling élite.

The professional economic bureaucracy, and in particular the Ministry of International Trade and Industry (MITI), has been a key force behind Japan's industrial success in the postwar era. As postwar reconstruction began, MITI targeted specific growth industries in the economy, and took steps to ensure that those areas would become successful. For example, the Japanese camera industry was carefully nurtured in its early years and shielded from overseas competition until it had become competitive.

MITI did not have total power to enforce compliance, and it made some errors of judgement. It could not prevent one company from developing transistors when MITI thought that the future still lay in valves! MITI's guidance is now becoming lighter as Japan's economy grows increasingly sophisticated and international. But in the earlier postwar decades, Japan was a good example of how the bureaucracy can guide economic development.

creator? Or of the politicians (ministers) who notionally control it? Or of the administrators who staff the ministry? The goals of these groups may be totally incompatible, thus rendering the idea of the purpose of the organisation as an integrated whole distinctly elusive.

A British television series called 'Yes Minister' provided a lighthearted insight into how bureaucracies can stress objectives other than their supposed purpose. The series showed how politicians and civil servants interacted in the mythical Ministry of Administrative Affairs. The

Table 14.1   *Structures of administration*

Basis of organisation	Definition	Examples and comment
Purpose	Departments are organised to pursue specific objectives in society.	Most central governments are largely organised on this basis, though departments may place their own interests before their ostensible goals.
Area	One department responsible for all the policies of central government in a particular locality.	The prefectoral systems of France, Italy and Japan.
Clientele	A single department provides all public services to (and often controls) a specific group.	War veterans and minority groups are often served on this basis. The department can outlast the group: Italy still has an agency for the widows and orphans of Garibaldi's campaign!
Process	All bureaucratic activities of a particular type are concentrated in a particular department.	Specialist activities such as computing and engineering are often organised in this way. Enables skills to be concentrated. Serves other departments rather than the public directly.

Source: G. Peters *The Politics of Bureaucracy* (London: Longman, 1984).

Minister is concerned with furthering his career prospects, while the administrators act to preserve their influence, and to promote the Ministry's interests against other departments. These interests frequently conflict, and only rarely coincide with those of the government as a whole. The popularity of the series with British politicians (notably Margaret Thatcher) is an indication of how close the fiction came to fact.

The other three types of bureaucratic organisation shown in Table 14.1 are more specific than functional organisation.

Organisation by **area** was exemplified by the system of British colonial rule under which a local commissioner was responsible for all the activities of the colonial government within a particular district.

Organisation by area can coexist alongside organisation by purpose, although this system of **dual control** often creates considerable problems of coordination.

The decentralised system practised (at times) in China is a good example of dual control in action. Because of China's sheer size the whole country cannot be ruled effectively from one place. For example, the province of Sichuan alone has a population of over 150 million people. Each provincial government has its own system of administration, but each ministry in the capital, Beijing, also has a branch office in the provincial capital. This branch office is therefore subordinate to two authorities. It is vertically responsible to the central ministry in Beijing, and at the same time horizontally responsible to the provincial government. By adhering to the provincial authority it may upset the central ministry, and vice versa.

Organisation by **clientele** is often introduced to coordinate the provision of services to groups that make heavy use of government programmes (for example, disabled war veterans in the United States) or deprived minorities (such as Aborigines in Australia).

The final basis of organisation is by **process**. This type of organisation is typically designed to achieve economies of scale within the administrative system. It centralises functions such as data processing, auditing and accounting.

■ Bureaucracy in the first world

A key feature of bureaucracy in the first world in the modern era has been the trend towards big government. At the beginning of the century there was one public official for every 300 Americans; now, the figure is closer to one in fifteen. In Britain the number of civil servants in central government has increased tenfold over the century. By way of comparison, the number of cabinet ministers in Britain barely doubled over the same period. In Canada, including provincial and municipal government employees, over a million people are on the public payroll – around 12 per cent of the total workforce.

The expansion of public services provided by the state explains at least part of this growth. In Sweden, where the state provides many welfare services, over 16 per cent of the workforce are public employees. By comparison in Japan, where the family is traditionally expected to provide such functions, the figure is only 4 per cent (Rowat 1988, pp. 443–5). Conservative governments in several countries in the 1980s attempted to 'roll back the frontiers of the state'. This strategy was led by Margaret Thatcher in Britain and Ronald Reagan in the United

States. In Britain, Thatcher's privatisation drive did succeed in returning many public *companies* to the private sector. However, public *services* (such as health, education and welfare) survived relatively intact. Employment in these services will now probably resume its upward growth.

Underlying these attempted cut-backs lay a powerful 'New Right' critique of bureaucratic growth and public expenditure (for an assessment, see Dunleavy 1991). This argued that bureaucrats working in the public sector seek to maximise budgets. In consequence public expenditure tends to inexorable growth unless held back by decisive political action.

The solution, argues the New Right, is to introduce competition and public choice into public administration. For example, the public should not have to attend whichever government office is nearest to their home. Instead they could choose to visit the office that they think is best at dealing with their problem. As the 'New Right' believe that 'money should follow the customer', this provides an incentive to offices to become more efficient in their competition to attract 'customers'.

As an addition or an alternative, services can be contracted out to the private sector. For example, several prisons in the United States are run by privately owned security firms. The public sector is not debarred from providing these services, but must prove itself an efficient provider by beating off competition from the private sector. As a result, it is argued that the taxpayers will receive better value, and better services, for their money.

☐ *Organisation*

There are also vast differences in the ways in which bureaucracies are organised in the first world. Perhaps the biggest difference in administration between liberal democracies is the degree of centralisation – the extent to which authority is located at the apex of the national administration. The concentration of power takes two forms – territorial and hierarchical concentration.

Territorial concentration refers to geographic considerations – the balance of power between central and local authorities. How much power and independence do subnational administrative units (such as regions, provinces and districts) have compared with the national government? **Hierarchical** concentration refers to the amount of discretion given to subordinate individuals within the administrative system. To what extent can officials make policy or apply policy to cases, without referring to their superiors for approval?

The United States provides the clearest example of both territorial and hierarchical decentralisation. The federal character of the American constitution has created a geographic dispersion of power. The fifty state governments have a high degree of autonomy, and centralising trends notwithstanding, government in Massachusetts is a world away from government in Alabama. For example, whether or not murderers can be sentenced to death depends on the state where the murder was committed.

Secondly, the American administration is much less hierarchical at the centre than is the case in other liberal democracies. Compared to its European counterparts, the US higher civil service is hollow at the centre. There is no central civil service hierarchy to impose order on the system. The departments, agencies, bureaux and commissions cultivate allies in Congress, try to keep on good terms with pressure groups, battle to protect their flanks from bureaucratic rivals and strive to maintain independence from presidential control. Federal administration in the United States is the classic example of bureaucratic politics.

In unitary liberal democracies such as Sweden and New Zealand, administrative organisation is more centralised than in federal countries such as Germany or Austria. Nevertheless, central–local conflicts do take place. In Britain, the Labour Party controlled many large cities during Margaret Thatcher's eleven years in national power. Conflict between Whitehall (or rather, Downing Street) and townhall was intense. However, the central government retained ultimate control over the localities. It imposed limits on their spending, took powers away from them, and even abolished some local authorities (such as the Greater London Council) altogether.

☐ Recruitment

Given the strategic importance of senior civil servants, the manner of their recruitment is an important topic. Liberal democracies differ in their general pattern of recruitment. The civil service in most countries is unified, recruiting through standardised procedures and controlled by a single system of rules and regulations. There are exceptions: in the Netherlands, for instance, there is no *national* civil service, rather an assortment of autonomous and culturally distinctive departments, each recruiting in its own way.

There are differences between countries in the extent of competition for entry. Public service in the United States is held in relatively low esteem. It therefore attracts fewer able candidates than in Britain and France, both of which rely on open examinations and interviews to select from a strong field of able candidates. Low pay and morale did reduce the attractiveness of a civil service career to bright young graduates in Britain in the 1980s, some of whom preferred the glamour (and salary) of a job in what was then the booming financial sector.

Again, civil services differ in their emphasis on specialist or generalist skills. Should the implementation of policy rest with technical experts with specialist knowledge of the subjects they are dealing with? Or is it better to have enlightened amateurs who compensate in breadth for what they lack in specialist knowledge? In Britain, the dominant view has long been strongly generalist. Administration is seen as an art of judgement, born of intelligence and experience in administration *per se*. Specialist knowledge should be sought by administrators – but they do not need to possess that specialised technical knowledge themselves.

By contrast, the New Zealand system, like most others, is dominated by functional specialists. Secondary school graduates are the main source of recruitment into the New Zealand civil service, and appointments to higher levels are commonly made through the promotion of **insiders**. An **outsider** can only be considered for a position if there is no internal candidate of equal capability. Furthermore, many permanent heads of department in New Zealand are appointed to departments in which they have served for twenty years or more. Thus, many agencies are headed by career bureaucrats who have had relevant training and experience in their field (Thyne 1988). Whereas an administrator in the transport department in the United Kingdom may be a classics graduate from Oxbridge, his or her counterpart in New Zealand will be a secondary school graduate who has worked up through the ranks.

Irrespective of differences in the recruitment of administrators, the social background of senior civil servants is invariably unrepresentative of the general population. The typical high-level civil servant is a male graduate, brought up in a city, from a middle or upper class family that was itself active in public affairs. Many of these qualities also apply to politicians, although sometimes less strongly. The comparisons between the social backgrounds of politicians and senior civil servants are shown in Table 14.2. This comes from a project which investigated qualities affecting entrance to (*a*) the political élite and (*b*) the bureaucratic élite in seven liberal democracies.

A legal training is common among bureaucrats and politicians. The Department of Law at Tokyo University is the dominant recruiting ground for career civil servants at the highest levels of the Japanese civil service. There is also a strong legal bias in recruitment to classic European bureaucracies such as Germany and France. Although the importance of a legal training has declined since the nineteenth century, bureaucrats with a legal training remain a large group within European

Table 14.2 *Background characteristics that increase the chances of entry into the bureaucratic and political élites in liberal democracies*

	Senior posts in public administration	Senior posts in political parties
Male	√√	√√
University education	√√	√
Middle or upper class family background	√√	√
Family involved in public affairs	√	√
From an urban area	√	—

Note: √√ indicates a strong advantage
√ indicates a weaker advantage
− indicates little effect

Source: adapted from J. Aberbach *et al.*, *Bureaucrats and Politicians* (Cambridge, Mass.: Harvard University Press, 1981, p. 80).

civil services. Similarly, many European members of parliament also have a legal background.

It is by no means clear that this bias in recruitment to the civil service produces the prejudice against the left which critics often allege. Certainly the Japanese bureaucracy does produce many people who end up as business leaders or as politicians for the conservative Liberal Democratic Party. However, left of centre allegiances are commonplace in France and Germany, where civil servants are allowed to pursue political careers. A third of the graduates from the French National School of Administration (which provides training and higher education for the nation's civil servants) elected to the French National Assembly in 1978 were members of the Socialist Party. Aberbach *et al.* (1981) found that the dominant ideology was centrist – bureaucrats were as sceptical of the far right as they were of the far left.

□ Political control

The various modes of controlling the bureaucracy can be divided according to whether they are formal or informal. As Table 14.3 shows, the informal controls can either be internal or external to the bureaucracy. The main *formal* control over the bureaucracy in liberal democracies is the political executive, headed by the president or premier. The extent and effectiveness of political direction depends on three factors:

1. The reach of political appointments;
2. Norms of ministerial responsibility;
3. The use of ministerial advisers.

The reach of political appointments

The extent to which political appointments extend into the bureaucracy varies substantially. As a general rule, the greater the penetration, the easier it is to ensure political control. In Britain, only the ministers who head departments are politically appointed; the rest are permanent professional civil servants. In Germany, the number of ministerial appointments is even smaller. However, this lack of penetration is offset in Germany by a system in which civil servants who are sympathetic to the ruling party are moved into sensitive administrative positions. The financial cost of this approach is substantial: civil servants who lose their jobs on political grounds take early retirement – on full pay.

This tendency to staff important ministries with loyal and sympathetic civil servants is even more marked in Finland. Vartola (1988

Table 14.3   *Modes of control over bureaucracies*

Formal	Informal
Political direction by ministers	EXTERNAL
Minister's advisory staff	Mass Media
Legislative scrutiny	Public opinion Interest groups
Judicial scrutiny	
Ombudsmen	INTERNAL
Citizen involvement (where legally necessary)	Professional standards Anticipated reactions Peer-group pressure Conscience

Source: adapted from F. Nadel and F. Rourke, 'Bureaucracies' in *The Handbook of Political Science*, vol. 5, ed. F. Greenstein and N. Polsby (Reading, Mass.: Addison-Wesley, 1975), Table 1.

p. 126) notes that the Finnish civil service has become more politicised since the Second World War. He goes as far as to suggest that: 'It has for a long time been very difficult for civil servants who are not committed politically to advance to leading posts in administration.'

Norms of ministerial responsibility

Political control over the bureaucracy also depends on notions of ministerial responsibility. It is easy for bureaucrats to escape both political and public scrutiny when ministers alone are formally responsible to parliament for the actions of their officials. This system is found in its extreme form in Britain. 'The buck stops' with the minister, but in practice ministers are rarely sacked for incompetence or wrongdoing in their department. So civil servants can exert power without being subject to public accountability.

The British stress on the anonymity of higher civil servants is not matched in other liberal democracies. In the United States, bureaucrats are much more likely to appear before Congressional committees than are British civil servants to be questioned by a House of Commons committee. American bureaucrats are also likely to give more open and candid replies than their British counterparts, who make a profession out of being 'economical with the truth'.

The use of political advisers

Political control of the bureaucracy can be aided by providing ministers with personal advisory staff. These advisers act as alternative sources of information and guidance to the formal bureaucracy. The Executive Office and White House staff of the American Presidency are the fullest expression of this approach. They almost represent a counter-bureaucracy within the political system – one much more likely to be ideologically driven than the formal bureaucracy and personally loyal to the president.

These advisers may help to control the administrators, but as political scandals in the United States in the 1970s and 1980s revealed, they themselves create problems of control. They are not subject to the electoral system, nor are they restrained by bureaucratic inhibitions about acting politically. Their outside business and personal contacts are not subject to the same scrutiny given to politicians and civil servants. Advisers' political views are often very close, perhaps too close, to those of the people that they are advising. Politicians do not appoint advisers to tell them that everything they do is wrong.

By contrast, British practice has traditionally favoured a close relationship between ministers and senior civil servants, unadulterated by personal advisers. However, in the 1980s, some ministers experimented with political advisers. Indeed, in 1989 the Chancellor of the Exchequer, Nigel Lawson, resigned his ministerial post, claiming that the Prime Minister's personal economic adviser had too great an input into government policy-making. The idea of ministerial 'irregulars' who can counterbalance the professionals has been inspired by the well-established French system of ministerial *cabinets* (see Exhibit 14.3).

Although ministerial direction is the main formal control, other constraints can come from the courts and through legislative scrutiny. A more recent addition to the armoury has been the spread of the Swedish **Ombudsman** system. The ombudsman is a bureaucratic watchdog – established to investigate cases of bureaucratic mismanagement in response to claims by citizens and groups who feel that they have been mistreated.

The role of the ombudsman varies throughout the first world. They are well established at national levels in the Scandinavian democracies (and in the Netherlands since 1982). By contrast, in Italy the ombudsman is only represented in eight regions, and possesses limited power. In Germany, the ombudsman system is organised on functional lines, with different officials appointed in various sensitive areas (for example, data protection and the armed forces). To be successful, an ombudsman must have strong powers of investigation. Although the ombudsman system has now extended beyond Scandinavia, both politicians and civil servants in more secretive governmental systems are reluctant to grant ombudsmen sufficient powers to do their jobs effectively.

Informal pressure can also be brought to bear on administration. Public opinion, especially when aroused through well-organised interest groups, can act as an informal ombudsman within the system. A vigorous mass media can also act as a check and balance on both the bureaucracy and the government. Investigative programmes on television networks throughout the first world now specialise in exposing public scandal or bureaucratic ineptitude.

However, the freedom of the media is not wholly enshrined in all liberal democracies. The habit of official secrecy is particularly strong in Britain, for instance. The British government pursued legal action both in Britain and Australia to try to prevent the publication of *Spycatcher*, the harmless (and dull) memoirs of an ex-secret-service employee – already freely on sale in the United States.

Exhibit 14.3 *Controlling the bureaucracy: a lesson from France?*

A device which has attracted international attention as a way of helping ministers to gain control of their departments is the French ministerial *cabinet*. This is a group of about fifteen to twenty people who form the minister's personal advisory staff and work directly under his or her control. Although the *cabinet* originally developed in the nineteenth century as a mechanism through which political favours were distributed to outsiders, it now acts as a pivot in minister–department relations; 90 per cent of *cabinet* members are civil servants and about half work in the *cabinet* of their home ministry. On average, members spend two to four years in a *cabinet* before moving to other duties inside or outside the bureaucracy.

The functions of *cabinets* vary with the personality of the minister but can include: acting as a brains-trust to help the minister formulate policy; helping the minister in political relationships with both party and constituency; providing the minister with additional eyes and ears through which he or she can supervise departmental activities; and undertaking the vitally important tasks of liaison and coordination, both among the internal sections of the department and with other departments.

Both the strength and the weakness of the *cabinet* system lie in its informality. In the absence of formal regulations about its role, the *cabinet* can respond to political opportunities with a speed and flexibility denied to the permanent administration. Given the factious nature of the French civil service, these opportunities have not been slow to arise. Indeed, there are many allegations from both the political and administrative arenas that the *cabinets* have usurped the power of politicians and civil servants, allegations which gain in credence from the informal and occasionally semi-secret fashion in which some *cabinet* members operate. Moreover, since the great majority of *cabinet* members are able and ambitious bureaucrats, it is arguable that the cabinet may instil bureaucratic interests into ministers as much as it imposes political values upon the bureaucracy. (For a full discussion of the *cabinet*, see Searls 1978).

Other informal controls are internal to the bureaucracy. Liberal democracies place considerable reliance on the internalised professional norms – the conscience – of civil servants. Yet bureaucratic cohesion can easily become excessive. The state tradition in France and Germany enhances the self-esteem of the bureaucracy to the point where many perceive it as an arrogant élite. The in-group mentality of bureaucrats can mean that defending one of their colleagues becomes more important than defending the public good. As H. Finer (1941) succinctly stated: 'To rely on a man's conscience is to rely on his accomplice.'

■ Bureaucracy in the second world

Two key differences separate administration in the communist world from the first world. The first was a matter of scale: the administrative machinery extended into society to an extent unknown in the West. The other was that whereas the first world has seen the bureaucratisation of politics, in the communist world the bureaucracy was politicised.

□ *Bureaucratic power in communist states*

Ruling communist parties had to rely on the bureaucracy for the implementation of their goals. Given the scale of the bureaucracy in communist states, the problems that faced leaders in controlling the administrators were magnified. One response to this problem was to reject the notion that government officials were in some sense impartial and even above politics. All bureaucrats, at whatever level of the administrative machinery, were expected to contribute to the achievement of the goals laid down by the party, whether they themselves were party members or not. At the highest levels of the bureaucracy, party membership was the norm. All the leading posts within the administrative machinery were staffed by leading party members – in essence, the ruling party told itself what to do.

Despite this politicisation of the bureaucracy, communist party states were not successful in ensuring total bureaucratic compliance with decisions made at the top. Both bureaucratic and local interests have impinged on administrators' willingness to follow policy coming down from central leaders. In the past, an impression of unanimity was presented to the outside world, but the struggle for influence and resources continued behind closed doors. However, in the late 1980s, these struggles came out into the open.

For example, in China since 1987 the press has carried many official editorials calling for local and bureaucratic interests to be subordinated to the national interest. Administrative agencies have blatantly flouted central directives, and government inspection teams have been sent to administrative and local offices to ensure that party policy is being followed. The Chinese example shows that despite the politicisation of the bureaucracy, individual departments struggle to gain approval for *their* projects and promote *their* interests. At the same time, they evade (and at times simply ignore) higher decisions that do not fit in with their bureaucratic interest.

☐ *Organisation in communist party states*

Wide differences existed between administration in different nations. Yugoslavia with its many different national groupings developed a decentralised federal system to incorporate the tensions inherent within the system. Such a system bore little resemblance to the highly centralised Soviet system under Stalin that became the blueprint for administration in most communist party states after the Second World War.

Furthermore, the experience of individual states changed over time – typically as the regime has tried to overcome the problems of the past. After coming to power in 1949, the Chinese communists adopted the highly centralised Stalinist model of administration. By the mid-1950s it had become clear that the Soviet pattern was too centralised, and concentrated too much power at the national level. Although the party élites agreed that the Soviet model should be replaced, there was no consensus on what should replace it. As a result, the Chinese have subsequently experimented with different forms of decentralised control. These varied between devolving some power to large regions, to the provinces, and to communes.

These experiments indicate a key contradiction in communist party states. The party needed to have skilled and expert personnel working in the administrative machinery to get the best information and advice. It further relied on these experts to ensure the effective implementation of party policy. However, the commitment of the experts to the party's goals was suspect. If control was too tight, then the experts did not have the discretion needed to work properly. If the controls were too lax, then the party's goals may be ignored or subverted by the experts.

This tension was particularly acute in the early years of the Soviet and Chinese states. Lacking sufficient loyal party members to staff the administrative machinery, the communists had little choice other than to rely on experts who had worked in the old pre-revolutionary bureaucracies. As a result, the communists had to exercise close guidance and control over the administrative machinery to ensure that party policy was not being blocked or altered by the bureaucrats.

These tensions were more successfully dealt with in the Soviet Union than in the People's Republic of China. In China, Mao Zedong's suspicion of experts and mania for 'redness' (holding 'correct' political values) was sparked by a fear that the professional bureaucrats would try to run the country for their own benefit. His greatest fear was that the revolution was being hijacked and that China was heading towards the return of capitalism. Mao could not sit idly by and watch his vision of the Chinese revolution being overturned.

With the aid of loyal army units and radical student activists, in 1966 Mao launched the Cultural Revolution – a nationwide witch-hunt of 'capitalist roaders' and 'counter-revolutionaries'. The Cultural Revolution returned Mao to power, but at the cost of bringing the entire political system to a standstill. With the nation in turmoil and a virtual civil war raging between rival student groups, the military stepped in to restore order. They quickly began to restore the administrative machinery and, by 1973, many of those who had been purged in 1966 (and had survived the excesses of the radical student Red Guards) had returned to their previous positions. The bureaucrats were again back behind their desks.

☐ *Bureaucracy in postcommunist states*

The collapse of communism in Eastern Europe heightened the issue of the political reliability of the bureaucracy. If the interests of the experts are not firmly linked with one-party rule, then the foundations of the party state begin to crumble. In Hungary during the 1980s, bureaucratic power had been transformed into economic power through the semi-privatisation of government enterprises. In the past, bureaucrats had gained their power and privilege through the very fact that they were bureaucrats. Once they became business people, their power and privilege no longer depended on communist party rule. On a much lesser scale, rural officials in China in the 1980s began a similar process of transforming their political power and prestige into economic power.

A key problem is the allegiance of administrators. Are bureaucrats working in Slovakia loyal to the Czechoslovak Federation, or to the Slovak Republic? In China, local officials, particularly in the south and south-east, appear to be working for the interest of their local area, which at times has conflicted with the national goals of the central party leadership. These problems are dwarfed, however, by the break-up of the Soviet Union, and the balkanised systems of administration that will result as ministers and bureaucrats of the various republics feud over territory and resources, nuclear weapons included.

The new governments in the postcommunist second world are now facing the same problem that faced communist regimes in their early years. It is impossible to introduce a new system of administration overnight. Just as the Chinese and Soviet communists were forced to rely on hand-me-downs from the old bureaucracy, so postcommunist states must rely on remnants of the old communist administration. It is not the communist values of the bureaucrats that create the problem, but the fact that they had grown accustomed to privilege. As such, the bureaucracy represents a potentially powerful group within society that has a self-interest in blocking fundamental changes.

■ Bureaucracy in the third world

In simple traditional societies, administrative roles were relatively underdeveloped. Indeed, specialised administrative staff may have been virtually absent. Authority was typically based on kinship and exercised by the family's oldest male. Almost all third world societies have now witnessed the gradual emergence of administrative roles and specialised offices. These positions were initially filled by the family of the ruler, thus binding political power and bureaucracy together in a small and cohesive central élite. Indeed, a feature of administration in the third world is the high degree of concentration at the centre, which limits penetration of peripheral areas.

□ *The colonial legacy*

Public administration is often imitative rather than innovative in contemporary developing societies. The stamp of colonial rule can still be found in the third world, even in places where the colonialists have long since departed. Bureaucratic institutions are often much more developed and 'modern' than the political institutions and parties they serve. This can act as a source of strength; the bureaucracy can play a valuable role as guardian of the state in politically unstable nations.

For example, Pakistan's civil service has been the mainstay of the state throughout its many political upheavals. When the government collapsed, the bureaucracy conducted the business of government itself. Much the same can be said of the Indian Administrative Service which is nothing less than the guardian of the Indian state. In both countries, the bureaucracy is closely modelled on the British colonial civil service. The strength of such **guardian bureaucracies** may be beneficial, but by definition, they are not amenable to political control.

However, the impact of colonialism was entirely destructive in other cases. Between 1910 and 1945, the Japanese totally dominated the Korean political and administrative system. Korean natives were only allowed to play minor roles, and were firmly subservient to their colonial masters. With defeat in the Second World War, the Japanese empire collapsed almost overnight. As a result, Korea was left with a political and administrative vacuum. In contrast to India, no domestic bureaucratic class was available to step into the shoes of the colonialists and take over the functions of government and administration.

☐ Patronage and privilege

The process of grafting a modern administrative system onto a traditional political culture has produced bureaucracies in the third world that depart sharply from Weber's ideas. For example, ties of kinship still pervade many African societies. Civil servants, politicians and military officials are all expected to use their positions to reward their families.

This problem is compounded by rising expectations. Those in positions of power feel entitled to Western-style living standards, even though they live in very poor societies. Public office is therefore an opportunity for personal enrichment to be vigorously exploited; the state becomes a device by which a political and adminstrative élite extracts resources from the rest of society.

Not surprisingly, such corruption becomes the focus of opposition. After each coup in Nigeria, extensive clean-up campaigns were conducted as the new regime tried to consolidate its rule. But corruption is endemic. Legal-rational norms of conduct are simply unable to contain the pressures towards corrupt behaviour. Wherever the state is the chief mechanism for obtaining access to scarce and desirable resources, officials use their 'gatekeeper' positions to distribute goods and resources to their patrons, friends and family. As the rampant state of corruption in the Chinese administration shows, such misuse of bureaucratic power is also found in the communist world.

Corruption is not just about depositing money in Swiss bank accounts. Certainly, some officials do abuse the system for their own gain, but families and local areas are also recipients of 'corrupt' practices. Families have to make great sacrifices to ensure that one of their number receives the education that is needed to get a government job. In return, officials are virtually *obliged* to reward their family and patrons for their help.

Furthermore, conflict over resources is endemic between different regions and ethnic groups in many third world nations. Officials from a particular region or tribe are often seen as *representatives* of that group. As such, the officials are expected to favour their own people.

Chronic unemployment has led to excess labour being absorbed into government employment in many third world nations. As a result, bureaucracies are overstaffed at lower levels. This aggravates the problem of bureaucratic red tape. As anyone who has bought a long-distance train ticket in India knows, the public often has to follow procedures of great complexity to gain the simplest kind of official authorisation.

Overstaffing can also exist at the higher levels of the administrative machinery. As a result, patterns of bureaucratic behaviour emerge that are something of a parody of Weber's model. Initiative is stifled, formal procedure is rigidly followed and authority is not delegated. Yet at the same time responsibility is diffused. The consequence is that the bureaucracy cannot act as an effective instrument for achieving the economic and social changes to which the regimes are notionally committed. An effective bureaucracy coupled with a vigorous modernising élite is a prerequisite for economic progress. In the third world, one of these two is usually absent; in too many cases, neither prerequisite exists.

Okoli (1980) describes administration in Africa as **premature bureaucratisation**. Europeans established and staffed the upper echelons of the bureaucracy in their African colonies. After independence, Africans moved into the existing administrative jobs. The machinery of administration was there, but the new bureaucrats had little or no experience of (or commitment to) Weberian norms. The development of modern *organs* of state power preceded the development of modern *attitudes* towards bureaucracy and power.

Furthermore, modern administrative machinery is based in principle on a notion of impartiality. However, the prevailing political cultures in African states placed a great emphasis on personal rule. Inevitably, bureaucratic norms gave way to a particularistic outlook.

Summary

1.   The bureaucracy is the institution that administers the functions of the state. Heady (1979) separates **classic** from **political** bureaucracies. Classic bureaucracies (e.g. Germany) are often professional and efficient, though they tend towards rigidity and aloofness. Political bureaucracies (e.g. the United States) are more amenable to political control.

2.   Top-level bureaucrats are important actors in the policy-making process. This power derives from their links with other departments and interest groups, from their permanence, from their involvement in carrying out policy and above all, from their proximity to ministers.

3.   The concept of bureaucratic politics suggests that civil servants act to defend the interest of their particular organisation. They seek to maximise their budgets and the size of their organisations, which is unlikely to be compatible with full efficiency.

4.   Power gravitates to the bureaucracy if there is a vacuum elsewhere in the political system. If politicians are unwilling or unable to govern, then civil servants will and can.

5.   The distribution of power in a bureaucracy can be either territorial or hierarchical. Territorial concentration refers to the distribution of authority across areas (for example, regions), whereas hierarchical concentration refers to the amount of discretion given to subordinate individuals within the administration.

6.   First world civil services differ in their emphasis on specialist or generalist skills. Specialists are technical experts with experience in and knowledge of the subjects they are dealing with. However Britain emphasises generalists – people who have experience of working in many different areas and who are 'specialists in the art of administration'.

7.   The extent and effectiveness of formal control over the bureaucracy depends on the reach of political appointments, norms of ministerial responsibility, and the extent to which ministerial advisers are used to supplement advice from the civil service.

8.   In the second world, ruling communist parties attempted to ensure effective control over the civil service by politicising the bureaucracy. Bureaucrats were a privileged stratum of society. The successful integration of this bureaucratic class into fledgling democracies is an important element of the process of state-building in the postcommunist world.

9.   In much of the third world, bureaucratic institutions imitate the administrative systems of the old colonial powers. They are often more 'modern' and developed than the political institutions and parties that they serve. They can step in to conduct the business of government themselves during political crises.

10. Bureaucrats in the third world are often perceived as representatives of their region, tribe or family. They are expected to favour their own kind at the expense of others whenever goods and resources are being distributed.

Discussion points

1. You are the leading civil servant in a government department. A new minister has been appointed who has proposed fundamental reform of the bureaucracy. How can you stop the minister?

2. Should bureaucrats and political advisers be accountable in public for their advice?

3. Would it be best for everyone if politicians simply gave up and let the bureaucrats run the country?

4. Too much political control of the bureaucracy reduces its efficiency; too little control gives the bureaucracy great power. Is there a solution to this?

5. Have the bureaucratic structures left by colonial powers been an aid or a hindrance to government in the third world?

Key reading

Heady, F. (1979) *Public Administration: A Comparative Perspective* (New York: Marcel Dekker). A comprehensive study of comparative administration.

Blau, P. and Meyer, M. (eds) (1987) *Bureaucracy in Modern Society*, 3rd edn (New York: Random House). An accessible introduction to the study of bureaucracy.

Rowat, D. (ed.) (1988) *Public Administration in Developed Democracies: A Comparative Study*, (New York: Marcel Dekker). A country-by-country study tied together by comparative chapters.

Harding, N, (ed.) (1984) *The State in Socialist Society*, (London: Macmillan). Contains much information on how bureaucracies were organised in communist party states.

Further reading

In addition to Heady (1979) on comparative administration, Peters (1984) is also useful, and considerably shorter. The collection edited by Suleiman (1984) contains several good pieces on individual countries.

On individual first world nations, C. Johnson (1982) provides an insight into bureaucratic power and policy-making in Japan. Self (1977) provides a perceptive comparison of French, American and British administration. Heclo and Wildavsky (1981) is a fascinating study of mandarin culture in Britain, while Aberbach *et al.* (1981) is a major comparative study of the values of civil servants and politicians in several Western countries.

For the bureaucratic model of communist states, see Meyer (1961 or 1965) and the discussion in Dawisha (1980). Schurmann's (1968, chs 3–5) introduction to the Chinese administrative system is still useful despite its age. Much information on the bureaucracy in communist states can be found in general discussions of the state in socialist society. See, for example, Harding (1984) and S. White *et al.* (1990, chs 3 and 6).

Okoli (1980) is a good (and short) introduction to bureaucratisation in postcolonial states in Africa. Potter's (1986) analysis of the Indian civil service is a cogent introduction to guardian bureaucracies in West Asia.

■ *Chapter 15* ■

The Military and the Police

■ The state in uniform

Whatever their political complexion, all regimes face the problem of coming to terms with non-elected institutions. The military and the police force play crucial roles not just in society, but also in politics. Military coups in the third world bear ample testimony to the impact of armed forces in domestic politics. However, the military also influence government in the first and second worlds, although in less dramatic ways.

Whereas the bureaucracy is involved in making and implementing laws, the police force is charged with upholding and enforcing the law. The term 'police' is cognate with 'politics' and 'policy' – the police are the guardians of the *polis*. In authoritarian states the police play an important role in controlling and suppressing political opposition – the police force are agents of the ruling élites, enforcing their political objectives. But even in liberal democracies, the independence of the police force has also been questioned. In particular, the surveillance role of secret police organisations has been the focus of criticism from civil rights groups.

Governments have their own priorities in responding to the problems of 'the state in uniform'. The threat of a military coup has long been a feature of political life in the third world, but has not been a dominant concern for first world governments. Notwithstanding these contrasts, the creation and maintenance of effective political control over these non-elected institutions is a central problem confronting all governments in the contemporary world.

■ The military: who guards the guards?

The military present special problems of political control in virtually every society. Not only are the armed forces specialists in the use of violence, but their organisational qualities of firm discipline, good communications and substantial *esprit de corps* make the military at least as important a political institution as the bureaucracy. The key difference is that the military's influence on politics sometimes remains latent. It may not have the same day-to-day impact on the political system as the bureaucracy has, but the military retains the capacity to seize power and hold on to it by force. This fact yields two key questions about the military. First, how can civilian rulers ensure control? Secondly, under what circumstances do the armed forces attempt to seize power?

□ The first world: the liberal model

The first world relies on a **liberal** model of civilian–military relations. According to this, civilian politicians take complete charge of society's affairs. The role of the military is to undertake the defence policy decided by the civilian leadership – politics is not the business of the military. In principle, the military does not formulate national security policy. The civilian leadership decides on policy, and the military's task is to decide how best to implement this policy.

Overall control of military affairs lies in the hands of civilian politicians. For example, the commander in chief of the American military is the president. In Britain, the formal commander is the Crown, though ministers are the real decision-makers. Under the liberal model, decisions relating to military affairs are ultimately subject to the electorate's verdict. If voters do not approve of the government's use of the military, they can register this disapproval in elections. The government, and not the military itself, is held responsible for the military's actions.

The military and policy-making

The liberal model of civil–military relations does not preclude a military role in policy-making. At the very least, military figures must be consulted regarding the viability of defence policy. Yet as US experience shows, the armed forces can play a larger role than this. Although there is no serious question of the Pentagon posing a direct challenge to the supremacy of the elected government, the armed forces are a powerful institutional group within the political system.

Military leaders are skilful players of Washington's political game, making full use of their status in society and technical expertise in their appearances before the Congressional Armed Services Committees, and in their participation in the National Security Council. Through their dealings with the media, the armed forces have also demonstrated considerable skill in mobilising public opinion behind their cause.

During the Cold War, the American military made considerable use of the potential threat from the Soviet Union to push for increased spending, especially on high-tech research. The political atmosphere allowed military leaders to exert influence so that the United States did not allow the Soviet Union to gain any advantage, real or imagined. Soviet military leaders exerted similar influence based on exactly the same fears among Soviet leaders. The resulting arms race ensured that military interests remained high on the decision-making agenda on both sides of the Iron Curtain.

First world nations spend billions of dollars every year on their armed forces. During the 1991 Gulf War, the British and US governments committed themselves to liberating Kuwait from Iraqi occupation. The cost of the Gulf War became the focus for criticism from left-wing critics who argued that the money would have been better spent improving education and health services. All governments have to make important choices regarding military spending. A nation only has limited financial resources at its disposal, and every pound, dollar or rouble spent on the military means that other areas of government spending will lose out. Although military spending in the first world is high in absolute terms, as Figure 15.1 demonstrates, many third world nations are higher spenders in relation to their GNP.

The relationship between military and civilian leaders is changing as a result of the collapse of communism and the end of the Cold War. Civilian politicians are facing expectations of 'the peace dividend' – a cut back on military spending with the savings used either to cut taxes or to increase public spending in non-military areas. Rather than pushing for increased military spending, the armed forces are now lobbying to limit the cutbacks. Furthermore, conflicts are emerging within the various branches of the armed forces. Even where cutbacks are accepted as inevitable, nobody wants *their* unit to be disbanded.

In the United States, relationships between the military, elected representatives and defence contractors have at times smacked of collusion rather than coalition. Considerable opposition to the Strategic Defence Initiative (more commonly called Star Wars) emerged in the late 1980s. The project still received firm backing from President Reagan and continued despite objections that it was a colossal waste of money. In general, however, America's armed forces pursue their objectives through means that are perfectly legitimate in the context of the liberal model of civil–military relations.

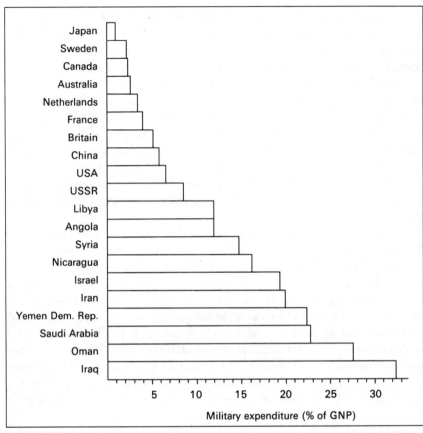

Source: World Bank (1990), *World Development Report 1989* (New York: World Bank, 1990).
Figure 15.1   *Military spending as a proportion of GNP, 1986 (selected countries)*

In contrast to the United States, Japanese military spending is limited by the constitution. After the Second World War, the American occupiers forced the Japanese to accept a constitutional clause stipulating that its defence spending could not exceed 1 per cent of Gross National Product. The growth of Japan's economy since then makes this figure more significant, and much defence research expenditure has been disguised by being channelled through other departments, such as the Education Ministry.

The military as a police force

Although the armed forces may not seek to intervene in the domestic politics of liberal democracies, such a role may be forced upon them by civilian politicians. The potential for military action to become political increases when the military is asked to undertake non-military tasks.

Britain is a good example. During industrial disputes involving the fire and ambulance services in the 1970s and 1980s, the military was brought in to undertake crucial lifesaving tasks. The British government is empowered to deploy the military for urgent work of national importance through the Emergency Powers Act of 1964 (Babington 1990). Although it was argued that the work being done was essential for public safety, the involvement of military personnel in strike situations remains a thorny issue.

The military is also 'politicised' when it is used to police domestic civil disturbances. American troops, for example, were used to implement federal desegregation orders during the civil rights struggle in the 1950s and early 1960s. In Britain, the army was introduced into Northern Ireland in 1969 because the police were unable to cope with the scale of civil disorder. More than twenty years later, it is still there.

The state must be perceived as legitimate for the military to be seen as apolitical. For the most part, this consensus does exist in the first world. In areas such as Northern Ireland, or the Basque areas of northern Spain, the consensus does not exist, and so the role of the military remains controversial, with some viewing it as an agency of occupation.

□ *The second world: the penetration model*

The penetration model of civilian control is the opposite of the liberal notion of a depoliticised military. The penetration model seeks to imbue the armed forces with the political ideals of the civilian leadership. This approach was taken furthest in communist party states. In the first world, the military is very much the army of the state. The values of many military officers may be right-wing, but the armed forces are not party political. They are defenders of the state rather than defenders of any one party. In the communist world, although the military is there to defend the state from foreign aggression, the armed forces are also defenders of the party.

The party in the army

The Soviet Union provided an influential example of the penetrative control of the military by the party – a model that was copied throughout the communist world. The communist party went to extraordinary lengths to ensure the political reliability of the military, even at the cost of weakening its efficiency as a fighting force. For example, Stalin's purge in 1937–38 of military officers perceived to be politically unreliable virtually destroyed the Red Army's professional leadership.

Stalin's paranoia provoked extreme measures to ensure political reliability. Less extreme but still extensive measures of political control were also employed. At each level of the military command structure, a deputy commander or political commissar was responsible for political affairs. These political officers reported to higher party officials, and thus created a two-tier chain of command within the armed forces. One chain of command went up to higher *military* officials, the other went up to higher *party* officials and ultimately to the party's central committee.

To further increase military reliability, conscripts were subject to intensive political indoctrination. Thus, the armed forces acted as a school for socialism. Furthermore, to become a career soldier, membership of the party or Young Communist League was a virtual prerequisite. Security agencies also undertook extensive surveillance within the armed services to keep tabs on 'unreliable' individuals.

The army in the party

Civilian penetration of the army results not only in the party placing itself in the army, but also in the army gaining a place within the party. This process was much more noticeable in China than in the Soviet Union. The party and military became closely intermingled in China. Revolution occurred as the result of a protracted military (or guerrilla) struggle, so party and army became almost indistinguishable. In China, military leaders believe that they have a right and indeed a duty to be involved in civilian politics. Furthermore, the demobilisation of the army in peacetime saw many old military leaders taking up positions within the civilian leadership.

Military and political leaders in China are bound together through a network of personal ties. Since 1949, the military has been deployed in China for reasons other than national defense. During the Cultural Revolution, the army was needed to restore order after virtual civil war had brought the country to a standstill between 1966 and 1969. Then, in June 1989, the military was brutally used to murder and disperse student demonstrators from Tiananmen Square.

When the military intervened in Chinese politics, its actions were not in conflict with party rule. Rather, the military acted as one element in a ruling élite that encompassed party, state and military. Its interventions were motivated by the need to restore order to a disintegrating society.

Military leaders gained immense power and status in all communist party states. In the Soviet Union, with party leaders and the KGB (the secret police force), they formed a ruling class that enjoyed extensive privilege – holiday homes, chauffered cars, access to scarce foreign imports, special medical care. No waiting in queues for the officers of the Red Army: for them, communism had already arrived.

Perhaps then, it should not have been too great a surprise when leaders of the 'three ugly sisters' – the party, the military and the security services – attempted to seize power and prevent the break-up of the old Soviet system in August 1991. Although the timing of the coup took the world by surprise, leading figures like Eduard Shevardnadze in the Soviet Union had been warning for months of the danger that the old guard might try to re-establish its position by force. However, as Exhibit 15.1 shows, the August coup was poorly conceived and badly executed – an excellent example of how not to stage a coup.

The military and the collapse of communism

The potential for military intervention is strongest when political authority collapses. During 1989 the communist world underwent massive changes. As popular challenges to communist party rule mounted, the reliability of the military as defenders of the ruling regime took on increased importance.

With the exception of Albania and Yugoslavia, national revolutionary movements played only minor roles in bringing communist parties to power in Eastern Europe. Elsewhere, the dominant factor was the 'liberation' of German-occupied territory by Soviet armed forces. To a large extent, communist party rule in Eastern Europe was underpinned by the threat of Soviet military intervention. Where the Red Army installed communist regimes from the outside, it fell to it to ensure that communist rule continued against domestic opposition. In 1956 and 1968 the Soviet Red Army removed reformist political leaders in Hungary and Czechoslovakia respectively. On each occasion, a regime more in tune with the Soviet Union's thinking was installed. The Red Army was also active in suppressing workers' uprisings in East Germany in 1953 and in Poland in 1956.

Given the weak foundations for communist rule in much of Eastern Europe, military backing provided an essential source of stability for communist leaders. However, this backing depended on the Soviet Union's adherence to the **Brezhnev Doctrine**. This doctrine asserted that 'the gains of socialism were irreversible': in other words, Moscow had the right to use any available means to ensure that Eastern European remained within the Soviet Union's sphere of influence.

Exhibit 15.1 *How not to stage your coup: the Soviet Union, August 1991*

'Over the years, President Gorbachev has got very tired. He needs some time to get his health back'. Gennady Yanayev, acting president of the Soviet Union, 19 August 1991.

'I said, "You are reckless adventurers. If you want to kill yourselves, that's your affair, but you will kill the country. Convey that to those who sent you"'. Mikhail Gorbachev, reaction to being placed under house arrest, 22 August 1991.

For sixty hours in August 1991, the Soviet Union teetered between its authoritarian past and an uncertain but very different future. President Gorbachev was placed under arrest in his holiday home by a self-styled 'Emergency Committee' of leading party, state and KGB officials. The conspirators aimed to turn the clock back and reverse many of the changes that had taken place in the Soviet Union since 1985. Their bungled coup attempt achieved the exact opposite. The break-up of the Soviet Union was accelerated, the KGB was dismantled and the communist party lost what was left of its grip on power.

The failure of the August coup gives some pertinent examples of how not to carry out your coup. First, the coup's leaders were divided and lacked a clear plan of action. Almost as soon as Gorbachev had been arrested, the new leadership began to fall apart. The spate of 'illnesses' that afflicted coup participants was a clear sign of lack of unity. Opponents were given the hope and resolution that the coup could be defeated if they stayed firm in their opposition.

Secondly, it is essential that a coup removes its targets from power. Although Gorbachev was arrested, Boris Yeltsin remained free to rally opposition against the coup. Had Yeltsin and Gorbachev been arrested simultaneously, then the coup would have had more chance of succeeding.

Thirdly, coups are more likely to succeed when there is a single centre of authority in a nation. By August 1991, much power had drained away from Moscow to leaders of the republics and city mayors. In essence, the coup came too late – it was impossible to seize all major centres of power in the country.

Fourthly, the new leadership must ensure that they use those levers of power at their disposal. KGB officers are reported to have sat around drinking tea, awaiting orders to carry out arrests that never

came. The coup leaders also failed to gain full control of communications, thus aiding their opponents who maintained contact with
the watching world outside.

Fifthly, the coup organisers needed the collaboration of those who
exercised direct command over the armed forces. General Grachev's
refusal to send his paratroopers against the Russian parliament
building was perhaps the final nail in the coup's coffin.

And finally, reports from a variety of sources indicated that some
of the coup's leading figures were drunk for much of their three days
in power. If you need one thing above all else to carry out a coup
successfully, it is a clear head.

By the summer of 1989, the threat of Soviet intervention in Eastern
Europe had become remote. In a speech at the Council of Europe in June
1989, Gorbachev spoke of the possibility of political and social change
in Eastern Europe, commenting that such change would be: 'exclusively
the affair of the peoples themselves, any attempts to limit the sovereignty of states . . . is impermissible.'

Gorbachev made clear to East European leaders that if their regime
had to be sustained by military power, then it would have to be by their
own armed forces, and not by the Soviet Union's. Although the use of
the **Chinese Option** (crushing the opposition movement by force) was
discussed in East Germany and Czechoslovakia, in the end the military
was not asked to intervene to defend the ruling party.

Even if the armed forces had been ordered to open fire on the
demonstrators, it is far from certain that these orders would have been
obeyed. Military leaders may have formed part of a privileged élite, but
ordinary soldiers (particularly conscripts) did not. They often had much
more in common with the demonstrators than they did with their
commanding officers. It is misleading to refer to the armed forces in
communist party states as a unified and coherent group, or of the
military as a single-interest group. Sharp divisions existed between the
interests of the military élites and those of the lower ranks who had less
to lose from the collapse of communist rule.

As a comparison between military intervention in China and
Romania in 1989 demonstrates, there is a very fine line between success
and failure in using the armed forces to suppress popular opposition
movements. In June 1989 the Chinese leadership sent the military into
Tiananmen Square in Beijing to clear the capital of protesters who had
been occupying the square since mid-April. The troops shot anybody

who got in their way, and tanks rolled over the makeshift tents occupied by sleeping protesters. From the party leadership's viewpoint, the exercise was a success. The streets were cleared and the party élite retained its hold on power.

In contrast, when Romanian troops were faced with demonstrators on the streets of Bucharest in December 1989, many decided to side with the protesters. A short but bloody conflict ensued between the army and Securitate (secret police) units loyal to Ceaucescu. After a hastily arranged trial, Nicolai and Elena Ceaucescu were executed, and the resistance from the Securitate slowly but surely petered out.

In both China and Romania, the élite's survival depended on the loyalty of the military. Some retired senior generals in China did oppose the use of military force against unarmed and peaceful protestors. There are also reports that individual soldiers were shot by their superiors for refusing to carry out orders. But, overall, the military's discipline remained firm and the regime won the day. In Romania, by contrast, many soldiers refused to carry out Ceaucescu's orders, and the regime fell.

Under *normal* conditions, controlling the military through the 'penetration' approach has proved successful. However, when normal conditions break down and the military are asked to intervene in domestic affairs, then the reliability of the armed forces cannot be ensured. The key to keeping the military under political control in communist party states was therefore maintaining political stability. While the armed forces were confined to barracks, their political reliability was not an issue.

☐ *The third world: military coups*

When political control of the military is not secured by the means outlined above, the danger of a coup becomes endemic. Such coups have been a feature of politics in the third world. Pinkney (1990, p. 11) identified 56 countries that have experienced military governments since 1960, the vast majority in the third world. Since the end of the Second World War, military intervention in politics has been the norm rather than the exception in the third world.

Types of military rule

Military coups do not, in the long run, always result in military governments. Often, once the old ruler or party is overthrown, the military hands power over to a new civilian leader. However, in these cases, the military usually acts as the effective ruler behind the scenes. Rouquie (1982) has called these regimes **supervised democracies**. Furthermore, even in states where the military retains power in its own hands, the style of military leadership varies enormously (Remmer 1989).

At the two extremes are **inclusionary** and **exclusionary** regimes. In the former, the military leaders try to build a base of popular support among the populace. Peron's military government in Argentina from 1946 to 1955 is a classic example of a populist regime. Peron undertook a policy of state-led industrialisation and social welfare, based on a strong trade union movement. According to Munck (1989, pp. 27–8) the central feature of **Peronism** was the concept of the 'providential person' – a benevolent leader attempting to build a strong, modern and wealthy Argentina.

In exclusionary regimes, military leaders attempt to limit popular participation in politics. For example in Chile between 1973 and 1989, General Augusto Pinochet suppressed all potential sources of popular involvement in politics (opposition political parties, trade unions, the media and so on). Power was concentrated in the hands of his ruling military clique.

Motives for military coups

S. Finer (1988, first pub. 1962) argues that coups occur when the military has both the opportunity and the disposition to intervene. Opportunities often arise when the civil authorities need the military to fight a war or act as a police force. But what of the initial disposition to intervene? Finer suggests five motives.

National motives are at work when military intervention is based on officers' conceptions of the national interest. For example, in Pakistan the threat of national disintegration prompted military intervention in October 1958. In 1977 the military under General Zia again intervened against the backdrop of political unrest. Although the Pakistan People's Party (PPP) had won a majority in a general election, the opposition parties refused to recognise the PPP's right to rule, claiming that wide-scale ballot-rigging had taken place. The military deposed the PPP government of Zulfikar Ali Bhutto and later executed him. In Thailand civilian incompetence in managing domestic affairs has proved the spark for military intervention on numerous occasions. For Thais, 'revolutions per minute' has more to do with the prevailing political situation than the speed at which records play.

Class motives may be part of the military creed. Soldiers may act on behalf of particular social interests. Needler (1968) suggested that in

Latin America military officers of middle-class background historically sided with the middle classes in their struggle to wrest power from the dominant landowning oligarchs. Right-wing military governments then emerged in opposition to the growth of mass left-wing political parties. Again, the example of Pinochet in Chile is pertinent here. An elected left-wing government was shot out of power to the applause of much of the middle class.

In post-colonial Africa, class interests are less important than **ethnic** affiliations. Many coups are outgrowths of ethnic, religious or regional tension within society. For example, the first Nigerian republic was destroyed by coups driven by ethnic and regional rivalries. Further examples of ethnic motives can be found in coups in other African states, among them Zaire, Uganda, Chad, Liberia (twice) and Guinea-Bissau.

Institutional interests can also provoke intervention. Threats to the military's budget, autonomy, living standards or prestige all provoke discontent in the armed forces. Six years after President Nkrumah was removed by a coup in Ghana in 1966, the military overthrew the reformist government of Dr Busia, which had been attempting to curb the extravagant lifestyle of military officers. In much of the third world, the military provides one of the few channels for ambitious young men of modest background to achieve status and financial reward in society. If these aspirations are frustrated, then a coup is more likely.

Finally, a military coup may be a vehicle for **personal ambition**. Such motives are rarely sufficient in themselves to provoke a successful coup. In Uganda, the authoritarian nature of Idi Amin's government between 1971 and 1979 was clearly shaped by his drive to attain personal power. However, he was aided in his seizure of power from Milton Obote by popular resentment against the civilian leadership, ethnic rivalries, and widespread military concern over its declining position (Decalo 1976, pp. 201–11).

Back to the barracks?

The 1980s saw a trend towards democratisation in the third world. Most notably in Latin America, but also in Asia and Africa, military governments handed power back to elected civilian leaders. This forms part of a worldwide trend epitomised by the collapse of dictatorship in Eastern Europe and the collapse of legitimate alternatives to democratic rule. As Hamburg (1988, p. 1) notes, just as the motivation for military

Exhibit 15.2 *How to stage your coup:
the mechanics of military takeover*

The coup d'état has been one of the main mechanisms for the transfer of power in the third world. But how exactly does one go about organising a military takeover? In a useful handbook, Luttwak (1969) provided a compendium of advice for the politically ambitious officer, concentrating on countries with a parochial political culture where seizing power is a relatively straightforward matter.

Luttwak suggests that the planning stage is in many ways the most dangerous. Those who ride to power on a coup are, by definition, expert in its mechanics, 'I came in on a tank', said the Iraqi Prime Minister in 1968, 'and only a tank will evict me'. Hence infiltration of the army is risky, though to some degree essential. The key army units are those based in or around the capital; the sympathetic officers will probably be those with frustrated career ambitions or a similar ethnic affiliation and political views to the conspirators. Even if officers cannot be won over, the support of key technicians is often sufficient to immobilise the unit while the coup is executed.

Essential elements in the coup itself include: seizing the presidential palace, if only for symbolic reasons; disrupting telecommunications; closing the airport; setting up road-blocks around the capital; establishing a physical presence in public buildings; arresting political opponents; and controlling the radio station. For your message to the people, Luttwak offers a choice of styles ranging from the messianic ('the bourgeoisie is abolished . . . a new era of equality between all citizens is inaugurated' – Colonel Bokassa, Central African Republic, 1966) – to the rational-administrative ('Nkrumah ruled the country as if it were his private property . . . We hope to announce measures for curing the country's troubles within the next few days' – Ghana National Liberation Council, 1966).

If the forces that remain loyal to the previous government are successfully dealt with, consolidation of the coup requires the development of the regime's legitimacy, both domestically and internationally. Military force will be as insufficient in maintaining the military in office as it was necessary for obtaining power in the first place. Generals who fail to become politicians very soon cease to be either.

intervention in politics varies from case to case, so military regimes depart in response to different pressures.

First, the military regime may respond to pressure from civilian life – either politicians or the population itself. Secondly, it may lose credibility by failing to perform the military's main task – to act as a fighting force. For example, the military junta in Argentina was thoroughly discredited by failure in the Falklands (Malvinas) War against Britain in 1982. Thirdly, the military may recognise that its domestic policies have failed: the army simply gives up. Fourthly, the military may decide that governing is not as easy as it seems; it therefore chooses to return to professional military activities. Finally, some regimes have been pressured by outside forces to hand power back to the civilians. The United States's immense economic leverage in Central and South America was successfully applied to the military regimes in Bolivia, El Salvador and Guatemala. International bodies such as the World Bank are also more comfortable with civilian government.

However, as Hamburg (1988, p. 1) further comments, 'military disengagement or withdrawal is rarely total or final'. The return to civilian leadership can often be short lived, particularly if the new regime does not give a high priority to the military's interests.

There have been many false starts on the road to demilitarisation. Between them, Argentina, Peru and Honduras have embarked on re-democratisation on no fewer than thirteen occasions since 1945 (Remmer 1989, p. 52). In any case, withdrawal may only be partial. When General Pinochet relinquished political power in Chile, he retained his position as head of the armed forces. Power may now be vested in the hands of civilian leaders in Chile, but Pinochet remains a looming presence within the political system. As Salvador Allende said, weeks before Pinochet's coup ousted him from power in 1973: 'It won't cost you much to get a military man in. But by heaven, it will cost you something to get him out!'

■ The police

Although the military is occasionally used by governments to deal with domestic disorder, its primary function is to pursue national defence. Except for cases of severe civil disorder, the task of upholding and enforcing the laws of the land belongs to the police.

There are two conflicting views of the police's role in society. In essence, these see the police as 'citizens in uniform' (liberal perspective) or as 'the state in uniform' (radical perspective).

☐ *Liberal and radical perspectives*

The **liberal** view sees the police as 'disinterested custodians of public order' (Brewer *et al.* 1988, p. 214). The police should be entirely independent of political control. Officers' personal political opinions should not affect how the police carry out their functions. All the laws of the land should be enforced irrespective of how members of the police view those laws.

For liberal theorists, policing is based on consent. The legitimacy of police actions stems from broadly agreed values in society. Some minorities may oppose certain police activities but, by and large, police actions are accepted by most of the population as necessary and fair.

In contrast, the **radical** perspective views the police as an instrument of domination. They are controlled by the state, and act to defend its interests. Police forces are not a part of society, but apart from society. They are agencies of state power – and of the interests that the state represents. Rather than being a product of consent, the police are an instrument of coercion. Whereas liberal theorists see the police as servants of the public, radical theorists perceive the police as servants of the state.

Liberal theorists agree that the radical perspective fits authoritarian political systems. In South Africa under white rule, or in Eastern Europe under communist party control, the police openly served the interests of their political masters. However, the radicals suggest that this is also a feature of policing in liberal democracies. Although the police's support for the ruling élites may be less overt than in authoritarian regimes, it is nevertheless a fact of political life.

☐ *Structure and organisation*

Police forces are usually either 'bottom-up' or 'top-down' in structure. The 'bottom-up' style is prevalent in those nations where police forces had their origins in rudimentary local patterns of law enforcement. Over the years, the various local styles of patrolling and enforcement have been merged, standardised and professionalised into a national system.

Although this process inevitably involves a degree of central control, bottom-up police forces are often decentralised. For example, there is no national police force in Britain (although the activities of the local forces are coordinated on a national level). The balance between central and local control is embodied in a tripartite division of power – central government, local police authorities, and chief police officers.

Table 15.1   *Police politics: a glossary*

Term	Description	
Perspectives		
Liberal	The police are disinterested custodians of public order – policing is based on consent.	
Radical	The police are agents of the state and an instrument of coercion.	
Organisation		*Example*
Bottom-up	Police forces originate from rudimentary local patterns of law enforcement. Characterised by decentralised control.	Britain USA
Top-down	The police are under the direct control of central government. Characterised by national rather than local police forces.	France
Approaches		
Community	Police force is part of the community. The entire community is part of the law enforcement process.	Japan
Reactive	'Heavy-handed' policing. Crime is prevented by ensuring that everyone is aware of the power of the police.	Authoritarian regimes
Control mechanism		
Internal	The police is responsible for its own discipline, and investigates accusations of wrongdoing by officers.	Most police forces
External	Representatives of the local community or elected civilian politicians play a major role in policing the police.	Sweden
Surveillance techniques		
Overt	The police makes sure that people know that their actions are being closely watched.	Communist party states
Covert	Secret surveillance of people who are deemed to be a danger to the state.	All countries

British police forces are financed through local authorities and are politically accountable to local communities. Furthermore, local police chiefs have considerable autonomy over operational tactics. Lacking the resources to cope with every area of law enforcement, police chiefs are forced to target priority areas or crimes.

The American system is a good example of **decentralised** control within a 'bottom-up' structure. Local police forces are directly accountable to locally elected or appointed police chiefs. There are around 40 000 police forces in America. Virtually every municipal area with a population of over 2500 has its own force. The vast majority of these forces are very small indeed, employing less than ten officers (Brewer *et al.* 1988, p. 110). The cost of local autonomy and control is the duplication of activities, and a lack of national coordination. For many petty criminals in the United States, a safe haven is only as far away as the state, or even the county, border.

In 'top-down' systems, the police are directly controlled by central government. The police force is seen as the guardian of the whole political system, not just of private property and individual safety. This system is the norm in much of continental Europe. Police forces are financially dependent on, and accountable to, central political institutions, rather than local organisations.

France provides a good example of 'top-down' policing. Although small local police forces under the control of the local mayor do exist, they only play a minor role in law enforcement. The major role is played by two national forces, the Police Nationale, under the civilian control of the Ministry of the Interior, and the Gendarmerie Nationale, under the military control of the Ministry of Defence (Ritchie 1992).

☐ *Specialisation*

As the police's tasks have grown and diversified, so has the need for specialisation within police forces. Most forces now contain many structural subdivisions dealing with specific tasks: for example, criminal investigation, anti-drugs squads and specially trained tactical weapons units.

With criminal activities spanning national boundaries, there is also an increased role for international cooperation in policing. At times, this takes the form of unilateral incursions into one country by another. American attempts to hit the narcotics trade at source by seizing drugs barons in Central America are a case in point. Due to their nature, such police actions are usually performed by military or quasi-military units.

However, cooperation rather than confrontation is increasingly the order of the day. From its headquarters in France, Interpol has long been the main institution for coordinating cross-European criminal investigation. Furthermore, bilateral contacts and investigations play an increasingly important role in the fight against drugs trading and international terrorism. National investigation agencies regularly swap information and even coordinate their activities to retain the crucial element of surprise. One example is the investigations in 1991 into world-wide financial irregularities and money-laundering by the Bank of Credit and Commerce International.

Although aspects of policing are becoming more international in the first world, law enforcement remains strongly local in the third world. Where police forces have not yet developed on a national scale, the responsibility for local policing often falls on the shoulders of community leaders. These 'big men' belong to families that have exercised power in the local community for many generations. In tight-knit local communities, their functions are usually more to do with adjudicating local conflicts and upholding local traditions than criminal investigation.

□ Community or reactive policing?

As well as differing in terms of structure, police forces also differ in terms of **philosophy**. On one side, there is the **community** approach, typified by the image of the local British bobby on the beat. This approach is favoured in Japan, which has one of the lowest crime rates and highest detection rates in the developed world.

On the other side is the **reactive** approach. This involves a much higher profile for the police force and a harder style. The community approach places a premium on preventing crime by making the entire community part of the law enforcement process. In contrast, the reactive approach is based on preventing crime through instilling feelings that the police is powerful and all-watching. This approach is the basis of paramilitary-style policing in authoritarian political systems. It also provides the basis of policing in some Western liberal democracies. American police officers make no attempt to hide the fact that they carry guns, and they will use them if required. In essence, the reactive approach is based on instilling fear in the minds of potential offenders.

Elements of both styles of policing can be found in most police forces. When the community approach fails to keep the peace, police chiefs have little alternative than to resort to a more heavy-handed policing style. However, it can prove extremely difficult to switch between

Exhibit 15.3   *Policing Japanese-style*

The integration of the police into the local community characterises policing in Japan. Police officers are assigned to police boxes (*koban*) or residential police stations (*chuzaisho*), which act as the grass-roots link between police and society. Japanese police officers are expected to know and visit all the families under their jurisdiction during the year – a feat that requires the ability to consume immense amounts of tea. Japanese citizens accept that their lives will be closely monitored by the local police officer. They also believe that the task of law enforcement is not the sole responsibility of the police. Citizens form themselves into local crime prevention associations, and meet regularly with their local officer to pass on information on suspected or potential offenders.

This community approach is more suited to (and successful in) rural areas rather than urban centres with more mobile populations. However, community policing is also practised in all Japanese cities. The urban neighbourhood police officer – known as Mr Walkabout (*omawari-san*) – is a common visitor at both the homes of local residents, and at workplaces which employ workers from outside the local area. In summary, police officers are highly regarded and respected members of the local community in Japan (see Ritchie 1992).

the two systems. A heavy-handed police force will not be easily trusted if it attempts to present itself as a community force. Furthermore, building confidence in the police force is much more difficult than losing it. Years of efficient community policing can easily be demolished by one or two instances of 'heavy' police action.

Community relations

All policing relies on the cooperation of the local population to be effective. Without information from the public, it is extremely difficult to bring offenders to book except in the most authoritarian regimes where trials are a mere formality. Such cooperation depends on the extent to which the police force is regarded as a legitimate actor. Put another way, it depends on the extent to which the police is perceived as a repressive agent of state power. This is most likely to be the case when the government itself is not accepted as legitimate. Under South African apartheid, the control of all significant levers of power by the white minority meant that the black population was fully aware of the police's role as an instrument of white domination.

Where there is conflict over sovereignty, the police may also be seen as an illegitimate force. For example, Basque separatists in northern Spain do not accept that their land should be part of Spain. As such, they view the police as an instrument of colonial occupation, and regard police officers as legitimate targets for attack. In such circumstances, the ability of the police to maintain the peace and enforce laws is severely impaired, and often gives way to paramilitary policing, or direct military control.

However, the system can also break down if the local community feels that its interests are not represented by the police force. This has been most clearly shown in the first world in the policing of minorities. In Northern Ireland, for example, the Roman Catholic minority has never had confidence in the local police force, which is predominantly staffed by Protestants. In the early 1970s, 'no-go' areas were created and barricades set up to keep the police force from entering Catholic areas. Within this policing 'vacuum', there was not a total breakdown in order. The illegal terrorist group, the Irish Republican Army (IRA), meted out its own special punishments – executions, beatings, 'tar-and-feathering' and 'kneecapping' (shooting somebody through the knee). These punishments are not reserved for those foolish enough to cross the IRA, but are also inflicted on 'normal' criminals.

☐ Policing the police

The notion of the accountability and control of police forces is a fundamental issue. Who controls the controllers, who surveys the surveillance agencies and who is to prevent beatings in police cells?

The degree of confidence in the police force depends on community perceptions of police accountablity. If there is no right to appeal against the actions of the police, then in general, there is likely to be a low level of confidence. This public attitude can all too easily become self-sustaining. If there is a low opinion of the police, it becomes difficult to attract enough high quality recruits to improve the standing of the force.

The relationship between the public and the police force is an unequal one. Citizens are often unaware of their rights, and police can invoke 'catch-all' offences (such as breach of the peace) to detain individuals. This places primacy on the need to have an effective complaints procedure to allow citizens to redress the balance, if only after the event.

However, most police forces favour and employ an internal complaints procedure. In essence, the police investigates itself through such bodies as the Internal Affairs Divisions in American police forces. Although the British Police Complaints Authority does contain an independent element, police representatives constitute a majority on these bodies. Attempts to open police forces to more public scrutiny have been opposed by the police. Most notably, the Belorgey reform proposals in France, which advocated a greater role for the public in monitoring police activities, encountered great hostility from all the major police unions, and ultimately met with failure.

In some third world regimes, the police act with virtual impunity. Police rapists in some parts of Asia are virtually invulnerable because a known rape victim loses all social status. If she does report the crime, there is often little to stop her being raped again by the police. In many third world societies, becoming a police officer is a way of gaining both income and status. Once inside the police force, a myriad of opportunities for increasing that income – bribery and corruption – open up. When a mass rape occurred at a Kenyan school in 1990, the police refused to turn up until they were given 'money to buy petrol' i.e. bribed.

Despite closer controls on officers in first world police forces, the abuse of police power is not confined to the third world. A key problem is the emergence of a police subculture. Nowhere are police officers renowned as namby-pamby soft-hearted liberals, and the view of the police as sexist, racist, authoritarian men persists through much of the first world. Despite belonging to the public sector, their politics (like those of the armed forces) are predominantly conservative.

In extreme cases, the existence of such a subculture can lead to the police imposing their own political agenda. The police in the southern states of the United States strove to maintain white supremacy in the face of anti-discrimination legislation by the federal government in Washington. More usually, this aspect of police subculture encourages stereotyping. Because deprived social groups (for example young male blacks in white societies, Aborigines in Australia, American Indians) provide more than their fair share of society's criminals, the police assume that all such people should be treated with suspicion. As a result, the treatment that people get from the police depends very much on their social status.

☐ The police and politics

Some police forces are more vulnerable to political interference than others. The more centralised a police force, the easier it is for politicians

---

Exhibit 15.4   *Civilian control of the police in Sweden*

Internal complaints procedures predominate in the first world. However, in the more consensual democracies of Scandinavia, where the tradition of ombudsmen acting as protectors of individuals is well entrenched, 'outsiders' do play a prominent role. For example, the Swedish police force is administered at the national level by the Rikspolisstyrelsen – the National Police Board. Of the eight ordinary members of the board, only two are representatives of the police. The remaining six are members of parliament.

This role for elected civilian representatives is reproduced in the 118 local police districts. The local police board (which controls finance, organisation and police appointments) is headed by the local police commissioner, with the remaining six to eight places filled by appointments made by the local council.

Furthermore, the Swedish police force attempts to build bridges with the local community from the earliest possible stage. Local police officers teach law and justice classes in local schools to create a feeling of common interests between the citizen and the police (Archer 1985). And, would you believe, police officers on the street still often give citizens a salute when responding to requests for information.

---

to influence and manipulate the actions of the police. In the Republic of Ireland, the Garda Siochana (the national police force) is headed by a Commissioner who is directly appointed by the Minister of Justice. This places the Commissioner in an extremely vulnerable position and makes the process of applying political pressure much easier than in decentralised systems (Brewer *et al*. 1988, pp. 87 and 226).

One source of political pressure on police chiefs is in response to violent crimes that have shocked the nation. Faced with a government wanting a quick conviction, it is not surprising that police forces sometimes act with undue haste. The convictions of several suspected IRA terrorists in Britain have been quashed on appeal as it became clear that the police's evidence was either fatally flawed or had been concocted to ensure a conviction. The fact that defendants spent many years in prison while previous appeals were rejected cast a cloud over the entire British criminal justice system.

In Sweden, the assassination of Premier Olaf Palme in 1987 led to political pressure on the police to find the culprit. A massive investigation failed to bear fruit for two years, as political impatience grew. When an arrest was finally made, the case against the defendant was so flimsy and riddled with inconsistencies that it was thrown out. Political pressure on police forces can therefore be seen as an obstacle to effective and efficient policing, and in the long run proves to be counter-productive.

☐ The secret police and surveillance

One crucial element in the relationship between politics and the police is the question of surveillance. The issue is not whether surveillance should take place – there is a high level of consensus that anti-terrorist operations are legitimate – but one of whom should be watched.

Defining who is an 'enemy of the state' is not easy. Terrorists are 'enemies' but civil rights activists surely are not? This area is difficult to control because surveillance has to be secret. People may suspect that they are under investigation, but if the intelligence agencies are doing their jobs properly, it is extremely difficult to prove. Secret policing, by its very nature, is the least accountable area of police operations.

Thus, surveillance activity can easily cross ill-defined boundaries and become political. Arguably, judgements on who is an appropriate and legitimate target for police surveillance should be made by politicians. Some surveillance agencies, however, defy political control. Indeed, there have been repeated allegations that elements in the British security services tried to destabilise the Labour Government of Harold Wilson in the mid-1970s – the very entity that was supposed to control those services.

The role of the police as an agent of political repression is most clearly seen in authoritarian regimes. In these cases surveillance of the population can be both overt and covert. **Overt surveillance** is employed to create a firm belief in the minds of the population that any heterodox or illegal activities will not avoid detection by the police, and that severe sanctions will follow. As the Chinese saying puts it, 'kill the chicken to scare the monkey'. In communist party states, this was reinforced by 'show trials' – widely reported trials of dissidents and political criminals to let the rest of the population know what was awaiting them if they too crossed the line.

Overt policing of this sort is usually backed up by a network of unpaid civilian informers. In China, representatives of neighbourhood committees keep close tabs on the activities of their neighbours. It is common to see the old women of a neighbourhood sitting outside, knitting for the grandchildren – and quietly noting any visitors to the area. After the suppression of the 1989 democracy movement in Beijing, activists were often turned over to the police by members of their family. Such cases were widely reported in the press to instil in the minds of the 'criminals' the sense that they could trust nobody, that they were alone in the world, and that even their families disapproved of their 'counter-revolutionary' activities. Similarly, the Iraqi regime of Saddam Hussein has been described by exiled dissidents as one where the entire population informs on itself.

Clearly, overt surveillance may not be sufficient to stamp out political dissidence. **Covert surveillance** is often, therefore, an important tool in political repression. As well as the unpaid civilian informers, members of the security police infiltrate all areas of society, reporting back to their superiors on potential troublemakers. The true extent of this secret police penetration into civilian society in Eastern Europe will probably never be known. However, it has become clear from the files found in the Stasi offices in East Germany and the Securitate headquarters in Romania that the network was vast. The Securitate played a major role in maintaining Ceaucescu's rule and, disregarding popular hatred of their organisation, resisted his overthrow until the end.

In communist party states, there was no separation of the secret police from the ruling party. The head of the surveillance machinery was a political appointment. Supreme loyalty to the party was expected and demanded of secret police officials. Managing the secret police machinery was an important stepping stone to holding political power in many communist party states. Yuri Andropov, who headed the KGB in the Soviet Union for fifteen years before becoming General Secretary of the Communist Party in 1982, is perhaps the best-known example. However he was not alone. Hua Guofeng in China, Honecker in East Germany and Kania in Poland also made the transition from police chief to party chief (Adelman 1984).

The use of the police to silence opposition is not limited to communist party states. It has been a feature of the role of the police in authoritarian regimes throughout the third world. Often organised on paramilitary lines, the police have played a key role in political repression in Latin America. It has been estimated, for example, that between 1973 and 1990 under the dictatorship of Pinochet in Chile, there were 15 000 assassinations, more than 2200 political detainees who subsequently 'disappeared', and 155 000 prisoners who were held in concentration camps throughout the country.

Similarly, after General Videla came to power in Argentina in 1976, state kidnapping, torture and murder of political opponents became systematic in the so-called 'dirty war'. Human rights organisations estimate that over 7000 people became *desaparecidos* (missing persons) at the hands of the police. Little attempt was made to hide the extent of the operation, with most being arrested in front of witnesses. What happened to these 'missing persons' has never been explained, although there is no doubt that most were eventually killed.

The reliance on police repression to maintain control over society has led to many states being described as 'police states'. The ruling élites rely not so much on building popular legitimacy for the security of their tenure, as on the fear instilled by the actions of the police and military forces. Such examples of police repression can be found throughout the third world.

However, more 'orthodox' policing also takes place in authoritarian states. People are robbed and murdered all over the world; traffic offences are not confined to liberal democracies. If the focus of policing in authoritarian states tends to be on repression, it should not be forgotten that police units also undertake more mundane functions of law enforcement. The main difference between policing in these states and in liberal democracies is the notion of what the police force is defending. In 'police states' the interests of the ruling élite – the ruling party or élites – are placed above notions of individual rights. The police force, with a varying degree of commitment, does defend the individual and the individual's property from attack. But personal freedoms are ultimately subservient to the task of keeping the ruling élite in power.

Summary

1. In the liberal model of civilian control over the military (the first world), civilian leaders take complete charge of society's affairs. The military is, to a degree, depoliticised. In the penetration model (communist party states), the civilian élites attempt to ensure that the armed forces share their political ideas, and they promote loyal party members to all key positions within the military establishment. The military are deliberately politicised.

. Military leaders in the first world have operational autonomy to pursue the national defence policy, under the control of the civilian leadership. However, the military also attempts to influence decision-makers and public opinion to support its own favoured policies.

. The civilian leadership in liberal democracies occasionally orders the military to intervene in domestic political situations. This is most likely to occur when an industrial dispute has led to essential services being withdrawn, or when the domestic police force fails to keep the peace during severe breakdowns in law and order.

4.   Military leaders in communist party states formed part of a powerful and privileged ruling élite. Their influence was not confined to military affairs, and many military leaders also held high office within the party leadership itself.

5.   The key to keeping the military out of civilian politics in communist party states was maintaining political stability. In times of political instability, the army's reliability becomes crucial for regime survival.

6.   Military regimes in the third world are either inclusionary or exclusionary. In the former, the military leaders try to build a base of popular support among the populace (Peron's Argentina). In exclusionary regimes, military leaders attempt to suppress all popular participation in politics (Pinochet's Chile).

7.   A key trend in contemporary third world politics is military withdrawal from politics. However, despite this move towards democratisation, the lesson of history is that military withdrawal is rarely final, and further military takeovers in the future cannot be discounted.

8.   The liberal view sees the police as disinterested and impartial custodians of public order. In contrast, the radical perspective views the police as an instrument employed by a dominant minority to defend their interests. Whereas liberal theorists see the police as public servants, radical theorists perceive the police as servants of the state.

9.   The police's role as an agent of political repression is most clearly seen in authoritarian regimes. Extensive surveillance of the population is combined with a high-profile heavy-handed policing style to instil fear into the population.

Discussion points

1.   Given their overwhelming coercive power, why do military regimes ever return power to civilians?

2.   Is the military in your country an 'interest group'?

3.   Which comes first, popular mistrust of the police force, or bad policing?

4.   What is more dangerous, a police force independent of political control, or one under tight political control?

5.   Is policing without consent coercion?

Key reading

Decalo, S. (1976) *Coups and Army Rule in Africa*, (New Haven, Conn.: Yale University Press). An excellent introduction to military rule in Africa, written near the peak period of military rule.
Munck, R. (1989) *Latin America: The Transition to Democracy*, (London: Zed). Analyses how and why military regimes have given way to civilian governments in Latin America.
Brewer, J. *et al.* (1988) *The Police, Public Order and the State* (Basingstoke: Macmillan). A comparative study of the police in Great Britain, Northern Ireland, the Irish Republic, the United States, Israel, South Africa and China.
Orwell, G. (1962) *Nineteen Eighty-Four* (London: Secker & Warburg). The classic nightmare vision of life in a police state.

Further reading

On the military, S. Finer's (1975) pioneering study sets the standards in terms of breadth and cogency. Nordlinger (1977) is the starting-point for studying civilian control, while Baynham (1986) is a useful update and Pinkney (1990) is a good up-to-date work on right-wing military regimes.

Clapham and Philip (1985) is a collection on civil–military relations in a number of third world countries. O'Brien and Cammack (1985) focus on the crisis of military rule in Latin America. For military withdrawal from politics, see Danopoulos (1988) for a general study, and Munck (1989) on Latin America. For a case study on military involvement in domestic politics, see Babington (1990) on the military in Britain.

Work on the military in the second world has been overtaken by the dramatic events of recent years. However, Colton (1986) is a useful introduction on the military in Soviet politics before *perestroika*. Joffe (1983) is similarly useful on the Chinese military.

Brewer *et al.* (1988) is a good comparative introduction to the police, while Ritchie (1992) is a useful introduction to law and order in Japan, France, Britain and the United States. Roach and Thomaneck (1985) is a collection on policing in Europe. Adelman (1984) is a good introduction to surveillance and secret police forces in the communist world.

■ PART 5 ■

POLICIES AND PERFORMANCE

Policies matter. In one country, government actions may be the principal cause of human misery. In another, public policies may help to create the conditions under which people can fulfil their potential. Ultimately, politics matters because it affects people's lives. In this final part, therefore, our focus shifts from the structures of government to the policies that governments pursue. We explore how the content and style of public policy varies not only between the three worlds but also within them, over time.

Chapter 16

The Policy Process

Most political science (and most of this book) discusses the framework of political institutions and processes within which government policies are formed. Little attention is given to the substance of these policies – their ideological flavour, their impact on society, their success or failure. Yet this is like describing a factory without mentioning the products it makes. Just as the purpose of a factory is to manufacture goods, so the development and implementation of policy is central to government activity. This point was belatedly recognised by political scientists in the 1980s. As a result, a large literature on policy analysis now exists. This chapter reviews this material.

■ The policy focus

One way to introduce the policy approach is to compare it with the study of decision-making (pp. 14–16). A policy is a more general notion than a decision. A policy covers a bundle of decisions. It involves a general predisposition to respond in a particular way. When a government says, 'our policy is to favour public transport', it is stating an intention to make specific decisions with this attitude in mind. It is not announcing a decision as such. (In fact, the practical 'decisions' may never arrive at all. Window-dressing is one reason for having policies).

Typically, a policy will evolve when (and if) it is put into practice. It will be modified in the field and have effects beyond those envisaged by its original designers. For example, a plan, drawn up in a government office, to reduce needle-sharing among drug addicts is likely to require modification in the light of practical difficulties trying to reach drug users and change their behaviour. A major advantage of a policy focus over the decision-making approach is that it traces a policy beyond the point of initiation to the point of delivery. It examines what goes on out there in the world. Whether or not this is what politics is about, it is

397

certainly what politics is for. In consequence, the policy focus also implies a concern with evaluating, and improving, public policy.

■ Synoptic and incremental models

Modern policy analysis is informed by two general models of decision-making – the rational or synoptic model, associated with H. Simon (1983) and the incremental model, associated with Lindblom (1979). The synoptic model requires decision-makers to examine a problem in a comprehensive way. Specifically policy-makers must

1. Rank all their values;
2. Formulate clear options;
3. Calculate all the results of choosing each option;
4. Select the alternative which achieves most values.

This is an unrealistic counsel of perfection. It lacks force even as a prescription of how policies should be made. It requires policy-makers to foresee the unforeseeable and measure the unmeasurable. So the advocates of synoptic models offer the notion of **bounded rationality** as a more feasible alternative. To make policy-making more manageable, this eliminates the comprehensiveness required by the full model. In bounded rationality decision-makers focus on a few 'good-looking' options and look only for a satisfactory rather than the best solution. For example, in deciding on school reorganisation, a minister of education will probably only consider the handful of options presented by civil servants. The minister will relate these to a few core objectives – improving numeracy among schoolchildren, say, or ensuring his or her promotion in the next reshuffle. And the minister will probably concentrate on the immediate implications of the reforms, ignoring indirect and therefore less predictable consequences.

The incremental model was developed by Lindblom in reaction to the synoptic model. Incremental policiy is change by small steps. Its central feature is that policy is continually made and remade in a series of small adjustments, rather than as a result of a single, comprehensive analysis. It represents what Lindblom calls the 'science of muddling through', an approach which may not lead to the achievement of grand objectives but which at least avoids the making of huge mistakes. In incremental policy-making, what matters is not that those involved should agree on objectives but that agreement should be reached on the next step to be taken, even when basic objectives differ. For instance, the education minister might hold discussions with various interests – teachers,

Exhibit 16.1   *The language of policy analysis*

The price of a new approach is a new jargon. Here is an abbreviated guide to the terms used in policy analysis; most are discussed fully in the text.

The earliest debate was between **rational** and **incremental** models of policy-making. The rational model (Simon 1983) holds that decision-makers should try to consider all the consequences of all options for all values before reaching a verdict. The incremental model (Lindblom 1979) maintains that policy-makers make small adjustments to patch up defects. They adopt a satisficing approach (satisfying and sufficing) based on what is good enough rather than what is best. The **mixed scanning** model (Etzioni 1976, pp. 90–6) is a middle way; it argues for careful scrutiny of key problems and routine monitoring elsewhere.

In analysing policy, it is important to identify the **policy community** or **network** – the interlocking groups of politicians, civil servants, local officials, quangos* and interest groups involved in a decision-making area. Ministries can become subservient to the **client group** affected by their decisions; client groups include service providers (such as doctors) who are generally more powerful than service consumers (such as patients).

Policy communities or even countries can develop their own **policy styles** (Richardson 1982) – their preferred, though not always realised, way of making policy. Policy style is influenced by the **assumptive worlds** (K. Young 1977) or **policy frames** (Hogwood and Gunn 1984, pp. 119–20) of the participants – that is, by their assumptions, values and implicit theories about how society works. The ability to control how an issue is discussed is a significant aspect of **agenda-setting**. Control over what issues are discussed is the other, and more important, aspect of agenda-setting.

The implementation of policy can be approached from a **top-down** perspective (how can our goals be implemented down the line?) or from the **bottom-up** (where those who apply the policy largely determine it). But all are agreed that it is vital to distinguish **policy outputs** (what government does) from **policy outcomes** (the consequences of government activity). Many outcomes are unintended; some contradict original objectives (Lewis and Wallace 1984).

* Quasi-autonomous non-governmental organisation: bodies carrying out public responsibilities but (officially) independent of government control.

administrators, professional associations – to try and sort out a solution to an immediate problem. Almost by accident, if at all, a series of such small changes might alter the direction of education policy.

What assessment should we give of these models? On a descriptive level, there is little doubt that Lindblom's incremental account is more accurate. Politicians rarely write on a blank sheet. Current policies are constrained by past decisions. Once construction of an orbital motorway has begun, it makes no sense to leave the job half done. Once a hospital has been built, it has to be staffed. The incremental approach is also more sensitive to the politics of policy-making, whereas the synoptic model is really an idealised account of individual rather than group decision-making.

However incrementalism is not a model of how policy should be made – at least not in all areas of government activity. As Lindblom himself points out, incremental decision-making is based on dealing with existing problems rather than avoiding future ones. Public policy is seen as remedial rather than innovative. But the threat of ecological disaster, for instance, has arisen precisely from human failure to consider the long-term cumulative impact of industry upon the environment. Different forms of policy-making, then, are called for in different areas in the public sector.

In the first world, incremental policy-making predominates. A distinctive characteristic of liberal democracies (in peacetime) is their lack of overall national goals. Government programmes chiefly reflect past commitments and budgetary considerations about what is possible. Policy mostly bubbles up to politicians from below rather than being formulated at the top. This upward flow of policy is accepted as the hallmark of a democracy even by politicians and civil servants themselves. The style of policy-making is incremental, not transformative.

Attempts to introduce more synoptic or at least disciplined forms of policy-making have generally ended in tears (for a remarkable illustration from the second world, see Exhibit 16.2). Failures include Britain's 'National Plan' in the 1960s, and various efforts to introduce comprehensive program-planning in the United States. Where economic planning has proved effective, as in France in the 1950s and 1960s, a rare combination of circumstances was required. In France these included: a strong state, a new generation of eager civil servants, effective political leadership and a society ripe for postwar modernisation. Strategic economic planning has also been practised in Japan, with close cooperation between government and business. However 'The Plan' has gradually been downgraded in both France and Japan since the 1960s. In both countries, leading firms have become more international

Exhibit 16.2   China's Great Leap Forward . . . into starvation

By 1957, the process of rebuilding China's economy after years of neglect and the ravages of war had been basically completed. For China's leader, Mao Zedong, this meant that it was time to move forwards and hasten the transition to communism – China was to take a Great Leap Forward.

Mao believed that if the masses were motivated to support a project, then there was nothing that they could not achieve. Whereas the capitalist world had developed by relying on capital equipment, expertise and professionalism, China would utilise ideological commitment, mass mobilisation and organisation.

In the countryside, the peasants were organised into large communes. Private property was pooled, and the distribution of all resources (food, clothing and so on) was based on individual needs. To aid industrial development, the rural population was exhorted to produce its own steel. Furnaces were hastily built in every available space, and work teams despatched to find available sources of coal and iron ore.

By the autumn of 1958, everything appeared to be progressing well. In particular, the grain harvests were far better than expected, and breaking record after record. Thinking that the country was awash with grain, the central planners ordered peasants to grow more cash crops (such as cotton and tobacco) and they transferred large amounts of grain to urban centres.

But the success was all a sham. Spurred on by the desire to prove their revolutionary commitment, party officials throughout the country exaggerated their grain production figures. Furthermore, much of the iron ore produced in the 'backyard' steel furnaces was poor quality and unusable. In some communes, pots, pans and farm utensils were melted down so that a high production figure for steel could be reported.

The 'Great Lie' came home to roost in 1959 and 1960. In the space of two years, half of all the cultivated land was hit by drought or floods. Food consumption had increased during 1958 when it appeared that there was more than enough to go around, so peasants had few or no stockpiles to fall back on. It also became evident that when property was being pooled in 1957 and 1958 many peasants had slaughtered and eaten their livestock rather than allow it to be turned over to the communes.

The exact extent of the famine that followed is unknown. Coale's (1981) estimate of 16.5 million deaths between 1958 and 1961 is one of the lowest figures. At the other extreme, Mosher (1983) suggests that as many as 30 million may have died in 1960 alone. The total figure for the period from 1958 to 1963 is probably in the region of 40 million deaths – a phenomenal price to pay for a utopian vision that went tragically and bizarrely wrong.

and so less subject to influence from the national government. National economic plans still state the government's priorities but without setting out clear mechanisms for achieving them.

■ Stages of the policy process

A distinction is often drawn between the four stages of the policy process shown in Figure 16.1. These are:

1. Initiation   – the 'decision to make a decision' in a particular area; otherwise known as agenda-setting.
2. Formulation   – the detailed development of a policy into concrete proposals.
3. Implementation – putting the policy into practice.
4. Evaluation   – appraising the consequences and success of the policy.

This classification can give an artificial sense of coherence to the policy process. These stages are analytical, not chronological. Bearing this in mind, we will discuss each stage individually.

□ *Initiation*

Why is health policy directed to treating illness rather than preventing it? Why did ecology suddenly emerge as an issue in Western democracies in the 1970s? Why is workers' control of industry not a major political

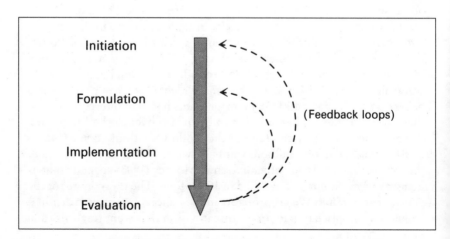

Figure 16.1   *Stages of the policy process*

concern? These are questions about the political agenda – about the issues on which policies are (or are not) initiated. In any complex society the agenda cannot be controlled by a single group; it is the product of debate between a variety of competing though often unequal forces.

As the incremental model suggests, policy-makers respond to problems more than they anticipate them. Annual budgets wrest priorities from governments reluctant to commit themselves. Manifest policy failings, perhaps highlighted by the media, force a rethink. Crises such as strikes, riots or major accidents demand immediate action. Except in regimes which set out to transform society, policy agendas are fluid and fast-flowing because they are made by events rather than by politicians or planners.

However, in analysing influences on the agenda, it is useful to distinguish between the general and specific priorities of government. General priorities are usually influenced and sometimes determined by public opinion. In the West, the fall in inflation in the early 1980s led to growing popular concern about unemployment, a shift in priorities to which governments attempted to respond, albeit with varying success. This responsiveness to public concern was increasingly apparent in communist states, too, though it came too late to save the regimes.

At a more specific level of policy initiation, the policy community rather than public opinion becomes crucial. The policy community is the network of interest groups, professionals, civil servants and politicians constructed around a common interest in a particular policy area such as education or defence. Routine policy-making springs from the policy community rather than being imposed on it by either public opinion or politicians. Australia is a good example of a country where policy communities are especially important. In numerous boards, agencies and quangos, the interests gather together to maintain their own traditional privileges, often to the detriment of the general good. Any group which wishes to influence the course of policy must become accepted as a member of the policy 'club'. In Australia, as elsewhere, non-members are organised out of policy-making just as effectively as participants are incorporated within it.

□ Formulation

Translating a feeling that 'something should be done' into precise legislation or administrative proposals, and then enacting them, is a core political craft. Like bringing a ship into harbour, many decisions must be made correctly and in sequence if the goal is to be achieved. There are essentially three tasks here:

1. Knowing when to proceed – the question of identifying the right moment.
2. Knowing what to propose – the question of understanding the problem so that the proposals will (apparently) ameliorate it.
3. Knowing how to proceed – the question of building a political consensus around the proposals. Even where the legislature is party-dominated, policies must be legitimately made to command acceptance: political skill and parliamentary expertise are indispensable for policy legitimation in liberal democracies.

☐ Implementation

The main achievement of policy analysis has been to direct attention to problems of implementation. Conventional political science generally stopped at the point where a government took a decision. Putting the policy into practice was regarded as a technical matter of administration. But this is much too simple. The failure of the social welfare programme in the United States in the mid-1960s illustrates how, to quote the subtitle of a pioneering study, 'great expectations are dashed in Oakland; or, why it's amazing that Federal programs work at all' (Pressman and Wildavsky 1973).

There are in fact a great number of conditions which must be met if a policy is to be implemented successfully. First, there must be sufficient time and resources, both overall and at particular 'bottlenecks' in the execution of policy. Secondly, there should ideally be few 'stations' where the policy has to sit, awaiting clearance from a variety of different groups, each with its own interests. Thirdly, those in authority must be able to achieve compliance from subordinates (Hogwood and Gunn 1984, ch.11).

Few of these conditions are met in the United States, where a complex network of federal, state and local governments is involved in each policy area. Yet even when all these criteria are fulfilled, the policy may still fail because of changes in external circumstances (bad luck) or because the policy is not actually based on valid assumptions about how to achieve particular objectives (bad policy).

The preceding paragraphs are based on a 'top-down' view of implementation. The problem is conceived as one of facilitating democracy by giving politicians the means of controlling unruly subordinates. But what if circumstances have changed since the policy was formulated? And what if the policy is just bad policy? Writers in the 'bottom-up' tradition (e.g. Barrett and Fudge 1981) argue that policy is more likely to succeed if its executors have flexibility over application – and hence, to an extent, over content. At 'street level' (i.e. the point where the policy is put into effect) policy emerges from interaction between local bureaucrats and groups affected by the policy. Here at the sharp end, the objectives of policy can often be better achieved by adapting its content to local conditions. For example, the practice of education, health care and policing must surely differ between the rural countryside and multi-cultural areas in the inner city.

Yet giving more scope to policy-implementers involves a risk. Once the centre loosens its control, policy may be distorted to serve the interests of administrators and professionals (teachers, doctors and police) rather than 'customers' (schoolchildren, sick people and crime victims). This trade-off between central control and flexibility in application is the major dilemma in policy implementation. Liberal democracies generally leave more discretion with those who apply policy than communist states, where in theory the plan decides all. But since the plan never worked as it should, administrators in communist states often ended up with more discretion in practice than their Western equivalents.

One solution to the dilemma of control versus flexibility is to construct organisations around policies rather than to add new objectives to existing institutions. Governments have achieved striking successes when a single new agency has been given total responsibility for solving a problem. Examples include the Japanese programme to eliminate tuberculosis, or the American programme to put a man on the moon by the end of the 1960s. When the responsibility is diffused, or added to departments which have already developed their own style, implementation problems become more acute. Of course the creation of new agencies indicates a political will to solve the problem. Once the spotlight moves to a different topic, as it soon does, the drive of street-level bureaucrats often begins to decay. Lewis and Wallace (1984) contend that consistent political direction is a major factor favouring successful implementation – but calling for this, cynics might contend, is like whistling in the wind.

Another problem with building organisations around objectives is that the organisation rarely folds up when the job is done. It often outstays its welcome. Ever since Neil Armstrong stepped onto the moon in 1969, the space agency NASA has been searching for new goals to justify its existence. There are in fact very few examples of agencies going into voluntary liquidation. Australia, surprisingly perhaps, supplies two. The Metric Conversion Board was abolished when its job was done and the Bicentennial Authority was dissolved after 1988 (Laffin 1989, p. 47).

□ *Evaluation*

The job of policy evaluation is to work out whether a policy has achieved its goals. Like the famous recipe for political stew which begins 'first catch your rabbit', this neatly sidesteps the problem of working out what the objectives of policy really were. As we have seen, the political motives behind a policy often differ from its ostensible purpose. But this does not detract from the importance of the task. Few governments have made much headway in building evaluation studies into the policy process. In the United States, President Carter did insist that at least 1 per cent of the funds for any project be devoted to its evaluation. The vast number of reports required meant a bonanza for photocopier manufacturers but did not noticeably improve the effectiveness of public policy. In general policy evaluation is most likely to carry weight in consensual democracies with an anticipatory policy style – that is, countries located in the top left of Figure 16.2. There are few such countries.

Policy evaluations must distinguish outputs (what government does) from outcomes (the effects, including the unintended consequences, of government activity). The connection between the two is often tenuous, especially when governments spend money with the supposed purpose of reducing inequalities. Le Grand (1982) has argued that almost all public expenditure in Britain on health, education, housing and transport benefits the better off more than the poor, even when the purpose is the exact opposite. Whether or not this claim is true, it is clear that outputs and outcomes are two different things – and that policy evaluation is therefore an important task which should become a routine part of the policy process.

■ The first world

Although policy-making in the first world is generally incremental rather than synoptic, there are marked differences between liberal democracies in how they reach decisions. Indeed, for the student of comparative politics, the concept of policy styles is one of the more interesting contributions of policy analysis.

□ *Policy styles*

In contrast to the abstract nature of synoptic and incremental models, the term 'policy styles' suggests that individual liberal democracies can be characterised according to their own national way of reaching decisions. Policy style is a preferred way of making policy ('a procedural ambition') which is not always adhered to in practice.

For example, Richardson *et al.* (1982) suggest that Britain has a predilection for consultation, especially with entrenched interests. Sweden also consults widely but as part of a more rational search for solutions to problems. The French policy style reflects secrecy and stagnation most of the time, with occasional bouts of radical change led by an assertive bureaucracy. (These oscillations in French policy-making are no longer so evident now that the country has modernised.)

Richardson suggests the two main dimensions of policy style are:

1. Whether the government has an anticipatory attitude towards policy-making (Sweden) or adopts a reactive, fire-brigade role (UK).
2. Whether the government attempts to reach a consensus with organised groups (United States) or is more inclined towards imposing decisions on society (France sometimes).

This yields the pattern shown in Figure 16.2. Most liberal democracies are concentrated on the right-hand side of the diagram – reacting to rather than anticipating problems. Compared to other forms of government, democracies also tend to congregate in the upper half – seeking to construct a consensus rather than impose policy.

Where does a country's policy-making style come from? What are its origins? The answer is partly historical. Crises call forth new procedures which then become part of a country's political process. For example, the depression of the 1930s forced most Western governments to adopt a stronger role in the management of the economy. Equally, the Second World War called forth national planning on a grand scale. It created close consultation between governments and producer groups, links which may have weakened, but have not disappeared.

There is also a cultural answer to the question, where do policy styles come form? Decision-making processes in government inevitably reflect wider cultural norms. For example, the Japanese policy-style seeks to suppress the open display of conflict and disagreement, a characteristic which is found in many non-state Japanese institutions, including the family. The more open and pluralistic approach of American policy-makers is also found among their local officials, educators and business people. The more frequently people move between public and private spheres, the greater the convergence of policy-making styles between the two sectors. In France and Japan, for instance, there is a tradition of movement from government to business.

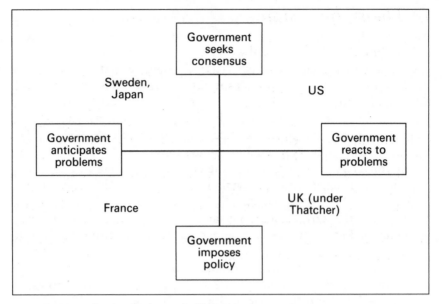

Note: Position of countries is merely illustrative.

Source: Adapted from J. Richardson *et al.* 'The Concept of Policy Style' in *Policy Styles in Western Europe*, ed. J. Richardson (London: Allen & Unwin, 1982), p. 13.

Figure 16.2   *Dimensions of national policy style*

   The international environment is now a strong influence on policy-making in the first world. Similar problems (such as an increase in crime) show up in different societies at a similar time. Some solutions (such as community policing) are also considered throughout the first world. The mass media and international conferences between experts both encourage the diffusion of policy. Thus, there is a tendency towards policy convergence. Broader shifts in priorities also echo round the democratic world. For example, in industrial policy, high-level negotiations between government and peak associations representing business and unions have become little more than talking shops in all but some of the smaller European consensus democracies. The 1990s is the decade of the competition state, rather than the corporate state.

   Styles of policy-making may well vary from one sector to another, however. It would be surprising, for example, if policy-making in the field of health-care exactly resembled that in, say, defence or transport. The policy communities are different. The problems and agendas are different – and so the styles of policy-making are also likely to vary.

☐ *The welfare state*

Defining the welfare state

The transformation of first world countries from nightwatchman states to welfare states was completed in the twentieth century. This perhaps is the single major policy achievement of the liberal democratic state. To understand public policy in liberal democracies, we must examine the welfare state, for welfare consumes most of the state's financial resources and much of the time of its officials.

What exactly is a 'welfare state'? It is usually defined as a state which takes a prime role in ensuring the provision of a minimum standard of welfare to all its citizens. The main aspects of 'welfare' are medical care, education, housing, income maintenance and personal social services. Several countries, such as France and Japan, now include a statement of welfare rights in their constitutions.

The United States is one of the few remaining first world countries which is not a welfare state. For example, it does not have a national scheme ensuring prompt access to medical care. The United States's policy style has generally preferred private solutions to public ones, and also to distribute the 'porkbarrel' among a few favoured groups rather than among the population as a whole.

The welfare state can be compared with the nightwatchman state which preceded it. The nightwatchman state had limited functions. These were mainly to maintain law and order, defend the country, and deal with unexpected problems. The state lacked the desire, resources and infrastructure to supply welfare services to people. Instead, these were provided by private, informal sources: the family, the church, and charities. With the possible exception of Japan, where the family is still exceptionally important, these agencies have now been overtaken by the state as the major supplier of services such as health, education and child allowances.

The development of the welfare state parallels the extension of the suffrage. In a sense, the welfare state is a *form* of the democratic state, implying as it does the right of all people to basic standards of welfare. It is an expression of citizenship. In the nightwatchman state, those who received public welfare through the poor laws were denied the vote. In the welfare state, a guaranteed minimum income is a benefit of citizenship.

Development of the welfare state

As with the extension of the suffrage, the welfare state expanded at a different rate at different times in different countries. It was a transformation in small steps, a classic example of how a series of incremental changes can bring about major change. The term 'the welfare state' originated in Britain during the Second World War as a contrast to Hitler's 'warfare state'. However, its origins lie further back, in the period before the First World War, ironically in Germany itself. Under Bismarck, Germany had pioneered social insurance schemes which 'collectivised' risks such as accident and illness, at least for industrial workers (see Table 16.1).

Building on such foundations, the period from the 1920s saw the gradual extension of welfare in first world countries to more areas of life (e.g. pensions and family allowances) and to more groups in the population (e.g. rural people and dependents of industrial workers). Public spending on welfare also grew rapidly during this period, partly due to the expanding cost of providing pensions to an ageing population. By the 1970s virtually the entire population was covered in most democracies for the main aspects of welfare.

Several theories purport to explain the emergence of the welfare state (Esping-Andersen 1990). These see the welfare state as:

1. A response to **industrialisation**. According to this, the transition to an industrial society diminished traditional welfare providers such as guilds and the extended family. The state filled the gap.

Table 16.1   *Introduction of social insurance, selected countries*

	Industrial accident	*Health*	*Pensions*	*Unemployment benefit*	*Family allowances*
Australia	1902	1945	1909	1945	1941
Austria	1887	1888	1927	1920	1921*
Canada	1930	1971	1927	1940	1944
Denmark	1898	1892	1891	1907	1952
Finland	1895	1963	1937	1917	1948
France	1898	1898	1895	1905*	1932
Germany	1871*	1883*	1889*	1927	1954
Italy	1898	1886	1898	1919	1936
Netherlands	1901	1929	1913	1916	1940
New Zealand	1900	1938	1898	1938	1926
Norway	1894	1909	1936	1906	1946
Sweden	1901	1891	1913	1934	1947

* = innovator.

Source: C. Pierson, *Beyond the Welfare State?* (Oxford: Polity, 1991) table 4.1.

2. A response to modern **bureaucracy**. The emergence of a national civil service, efficient and expansive, was the key device which made a universal welfare service feasible.
3. A response to **democracy**. People are averse to risks and will seek to collectivise them when possible. Collective welfare funding and/or provision is therefore a consequence of extending the suffrage. As Churchill put it, social insurance 'brings the magic of averages to the aid of the millions.'
4. A response to **working-class** interests. The welfare state pushes back the frontiers of the market. It takes services such as education out of the market. The welfare state is therefore used by the working class, and the social democratic parties representing it, to further its own interests.
5. A response to **capitalism**. The market requires its failures to be taken care of. Capitalism therefore gives the state some autonomy to engage in welfare activities, even though these do not contribute directly to profit.

The welfare state is probably best seen as part and parcel of the overall process of transformation to modern, national and democratic politics. Seeking a single, specific explanation is fool's gold. However, it seems unlikely that the origins of the welfare state lie purely in the demands of capitalism since communist party states also introduced extensive systems of welfare provision.

Even if the welfare state was originally an aspiration of the working class, the middle classes have proved adept at getting more than their fair share. In many countries, newer benefits, such as subsidies for higher education and house purchase, are heavily biased to the more affluent. Furthermore, the postwar extension of the welfare state to the whole population brought many affluent people within the net who had previously been excluded from means-tested schemes (Goodin and Le Grand 1987). This is an example of how policies can have unintended, indeed surprising, consequences. It also shows how policies can, in practice, be 'bent' towards influential groups.

Classifying welfare states

Now that most democracies have built their welfare states, we can see that their constructions vary. For one thing, some are kitted out more lavishly than others. What explains this variation? Why do some countries spend more than others on their welfare state? Research shows that the proportion of gross national product spent by a country on welfare depends first and foremost on its level of affluence. Richer countries spend a higher *proportion* of their national income on welfare than do poorer countries.

By comparison, the political characteristics of a country, such as the ideological flavour of its governing parties, are less important (Wilensky 1984). However, after some vigorous debate within the discipline, many political scientists now believe that political factors do play at least a secondary role in influencing spending levels. Centralised states (such as Britain) and those where parties of the left have predominated in office (such as Sweden) tend to be high spenders. The same applies to countries (such as Austria) in which Catholic parties have been a major governing force. By contrast, low spenders include several federal states (such as the United States) and those where the right has been more influential (such as Italy).

But the qualitative distinctions between welfare states are more important than these simple expenditure figures. These affect the whole edifice of the welfare state and how citizens approach it. Esping-Andersen (1990) distinguishes three different types of welfare state found in the first world today:

1.   **The liberal (or limited) welfare state.** Here the rules for gaining benefit are strict and benefits are equally modest. Claimants are a small, workless section of the population. This is not so much a welfare state as state welfare. The traditional examples of these 'residual' welfare states were the United States, Canada and Australia.

2.   **The conservative (or corporate) welfare state.** Here the state is the major provider but benefits are linked to jobs, depend on the 'paying in' principle, and are benefits distributed in line with salary. Occupations which serve the state, especially civil servants, often receive generous treatment in sickness benefit and pensions. Germany is the classic example of this type of welfare state. It is the predominant type in continental Europe.

3.   **The social democratic (or Beveridge) welfare state.** This is based on the principle of equal, flat-rate benefits for all citizens. It was advocated in an influential report by Lord Beveridge in wartime Britain. A full-employment policy may also form part of the welfare state. If benefits are to be reasonable, this is an expensive system. Unless contributions are kept very high (as in Sweden), the effect tends to be a two-tier system in which minimum state benefits are topped up by, for example, company pensions.

A crisis of the welfare state

The 1980s witnessed the first real setbacks to the welfare state. The underlying problem was financial: welfare states are expensive. As the average age of the population increases, so the total cost of pensions, medical care and support services goes up. But the working population, which shoulders the burden, declines in number.

Further, demand on the welfare state increases when supply is low. For instance, when unemployment goes up, so does expenditure on unemployment pay – but the tax collected from the workforce goes down. Thus the recession of the early 1980s caused severe problems for welfare states.

An additional difficulty is that the welfare state is based on open-ended commitments. The state guarantees to educate all young people, to treat all people with AIDS, to give a pension to all people over sixty-five. In so doing, some of life's risks are removed from the individual but they are just placed on the state instead. And sometimes the state miscalculates the odds. Even the best-informed actuaries cannot foretell the future.

International pressures also matter. If the cost of one country's welfare system is higher than all the rest, the economy loses its international competitiveness suffers. Pierson (1991, p.188) suggests that the move to a more open international economy 'has curtailed opportunities for the further development of national welfare states'. Given Japan's importance in world trade, the relatively low cost of its welfare state reduces the possibilities of extending the welfare state in competitor countries. International pressures are forcing several Scandinavian countries to reconsider their high levels of welfare provision, pressures which will intensify as these countries join the EC.

Though often not addressed directly, the impact of welfare provision on willingness to work is also a factor in the current problems confronting welfare states. In Sweden, for example, more than 20 per cent of employed women are off work, with pay, on any given day. As Esping-Andersen delicately puts it (1990, p. 155), 'In Scandinavia, the welfare state has taken upon itself to permit employees to pursue non-work-related activities within the work contract.' Whatever the significance of these figures (and some women are simply away having children), such statistics influence the views of a public which has to forgo a substantial chunk of its earnings in tax deductions in order to pay for such benefits. In Scandinavia, public support for the welfare state declined in the 1970s. Politicians began to fear 'taxpayers' revolts'.

These problems led to some retrenchment of the welfare state in the 1980s. Benefits were reduced, at least at the margin; eligibility rules were tightened, especially by raising the pension age; charges were introduced for services such as medical treatment; few new commitments were taken on; and the state made an effort to revive the old caring agencies, such as charities and the church. Some of this was done in the name of **subsidiarity**, a German notion which means that welfare should be provided at the lowest practical level. This edging away from a fully comprehensive welfare state also reflected a general shift in the priorities of governments from the social to the economic.

In New Zealand, cutting back the many branches of its welfare state proved especially painful. New Zealand faced the unenviable combination of a declining economy, an ageing population, and a population accustomed to a high level of benefit. In 1972 a Royal Commission had made a crucial recommendation: 'anyone receiving benefits should be able to enjoy a standard of living much like that of the rest of the community, and thus be able to feel a sense of participation in, and belonging to, the community.' Nearly twenty years later, undoing that knot required what the finance minister called the 'mother of all budgets' in 1991.

Elsewhere, the welfare state experienced a correction rather than a crisis. On the whole, taxpayers' revolts have not materialised; the basic structures of the welfare state remain in place. In Scandinavia, public support for the welfare state increased again in the 1980s (Alber 1988). In the Netherlands, which moved from a low-spending to a high-spending state in the two decades after the war, social security benefits were reduced in the 1980s but unemployment benefits remained the highest in Western Europe, almost three times those in the United Kingdom (Gladdish 1991, p. 156). The principle of citizenship is touted less often in the 1990s than in the 1960s but its cash value remains substantial.

■ The second world

Communist states differed enormously from liberal democracies in their policy styles. Communist states were planned societies, totally different from the liberal, pluralistic, market-based countries in the first world. Few would quibble with the point that economic failure played a significant role in the collapse of communism in Eastern Europe and the Soviet Union. But why did planning fail? And did it achieve anything before it did? To answer these questions, we must first look at how planning worked. The Soviet Union is the clearest example because, under communist party rule, it ran the most planned economy on earth.

☐ *The planned economy*

The Soviet Union was the land of The Plan. GOSPLAN, the State Planning Committee, drew up annual and five-year plans which were given the status of law once they had received political approval. Implementation was the responsibility of ministries which controlled individual enterprises through a complex administrative network. Detailed planning was forced by a command economy. A factory could not buy its components on the market when there was no market. Instead arrangements had to be made for another factory to manufacture the parts and deliver them on time – and that factory in turn had to be supplied with raw materials.

The flaw was obvious. For anything to go right everything had to go right – and inevitably something went wrong! The right components did not arrive at the right time so all sorts of informal, often illegal, deals had to be fixed up to ensure the (often arbitrary) production quota was met. Further, the whole system was dominated by planners and producers, rather than customers. The centre, not the consumer operating in a market, decided how many goods should be produced at what price. Targets were based on quantity, not quality. As a result, goods were shoddy when they were produced at all (see Exhibit 16.3, p. 416). Local managers did not have any room for initiative, even though they were often in the best position to see what needed to be done. Many factories were 'value subtracting' – the value of the goods going out was less than that of the raw materials coming in. In the end, the planned economy just produced a shrug of the shoulders.

☐ *What did the planned economy achieve?*

So was the planned economy an unmitigated disaster? In the Soviet Union and elsewhere, it did prove very successful at building the foundations of industrial development, albeit at an often sizeable human price. Heavy industry was the great success of the planned economy. This was the case both in communist states which were undergoing industrialisation for the first time, and in those which were rebuilding after the ravages of the Second World War.

This success derives from the philosophy of the 'big push'. Stalin's big push on industrialisation meant that between 1928 and 1938 industrial production in the Soviet Union rose from 7 per cent to 45 per cent of the American output (which was still below its full capacity in 1938 because of the depression). More recently China and Cuba have applied the

| Exhibit 16.3   *'Private enterprise' in the Soviet Union* |

In the Soviet Union under communist rule the successful shopper had to be an expert in the art of queuing. People would join a queue even before they knew what it was for. They always had string bags in their pocket, 'just in case'. A queue meant there must be something to buy. You could only hope that they didn't run out of whatever it was before you got to the front. Soviet women – rarely men – spent an average of three hours a day queuing, probably longer than even the most conscientious consumers in the United States. The difference is that Americans went shopping while Russians went queuing (Macqueen 1989).

With goods and services in short supply, the providers become very powerful figures. They become the entrepreneurs of the planned economy. If you can persuade them to tell you when a delivery is due, you can be first in the queue in the morning. People join queues partly because they assume that the person at the front has been tipped off. Or even better, if you get to know the warehouse storeman, you can go straight to him and avoid the queues altogether.

Even if you were at the front of the queue, you might still only get a rough scrag of meat hanging off a bone, unless you have greased the right palms. By 1990, roubles had become a currency of last resort in the Soviet Union. A packet of foreign cigarettes can get you the best cut of meat and a bottle of vodka ensures that non-existent train tickets suddenly become available. Dollars will get you anything.

But even this may not be enough. A manager may have control over meat supplies, but how does he or she get access to other scarce resources? The obvious solution is for the providers to trade with each other. If the car mechanic always gets a nice fresh salami from the butchery, then the manager knows that he or she can always count on getting spare parts for the car. If the stationmaster's daughter gets high marks at school, then the teacher knows that train tickets will materialise. As a result of this siphoning off, there is even less left for those, such as pensioners, who have no favours to offer.

So where does all this leave the ordinary man or woman on the street? On the street, queuing for three hours a day.

philosophy of the big push to their own societies, again with spectacular results. They have given high priority to specific objectives (adequate housing, say, or improved life expectancy) and have allocated as many resources as are needed to meet the goal. Certainly massive changes such as these could never have resulted from incremental policy-making as practised in liberal democracies. The big push is focused, not synoptic, planning. Absolute priority is given to a single goal and blow other consequences. Objectives determine budgets rather than vice versa. The big push is a deliberately blinkered approach which ignores the overall view.

Yet once the heavy industrial base had been constructed, the planned system proved far less successful in generating light industrial and consumer goods. Galbraith (1990) argues that the socialist system did succeed in attaining its initial goals, but did not adapt to the new challenges and requirements placed upon it: 'Capitalism in its original or pristine form could not have survived. But under pressure it did adapt. Socialism in its original form and for its first tasks did succeed. But it failed to adapt.'

The Korean case neatly illustrates both the initial success of the planned economy and its subsequent failure. The communist north and capitalist south have existed as unfriendly neighbours since the north's attempt to reunify Korea by force ended in failure in 1953. Since then, the rival regimes have competed with each other on other fronts. The economy has been a key area of competition. Until the mid-1970s, the planned economy of North Korea outperformed the capitalist south. Yet once it had recovered from war damage and built a heavy industrial base, economic growth in the north slowed drastically. By about 1973, the south surpassed its communist neighbour, and has been racing ahead ever since.

Can a case be made in defence of the planned economy in communist states? There are at least a few extenuating circumstances. First, massive resources were diverted to military spending. Even in 1991, around 30 per cent of the Soviet Union's total industrial production was for defence-related industries. The 'first world' quality of the Soviet Union's military research contrasted sharply with the 'third world' quality of life for the ordinary citizen.

Secondly, some communist states did sometimes choose a more equal distribution of growth rather than the fastest possible growth. In 1990, a World Bank report on China suggested that the egalitarian nature of growth was one of the few successes of its planned economy.

Thirdly, although the record of economic development in the second world is poor compared to the first world, such comparisons are not always fair. China's economy does not appear in a favourable light when compared with Germany's, the United States's or Japan's. In comparison with many nations in the third world, China has not done badly. The starting-point of development under the planned economy must be considered.

Finally, most communist states had to do without American aid after 1945. Only Yugoslavia accepted American aid, an action that confirmed its break with the Soviet Union. Economic isolation from the non-communist world reduced the benefits of trade for communist party states. In some cases, as in China during the Cultural Revolution, such integration was not sought. At other times, it was denied by the West, as for example in restrictions on technology transfer.

☐ Dismantling the planned economy

It was clear by the early 1980s that the planned economy had run its course in industrial societies. Even leaving aside its implications for individual freedom, it was simply not delivering the goods. Most of the nations that had built their economies on a planned system were turning towards the market as a way of kick-starting their economies back to life. In Eastern Europe, movements to introduce market mechanisms and break down the planning system were under way long before the revolutions of 1989. In Hungary, the state relinquished many of its direct controls over economic enterprises, and allowed market forces to set the prices of some products.

In China, the reform process became caught between two stools. Having pushed ahead with market reforms during the early 1980s, there have now been some periods of retrenchment. Though private enterprise flourishes in the coastal regions and in agriculture, inefficient state-owned industries have not yet been reformed and continue to drain the state budget. Thus the Chinese economy has lost some of the benefits of the planned system, but has not yet gained the full benefits of the market system.

With the end of communist power in Eastern Europe, any remaining constraints on moving towards a market economy, and integration with the world economy, were removed. Yet initially there was no unrestrained dash to the market. Partly this was because of lingering scepticism about capitalism. This sentiment was best summed up by Jan Urban (1990), a member of Charter '77 and later Chief of Staff of Civic Forum in Czechoslovakia. He said, 'There is much that we want and need from the west, but there is one thing which I do not want:

carelessness with people.' Like many others, he was reluctant to give up completely the 'equality of poverty' which communist party rule had produced. Many wanted to search for a (mythical?) 'third way' before committing themselves to the capitalist road.

In addition, there was the question of what to do with the functionaries of the planned economy. They could hardly be marched into a lecture room through a door marked 'planners' and marched out an hour later through a door labelled 'entrepreneurs'. Their job descriptions might have changed but their outlook and knowledge were unaltered. Their potential to stir up trouble was also unchanged. It was a difficult problem.

By the early 1990s, some postcommunist states were grasping the nettle of the transition. They were beginning the new and enormous task of dismantling a planned economy. This is an example of a task where an incremental approach is clearly inappropriate. Postcommunist economies need a rebirth rather than a recovery. 'Marketisation' is a long-term objective which must take priority over others. You cannot run both a planned economy and a market economy alongside each other. In the Soviet Union, where the planned economy collapsed but nothing immediately replaced it, the economy was shrinking by about 1 per cent *each month* in the second half of 1991. Dismantling a planned economy requires almost as much discipline as constructing it, except that popular preferences can no longer be overridden so easily. Yet the human and political problems caused by the transition are substantial. The prices of previously subsidised goods have to go up if they are to match production costs. People in inefficient factories have to lose their jobs if production costs are to go down. Inevitably, some postcommunist governments (Romania, Bulgaria?) will flinch at the task. Popular attitudes to capitalism in postcommunist states are ambivalent, supporting the principle but cautious about the practical effect (see Exhibit 16.4).

But some postcommunist countries have made surprising progress. The private sector's share of GNP in Poland, Hungary and Czechoslovakia rose from less than one-fifth in 1989 to a third in 1991. Poland has liberalised its banking system and sought to privatise 90 per cent of its economy within five years. (In the 1980s Britain took twice as long to privatise about a tenth of that amount.) Hungary also continued its development of the market. Yet with the collapse of the Soviet economy to the east, and a reluctance by the EC to open its doors immediately, the international environment remained difficult. Even the most anti-communist postcommunist must occasionally look back with nostalgia to the false certainties of The Plan.

Exhibit 16.4   *Mixed views about the market*

A successful transition to a market economy in Eastern Europe depends on popular attitudes as much as on government measures. A large scale opinion poll (13,000 people) carried out in nine European countries and three Soviet republics in 1991 suggested that the free market system had strong majority support in most of Eastern Europe. But most East Europeans would prefer a market economy along Swedish rather than American lines. In other words, people want capitalism with welfare guarantees and substantial government involvement (see Figure 16.3).

As the report puts it,

'while most East Europeans endorse the idea of a free market economy, they don't trust the private sector to manage it. They want the state to run heavy industries, transportation and telecommunications, and to be involved in health care, banking, farming, consumer goods manufacturing, newspapers, radio and television' (*Atlantic Outlook* 1991).

As one might expect, younger people were more enthusiastic about the market and in more of a hurry to shift to it than older ones. But the transition to the market economy is going to encounter considerable obstacles in popular attitudes. For instance, large minorities in Czechoslovakia, Poland, Russia and Lithuania favoured government-set limits on profits. Figure 16.3 shows the extent of suspicion of business. In Russia, Ukraine and Lithuania entrepreneurs tend to be viewed in the same negative light as black marketeers. After decades of anti-market propaganda, this is not surprising. At the same time, attitudes to business in the East European countries are much more positive. These are the countries which have taken the fastest strides towards market economies.

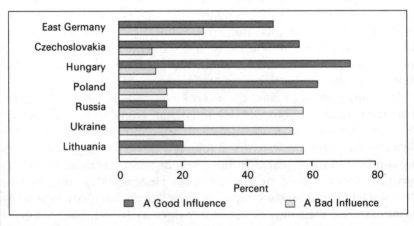

Figure 16.3   *Attitudes towards business people in eastern Europe*

Source: Adapted from Times-Mirror Center for the People & the Press (republished in *Atlantic Outlook*, no. 18, November 1991).

■ The Third World: policy stagnation

The key determinant of policy style in most of the third world is lack of government capacity. In the first world, local agencies of the state allow the centre to influence the periphery. Decisions reached in Stockholm or Paris carry through to Malmo or Bordeaux. The state penetrates society. In the second world, dominant communist parties operated within closed societies, conditions which were even more favourable to central policy-making.

But in much of the third world governments lack the capacity to implement their policies throughout the territory. They lack numbers on the ground and must often rely on traditional local leaders who are therefore able to veto the implementation of radical policies. Even at the centre, the state is often taken over by dominant groups (military, ethnic or class-based) which exploit the state's resources for their own benefit. And the peripheral position of most third-world countries in the international economy means serious attempts at policy-making are frequently blown off course by the vagaries of international markets. For instance, Tanzania's course towards Uja'ma (African village socialism) lost headway, partly because of resistance and inefficiency but partly because of crippling external constraints. Real policy-making stops and the state sits becalmed in the water, drifting in response to the forces acting upon it but lacking any momentum of its own.

Of course the formalities of planning continue but without any effective contact with reality. Ambitious national plans are made because of their public relations value, especially with international development agencies; because they allow a swollen bureaucracy to justify its existence; and because they legitimise the distribution of resources to powerful groups and favoured areas. But the synoptic veneer does not obscure the harsher realities.

Fortunately this gloomy portrait does not fit all the third world. Some countries (e.g. India) are sufficiently large in population or production to have achieved some insulation from the international economy. Others (e.g. South Korea) have gained a more secure niche in the international system by offering a manufacturing capacity rather than just commodities. And a few communist regimes (e.g. China) acquired the grip on society which meant that central policies do matter. But for small, poor, noncommunist states, effective policy-making remains an aspiration not a reality.

Nonetheless, are third world states making progress in improving the length and quality of life? Are the trends at least moving in the right direction? Some social indicators are showing signs of an improvement.

Life expectancy is growing as the developing world adopts basic programmes of preventive medicine, though in much of sub-Saharan Africa this is now threatened by the AIDS epidemic. Elementary education has also expanded, increasing the proportion of the world's population that can read and write. The birth rate has fallen though the world's population is still growing.

But economic advance, which ultimately underpins social progress, has slowed. Between 1945 and 1971 economic growth in the developing world did at least match the industrial world. Indeed Brett (1985) argues that the economic performance of the third world during this period compared favourably with the developed countries during their transition to industrial society. Growth was uneven, both within and between developing countries, but it did take place.

In the 1970s and early 1980s, however, progress slowed and in some countries went into reverse. The causes included: the collapse of the fixed exchange rate system; the rapid increase in oil prices; the recession in the Western world; the decline in commodity prices; and the rise in interest rates at a time when the third world was falling into greater debt. The newly industrialising countries, and those immediately beneath them, coped well, but in the least developed countries ('the fourth world') the situation became bleaker. In Africa, the gross national product of 15 countries actually fell in the 1970s, and in many continued to drop in the 1980s. Food production per head also declined in sub-Saharan Africa, leading to a virtual collapse of the formal economy as people resorted to the black market to ensure their own survival. For the least developed countries, the disease of underdevelopment intensified. More market-based economic policies, linked to loans from agencies such as the World Bank, offer the main practical hope for the 1990s.

Summary

1.   A public policy covers the general stance of government towards problems, as well as its specific programmes. A focus on policy broadens our appreciation of politics because it involves looking at how policies are put into practice, and whether they work.

2.   The synoptic model of policy holds that a policy-maker should consider all the consequences of all the options before reaching a verdict. It is not a practical proposition at all. The incremental model prefers change by small steps, both as a description of how policy is made and as a model of how it ought to be made. The main danger of incremental policy-making is that long-term cumulative consequences are ignored.

3.   The four stages of the policy process are initiation, formulation, implementation and evaluation. However, in practice these stages often occur together; policy-making is not a tidy world. The latter two stages – implementation and evaluation – are a distinctive concern of students of policy.

4.   The policy style of a government is its preferred, if not always realised, way of reaching decisions. For example, the Swedish policy style involves widespread consultation as part of a careful search for solutions. Two dimensions of policy style are (*a*) whether a government seeks to reach a consensus or to impose policy; and (*b*) whether it anticipates or reacts to problems.

5.   Policy styles in the first world are generally incremental, with policy bubbling up from below and with many groups given a say in both forming, and implementing, policy.

6.   The welfare state is a major policy achievement of first world states. Measured by expenditure, welfare is now the major activity of most first world states. Welfare states divide into liberal, conservative and social democratic forms. All have faced difficulties from rising costs, and increasing competition in the global economy. Most have only needed to trim at the margins.

7.   Under communist party rule, second world countries adopted a synoptic approach, with centrally planned economies. These proved effective at developing heavy industry but failed to adapt to a more sophisticated era of light industry and consumer goods. Economic weakness was one factor in the collapse of communist power.

8.   Policy-makers in postcommunist states face an enormous task in dismantling the planned economy. A market economy will cause medium-term increases in prices and unemployment, yet postcommunist rulers do not have the freedom to override public opinion which their predecessors possessed.

9.   Except for countries which establish a niche in the world economy, third world states tend to policy stagnation. The state lacks the combination of autonomy from, and penetration through, society needed for effective leadership. The result is often drift. However, much of the third world has made progress in reducing the birth rate and illiteracy. This progress has not been matched in sub-Saharan Africa, where many countries now also face the catastrophe of AIDS.

Discussion points

1.   You have been appointed Minister of Education in your government. What are your priorities? How will your knowledge of policy analysis affect how you will go about putting them into effect?

2.   Where would you put your country in the map of policy styles on p. 408? Has the country's position changed over the past ten years?

3.   What are the implications of the failure of the planned economy in communist party states for policy-making in the third world?

4.   Is the synoptic or incremental model more appropriate for (*a*) transport policy (*b*) education policy (*c*) ecological policy?

5.   Do you agree with Zbigniew Brzezinski that 'communism is the grand failure of the twentieth century'?

Key reading

Anderson, J. (1984) *Public Policy-making* (Orlando, Fla.: Holt, Rinehart & Winston). A short and succinct introduction to policy analysis.

Hogwood, B. and Gunn, L. (1984) *Policy Analysis for the Real World* (Oxford: Oxford University Press). An excellent discussion of the concepts used in policy analysis.

Pierson, C. (1991) *Beyond the Welfare State?* (Oxford: Polity). A valuable comparative review of welfare states and their prospects.

Bertsch, G. (1990) *Reform and Revolution in Communist Systems* (New York: Macmillan). Looks at the reasons for and course of the crisis that broke out in the 1980s.

Further reading

The reader edited by McGrew and Wilson (1982) is a useful introduction to policy analysis. For an application of policy analysis to sectors, see Heidenheimer, Heclo and Adams (1990). On policy styles, Richardson (1982) is the main source, though restricted to Western Europe.

On implementation, the starting-point is the classic American study by Pressman and Wildavsky (1973) while Barrett and Fudge (1981) is a more recent British work. A very intriguing example of policy evaluation is Le Grand's (1982) book on the outcomes of British social policy.

The welfare state is well served with several outstanding comparative books. These include Flora and Heidenheimer (1981) and Esping-Andersen (1990) as well as Pierson (1991).

There are now several books which apply the policy approach to particular countries: see Burch and Wood (1990) for Britain and Peters (1986) on the United States. Harrop (1992) is an application of policy analysis to France, Japan, the United Kingdom and the United States.

For a more detailed introduction to the policy process in three worlds, see the relevant chapters of Bertsch, Clarke and Wood (1992).

■ *Appendix* ■

Information Sources for Political Students

■ Books about specific countries and regions

A selection of introductions to the politics of particular countries and regions. For author and publication details, see References (pp. 432ff.).

Afghanistan
Gupta (1986).

Africa
Chazan *et al*. (1988).

Algeria
Fattah (1988).

Asia, East
Fairbank *et al*. (1989)
(China, Japan, Korea, Vietnam).

Asia, South
Baxter *et al*. (1991)
(Bangladesh, Bhutan, India,
Maldives, Nepal, Pakistan,
Sri Lanka).

Australia
Emy and Hughes (1991); Smith and
Watson (1989).

Austria
Fitzmaurice (1991).

Belgium
Fitzmaurice (1991).

Benin
Allen *et al*. (1987).

Botswana
Harvey and Lewis (1990).

Brazil
Skidmore (1988).

Bulgaria
Bell, J. (1986).

Burkina Faso
Allen *et al*. (1987).

Cameroon
DeLancey (1989).

Canada
Dawson (1987); Fox and White
(1991).

Central African Republic
O'Toole (1986).

Chile
Garreton (1989).

China, People's Republic of
Rodzinski (1988); Gray (1990).

426

Colombia
Pearce (1990).

Congo
Allen *et al.* (1987).

Cuba
Azicri (1988).

Czechoslovakia
Wolchik (1991).

Denmark
Fitzmaurice (1988); Miller, K. (1991).

Dominican Republic
Black (1986).

Egypt
Tripp and Owen (1989).

Ethiopia
Clapham (1988).

Europe (East)
White, S. *et al.* (1990); Blatt (1991).

Europe (West)
Kesselman *et al.* (1987); Lane, J. and
Ersson (1991); Meny (1990);
Smith, G. (1989).

European Community
Nugent (1991); Archer (1990).

Finland
Arter (1987).

France
Wright, V. (1989); Ehrman (1983).

Gabon
Aicardi de Saint-Paul (1989).

Germany
Smith, G. *et al.* (1992); Rotfeld and
Stutzle (1991).

Germany (East)
Dennis (1987).

Germany (West)
Conradt (1986); Paterson and
Southern (1991).

Ghana
Pellow and Chazan (1986).

Greece
Featherstone and Katsondas (1987).

Gulf
Bulloch (1984); Sandwick (1987).

Guyana
Hintzen (1989).

Hong Kong
Miners (1981).

Hungary
Heinrich (1986).

India
Brass (1990); Kohli (1988).

Indonesia
Crouch (1988).

Iran
Chelabi (1990).

Iraq
Khalil (1990).

Ireland
Chubb (1982).

Israel
Pevetz (1984).

Italy
La Palombara (1987); Sassoon (1986).

Japan
Richardson, B. and Flanagan (1984);
Curtis (1988).

Korea
Kihl (1984).

**Korea (North: Democratic People's
Republic of Korea)**
Scalapino and Lee (1971).

Korea (South: Republic of Korea)
Macdonald, D. (1988).

Kuwait
Bulloch (1984).

Laos
Stuart-Fox (1986).

Latin America
Wynia (1990); Lehmann (1990).

Lesotho
Bardill (1985).

Malaysia
Ahmad (1987).

Maldives
Baxter *et al.* (1991).

Mali
Imperato (1989).

Mexico
Story (1987).

Middle East
Bill and Springborg (1990).

Mongolia
Sanders (1987).

Mozambique
Torp (1989).

Nepal
Baxter *et al.* (1991).

Netherlands
Daalder and Irwin (1989); Gladdish
(1991).

New Zealand
Gold, H. (1989); Wood (1988).

Nicaragua
Close (1988).

Niger
Charlick (1991).

Nigeria
Adekson (1981); Graf (1988).

Pakistan
Hyman (1990); Lamb (1991).

Paraguay
Lewis, P. (1982).

Philippines
Wright, M. (1988).

Poland
Ash (1991); Kominski (1991).

Portugal
Opello (1989).

Qatar
Bulloch (1984).

Romania
Gilberg (1990).

Sao Tome and Principe
Torp (1989).

Saudi Arabia
Farsy (1986).

Scandinavia
Elder, Thomas and Arter (1982).

Singapore
Quah *et al.* (1989).

Somalia
Laitin and Samatar (1987).

South Africa
Price (1991).

Soviet Union
Hill (1989); Smith, G. (1992); White,
S., Pravda and Gitelman (1990).

Spain
Moxol-Browne (1989).

Sri Lanka
Tambiah (1986).

Sudan
Niblock (1987).

Sweden
Milner (1990).

Syria
Moaz and Yaniv (1987).

Taiwan (Republic of China)
Gold, T. (1986).

Tanzania
Bokoko (1988).

Thailand
Xuto (1987).

Third World
Cammack, Poole and Tordoff (1988);
   Clapham (1985).

Trinidad and Tobago
Hintzen (1989).

Turkey
Heper and Landau (1991).

Uganda
Otunno (1987).

United Arab Emirates
Bulloch (1984).

United Kingdom
Kingdom (1991); Norton (1991).

United States
Flammang *et al.* (1990); King (1990);
   Peele, Bailey and Cain (1992).

Uruguay
Taylor (1984).

Venezuela
Blank (1984).

Vietnam
Beresford (1988).

Yugoslavia
McFarlane (1988).

Zaire
Callaghy (1984).

Zambia
Gertzel (1984).

Zimbabwe
Herbst (1990).

■ Reference Books

Bogdanor (1987) *Blackwell Encyclopaedia of Political Institutions* (Oxford: Basil Blackwell).
Day (1988) *Political Parties of the World* (Harlow: Longman).
Instituto del Tercer Mundo (1990) *Third World Guide 91/92* (Montevideo: Instituto del Tercer Mundo).
Kidron and Segal (1981) *The State of the World Atlas* (London: Heinemann).
Mackie and Rose (1982) *The International Almanac of Electoral History* (Basingstoke: Macmillan).
Miller, D. *et al.* (1991) *The Blackwell Encyclopaedia of Political Thought* (Oxford: Basil Blackwell).
Shils (1979) *International Encyclopaedia of the Social Sciences* (18 vols) (New York: Macmillan).

Reference books that are updated annually

Banks, A. (ed.) *Political Handbook of the World* (Binghamton, N.Y.: New York State University, Centre for Social Analysis).
Central Intelligence Agency (CIA), *The World Factbook* (Washington D.C.: CIA).
Worldwatch Institute, *State of the World* (London, Sydney and Wellington: Unwin Hyman).

The Europa Yearbook (London: Europa).
The Middle East and North Africa (London: Europa).
The Far East and Australasia (London: Europa).
Africa South of the Sahara (London: Europa).
Statesman's Yearbook (London: Macmillan).

■ Keeping up to date

Keesings Contemporary Archives (London: Longman). A digest of current affairs drawn from the press. An excellent index.
Facts on File (New York: Facts on File Inc.) An American publication, similar in character and quality to Keesings.
The Times Index (Reading, Berks.: Research Publications). A comprehensive index to everything printed in the London *Times*. Most quality newspapers now publish regular indexes.
The Economist Index (London: The Economist Newspaper). A good starting-point for information on economic affairs around the world.

■ Starting a literature search

International Bibliography of the Social Sciences: Political Science (London: Tavistock). An annual list of international books and articles on politics. Listed by subject.
International Political Science Abstracts (Paris: International Political Science Association). An annual and comprehensive international list of books and articles on politics, indexed by subject and author, with short summaries of the contents of each work.
British Books in Print (London: Whitaker). Listed by author and subject.
American Books in Print (New York: Bowker). Listed by author and subject.
Subject Guide to Books in Print (New York: Bowker). Over a million entries. Listed by subject.

■ Books for the beach

A brief list of interesting and readable paperbacks. They should all entertain; if you reflect on their contents, they will also inform.

Conrad, J. (1963) *The Secret Agent* (London: Nelson).
Eco, U. (1983) *The Name of the Rose* (London: Secker & Warburg).
Garcia Marquez, G. (1970) *One Hundred Years of Solitude* (New York: Harper & Row).
Golding, W. (1954) *Lord of the Flies* (London: Faber & Faber).

Huxley, A. (1955) *Brave New World* (Harmondsworth: Penguin).

Koestler, A. (1973) *Darkness at Noon* (London: Hutchinson).

Orwell, G. (1962) *Nineteen Eighty-Four* (London: Secker & Warburg).

Orwell, G. (1972) *Animal Farm* (London: Heinemann).

Paton, A. (1959) *Cry, The Beloved Country* (Harmondsworth: Penguin).

Swift, J. (1975) *Gulliver's Travels* (New York: Dutton).

Tressel, R. (1969) *The Ragged Trousered Philanthropists* (London: Lawrence & Wishart).

Turnbull, C. (1984) *The Mountain People* (London: Triad).

Vargas Llosa, M. (1987) *Captain Pantoja and the Special Service* (London: Faber).

References

Aberbach, J. (1981) *Bureaucrats and Politicians* (Cambridge, Mass.: Harvard University Press).

Abercrombie, W., Hill, S. and Turner, B. (1980) *The Dominant Ideology Thesis* (London: Allen & Unwin).

Adekson, J. (1981) *Nigeria in Search of a Stable Civil/Military System* (Aldershot: Gower).

Adelman, J. (1984) 'Introduction' in *Terror and Communist Politics: The Role of the Secret Police in Communist States*, ed. J. Adelman (Boulder, Colo.: Westview).

Ahmad, Z. (1987) *The Government and Politics of Malaysia* (Oxford: Oxford University Press).

Aicardi de Saint-Paul, M. (1989) *Gabon: The Development of a Nation* (London: Routledge).

Alber, J. (1988) 'Is there a Crisis of the Welfare State?', *European Sociological Review* (4) 181–207.

Alford, R. and Friedland, R. (eds) (1985) *Powers of Theory: Capitalism, the State, Democracy* (Cambridge: Cambridge University Press).

Allen, C. *et al.* (1987) *Benin, The Congo and Burkina Faso: Politics, Economics and Society* (London: Pinter).

Almond, G. and Powell, G. (1978) *Comparative Politics* (Boston, Mass.: Little, Brown).

Almond, G. and Powell, G. (1988) *Comparative Politics Today: A World View* (Chicago: Scott, Foresman).

Almond, G. and Verba, S. (1963) *The Civic Culture* (Princeton, N.J.: Princeton University Press).

Almond, G. and Verba, S. (eds) (1980) *The Civic Culture Revisited* (Princeton, N.J.: Princeton University Press).

Altshuter, A. (1973) 'The Goals of Comprehensive Planning' in *A Reader in Planning Theory*, ed. A. Faludi (Oxford: Pergamon), pp. 188–207.

Amin, S. (1977) *Imperialism and Unequal Development* (Hassocks, Sussex: Harvester).

Anderson, J. (1984) *Public Policy-making* (Orlando, Florida: Holt, Rinehart & Winston).

Andeweg, R. (1991) 'The Dutch Prime Minister: Not Just Chairman, Not Yet Chief?', *West European Politics* (14) 116–32.

Archer, C. (1990) *Organizing Western Europe* (London: Edward Arnold).

Aristotle (1962) *The Politics* (Harmondsworth: Penguin).

Arter, D. (1984) *The Nordic Parliaments: A Comparative Analysis* (London: Hurst).

Arter, D. (1990) *Politics and Policy-making in Finland* (Sussex: Wheatsheaf).

Ash, T. (1991) *The Polish Revolution* (London: Granta).

Astin, A. (1977) *Four Critical Years: Effects of College on Beliefs, Attitudes and Knowledge* (San Francisco: Jossey-Bass).

Avineri, S. (1968) *The Social and Political Thought of Karl Marx* (Cambridge: Cambridge University Press).

Azicri, M. (1988) *Cuba: Politics, Economics and Society* (London: Pinter).

Babington, A. (1990) *Military Intervention in Britain*, (London: Routledge).

Bachrach, P. and Baratz, M. (1962) 'Two Faces of Power', *American Political Science Review*, (56) 947–52.

Bachrach, P. (1967) *The Theory of Democratic Elitism: A Critique* (Boston, Mass.: Little, Brown).

Bagehot, W. (1963, first pub. 1867) *The English Constitution* (London: Fontana).

Bailey, C. (1989) *The US Congress* (Oxford: Basil Blackwell).

Bakhash, S. (1985) *The Reign of the Ayatollahs* (London: Tauris).

Ball, A. and Millward, F. (1986) *Pressure Politics in Industrial Societies: A Comparative Introduction* (London: Macmillan).

Banting, K. and Simeon, R. (eds) (1985) *The Politics of Constitutional Change in Industrial Nations: Redesigning the State* (London: Macmillan).

Barber, J. (1977) *The Presidential Character: Predicting Presidential Performance in the White House* (Englewood Cliffs, N.J.: Prentice-Hall).

Bardill, J. (1985) *Lesotho: Dilemmas of Dependence in Southern Africa* (Boulder, Colo.: Westview).

Barkan, J. (1987) 'The Electoral Process and Peasant–State Relations in Kenya' in *Elections in Independent Africa*, ed. F. Hayward (Boulder, Colo.: Westview) 213–37.

Barnes, S. and Kaase, M. (1979) *Political Action: Mass Participation in Five Western Democracies* (London: Sage).

Barrett, S. and Fudge, C. (1981) *Policy and Action* (London: Methuen).

Barry, B. (1978) *Sociologists, Economists and Democracy* (Chicago, Ill.: Chicago University Press).

Baxter, C. *et al.* (1991) *Government and Politics in South Asia* (Boulder, Colo.: Westview).

Baynham, R. (ed.) (1986) *Military Rule in Black Politics* (London: Croom Helm).

Bebler, A. and Seroka, J. (eds) (1990) *Contemporary Political Systems: Classifications and Typologies* (Boulder, Colo.: Lynne Rienner).

Beer, S. (1967) 'The British Legislature and the Problems of Mobilising Consent' in *Essays on Reform* ed. B. Crick (Oxford: Oxford University Press).

Bell, D. (1973) *The Coming of Post-industrial Society* (New York: Basic Books).

Bell, J. (1986) *The Bulgarian Communist Party from Blagoev to Zhivkov* (Stanford, Calif.: Hoover Institution).

Beresford, M. (1988) *Vietnam: Politics, Economics and Society* (London: Pinter).

Bertsch, G. (1990) *Reform and Revolution in Communist Systems* (New York: Macmillan).

Bertsch, G., Clarke, R. and Wood, D. (1992) *Comparing Political Systems: Power and Policy in Three Worlds* 4th edn (New York: Macmillan).

Bianchi, R. (1986) 'Interest Group Politics in the Third World', *Third World Quarterly* (8) 507–39.

Bill, J. and Springborg, R. (1990) *Politics in the Middle East* (Boston, Mass.: Little, Brown).

Birk-Schlosser, D. (1990) 'Typologies of Third World Political Systems' in *Contemporary Political Systems: Classifications and Typologies*, ed. A. Bebler and J. Seroka (Boulder, Colo.: Lynne Rienner), pp. 173–201.

Black, J. (1986) *The Dominican Republic: Politics and Development in an Unsovereign State* (Boston, Mass.: Allen & Unwin).

Blake, D. and Walters, R. (1976) *The Politics of Global Economic Relations* (Englewood Cliffs, N.J.: Prentice-Hall).

Blank, D. (1984) *Venezuela: Politics in a Petroleum Republic* (New York: Praeger).

Blatt, J. (1991) *East Central Europe from Reform to Transformation* (London: Pinter).

Blau, P. (1963) *The Dynamics of Bureaucracy* (Chicago, Ill.: Chicago University Press).

Blau, P. and Meyer, M. (eds) (1987) *Bureaucracy in Modern Society* 3rd edn. (New York: Random House).

Blecher, M. (1986) *China, Politics, Economics, and Society* (London: Pinter).

Blondel, J. (1973) *Comparative Legislatures* (Englewood Cliffs, N.J.: Prentice-Hall).

Blondel, J. (1990) *Comparative Government: An Introduction* (Hemel Hempstead: Philip Allan).

Bogdanor, V. (1983) 'Introduction' in Bogdanor and Butler (eds) *see below*.

Bogdanor, V. (1987) (ed.) *Blackwell Encyclopaedia of Political Institutions* (Oxford: Basil Blackwell).

Bogdanor, V. (1988) 'Introduction' in *Constitutions in Democratic Politics*, ed. V. Bogdanor (Aldershot: Gower), pp. 1–13.

Bogdanor, V. and Butler, D. (eds) (1983) *Democracy and Elections: Electoral Systems and Their Consequences* (Cambridge: Cambridge University Press).

Bogdanor, V. (1984) *What is Proportional Representation? A Guide to the Issues* (Oxford: Martin Robertson).

Bogdanor, V. (1990) 'Founding Elections and Regime Change', *Electoral Studies* (9) 295–302.

Bokoko, K. (1988) *Socialism and Self-Reliance in Tanzania* (London: Kegan Paul International).

Boulding, K. (1989) *Three Faces of Power* (London: Sage).

Bowman, M. and Hampton, W. (eds) (1983) *Local Democracies* (Melbourne: Longmans).

Boyce, J. (1990) 'Why the Debt Cannot be Paid' in *Instituto del Tercer Mundo, Third World Guide*, Montevideo.

Brass, P. (1990) *The Politics of India since Independence* (Cambridge: Cambridge University Press).

Brett, K. (1985) *The World Economy Since the War: the Politics of Uneven Development* (New York: Praeger).

Brewer, J., Guelke, A., Hume, I., Moxon-Browne, E. and Wilford, R. (1988) *The Police, Public Order and the State* (Basingstoke: Macmillan).

Brinton, C. (1938, repub. 1965) *The Anatomy of Revolution* (New York: Random House).

Brown, A. (ed.) (1984) *Political Culture and Communist Studies* (Armonk, N.Y.: M. E. Sharpe and London: Macmillan).

Brown, A. and Gray, J. (eds) (1979) *Political Culture and Political Change in Communist States* (London: Macmillan).

Bull, M. (1991) 'The Unremarkable Death of the Italian Communist Party' in *Italian Politics: A Review*, vol. 5, ed. F. Sabetti and R. Catanzaro (London: Pinter), pp. 23–39.

Bulloch, J. (1984) *The Gulf: A Portrait of Kuwait, Qatar, Bahrain, and the UAE* (London: Century).

Burch, M. and Wood, B. (1990) *Public Policy in Britain* (Oxford: Robertson).

Burgess, M. (ed.) (1985) *Federalism and Federation in Western Europe* (London: Croom Helm).

Butler, D., Penniman, H., and Ranney, A. (eds) (1981) *Democracy at the Polls* (Washington, DC: AEI).

Cain, B., Ferejohn, J. and Fiorina, M. (1987) *The Personal Vote: Constituency Service and Electoral Independence* (Cambridge, Mass.: Harvard University Press).

Callaghy, T. (1984) *The State–Society Struggle: Zaire in Comparative Perspective* (New York: Columbia University Press).

Calvert, P. (1970) *A Study of Revolution* (Oxford: Clarendon).

Calvocoressi, P. (1991) *World Politics since 1945* (London: Longmans).

Cammack, P., Pool, D. and Tordoff, W. (1988) *Third World Politics: A Comparative Introduction* (Basingstoke: Macmillan).

Campbell, A., Converse, P., Miller, A. and Stokes, D. (1960) *The American Voter* (New York: Wiley).

Carnoy, M. (1984) *The State and Political Theory* (Princeton, N.J.: Princeton University Press).

Cartwright, J. (1983) *Political Leadership in Africa* (New York: St. Martin's Press).

Castles, F. (ed.) (1989) *The Comparative History of Public Policy* (Oxford: Polity).

Castles, F. and Wildemann, R. (eds) (1986) *The Future of Party Government*, vol. 1 (Berlin: Gruyter).

Cawson, A. (1986) *Corporatism and Political Theory* (Oxford: Basil Blackwell).

Cerny, P. (1990) *The Changing Architecture of Politics* (London: Sage).

Chan, S. (1987) *Issues in International Relations: A View From Africa* (Basingstoke: Macmillan).

Charlick, R. (1991) *Niger: Personal Rule and Survival in the Sahel* (Boulder, Colo.: Westview).

Chazan, N. *et al.* (1988) *Politics and Society in Contemporary Africa* (Basingstoke: Macmillan).

Chehabi, H. (1990) *Iranian Politics and Religious Modernism* (London: Tauris).

Christensen, R., Engel, A., Jacobs, D., Rejai, M. and Waltzer, H. (1971) *Ideologies and Modern Politics* (New York: Dodd Mead).

Chubb, B. (1982) *The Government and Politics of Ireland* (Stanford, Calif.: Stanford University Press).

CIA (Central Intelligence Agency) (1991) *The World Factbook* (Washington, D.C.: US Govt).

Cigler, C. and Loomis, B. (eds) (1985) *Interest Group Politics* (Washington, D.C.: Congressional Quarterly Press).

Clapham, C. (ed.) (1982) *Private Patronage and Public Power: Political Clientelism in the Modern State* (London: Pinter).

Clapham, C. (1985) *Third World Politics: An Introduction* (Beckenham, Kent: Croom Helm).

Clapham, C. (1988) *Transformation and Continuity in Revolutionary Ethiopia* (Cambridge: Cambridge University Press).

Clapham, C. and Philip, G. (eds) (1985) *The Political Dilemmas of Military Rule* (London: Croom Helm).

Clarke, M. (1992) *British External Policy-Making in the 1990s* (Basingstoke: Macmillan).

Claude, I. (1971) *Swords into Ploughshares* (New York: Random House).

Close, D. (1988) *Nicaragua: Politics, Economics and Society* (London: Pinter).

Coale, A. (1991) 'Population Trends, Population Policy and Population Studies in China', in *Population and Development Review* (7) 85–97.

Cohan, A. (1975) *Theories of Revolution* (London: Nelson).

Collier, D. (1991) 'The Comparative Method: Two Decades of Change' in *Comparative Political Dynamics: Global Research Perspectives*, ed. D. Rustow and K. Erickson (New York: HarperCollins).

Colton, T. (1986) 'The Impact of the Military on Soviet Society', in *Communist Politics: A Reader*, ed. S. White and D. Nelson (London: Macmillan), pp. 243–59.

Conradt, D. (1986) *The Germany Polity* (New York: Longman).

Converse, P. and Markus, G. (1979) 'Plus Ça Change . . . The New CPS Election Study Panel', *American Political Science Review* (73) 32–49.

Crampton, R. (1990) 'The Bulgarian Elections of 1990', *Representation* (29) 33–35.

Crewe, I. (1981) 'Electoral participation' in *Democracy at the Polls*, ed. D. Butler *et al.* (Washington, D.C.: AEI), pp. 216–63.

Crewe, I. and Denver, D. (eds) (1985) *Electoral Change in Western Democracies* (Beckenham, Kent: Croom Helm).

Crick, B. (1982) *In Defence of Politics* (Harmondsworth: Penguin).

Crouch, H. (1988) *The Army and Politics in Indonesia* (Ithaca, N.Y.: Cornell University Press).

Crouse, T. (1973) *The Boys on the Bus* (New York: Random House).

Curtis, G. (1988) *The Japanese Way of Politics* (New York: Columbia University Press).

Daalder, H. and Mair, P. (eds) (1983) *Western European Party Systems* (London: Sage).

Daalder, H. and Irwin, G. (1989) *Politics in the Netherlands* (London: Frank Cass).

Dahl, R. (1957) 'The Concept of Power', *Behavioural Science* (2) 201–15.

Dahl, R. (1961) *Who Governs? Democracy and Power in an American City* (New Haven, Conn.: Yale University Press).

Dahl, R. (1971) *Polyarchy: Participation and Opposition* (New Haven, Conn.: Yale University Press).

Dahl, R. (1982) *Dilemmas of Pluralism* (New Haven, Conn.: Yale University Press).

Dahl, R. (1983) 'Federalism and the Democratic Process', *Nomos*, vol. 25, pp. 95–108.

Dahl, R. (1984) *Modern Political Analysis* (Englewood Cliffs, N.J.: Prentice-Hall).

Dalton, R. Flanagan, S. and Beck., P. (eds) (1984) *Electoral Change in Advanced Industrial Societies* (Princeton, N.J.: Princeton University Press).

Danapoulos, C. (ed.) (1988) *Military Disengagement From Politics* (London: Routledge).

Daniels, P. (1992) 'Industrial Policy' in *Power and Policy in Liberal Democracies*, ed. M. Harrop (Cambridge: Cambridge University Press), pp. 123–49.

Davies, J. (1962) 'Toward a Theory of Revolution', *American Sociological Review* (27) 5–18.

Davis, H. (1987) 'Class' in *The Media in British Politics*, ed. J. Seaton and B. Pimlott (Aldershot: Gower).

Dawisha, K. (1980) 'The Limits of the Bureaucratic Politics Model: Observations on the Soviet Case', *Studies in Comparative Communism* (13) 300–26.

Dawson, R. (1987) *The Government of Canada* (Toronto, Ont.: Toronto University Press).

Dawson, R., Prewitt, K. and Dawson, K. (1977) *Political Socialisation* (Boston, Mass.: Little, Brown).

Day, A. (ed.) (1988) *Political Parties of the World* (Harlow: Longman).

Dearlove, J. and Saunders, P. (1984, 1991) *An Introduction to British Politics* (Cambridge: Polity).

Decalo, S. (1976) *Coups and Army Rule in Africa* (New Haven, Conn.: Yale University Press).

DeLancey, M. (1989) *Cameroon: Dependence and Independence* (Boulder, Colo.: Westview).

Dennis, M. (1987) *German Democratic Republic: Politics, Economics and Society* (London: Pinter).

Denver, D. (1989) *Elections and Voting Behaviour in Britain* (Hemel Hempstead: Philip Allan).

Derbyshire, J. and Derbyshire, I. (1991) *Spotlight on World Political Systems: An Introduction to Comparative Government* (Edinburgh: Chambers).

Diamond, L. and Linz, J. (1989) 'Introduction' in Diamond, Linz and Lipset (eds) (1989) *see below*, vol. 4.

Diamond, L., Linz, J. and Lipset, S. (eds) (1989) *Democracy in Developing Countries*, 4 vols (Boulder, Colo.: Lynne Rienner).

Djilas, M. (1957) *The New Class: An Analysis of the Communist System* (New York: Praeger).

Dogan, M. and Pelassy, G. (1990) *How to Compare Nations* (Chatham, N.J.: Chatham House).

Domes, J. (1985) *The Government and Politics of the PRC* (Boulder, Colo.: Westview).

Downs, A. (1957) *An Economic Theory of Democracy* (New York: Harper).

Dreyfus, F. (1990) 'The Conseil D'Etat' in *Developments in French Politics*, ed. P. Hall, J. Hayward and H. Machin (Basingstoke: Macmillan), pp. 133–51.

Duchacek, I. (1970) *Federalism: The Territorial Dimension of Politics* (New York: Holt, Rinehart & Winston).

Duchacek, I. (1973) *Power Maps: The Comparative Politics of Constitutions* (Santa Barbara, Calif.: ABC Clio).

Du Fresne, K. (1989) 'Lobbying New Zealand Style' in *New Zealand Politics in Perspective*, ed. H. Gold (Auckland: Longman Paul), pp. 312–19.

Dunleavy, P. (1990) 'Government at the Centre' in *Developments in British Politics 3*, ed. P. Dunleavy, A. Gamble and G. Peel (London: Macmillan), pp. 96–125.

Dunleavy, P. (1991) *Democracy, Bureaucracy and Public Choice* (Hemel Hempstead: Harvester Wheatsheaf).

Dunleavy, P. and O'Leary, B. (1987) *Theories of the Liberal Democratic State* (London: Macmillan).

Duverger, M. (1954, 1964) *Political Parties* (London: Methuen).

Dyson, K. (1980) *The State Tradition in West Europe* (Oxford: Martin Robertson).

Easton, D. (1957) 'An Approach to the Analysis of Political Systems, *World Politics* (10) 383–400.

Easton, D. (1965a) *A Framework for Political Analysis* (Englewood Cliffs, N.J.: Prentice-Hall).

Easton, D. (1965b) *A Systems Analysis of Political Life* (New York: Wiley).

Eberle, J. (1990) 'Understanding the Revolutions in Eastern Europe' in *Spring in Winter: The 1989 Revolutions*, ed. G. Prins (Manchester University Press).

Eccleshall, R. *et al.* (1984) *Political Ideologies: An Introduction* (London: Hutchinson).

The Economist Book of Vital World Statistics (1990) (London: Hutchinson).

Edelman, M. (1964) *The Symbolic Uses of Politics* (Urbana, Ill.: University of Illinois).

Ehrmann, H. (1971) 'Interest Groups and the Bureaucracy in Western Democracies' in *European Politics: A Reader*, ed. M. Dogan and R. Rose (Basingstoke: Macmillan).

Ehrmann, H. (1976) *Politics in France* (Boston, Mass.: Little, Brown).

Eisenstadt, S. and Lemarchand, R. (eds) (1981) *Political Clientelism, Patronage and Development* (London: Sage).

Elazar, D. (1985) 'Constitution-making: The Pre-eminently Political Act' in *The Politics of Constitutional Change in Industrial Nations*, ed. K. Banting and R. Simeon (London: Macmillan).

Elder, N., Thomas, A. and Arter, D. (1982) *The Consensual Democracies?: The Government and Politics of the Scandinavian States* (Oxford: Martin Robertson).

Emy, M. and Hughes, O. (1991) *Australian Politics: Realities in Conflict* (South Melbourne: Macmillan).

Epstein, L. (1967, 1980) *Political Parties in Western Democracies* (New Brunswick: Transaction).

Esping-Andersen, G. (1990) *The Three Worlds of Welfare Capitalism* (Oxford: Polity).

Etzioni, A. (1976) *Social Problems* (Englewood Cliffs, N.J.: Prentice-Hall).

Evans, P. Rueschemeyer, D. and Skocpol, T. (eds) (1985) *Bringing The State Back In* (Cambridge: Cambridge University Press).

Fairbank, J. *et al.* (1989) *East Asia: Tradition and Transformation* (Boston, Mass.: Houghton Mifflin).

Farsy, F. (1986) *Saudi Arabia: A Case Study in Development* (London and New York: Kegan Paul International).

Fattah, A. (ed.) (1988) *Politics and Government in Algeria* (New York: State Mutual).

Featherstone, K. and Katsoudas, D. (1987) *Political Change in Greece: Before and After the Generals* (New York: St. Martin's).

Finer, H. (1941) 'Administrative Responsibility in Democratic Government', *Public Administration Review* (1) 335–50.

Finer, S. (1966) *Vilfredo Pareto: Sociological Writings* (Oxford: Basil Blackwell).

Finer, S. (1958, 1966) *Anonymous Empire: A Study of the Lobby in Great Britain* (London: Pall Mall).

Finer, S. (1988, first pub. 1962) *The Man on Horseback: The Role of the Military in Politics* (Boulder, Colo.: Westview).

Fiorina, M. (1981) *Retrospective Voting in American National Elections* (New Haven, Conn.: Yale University Press).

Fitzmaurice, J. (1981) *Politics in Denmark* (London: Hurst).

Fitzmaurice, J. (1988) *The Politics of Belgium: Crisis and Compromise in a Plural Society* (London: Hurst).

Fitzmaurice, J. (1991) *Austrian Politics and Society Today* (London: Macmillan).

Flammang, J., Gordon, D., Lukes, T. and Smorsten, K. (1990) *American Politics in a Changing World* (Pacific Grove, Calif.: Brooks/Cole).

Flora, P. and Heidenheimer, A. (eds) (1981) *The Development of Welfare States in Europe and America* (New Brunswick, N.J.: Transaction).

Forsyth, M. (1989) *Federalism and Nationalism* (Leicester: Leicester University Press).

Fox, P. and White, G. (eds) (1991) *Politics: Canada*, 7th edn (Toronto: McGraw-Hill Ryerson).

Frank, A. (1969) *Capitalism and Underdevelopment in Latin America* (New York: Monthly Review Press).

Frank, A. (1981) *Crisis In The Third World* (London: Heinemann).

Franklin, M. (1985) *The Decline of Class Voting* (Oxford: Oxford University Press).

Franks, C. (1971) 'The Dilemma of the Standing Committees of the Canadian House of Commons', *Canadian Journal of Political Science* (4) 461–76.

Frears, J. (1990) 'The French Parliament: Loyal Workhorse but Poor Watchdog' in *Parliaments in Western Europe*, ed. P. Norton (London: Frank Cass), pp. 32–56.

Friedgut, T. (1979) *Political Participation in the USSR* (Princeton, N.J.: Princeton University Press).

Fukuyama, F. (1989) 'The End of History', *National Interest* (16).

Furlong, P. (1990) 'Parliament in Italian Politics' in *Parliaments in Western Europe*, ed. P. Norton (London: Cass), pp. 52–67.

Galbraith, J. (1990) 'Revolt in our Time: The Triumph of Simplistic Ideology', in *Spring in Winter: The 1989 Revolutions*, ed. G. Prins (Manchester: Manchester University Press), pp. 1–12.

Garreton, M. (1989) *The Chilean Political Process* (London: Unwin Hyman).

Garson, G. (1978) *Group Theories of Politics* (London: Sage).

Gasper, D. (1982) 'The Chinese National People's Congress' in *Communist Legislatures in Comparative Perspective*, ed. D. Nelson and S. White, pp. 160–90.

Gayle, D. and Goodrich, G. (1990) *Privatisation and Deregulation in Global Perspective* (London: Pinter).

Geertz, C. (1964) 'Ideology as a Cultural System' in *Ideology and Discontent*, ed. D. Apter (New York: Free Press), pp. 47–76.

Gellner, E. (1983) *Nations and Nationalism* (Oxford: Basil Blackwell).

George, S. (1988) *A Fate Worse Than Debt* (Harmondsworth: Penguin).

Gerth, H. and Mills, C. (1948) *From Max Weber* (London: Routledge and Kegan Paul).

Gertzel, C. (1984) *The Dynamics of the One-Party State in Zambia* (Manchester: Manchester University Press).

Gibbins, J. (ed.) (1989) *Contemporary Political Culture: Politics in a Postmodern Age* (London: Sage).

Gilberg, T. (1990) *Nationalism and Communism in Romania: The Rise and Fall of Ceaucescu's Personal Dictatorship* (Boulder, Colo.: Westview).

Ginsberg, B. (1982) *The Consequences of Consent* (Reading, Mass.: Addison Wesley).

Gladdish, K. (1991) *Governing from the Centre: Politics and Policy-Making in the Netherlands* (London: Hurst).

Glasgow University Media Group (1982) *Really Bad News* (London: Writers' and Readers' Publishing Group).

Glenny, M. (1990) *The Rebirth of History: Eastern Europe in an Age of Democracy* (London: Penguin).

Gold, H. (ed.) (1989) *New Zealand Politics in Perspective* (Auckland: Longman Paul).

Gold, T. (1986) *State and Society in the Taiwan Miracle* (Armonk, N.Y.: M. E. Sharpe).

Goodin, R. and le Grand, J. (1987) *Not Only the Poor: the Middle Classes and the Welfare State* (London: Allen & Unwin).

Goodwin, A. (1987) *The French Revolution* (London: Hutchinson).

Goodwin, B. (1987) *Using Political Ideas*, 2nd. edn (Chichester: Wiley).

Graf, W. (1988) *The Nigerian State* (London: James Currey).

Gramsci, A. (1971) *Selections From the Prison Notebooks* (London: Lawrence & Wishart).

Grant, W. (1985) 'Introduction', in *The Political Economy of Corporatism*, ed. W. Grant (London: Macmillan).

Grant, W. (1990) 'Industrial Policy' in *The State in Action*, ed. J. Simmie and R. King (London: Pinter), pp. 25–42.

Grant, W., Paterson, W. and Whitson, C. (1988) *Government and the Chemical Industry* (Oxford: Clarendon).

Gray, J. (1979) 'Conclusions' in *Political Culture and Political Change in Communist States*, ed. A. Brown and J. Gray (London: Macmillan).

Gray, J. (1990) *Rebellions and Revolutions: China from the 1800s to the 1980s* (Oxford: Oxford University Press).

Greenstein, F., Herman, V., Stradling, R. and Zureik, E. (1974) 'The Child's Conception of the Queen and Prime Minister', *British Journal of Political Science* (4) 257–88.

Griffith, J. (1977) *The Politics of the Judiciary* (London: Fontana).

Gupta, B. (1986) *Afghanistan: Politics, Economics and Society* (London: Pinter).

Gurr, T. (1972) 'Psychological Factors in Civil Violence', in *Anger, Violence and Politics: Theories and Research*, ed. I. Feierabend, R. Feierabend and T. Gurr (Englewood Cliffs, N.J.: Prentice-Hall).

Gurr, T. (1980) *Why Men Rebel* (Princeton, N.J.: Princeton University Press).

Gwertzman, B. and Kaufman, M. (eds) (1990) The Collapse of Communism (New York: Times Books).

Hamburg, R. (1988) 'Military Withdrawal from Politics' in *Military Disengagement from Politics*, ed. C. Danapoulos (London: Routledge).

Hancock, W. (1961, first published 1930) *Australia* (Brisbane: Jacaranda).

Hankiss, E. (1990) 'What the Hungarians Saw First' in *Spring in Winter: The 1989 Revolutions*, ed. G. Prins (Manchester University Press), p. 33.

Harding, N. (ed.) (1984) *The State in Socialist Society* (London: Macmillan).

Harrison, M. (1984) *Corporatism and the Welfare State* (Aldershot: Gower).

Harrison, M. (1985) *TV News: Whose Bias?* (Hermitage, Berks: Policy Journals).

Harrison, M. (1990), 'The French Constitutional Court: A Study in Institutional Change', *Political Studies* (38) 603–19.

Harrop, M. (1987) 'Voters' in *The Media in British Politics*, ed. J. Seaton and B. Pimlott (Aldershot: Gower) 45–63.

Harrop, M. (1992) 'Health Policy' in *Power and Policy in Liberal Democracies*, ed. M. Harrop (Cambridge: Cambridge University Press).

Harrop, M. and Miller, W. (1987) *Elections and Voters: A Comparative Introduction* (London: Macmillan).

Harvey, C. and Lewis, S. (1990) *Policy Choice and Development Performance in Botswana* (Basingstoke: Macmillan).

Harvey-Jones, J. (1991) 'Market Medicine for a Brave New World', *The Observer*, 25 August 1991, p. 26.

Heady, F. (1966, 1991) *Public Administration: A Comparative Perspective* (New York: Marcel Dekker).

Heath, A. and Topf, R. (1987) 'Political Culture' in *British Social Attitudes: The 1987 Report*, ed. R. Jowell, S. Witherspoon and L. Brook (Aldershot: Gower), pp. 51–68.

Heclo, H. (1974) *Modern Social Policies in Britain and Sweden* (New Haven, Conn.: Yale University Press).

Heclo, H. and Wildavsky, A. (1981) *The Private Government of Public Money* (Berkeley, Calif.: University of California Press).

Heidenheimer, A., Heclo, H. and Adams, C. (1990) *Comparative Public Policy: The Politics of Social Choice in Europe and America* (London: Macmillan).

Heinrich, H. (1986) *Hungary: Politics, Economics and Society* (London: Pinter).

Held, D. (1987) *Models of Democracy* (Cambridge: Polity).

Heper, M. and Landau, J. (eds) (1991) *Political Parties and Democracy in Turkey* (London: Tauris).

Herbst, J. (1990) *State Politics in Zimbabwe* (Berkeley, Calif.: University of California Press).

Hermet, G., Rose, R. and Rouquie, A. (eds) (1978) *Elections Without Choice* (London: Macmillan).

Higgott, R. (1983) *Political Development Theory: The Contemporary Debate* (New York: St. Martin's Press).

Hill, R. (1989) *The Soviet Union: Politics, Economics and Society* (London: Pinter).

Hill, R. and Frank, P. (1983) *The Soviet Communist Party* (London: Allen & Unwin).

Hine, D. (1981) 'Thirty Years of the Italian Republic', *Parliamentary Affairs* (34) 63–80.

Hine, D. (1982) 'Factionalism in West European Parties: A Framework for Analysis', *West European Politics* (5) 36–53.

Hine, D. (1986) 'Leaders and Followers: Democracy and Manageability in the Social Democratic Parties of Western Europe' in *The Future of Social Democracy*, ed. A. Thomas and W. Paterson (Oxford: Oxford University Press), pp. 261–90.

Hine, D. and Finocchi, R. (1991) 'The Italian Prime Minister', *West European Politics* (14) 79–96.

Hintzen, P. (1989) *The Costs of Regime Survival: Racial Mobilization, Elite Domination, and Control of the State in Guyana and Trinidad* (Cambridge: Cambridge University Press).

Hockling, B. and Smith, M. (1990) *World Politics* (New York: Harvester Press).

Hodges, D. and Gandy, R. (1983) *Mexico 1910–1982: Reform or Revolution?* (London: Zed Press).

Hodgkins, B., Wright, D. and Heick, H. (eds) (1978) *Federalism in Canada and Australia: The Early Years* (Waterloo, Ont.: Wilfrid Laurier University Press).

Hogwood, B. and Gunn, L. (1984) *Policy Analysis for the Real World* (Oxford: Oxford University Press).

Holmes, L. (1986) *Politics in the Communist World* (Oxford: University Press).

Hough, J. (1983) 'Pluralism, Corporatism and the Soviet Union' in *Pluralism in the Soviet Union*, ed. S. Solomon, pp. 37–60.

Hough, J. and Fainsod, M. (1979) *How the Soviet Union is Governed* (Cambridge, Mass.: Harvard University Press).

Hunter, F. (1953) *Community Power Structure* (Chapel Hill, N.C.: University of North Carolina Press).

Huntington, S. and Nelson, J. (1976) *No Easy Choices: Political Participation in Developing Countries* (Cambridge, Mass.: Harvard University Press).

Hyman, A. (1990) *Pakistan: Towards a Modern Muslim State?* (Research Institute for the Study of Terrorism and Conflict).

Iba, M. (1990) 'Transnationals: The Same Old Trends' in *Instituto del Tercer Mundo*, Third World Guide 91/92 (Montevideo: Instituto del Tercer Mundo).

Imperato, P. (1989) *Mali: A Search for Direction* (Boulder, Colo.: Westview).

Inglehart, R. (1971) 'The Silent Revolution in Europe: Intergenerational Change in Post-industrial Societies', *American Political Science Review* (65) 991–1017.

Inglehart, R. (1988) 'The Renaissance of Political Culture', *American Political Science Review* (82) 1203–30.

Inglehart, R. (1990) *Culture Shift in Advanced Industrial Society* (Princeton, N.J.: Princeton University Press).

Instituto del Tercer Mundo (1990) *Third World Guide 91/92* (Montevideo: Instituto del Tercer Mundo).

Jackson, R. and Rosberg, C. (1982) *Personal Rule In Black Africa: Prince, Autocrat, Prophet, Tyrant* (Berkeley, Calif.: University of California Press).

Jayanntha, D. (1991) *Electoral Allegiance in Sri Lanka* (Cambridge: Cambridge University Press).

Jenkins, R. (1987) *Transnational Corporations and Uneven Development* (London: Methuen).

Joffe, E. (1983), 'Party and Military in China: Professionalism in Command?', *Problems of Communism*, vol. 32, no. 5, pp. 48–63.

Johnson, C. (1966) *Revolutionary Change* (Boston, Mass.: Little, Brown).

Johnson, C. (1982) *MITI and the Japanese Miracle: the Growth of Industrial Policy, 1925–75* (Stanford, Calif.: Stanford University Press).

Johnson, N. (1979) 'Committees in the West German Bundestag' in *Committees in Legislatures: A Comparative Analysis*, ed. J. Lees and M. Shaw (Durham, N.C.: Duke University Press), pp. 102–47.

Jones, G. (1991) (ed.) *West European Prime Ministers* (London: Cass).

Kashyap, S. (1979) 'Committees in the Indian Lok Sabha', in *Committees in Legislatures: A Comparative Perspective*, ed. J. Lees and M. Shaw (Durham, N.C.: Duke University Press), pp. 288–326.

Katz, R. (1986) 'Party Government: A Rationalistic Conception' in *The Future of Party Government*, vol. 1, ed. F. Castles and R. Wildenmann (Berlin: Gruyter), pp. 31–71.

Katzenstein, P. (1984) *Corporatism and Change: Austria, Switzerland and the Politics of Industry* (Ithaca, N.Y.: Cornell University Press).

Kaufman, G. (1980) *How to Become a Minister* (London: Sidgwick & Jackson).

Kautsky, J. (1972) *The Political Consequences of Modernisation* (New York: John Wiley).

Keddie, N. (1991) 'The Revolt of Islam and its Roots' in *Comparative Political Dynamics*, ed. D. Rustow and K. Erickson (New York: HarperCollins) 292–308.

Kennedy, P. (1988) *The Rise and Fall of the Great Powers* (London: Unwin Hyman).

Keohane, R. and Nye, J., (eds) (1972) *Transnational Relations and World Politics* (Cambridge, Mass.: Harvard University Press).

Keohane, R. (1984) *After Hegemony: Cooperation and Discord in the World Political Economy* (Princeton, N.J.: Princeton University Press).

Kesselman, M., Krieger, J. and Allen, C. (1987) *European Politics in Transition* (Lexington, Mass.: D. C. Heath).

Khalil, S. (1990) *Republic of Fear: Saddam's Iraq* (London: Hutchinson Radius).

Kidron, M. and Segal, R. (eds) (1981) *The State of the World Atlas* (London: Heinemann).

Kihl, Y. (1984) *Politics and Policies in Divided Korea* (Boulder, Colo.: Westview).

Kim, C., Barkan, J. Turan, I. and Jewell, M. (1984) *The Legislative Connection: The Politics of Representation in Kenya, Korea and Turkey* (Durham, N.C.: Duke University Press).

King, A. (1975) 'Executives' in *The Handbook of Political Science*, vol. 5, ed. F. Greenstein and N. Polsby (Reading, Mass.: Addison-Wesley), pp. 173–256.

King, A. (ed.) (1985) *The British Prime Minister*, 2nd edn (London: Macmillan).

King, A. (ed.) (1990) *The New American Political System* (Washington, D.C.: American Enterprise Institute).

Kingdom, J. (1991) *Government and Politics in Britain* (Cambridge: Polity).

Kircheimer, O. (1966) 'The Transformation of the Western European Party Systems' in *Political Parties and Political Development*, ed. J. La Palombara and M. Weiner (Princeton, N.J.: Princeton University Press), pp. 177–200.

Knutsen, O. (1990) 'Materialist and Postmaterialist Values and Social Structure in the Nordic Countries', *Comparative Politics* (23) 85–101.

Kochan, L. (1970) *Russia in Revolution* (London: Paladin).

Kohli, A. (ed.) (1988) *India's Democracy: An Analysis of Changing State–Society Relations* (Princeton, N.J.: Princeton University Press).

Kohli, A. (1990) *Democracy and Discontent: India's Growing Crisis of Governability* (Cambridge: Cambridge University Press).

Kominski, B. (1991) *The Collapse of State Socialism: The Case of Poland* (Princeton, N.J.: Princeton University Press).

Kudrle, R. and Marmor, T. (1981) 'The Development of Welfare States in North America' in *The Development of Welfare States in Europe and America*, ed. P. Flora and A. Heidenheimer (New Brunswick, N.J.: Transaction Books), pp. 187–236.

Laffin, M. (1989) 'Public Policy Making' in *Politics in Australia*, ed. R. Smith and L. Watson (North Sydney: Unwin Hyman), pp. 38–48.

Laitin, F. and Samatar, S. (1987) *Somalia: a Nation in Search of a State* (Boulder, Colo.: Westview).

Lamb, C. (1991) *Waiting for Allah: Pakistan's Struggle for Democracy* (London: Penguin).

Lampert, N. (1990) 'Patterns of Participation', in *Developments in Soviet Politics*, ed. S. White, A. Pravda and Z. Gitelman (Basingstoke: Macmillan), pp. 120–36.

Landes, R. (1985) *The Canadian Polity: A Comparative Introduction* (Englewood Cliffs, N.J.: Prentice-Hall).

Lane, D. (1986) 'Human Rights under State Socialism', in *Communist Politics: A Reader*, ed. S. White and D. Nelson (London: Macmillan), pp. 326–45.

Lane, J. and Ersson, S. (1991) *Politics and Society in Western Europe* (London: Sage).

La Palombara, J. (1974) *Politics Within Nations* (Englewood Cliffs, N.J.: Prentice-Hall).

La Palombara, J. (1987) *Democracy Italian Style* (New Haven, Conn.: Yale University Press).

La Palombara, J. and Weiner, M. (1966) *Political Parties and Political Development* (Princeton, N.J.: Princeton University Press).

Lasswell, H. (1958, first pub. 1936) *Politics: Who Gets What, When, How* (Cleveland, Ohio: Meridian).

Lawson, K. (ed.) (1980) *Political Parties and Linkage: A Comparative Perspective* (New Haven, Conn.: Yale University Press).

Laver, M. (1983) *Invitation to Politics* (Oxford: Basil Blackwell).

Lees, J. and Shaw, M. (eds) (1979) *Committees in Legislatures: A Comparative Perspective* (Durham, N.C.: Duke University Press).

Le Grand J. (1982) *The Strategy of Equality: Redistribution and the Social Services* (London: Allen & Unwin).

Lehmann, P. (1990) *Democracy and Development in Latin America* (Philadelphia: Temple University Press).

Lenin, V. (1917, many editions) *The State and Revolution* (Moscow: Foreign Languages Publishing House).

Levine, S. (ed.) (1978) *Politics in New Zealand* (London: Allen & Unwin).

Levy, D. (1989) 'Mexico: Sustained Civilian Rule without Democracy' in *Democracy in Developing Countries: Latin America*, ed. L. Diamond, J. Linz, and S. Lipset (Boulder, Colo.: Lynne Rienner).

Lewis, D. and Wallace, H. (eds) (1984) *Policies into Practice* (London: Heinemann).

Lewis, P. (1982) *Socialism, Liberalism and Dictatorship in Paraguay* (New York: Praeger).

Lewis, P. and Potter, D. (eds) (1973) *The Practice of Comparative Politics* (London: Longman/Open University).

Liebert, U. and Cotta, M. (eds) (1990) *Parliament and Democratic Consolidation in Southern Europe* (London: Pinter).

Lijphart, A. (1971) 'Comparative Politics and Comparative Method', *American Political Science Review* (65) 682–93.

Lijphart, A. (1975) *The Politics of Accommodation: Pluralism and Democracy in the Netherlands* (Berkeley, Calif.: University of California Press).

Lijphart, A. (1977) *Democracy in Plural Societies: A Comparative Exploration* (Berkeley, Calif.: University of California Press).

Lijphart, A. (1984a) *Democracies: Patterns of Majoritarian and Consensual Government in Twenty One Countries* (New Haven, Conn.: Yale University Press).

Lijphart, A. (1984b) *Choosing an Electoral System: Issues and Alternatives* (New York: Praeger).

Lijphart, A., (1990) 'Democratic Political Systems', in *Contemporary Political Systems: Classifications and Typologies*, ed. A. Bebler and J. Seroka (Boulder, Colo.: Lynne Rienner), pp. 71–87.

Lindblom, C. (1977) *Politics and Markets: The World's Political Economic Systems* (New York: Basic Books).

Lindblom, C. (1979) 'Still Muddling, Not Yet Through', *Public Administration Review* (39) 517–26.

Lippman, W. (1922) *Public Opinion* (London: Allen & Unwin).

Lipset, S. (1983, first pub. 1960) *Political Man* (New York: Basic Books).

Lipset, S. and Rokkan, S. (1967) 'Cleavage Structures, Party Systems and Voter Alignments' in *Party Systems and Voter Alignments*, ed. S. Lipset and S. Rokkan (New York: Free Press).

Little, R. and Smith, M. (eds) (1991) *Perspectives on World Politics* 2nd edn (London: Routledge).

Loewenberg, G. and Patterson, S. (1979) *Comparing Legislatures* (Boston, Mass.: Little, Brown).

Lukes, S. (1974) *Power: A Radical View* (London: Macmillan).

Lukes S. (ed.) (1986) *Power* (Oxford: Basil Blackwell).

Luttwak, E. (1969) *Coup d'Etat* (Harmondsworth: Penguin).

Lynd, R. and Lynd, H. (1929) *Middletown* (New York: Harcourt Brace).

McCauley, M. and Carter, S. (eds) (1986) *Leadership and Succession in the Soviet Union, Eastern Europe and China* (London: Macmillan).

Macdonald, D. (1988) *The Koreans: Contemporary Politics and Society* (Boulder, Colo.: Westview).

MacDonald, F. (1991) 'Who is on Top? Ministers or the Mandarins?' in *Politics: Canada*, 7th edn, ed. P. Fox and G. White (Toronto: McGraw-Hill Ryerson) pp. 395–9.

McFarlane, B. (1988) *Yugoslavia: Politics, Economics and Society* (London: Pinter).

McGrew, A. and Wilson, M. (eds) (1982) *Decision-Making: Approaches and Analysis* (Manchester: Manchester University Press).

McKenzie, R. (1955, 2nd edn 1963, 3rd edn 1967) *British Political Parties* (London: Heinemann).

Mackie, T. and Hogwood, B. (eds) (1985) *Unlocking the Cabinet: Cabinet Structures In Comparative Perspective* (London: Sage).

Mackie, T. and Rose, R. (eds) (1982) *The International Almanac of Electoral History* (Basingstoke: Macmillan).

McKinlay, R. and Little, R. (1986) *Global Problems and World Order* (London: Pinter).

McLean, I. (1986) 'Some Recent Work in Public Choice', *British Journal of Political Science* (16) 377–94.

Macqueen, A. (1989) 'The Art of Shopping' in *Soviet Union: The Challenge of Change*, ed. M. Wright (Harlow: Longman).

Macridis, R. and Brown, B. (eds) (1990) *Comparative Politics: Notes and Readings*, 7th edn (Belmont, Calif.: Brooks/Cole).

Mair, P. (1990) *The West European Party System* (Oxford: Oxford University Press).

Mannheim, K. (1954) *Ideology and Utopia* (London: Routledge & Kegan Paul).

Marin, B. (1983) 'Organising Interests by Interest Associations: Organisational Prerequisites of Corporatism in Austria', *International Political Science Review* (4) 197–216.

Markus, G. and Converse, P. (1979) 'A Dynamic Simultaneous Equation Model of Electoral Choice', *American Political Science Review* (73) 1055–70.

Marsh, A. (1990) *Political Action in Europe and the USA* (Basingstoke: Macmillan).

Marx, K. and Engels, F. (1848, many editions) *The Communist Manifesto* (Moscow: Foreign Languages Publishing House).

Matthews, T. (1989) 'Interest Groups' in *Politics in Australia*, ed. R. Smith and L. Watson (Sydney: Allen & Unwin), pp. 211–27.

Mayhew, D. (1974) *Congress: The Electoral Connection* (New Haven, Conn.: Yale University Press).

Mayntz, R. (1980) 'Executive Leadership in Germany: Dispersion of Power or "Kanzlerdemokratie"?' in *Presidents and Prime Ministers*, ed. R. Rose and E. Suleiman (Washington, D.C.: AEI), pp. 139–70.

Meny, Y. (1990) *Government and Politics in Western Europe: Britain, France, Italy, West Germany* (Oxford: Oxford University Press).

Merkl, P. (ed.) (1980) *Western European Party Systems: Trends and Prospects* (New York: Free Press).

Meyer, A. (1965) *The Soviet Political System: An Interpretation* (New York: Random House).

Mezey, M. (1979) *Comparative Legislatures* (Durham, N.C.: Duke University Press).

Michels, R. (1915, 1949) *Political Parties* (Glencoe, Ill.: Free Press).

Milbrath, L. (1981) 'Political Participation' in *The Handbook of Political Behaviour*, vol. 4, ed. S. Long (New York: Plenum Press), pp. 197–240.

Miliband, R. (1969) *The State in Capitalist Society* (London: Weidenfeld & Nicolson).

Miller, D. *et al.* (eds) (1987) *The Blackwell Encyclopaedia of Political Thought* (Oxford: Basil Blackwell).

Miller, K. (1991) *Denmark: A Troubled Welfare State* (Boulder, Colo.: Westview).

Miller, W. and Levitin, T. (1976) *Leadership and Change: the New Politics of the American Electorate* (Cambridge, Mass.: Winthrop).

Mills, C. Wright (1956) *The Power Elite* (New York: Oxford University Press).

Milner, H. (1990) *Sweden: Social Democracy in Practice* (Oxford: Oxford University Press).

Miners, N. (1981) *Government and Politics of Hong Kong* (Hong Kong: Oxford University Press).

Moaz, H. and Yaniv, A. (eds) (1987) *Syria under Assad* (Beckenham, Kent: Croom Helm).

Mosca, G. (1939, 1958) *The Myth of the Ruling Class* (Ann Arbor, Mich.: University of Michigan Press).

Mosher, S. (1983) *Broken Earth: The Rural Chinese* (New York: Free Press).

Mouzelis, N. (1986) *Politics in the Semi-Periphery: Early Parliamentarism and Late Industrialisation in the Balkans and Latin America* (London: Macmillan).

Moxon-Browne, E. (1989) *Political Change in Spain* (London and New York: Routledge).

Munck, R. (1989) *Latin America: The Transition to Democracy* (London: Zed).

Nadel, F. and Rourke, F. (1975) 'Bureaucracies' in *The Handbook of Political Science*, vol. 5, ed. F. Greenstein and N. Polsby (Reading, Mass.: Addison-Wesley), pp. 373–440.

Neary I. (1992a) 'Japan' in *Power and Policy in Liberal Democracies*, ed. M. Harrop (Cambridge: Cambridge University Press), pp. 48–70.

Neary, I. (1992b) 'Ethnic Minorities' in *Power and Policy in Liberal Democracies*, ed. M. Harrop (Cambridge: Cambridge University Press), pp. 174–94.

Needler, M. (1968) *Political Development in Latin America* (New York: Random House).

Nelson, D. (1982) 'Communist Legislatures and Communist Politics', in Nelson and White (1982) *see below*.

Nelson, D. (ed.) (1983) *Communism and the Politics of Inequalities* (Lexington, Va.: Lexington Books).

Nelson, D. and White, S. (eds) (1982) *Communist Legislatures in Comparative Perspective* (London: Macmillan).

Neustadt, R. (1960, 1980) *Presidential Power: The Politics of Leadership from FDR to Carter* (New York: Wiley).

Nevitte, N. and Gibbins, R. (1990) *New Elites in Old States: Ideologies in the Anglo-American Democracies* (Ontario: Oxford University Press).

Niblock, T. (1987) *Class and Power in Sudan* (Basingstoke: Macmillan).

Nicholson, B. (1989) 'Increasing Women's Parliamentary Representation: The Norwegian Experience' (Newcastle upon Tyne: Centre for Scandinavian Studies).

Nie, N., Verba, S. and Petrocik, J. (1979) *The Changing American Voter* (Cambridge, Mass.: Harvard University Press).

Nordlinger, E. (1977) *Soldiers in Politics: Military Coups and Governments* (Englewood Cliffs, N.J.: Prentice-Hall).

Norton, P. (ed.) (1985) *Parliament in the 1980s* (Oxford: Basil Blackwell).

Norton, P. (ed.) (1990a) *Legislatures* (Oxford: Oxford University Press).

Norton, P. (ed.) (1990b) *Parliaments in Western Europe* (London: Frank Cass).

Norton, P. (1991) *The British Polity* (New York: Longman).

Nugent, N. (1991) *The Government and Politics of the European Community* (Basingstoke: Macmillan).

O'Brien, D. (1986) *Storm Center: The Supreme Court in American Politics* (New York: Norton).

O'Brien, P. and Cammack, P. (eds) (1985) *Generals in Retreat: The Crisis of Military Rule In Latin America* (Manchester: Manchester University Press).

Observer, The (1990) *Tearing Down the Curtain* (London: Hodder & Stoughton).

Okoli, F. (1980) 'The Dilemma of Premature Bureaucratisation in the New States of Africa', *African Studies Review* (23) 1–16.

Olsen, D. and Mezey, M. (eds) *Legislatures in the Policy Process: The Dilemmas of Economic Policy* (Cambridge: Cambridge University Press).

Olson, M. (1982) *The Rise and Decline of Nations* (New Haven, Conn.: Yale University Press).

Opello, W. (1986) 'Portugal's Parliament: An Organisational Analysis of Legislative Performance', *Legislative Studies Quarterly* (11) 291–320.

Opello, W. (1989) *Portugal: From Monarchy to Pluralist Democracy* (Boulder, Colo.: Westview).

Orwell, G. (1948, 1962) *Nineteen Eighty Four* (London: Secker & Warburg).

O'Sullivan, N. (ed.) (1983) *Revolutionary Theory and Political Reality* (Brighton: Harvester Press).

O'Toole, T. (1986) *The Central African Republic: The Continent's Hidden Heart* (Boulder, Colo.: Westview).

Otunno, A. (1987) *Politics and the Military in Uganda* (Basingstoke: Macmillan).

Ozbudun, E. (1989) 'Turkey: Crises, Interruptions and Reequilibrations' in *Democracy in Developing Countries: Asia*, ed. L. Diamond, J. Linz and S. Lipset (Boulder, Colo.: Lynne Rienner).

Packenham, R. (1970) 'Legislatures and Political Development' in *Legislatures in Developmental Perspective*, ed. A. Kornberg and L. Musolf (Durham, N.C.: Duke University Press), pp. 546–76.

Paldam, M. (1981) 'A Preliminary Survey of the Theories and Findings on Vote and Popularity Functions', *European Journal of Political Research* (9) 181–200.

Parkin, F. (1971) *Class, Inequality and Political Order* (London: MacGibbon & Kee).

Parkin, S. (1989) *Green Parties: An International Guide* (London: Heretic Books).

Parry, G. (1969) *Political Elites* (London: Allen & Unwin).

Parry, G. and Moyser, G. (1991) *Political Participation in Britain* (Cambridge: Cambridge University Press).

Parsons, T. (1967) 'On the Concept of Political Power' in *Sociological Theory and Modern Society*, eds. T. Parsons (New York: Free Press).

Pateman, C. (1980) 'The Civic Culture: A Philosophic Critique' in *The Civic Culture Revisited*, ed. G. Almond and S. Verba (Princeton, N.J.: Princeton University Press), pp. 57–102.

Paterson, W. and Southern, D. (1991) *Governing Germany* (Oxford: Basil Blackwell).

Pearce, J. (1990) *Colombia: Inside the Labyrinth* (London: Latin American Bureau).

Peele, G., Bailey, C. and Cain, B. (eds) (1992) *Developments in American Politics* (Basingstoke: Macmillan).

Peeler, J. (1985) *Latin American Democracies: Colombia, Costa Rica, Venezuela* (Chapel Hill: University of North Carolina Press).

Peil, M. (1976) *Nigerian Politics: The People's View* (London: Cassell).

Pellow, D. and Chazan, N. (1986) *Ghana: Coping with Uncertainty* (Boulder, Colo.: Westview).

Peretz, D. (1984) *The Government and Politics of Israel* (Boulder, Colo.: Westview).

Peters, G. (1984) *The Politics of Bureaucracy* (London: Longman).

Peters, G. (1986) *American Public Policy: Promise and Performance*, 2nd edn (Basingstoke: Macmillan).

Pierson, C. (1991) *Beyond the Welfare State?* (Oxford: Polity).

Pinkney, R. (1990) *Right-wing Military Government* (London: Pinter).

Polsby, N. (1963) *Community Power and Social Theory* (New Haven, Conn.: Yale University Press).

Polsby, N. and Wildavsky, A. (1984) *Presidential Elections* (New York: Scribner's).

Pomper, G. and Lederman, S. (1985) *Elections in America: Control and Influence in Democratic Politics* (New York: Longman).

Potter, D. (1986) *India's Political Administrators 1919–1982* (Oxford: Clarendon).

Powell, B. (1982) *Contemporary Democracies* (Cambridge, Mass.: Harvard University Press).

Pravda, A. (1986) 'Elections in Communist Party States' in *Communist Political Systems: A Reader*, ed. S. White and D. Nelson (London: Macmillan), pp. 27–54.

Pressman, J. and Wildavsky, A. (1973) *Implementation* (Berkeley, Calif.: University of California Press).

Price, R. (1991) *Political Transformation in South Africa, 1975–1990* (New York: Oxford University Press).

Prins, G. (ed.) (1990) *Spring in Winter: The 1989 Revolutions* (Manchester University Press).

Putnam, R. (1976) *The Comparative Study of Political Elites* (Englewood Cliffs, N.J.: Prentice-Hall).

Pye, L. and Verba, S. (eds) (1965) *Political Culture and Political Development* (Princeton: University Press).

Quah, J. *et al.* (eds) (1989) *The Government and Politics of Singapore* (Singapore: Oxford University Press).

Rae, D. (1967, 1971) *The Political Consequences of Electoral Laws* (New Haven, Conn.: Yale University Press).

Randall, V. (ed.) (1988) *Political Parties in the Third World* (London: Sage).

Ranney, A. (1981) 'Candidate selection' in *Democracy at the Polls*, ed. D. Butler, H. Penniman and A. Ranney (Washington, DC: AEI), pp. 107–37.

Ray, J. (1990) *Global Politics* (Boston, Mass.: Houghton Mifflin).

Reagan, M. and Sanzone, J. (1982) *The New Federalism*, 2nd edn (New York: Oxford University Press).

Remmer, K. (1989) *Military Rule in Latin America* (Boston, Mass.: Unwin Hyman).

Richardson, B. and Flanagan, S. (1984) *Politics in Japan* (Boston, Mass.: Little, Brown).

Richardson, J. and Jordan, G. (1979) *Governing Under Pressure* (Oxford: Martin Robertson).

Richardson, J. (ed.) (1984) *Policy Styles in Western Europe* (London: Allen & Unwin).

Richardson, J. (1984) 'The concept of policy style' in *Policy Styles in Western Europe*, ed. Richardson *see above*.

Riker, W. (1975) 'Federalism' in *The Handbook of Political Science*, vol. 5, ed. F. Greenstein and N. Polsby (Reading, Mass.: Addison-Wesley).

Ritchie, E. (1992) 'Law and Order' in *Power and Policy in Liberal Democracies*, ed. M. Harrop (Cambridge: Cambridge University Press), pp. 195–217.

Roach, J. and Thomaneck, J. (1985) *Police and Public Order in Europe* (London: Croom Helm).

Rodzinski, W. (1988) *The People's Republic of China: Reflections on Chinese Political History since 1949* (London: Collins).

Robertson, D. (1985) *The Penguin Dictionary of Politics* (Harmondsworth: Penguin).

Rokkan, S. (1970) *Citizens, Elections, Parties* (New York: McKay).

Rose, R. (1976) *The Problem of Party Government* (Harmondsworth: Penguin).

Rose, R. (1984) *Do Parties Make a Difference?* (London: Macmillan).

Rose, R. (1987), *The Postmodern Presidency: The White House Meets the World* (New York: Chatham House).

Rose, R., Page, E., Parry, R., Peters, G., Pignatelli, A. and Schmidt, K. (1985) *Public Employment in Western Nations* (Cambridge: Cambridge University Press).

Rose, R. and Suleiman, E. (eds) (1980) *Presidents and Prime Ministers* (Washington, D.C.: AEI).

Rose, R. and Urwin, D. (1969) 'Social Cohesion, Political Parties and Strains in Regimes', *Comparative Political Studies* (2) 7–67.

Roskin, M. (1977) *Other Governments of Europe: Sweden, Spain, Italy, Yugoslavia and East Germany* (Englewood Cliffs, N.J.: Prentice-Hall).

Rotfeld, A. and Stutzle, W. (1991) *Germany and Europe in Transition* (Oxford: Oxford University Press).

Rouquie, R. (1982) *Demilitarisation and the Institutionalization of Military-dominated Politics in Latin America*, working paper no. 110, (Washington: Woodrow Wilson Center for Scholars).

Rowat, D. (1988) 'Comparisons and Trends' in *Public Administration in Developed Democracies: A Comparative Study*, ed. D. Rowat (New York: Marcel Dekker).

Rush, M. (ed.) (1990) *Parliament and Pressure Politics* (Oxford: Clarendon).

Rusk, J. (1991) 'Government-Relations Firms are now Part of the System' in *Politics: Canada*, ed. P. Fox and G. White (Toronto: McGraw-Hill Ryerson), pp. 241–4.

Rustow, D. and Erickson, K. (eds) (1991) *Comparative Political Dynamics: Global Research Perspectives* (New York: Harper Collins).

Saich, T. (1981) *China: Politics and Government* (London: Macmillan).

Sanders, A. (1987) *Mongolia: Politics, Economics and Society* (London: Pinter).

Sandwick, J. (1987) *The Gulf Cooperation Council: Moderation and Stability in an Interdependent World* (Boulder, Colo.: Westview).

Sartori, G. (1970) 'Concept Misformation in Comparative Politics', *American Political Science Review* (54) 1033–53.

Sartori, G. (1976) *Parties and Party Systems: A Framework for Analysis* (Cambridge: Cambridge University Press).

Sartori, G. (ed.) (1985) *Social Science Concepts: A Systematic Analysis* (Newbury Park, Calif.: Sage).

Sassoon, D. (1986) *Contemporary Italy: Politics, Economics and Society since 1945* (New York: Longman).

Saunders, P. (1979) *Urban Politics: A Sociological Interpretation* (London: Hutchinson).

Scalapino, R. and Lee, C. (1971) *Communism in Korea* (Berkeley, Calif.: University of California Press).

Schaffer, H. (1988) 'Austria' in *Public Administration in Developed Democracies*, ed. D. Rowatt (New York: Marcel Dekker).

Schattschneider, E. (1942) *Party Government* (New York: Farrar & Reinhart).

Schmitter, P. and Lehmbruch, G. (eds) (1979) *Trends Towards Corporatist Intermediation* (London: Sage).

Schöpflin, G. (1990) 'Why Communism Collapsed', *International Affairs* (66) pp. 3–17.

Schubert, G. (1972) 'Judicial Process and Behaviour during the Sixties', *Political Science* (5) 6–15.

Schulz, D. (1981) 'On the Nature and Functions of Participation in Communist States' in *Political Participation in Communist Systems*, ed. D. Schulz and J. Adams, 26–78.

Schulz, D. and Adams, J. (eds) (1981) *Political Participation in Communist Systems* (New York: Pergamon).

Schumpeter, J. (1943) *Capitalism, Socialism and Democracy* (New York: Harper & Row).

Schurmann, F. (1968) *Ideology and Organization in Communist China* (Berkeley, Calif.: University of California Press).

Schwartz, B. (1960) 'The legend of the "Legend of 'Maoism'"' *China Quarterly* (2) pp. 35–42.

Scruton, R. (1983) *A Dictionary of Political Thought* (London: Pan).

Searls, E. (1978) 'The Fragmented French Executive: Ministerial *Cabinets* in the Fifth Republic', *West European Politics* (1) 161–76.

Segal, G. (1991) *The World Affairs Companion* (London: Simon and Schuster).

Self, P. (1977) *Administrative Theories and Politics* (London: Allen & Unwin).

Semetko, H., Blumler, J., Gurevitch, M. and Weaver, D. (1991) *The Formation of Campaign Agendas: A Comparative Analysis of Party and Media Roles in Recent British and American Elections* (Hillsdale, N.J.: Lawrence Erlbaum).

Shapiro, M. (1990) 'The Supreme Court from Early Burger to Early Rehnquist' in *The New American Political System*, 2nd edn, ed. A. King (Washington, D.C.: AEI).

Shaw, M. (1979) 'Conclusions' in *Committees in Legislatures*, ed. J. Lees and M. Shaw (Durham, N.C.: Duke University Press).

Shaw, M. (1983) 'Reform of the American Congress' in *The Politics of Parliamentary Reform*, ed. D. Judge (London: Heinemann), pp. 129–46.

Shaw, M. (ed.) (1987) *Roosevelt to Reagan: The Development of the Modern Presidency* (London: Hurst).

Sherrill, R. (1974) *Why They Call it Politics* (New York: Harcourt, Brace, Jovanovich).

Shils, E. (ed.) (1979) *International Encyclopaedia of the Social Sciences* (18 vols) (New York: Macmillan).

Skidmore, T. (1988) *The Politics of Military Rule in Brazil, 1964–1985* (New York: Oxford University Press).

Simon, H. (1983) *Reason in Human Affairs* (Oxford: Basil Blackwell).

Simon, R. (1982) *Gramsci's Political Thought: An Introduction* (London: Lawrence & Wishart).

Skilling, G. (1986) 'Interest Groups and Communist Politics Revisited' in *Communist Politics: A Reader*, ed. S. White and D. Nelson (London: Macmillan), pp. 221–42.

Skilling, G. and Griffiths, F. (eds) (1973) *Interest Groups in Soviet Politics* (Princeton, N.J.: Princeton University Press).

Skocpol, T. (1979) *States and Social Revolutions: A Comparative Analysis of France, Russia and China* (Cambridge: Cambridge University Press).

Skocpol, T. (1982) 'Rentier State and Shi'a Islam in the Iranian Revolution', *Theory and Society* (11) 265–84.

Skocpol, T. (1984) *Vision and Method in Historical Sociology* (New York: Cambridge University Press).

Skocpol, T. (1985) 'Bringing the State Back In: Strategies of Analysis in Current Research', in *Bringing The State Back In* ed. P. Evans et al, (Cambridge: Cambridge University Press), pp. 3–43.

Smith, G. (1989) *Politics in Western Europe* (Aldershot: Gower).

Smith, G. (1992) *Soviet Politics: Struggling with Change* (New York: St. Martin's Press).

Smith, G., Paterson, W., Padgett, V. and Merkl, P. (1992) *Developments in German Politics* (Basingstoke: Macmillan).

Smith, N. (1984) *Uneven Development: Nature, Capital and the Production of Space* (Oxford: Basil Blackwell).

Smith, R. and Watson, L. (eds) *Politics in Australia* (North Sidney: Allen & Unwin).

Solomon, S. (ed.) (1983) *Pluralism in the Soviet Union* (London: Macmillan).

Sorauf, F. (1985) *Party Politics in America* (Boston, Mass.: Little, Brown).

Spero, J. (1977) *The Politics of International Economic Relations* (London: Allen & Unwin).

Story, D. (1987) *Mexico's Ruling Party: Stability and Authority* (Boulder, Colo.: Westview)

Stouffer, S. (1966) *Communism, Conformity and Civil Liberties* (New York: Wiley).

Strange, S. (1986) *Casino Capitalism* (Oxford: Basil Blackwell).

Strange S. (1988) *States and Markets: An Introduction to International Political Economy* (London: Pinter).

Stuart-Fox, M. (1986) *Laos: Politics, Economics and Society* (London: Pinter).

Suleiman, E. (ed.) (1984) *Bureaucrats and Policy-making: A Comparative Overview* (New York: Holmes & Meier).

Sullivan, J., Pierson, J. and Marcus, G. (1982) *Political Tolerance and American Democracy* (Chicago, Ill.: Chicago University Press).

Tambiah, S. (1986) *Sri Lanka: Ethnic Fratricide and the Dismantling of Democracy* (Delhi: Oxford University Press).

Taylor, P. (1984) *The Government and Politics of Uruguay* (London: Greenwood).

Thomas, A. and Paterson, W. (eds) (1986) *The Future of Social Democracy* (Oxford: Oxford University Press).

Thompson, J. (1990) *Ideology and Modern Culture: Critical Social Theory in the Era of Mass Communication* (Oxford: Polity).

Thyne, I. (1988) 'New Zealand' in *Public Administration in Developed Democracies: A Comparative Study*, ed. D. Rowat (New York: Marcel Dekker).

Tocqueville, A. de (1954, first pub. 1835) *Democracy in America* (New York: Vintage Books).

Tocqueville, A. de (1966, first pub. 1856) *The Ancien Regime and the Revolution in France* (London: Fontana).

Tordoff, W. (1984) *Government and Politics in Africa* (London: Macmillan).

Torp, J. (1989) *Mozambique, Sao Tome and Principe: Politics, Economics and Society* (London: Pinter).

Townsend, J. (1980) *Politics in China*, 2nd edn, (Boston, Mass.: Little, Brown).

Tripp, C. and Owen, R. (1989) *Egypt under Mubarak* (London: Routledge).

Truman, D. (1951) *The Governmental Process: Political Interests and Public Opinion* (New York: Knopf).

Tucker, R. (1970) *The Marxian Revolutionary Idea* (London: Allen & Unwin).

Tucker, R. (1987) *Political Culture and Leadership in Soviet Russia: From Lenin to Gorbachev* (New York: Norton).

Turner, K. (1989) 'Parliament' in *Politics in Australia*, ed. R. Smith and L. Watson (Sydney: Allen and Unwin).

Urban, J. (1990) 'Czechoslovakia: The Power and Politics of Humiliation' in *Spring in Winter: the 1989 Revolutions*, ed. G. Prins (Manchester University Press), pp. 99–138.

Vartola, J. (1988) 'Finland' in *Public Administration in Developed Democracies: A Comparative Study*, ed. D. Rowat (New York: Marcel Dekker), pp. 117–32.

Verba, S. and Nie, N. (1972) *Participation in America: Political Democracy and Social Equality* (New York: Harper & Row).

Verba, S., Nie, N. and Kim, J. (1978) *Participation and Political Equality: A Seven-Nation Comparison* (Cambridge: Cambridge University Press).

von Beyme, K. (1985) *Political Parties in Western Democracies* (Aldershot: Gower).

Waisman, C. (1989) 'Argentina: Autarkic Industrialization and Illegitimacy' in *Democracy in Developing Countries: Latin America*, ed. L. Diamond, J. Linz, and S. Lipset (Boulder, Colo.: Lynne Rienner).

Walkland, S. (1968) *The Legislative Process in Great Britain* (London: Allen & Unwin).

Wallas, G. (1908, 1948) *Human Nature in Politics* (London: Constable).

Wallerstein, I. (1974, 1980) *The Modern World System*, 2 vols (New York: Academic Press).

Wallerstein, I. (1979) *The Capitalist World-Economy* (Cambridge: Cambridge University Press).

Warner, L. and Lunt, P. (1941) *The Social Life of a Modern Community* (New Haven, Conn.: Yale University Press).

Warnock, J. (1987) *The Politics of Hunger* (Toronto: Methuen).

Watson, L. (1989) 'The Constitution' in *Politics in Australia*, ed. R. Smith and L. Watson (North Sydney: Allen & Unwin), pp. 51–64.

Watt, E. (1982) *Authority* (London: Croom Helm).

Watts, R. (1991) 'Canada's Constitutional Options: An Outline' in *Options for a New Canada*, ed. R. Watts and D. Brown (University of Toronto Press), pp. 15–33.

Webb, S. and Webb, B. (1935) *Soviet Government: A New Civilisation?* (London: published by the authors).

Weber, M. (1930) *The Protestant Ethic and the Spirit of Capitalism* (London: Allen & Unwin).

Weber, M. (1957, first pub. 1922) *The Theory of Economic and Social Organisation* (Berkeley, Calif.: University of California Press).

Weller, P. (1985) *First Among Equals: Prime Ministers in Westminster Systems* (Sydney: Allen & Unwin).

Wheare, K. (1946, 4th edn 1963) *Federal Government* (Oxford: Oxford University Press).

Wheare, K. (1968) *Legislatures* (Oxford: Oxford University Press).

White, G. (1991) 'Functions of the House of Commons' in *Politics: Canada* (Toronto: McGraw-Hill Ryerson), pp. 407–17.

White, S. (1979) *Political Culture and Soviet Politics* (London: Macmillan).

White, S. (1982) 'The USSR Supreme Soviet: A Developmental Perspective' in *Communist Legislatures in Comparative Perspective*, ed. D. Nelson and S. White (London: Macmillan), pp. 125–59.

White, S. (1986) 'The Supreme Soviet and Budgetary Politics in the USSR', in *Communist Politics: A Reader* ed. S. White and D. Nelson (London: Macmillan).

White, S., Gardner, J., Schöpflin, G. and Saich, A. (1990) *Communist and Postcommunist Political Systems*, 3rd edn (Basingstoke: Macmillan).

White, S., Pravda, A. and Gitelman, Z. (eds) (1990) *Developments in Soviet Politics* (Basingstoke: Macmillan).

White, W., Wagenburg, R. and Nelson, R. (1991) *Introduction to Canadian Politics and Government* (Toronto: Holt, Rinehart & Winston).

Wightman, G. (1990) 'The June 1990 Elections in Czechoslovakia', *Representation* (29) pp. 18–22.

Wilcox, K. (1989) 'Australian Federalism' in *Politics in Australia*, ed. R. Smith and L. Watson (North Sydney: Allen & Unwin), pp. 140–153.

Wilensky, H. (1984) *The Welfare State and Equality* (Berkeley, Calif.: University of California Press).

Williamson, P. (1985) *Varieties of Corporatism: A Conceptual Discussion* (Cambridge: University Press).

Wilson, G. (1985) *Business and Politics: A Comparative Introduction* (London: Macmillan).

Wilson, G. (1990) *Interest Groups* (Oxford: Basil Blackwell).

Wiseman, J. (1990) *Democracy in Black Africa: Survival and Revival* (New York: Paragon House).

Wiseman, J. (1991) 'Democratic Resurgence in Black Africa', *Contemporary Review* (259) pp. 7–13.

Wolchik, S. (1991) *Czechoslovakia in Transition: Politics, Economics, and Society* (London: Pinter).

Wolinetz, R. (1979) 'The Transformation of West European Parties Revisited', *West European Politics* (4) 4–28.

Wood, G. (1988) *Governing New Zealand* (Auckland: Longman Paul).

World Bank (1985) *The World Bank Atlas* (Washington D.C.: World Bank).

World Bank (1990) *World Development Report 1990* (New York: World Bank).

Worldwatch Institute (1990) *State of the World 1990* (London: Unwin Hyman).

Wright, D. (1988) *Understanding Intergovernmental Relations* (Pacific Grove, Calif.: Brooks Cole).

Wright, M. (1988) *Revolution in the Philippines?* (Harlow: Longman).

Wright, V. (1989) *The Government and Politics of France*, 3rd edn (London: Unwin Hyman).

Wynia, G. (1990, 3rd edition) *The Politics of Latin American Development* (Cambridge: Cambridge University Press).

Xuto, S. (ed.) (1987) *Government and Politics of Thailand* (Singapore: Oxford University Press).

Young, C. (1982) *Ideology and Development in Africa* (New Haven, Conn.: Yale University Press).

Young, H. (1991) *One of Us: A Biography of Mrs Thatcher* (London: Macmillan).

Young, K. (1977) 'Values in the Policy Process', *Policy and Politics* (5) 1–22.

Zaslavsky, K. and Brym, J. (1978) 'The Functions of Elections in the USSR', *Soviet Studies* (30) 362–71.

Zolberg, A. (1966) *Creating Political Order* (Chicago: Rand McNally).

Glossary of Concepts

Agenda-setting 1. The ability to include (or exclude) issues for discussion and decision within a political organisation, and thus an important political resource. 2. The idea that the media in general, and television in particular, influence what we think about, if not what we think.

Agitprop Short for agitation and propaganda activities. A term mainly used in reference to communist party states.

Apparatchiki Literally 'the men of the apparatus', from the Russian. The full-time party officials in communist party states who acted as watchdogs and troubleshooters, enforcing party control over all areas of policy.

Assembly A multi-membered body which considers questions of public policy, and with constitutional powers to make law. Assemblies (or legislatures) have one core, defining function: 'They give assent, on behalf of a political community that extends beyond the executive authority, to binding measures of public policy' (Norton, 1990a, p. 1).

Authoritarian Any form of rule which pays little or no attention to public opinion, individual rights or government by consent. Authoritarian governments brook no opposition, and simply impose their will on the population.

Authority Basically the right to make lawful commands. Authority enables rulers, or those empowered by them, to secure compliance on grounds accepted as legitimate by those affected. The bases of authority may vary: see *charismatic authority, legal rational authority* and *traditional authority*.

Balkanisation Originally referred to the division of the Balkan region into several small, mutually hostile and frequently warring states. Now applied to any country, region or organisation that fragments with similar consequences.

Basic Law The constitution of the Federal Republic of Germany. Used more generally to mean a framework or outline law.

Bicameral Two-chambered, usually of assemblies.

Bretton Woods The postwar system of international financial regulation, devised at Bretton Woods, New Hampshire, USA, in 1944. It was based on fixed exchange rates, pegged to the US$, which was freely convertible into gold. The Bretton Woods system broke down in the 1970s.

Brezhnev doctrine   The assertion that the 'international gains of socialism' were irreversible. In effect, the Soviet Union claimed the right to ensure by force, if necessary, that the communist party states of Eastern European remained within the Soviet sphere of influence. This doctrine was renounced by Gorbachev, with shattering results.

Bureaucracy   Popularly an epithet for verbiage and 'red tape', and, literally, the rule of officials. The complex of public organisations carrying out administrative functions and responsibilities in the name of the state – in effect, the engine-room of the state.

Bureaucratic politics   The idea that, as civil servants' careers are linked with the fate of their department, they will act to promote the status of their department (and so their jobs). For example, bureaucrats will seek to maximise their department's budgets and resist reforms which diminish their importance.

Cabinet   A committee of senior government ministers which meets to discuss business confidentially. The leading executive body in parliamentary systems of government.

Capitalism   See Exhibit 4.2 on pp. 92–4.

Case study   The detailed study of a specific example within a broader category. A method of study widely employed in political science.

Catch-all parties   Parties that trawl the electoral market in search of whatever support they can find. Electoral success is more important for catch-all parties than consistency of policy or principle.

Charismatic legitimacy   This reflects mass devotion to a leader whose extraordinary personal qualities entitle him or her to rule. Charismatic leaders are obeyed because they inspire the population.

Chinese option   Refers to the use of military force to clear Tiananmen Square of students calling for democratic reforms in Beijing in June 1989. The Chinese option was one of the alternatives considered by Eastern European leaders but discarded, when faced with similar demonstrations later in that year.

Cohabitation   Used to describe a power sharing arrangement where representatives of different parties hold leading posts in government. The term originated in France, where the President may represent one party, while the Prime Minister represents another.

Collective responsibility   Ministers share public responsibility for the decisions agreed by the Cabinet.

Communism   See Exhibit 4.2 on pp. 92–4.

Communist federalism A device by which communist regimes allowed cultural, but not political, autonomy to national minorities.

Community policing A style of policing that emphasises close contacts with the community, and fosters the idea that the police are not apart from but a part of the community. Exemplified by policing in Japan.

Comparative history An approach to explaining key political developments (such as revolutions) through the analysis of a small number of examples.

Competition state A phrase describing how, in an interdependent modern world, the state fights for investment, markets and trade to enhance the nation's international competitiveness.

Confederalism A weak form of political association between sovereign states – for example, the Commonwealth of Independent States that replaced the Soviet Union.

Consensus democracy A political system in which power is diffused throughout the government and the parties. Executive authority is shared among members of a formal or informal coalition, drawn from various parties. The executive does not dominate the legislature as it does under majority democracy. There is a multi-party, rather than a two-party, system. The party system reflects several dimensions of cleavage rather than only one. Elections are typically held under proportional representation rather than first-past-the-post.

Conservatism See Exhibit 4.2 on pp. 92–4.

Constitution A set of rights, powers and procedures regulating the structure of, and relationships among, the public authorities, and between the public authorities and the citizens. Constitutions are the laws that govern the governors.

Corporatism In the traditional sense, corporatism is a system in which the state organises a series of 'corporations', each of which represents groups of workers and employers, although remaining subordinate to the state. As applied to modern states, corporatism refers to the tendency for policy to result from negotiations between the government and organised, officially recognised interests.

Coup d'état The overthrow of a political leader or regime by military force.

Cult of personality The promotion of a leader as the epitome of the revolution. Adulation of the wisdom and greatness of the leader on an all-embracing scale.

Cultural imperialism The promotion of international influence by cultural means (e.g. ideas, films and TV, lifestyle) rather than by military, economic or political power. Most often used to refer to the worldwide influence of US culture, though other countries like France and Britain also attempt to project their culture internationally to some extent.

Customary interest groups Natural social units such as the family which are still important in the politics of many societies. For example, in much of the third world, politicians and officials are expected to use their office to benefit their family or ethnic group.

De-aligned electorate Where social groups do not determine how people vote, and where people lack strong ties to parties.

Dependency theory Suggests that the whole international economy operates to the disadvantage of the third world, because ex-colonies remain economically tied to and dependent upon former imperialist powers. The theory argues that the third world has been systematically 'underdeveloped' by advanced capitalist nations for their own benefit.

Deregulation The removal of controls on economic activity to allow market forces to act unhindered by government intervention. A relative rather than an absolute concept – intervention is reduced rather than totally removed.

Desaparecidos From the Spanish, literally the disappeared ones. Refers to individuals picked up by the police or security forces in Latin America under authoritarian regimes, and subsequently never heard of again. They were almost certainly murdered by their captors.

Deviant cases The study of an atypical or unique case – a case that diverges from the expected pattern. By understanding why the case is unique, the study attempts to explain why other cases conform to a 'normal' type.

Deviating election The majority party loses the election due to short-term factors such as candidate appeal. However, the presumption is that voters who deviate from their normal choice retain their underlying allegiance and return to it in later contests.

Direct elections Where elected representatives are directly voted into office by the mass electorate, and not by lower-level representatives as with indirect elections.

Dominant party states Where a single party controls politics for a considerable period of time. Although opposition parties do exist, they are tolerated only as long as they show no signs of winning any elections that matter. Dominant parties use patronage, control of the media and ballot-rigging to maintain their position in a formally competitive party system. Examples include the Partido Revolucionario Institucional in Mexico and the People's Action Party in Singapore.

Dual control   Where administrative units come under the control of both the local and national government. For example, a provincial administrative office in China is responsible to both the provincial government and to a ministry of the central government.

Elected dictatorship   Where an elected government with a large majority can effectively do what it likes, within the confines of a desire to be re-elected at the next election.

Elitism   An approach to studying politics that stresses the importance of decision-makers and power holders, as opposed to the mass of the population. Even in liberal democracies, there is inevitably a ruling élite. This élite may incorporate economic as well as political and military leaders, though it may also be prone to splits and to opposition from counter-élites.

Evolutionary change   Gradual and incremental change that can, over time, transform the way a government works.

Executive   The structure of political roles at the highest level of government, i.e. the president or prime minister, plus other ministers and top decision-makers. In effect, the executive includes those positions occupying the commanding heights of government.

Externally created parties   Parties that had their origins in demands for the ballot and for legislative representation by excluded strata of the populations – for example, the working-class socialist parties which spread across Europe at the start of the twentieth century.

Faction   An organised group with a reasonably stable membership inside a larger body. Factions are most common in political parties.

Factionalism   A state of competition between different factions within a larger political unit. Factionalism can be motivated by different factors – for example, ideology, spoils, personal attachment, regional identity etc.

Fascism   See Exhibit 4.2 on pp. 92–4.

Federalism   A constitutionally guaranteed sharing of power between levels of government – some powers of decision are granted to provincial (sub-national) governments, while others remain the sole concern of the national government. The degree of independence for provincial governments (and conversely, the power of the national government) varies from country to country. Citizens of a federal system remain subject to the authority of both the central and the provincial governments, each of which acts directly on the citizen.

Focused comparison A comparison based on a small number of countries, typically just two (a *paired comparison*). Most often the comparison concentrates on particular rather than on all aspects of the countries' politics.

Functionalism 1. An approach to studying politics which concentrates on the functions which any political system must perform if it is to survive and operate effectively. Specifying these functions is extremely difficult. In practice, functionalist explanation dwells upon the wider consequences for society of particular political practices and institutions. 2. An approach to explaining revolutionary change that concentrates on a government's failure to perform the functions expected of it.

Fundamentalism See Exhibit 4.2 on pp. 92–4.

Glasnost From the Russian, literally translates as 'openness'. Initially referred to the policy introduced by Gorbachev of allowing frank and open discussion of public issues in the Soviet Union. The term has now passed into the language of international politics.

Global village The notion that the world has so shrunk through expanded contacts and the spread of mass media that it now resembles a village. Everybody knows what everybody else is doing, and the actions of one inhabitant can affect the lives of many others.

Government Has several related meanings, of which the most important are: 1. any settled pattern of decision-making within and for a group; 2. the structure of offices and institutions which performs this task; 3. the incumbents of the major offices within this structure ('the Government').

Guardian bureaucracy Where the national bureaucracy, mainly in third world countries, sees itself as the main guarantor of the survival and integrity of the state, against the instability and debilitating effects of party competition and electoral politics. Under these circumstances, the bureaucrats may take over most of the functions normally performed by elected governments.

Hegemony The predominance of one group, class or nation over others, usually by means other than brute force.

Ideal-type A description of the essential characteristics of a concept in heightened, even extreme form, but which recognises that few, if any, real-world cases will possess all of these characteristics.

Ideology The basic values and ideas which people hold about the nature of society, and the role of politics and government within it. For brief descriptions of major ideologies, see Exhibit 4.2 on pp. 92–4.

Incremental model of policy making   Changes in policy by small steps. Policy is continually made and remade in a series of small adjustments, rather than in bold sweeps.

Indirect elections   A system of elections of two or more levels, where representatives are chosen by those who are themselves directly elected. The US president, for example, is technically chosen by the electoral college, elected by the American people.

Institutional interest groups   Formal organisations acting as interest groups *within* government, i.e. sections of the bureaucracy or armed forces seeking to promote their values, priorities and objectives. Because of their proximity to the decision-making process, they can have major impact upon policy-making.

Interdependence   The expanding range of international commitments taken on by nation states reduces the room for manoeuvre available to governments. Economically and politically, the action of any nation state will be constrained by, and have an impact on, the politics and economy of other nation states. Global warming and ozone depletion illustrate the extent of interdependence in the world today.

Interest aggregation   The process of combining demands on government and turning them into a manageable number of alternatives. In effect, this means that some demands are selected and many are ignored.

Interest articulation   The expression by groups and individuals of needs, wants and demands to government. Interest articulation occurs to some degree even under authoritarian regimes, but is a prominent and highly organised feature of politics in liberal democracies.

Interest group   Independent organisations which try to influence public policy. Interest groups seek to influence government, but, unlike political parties, they do not aspire to become it.

Interest theory   Maintains that the function of ideology is to rationalise interests. Ideology is essentially a gloss upon self-interest, advancing a case for (or against) particular groups within society.

Internally created parties   Parties that were formed by cliques within an assembly joining together for electoral purposes. Such parties were typically dominated (originally) by upper class politicians.

Least developed countries   The poorest third world countries, many in Africa, which have per capita incomes below $1000 a year. They almost entirely lack a manufacturing base, and usually depend heavily on one or two commodities for export earnings. See also *less developed countries*.

Legal rational authority That based on a framework of laws or clearly specified rules. Legal rational authority, typical in modern societies, belongs to the office, not personally to the office-holder. There is normally a right to appeal against decisions which exceed or misuse the authority granted.

Legitimacy In political science, mostly used in a descriptive sense to indicate acceptance by the ruled of the ruler's authority – that is, the ruler is seen as having the right to govern. A legitimate government is not necessarily a just or worthy or even popular government.

Less developed countries Those third world countries where significant economic development has taken place, but the modern sector of the economy is internationally uncompetitive (unlike the NICs) or dominated by transnational companies. See also *least developed countries, newly industrialising countries*.

Liberal democracy A qualified form of democracy based on popular elections and representative government but with strong concern for individual rights. The concept of a liberal democracy is in essence protective. Government derives from and is accountable to the people but its powers are limited in various ways, so that the rights of individuals and minorities are balanced against majority rule.

Liberalism See Exhibit 4.2 on pp. 92–4.

Majority democracy Sometimes referred to as the Westminster model. A single party forms the government and wields extensive executive powers until the voters offer their verdict at the next election. Thus only the self-restraint of the ruling party stands between majority democracy and elected dictatorship.

Mass media Refers to methods of communication which can reach large numbers of people at the same time. Television and newspapers are the most important; others are posters, radio, books, magazines and cinema.

Moderate multi-party systems Those systems characterised by governing coalitions made up of parties of similar ideological persuasion. Hence they are said to be centripetal – strengthening the centre. Coalition members come and go but continuity of policy is maintained. Examples include the Netherlands and the Scandinavian countries most of the time.

Nationalism See Exhibit 4.2 on pp. 92–4.

New politics A style of political participation which goes beyond, and sometimes even excludes, traditional participation through political parties and election campaigns. Advocates of new politics are often willing to consider unorthodox forms of participation: demonstrations, sit-ins and sit-downs, boycotts and political strikes. New politics tends to be associated with broad, rather than class-based, objectives, for example, nuclear disarmament, feminism, protection of the environment.

Newly industrialising countries (NICs)   Rapidly developing nations in the third world. Most are found in the Pacific Rim of East Asia (South Korea, Taiwan, Singapore, Hong Kong). They combine a stable, if often authoritarian, political system with a coherent development strategy.

Night watchman state   A state which performs only limited functions. These were mainly to maintain law and order, defend the country and deal with unexpected problems.

NIMBY   Acronym for Not In My Back Yard. Refers to usually localised groups formed to oppose changes in their vicinity, for example, the construction of a new motorway or power station.

Nomenklatura   Literally a list of names, from the Russian. The system in communist party states whereby the party vetted appointments to all major posts in society, drawing them from a list of suitable candidates. This helped to ensure party domination of all significant positions in both government, and society at large.

Normal elections   An election in which voting directly reflects partisanship and the party with the greatest share of party identifiers (formerly, for example, the Democrats in the USA) wins the election.

Oligarchy   The rule of a few. A tiny elite dominates political life and the mass of the population are inactive. In a competitive oligarchy, there is a more complex structure involving some degree of competition for power, but popular involvement remains limited.

Ombudsman   A post of Scandinavian origin, widely adopted elsewhere, to investigate cases of bureaucratic mismanagement or cases where individuals feel that they have been mistreated by government. In effect, a bureaucratic watch-dog.

One-party state   Where politics is dominated by a single party, e.g. communist party states. Other parties sometimes exist, but are not allowed to challenge the dominance of the ruling party in any serious way.

Parochial political culture   A condition, once widespread but probably now rare, in which people are unaware or only vaguely aware of the existence of central government.

Participant political culture   Citizens know that they are affected by the political system but also believe that they can influence it.

Partisan dealignment Refers to the weakening of traditional bonds between voters, parties and social groups.

Patronage The practice of politicians, civil servants and military officials exploiting their access to government resources to benefit their families and supporters.

Patron–client relationship A relationship in which the 'patron' provides protection, services or rewards to the 'clients' (usually individuals of lower status) who become the patron's political followers.

Peace dividend The expectation that with the end of the Cold War military spending can be reduced and the savings used to reduce taxes or improve welfare and other public services.

Peak organisations A conglomeration of interest groups organised into a national centre, in order to have the maximum leverage on government decision making, e.g the Confederation of British Industry or the Swedish Landsorganisationen (national trade union federation).

Perestroika From the Russian, meaning 'reconstruction'. A term popularised by Gorbachev and referring to the wholesale transformation of the neo-Stalinist Soviet economic and political system.

Peronism A classic example of a successful populist movement. Between 1944 and 1955 in Argentina Juan Peron constructed a nationalist and welfare-oriented authoritarian regime based on lower-class support. Peronism remained a significant force decades after Peron's overthrow by the military.

Pluralism A form of rule in which many people and interests are involved in decision-making, with different people and interests influential in different areas of policy. Where élitism focuses on rule by *a* minority, pluralism emphasises rule by *minorities*, i.e. no single group dominates decision-making.

Polarisation The intensity of ideological differences between parties.

Polarised multi-party systems Those party systems where ideological differences between the parties are so wide and deep that they severely limit the number of feasible coalitions. Some parties, typically the Communists, are excluded from government altogether. Until the 1970s Italy was an example of a polarised multi-party system.

Policy The word has many uses, but a simple definition is that policy is any course of action designed to promote, maintain or prevent some state of affairs.

Policy evaluation   Appraising the consequences and degree of success of a policy in achieving its objectives.

Policy formulation   The detailed development of a policy into concrete proposals.

Policy implementation   Putting policy into practice.

Policy initiation   The 'decision to make a decision' in a particular area; otherwise known as agenda-setting.

Policy style   This suggests that political systems can be characterised according to their own national way of reaching decisions. Policy style is a preferred way of making policy – a procedural ambition – which is not always adhered to in practice.

Political culture   What people think about politics – their beliefs, values and emotions. It does not refer to actual political behaviour – indeed behaviour may conflict with prevailing attitudes.

Political party   The defining characteristics of a political party are a conscious aim (realistic or not) to capture decision-making power, alone or in coalition; seeking popular support through elections or other means; and a permanent organisation.

Political participation   Activity by individuals or groups intended to influence who governs or how they do so.

Political system   Broadly, the political arrangements of a society, embracing all factors influencing collective decisions, The political system thus includes processes of recruitment and socialisation, parties, voters and social movements which are not a formal part of government.

Politics   Defining what 'politics' is has been the object of much controversy. We define it here as the process by which groups of people, of whatever kind or size, make collective decisions.

Populism   See Exhibit 4.2 on pp. 92–4.

Postindustrial   A term used to describe how power and wealth generation in the advanced industrial countries are increasingly based on knowledge, education and service industries rather than on the property ownership and manufacturing industry associated with industrial capitalism. The class-based politics of the latter is increasingly giving way to postmaterial politics, reflecting non-acquisitive values. See also *postmaterialism*.

Postmaterialism A political outlook that takes material well-being for granted and concentrates on 'higher-order' values, for example life-style issues such as ecology, nuclear disarmament and feminism. Postmaterialism tends to be stronger among younger, better-off, well-educated people.

Poverty trap A situation in which poor people find that any increase in income is cancelled out by loss of welfare benefits or increased taxation. Thus they are often unable to work their way out of poverty. A similar trap affects poor countries: as they reach a certain level of development, they cease to receive aid or preferential treatment from international aid donors.

Power A central but much disputed concept of politics. Defined here as the production of intended effects – the capacity of an individual, group, party, class, etc. to get what it wants by securing the compliance of others through whatever means.

Power deflation Describes the situation when a political system is unable to cope with the pace and number of pressures for change. Leaders become swamped by the demands placed upon them, and are unable to satisfy popular expectations. As a result, legitimacy is lost, and a progressive reduction of system effectiveness follows.

Premature bureaucratisation Refers to third world states where modern bureaucratic structures were bequeathed by departing colonial powers but without the modern political system and culture needed for the bureaucracy to function effectively.

Promotional interest groups Sometimes called *attitude*, *cause* or *campaign* groups, these are set up to promote common ideas, values or activities. Environmental pressure groups are examples.

Proportional representation (PR) A class of electoral systems which are designed to, and generally do, produce a more equal relationship between votes and seats than the various majority systems.

Protective interest groups Sometimes called *sectional* or *functional* groups, these are formally organised groups which exist to protect the material interests of their members, be they miners, college lecturers or managing directors. Trade unions and employers' organisations are prime examples of protective groups.

Public opinion An often cited definition is that public opinion is 'those opinions held by private individuals that government finds it prudent to heed'. More broadly, it is the views shared by a community of people (whether a village or a nation) on matters of controversy.

Public opinion poll   A scientific way of measuring the views and attitudes of the mass public by administering questionnaires to samples of individuals chosen according to strict criteria. Opinion polls have revolutionised our understanding of public opinion, and give both governments and their opponents far more accurate information about what ordinary people think of them.

Realigning ('critical') election   An election that changes the underlying strength of parties and redefines the relationships between parties and social groups. Realigning elections are important events, for example the New Deal victory of the Democratic Party in the USA in 1932.

Redemocratisation   The process of rebuilding civilian democratic control over society after the end of a period of military rule. Also referred to as 'post-military politics'.

Regimented participation   People are forced to participate in politics whether they want to or not. A stage-managed display of support for the ruling party. Common in the second world under communist party rule.

Reinforcement thesis   The concept that the mass media strengthens but can not transform the political attitudes and behaviour of the electorate.

Relative deprivation   Describes the gap between what people think they are entitled to (their value expectation) and what they are actually getting (their value capability).

Retrospective voting   Casting one's ballot in response to government performance. The phrase conveys much of the character of contemporary voting behaviour. Electors form an overall assessment of the government's record and, increasingly, they vote accordingly.

Revolutionary change   Any wide-ranging change may be loosely defined as revolutionary. However, a tighter definition of political revolutions concentrates on whether there is a fundamental and long-lasting change in the distribution of power in the nation concerned.

Sinatra doctrine   The popular term to describe Gorbachev's hands-off attitude to Eastern Europe, renouncing any further intervention by the Soviet Union. The leader of each of the countries of Eastern Europe could now claim that he was free to 'do it my way'.

Social group   A focus of identity for individuals which binds them together in some way. The determining factor – the glue that produces group cohesion – varies. It may be class, religion, region, family, etc.

Social movements Social movements are broader, and less organised, than interest groups. They seek, and emerge from, changes in attitude and awareness across large segments of the public. Social movements are promotional in character but they are not in themselves interest groups, for example the women's movement.

Socialisation The transmission of values, attitudes and beliefs across generations. The study of what, when and how people learn about politics.

Socialism See Exhibit 4.2 on pp. 92–4.

Sovereignty The ultimate source of legitimate power in society. Sovereignty belongs to the body which has the right to make laws for a country. Also refers to the independence claimed by every nation state. The extent of sovereignty is often in practice restricted, in both respects.

Spiritual pollution A term used by the Chinese communists to describe the spread of 'decadent bourgeois' ideas from the west, polluting the purportedly socialist ethics of the population.

State An umbrella term that covers the whole range of offices which make and enforce collective decisions for society. Ministers, judges, legislators, bureaucrats, generals and the police all form part of a single organisation of public offices known as the state.

State-centred An approach to studying politics that originally examined the institutions and constitutions of government, in isolation from society. It has now evolved to emphasise the impact of the state on society.

Strain theory The concept that ideologies arise in response to social dislocation. They are seen as symptoms of a malfunctioning society, for example the rise of fascism in interwar Germany.

Subject political culture Where people see themselves as affected by government but not able to influence it – as with people living under a dictatorship.

Supervised democracies Where military regimes hand power over to civilian leaders, but remain in control by manipulating the civilians behind the scenes.

Subsidiarity A principle derived from German federalism, that services should be provided at the lowest practical level of government. Now often used in the context of the European Community to mean that decisions should be made and implemented at lower levels where possible.

Synoptic policy-making The view that policy-makers should consider all the consequences of all the options before reaching policy decisions.

Totalitarianism   A totalitarian regime attempts to control and reshape *all* aspects of society. Exemplified by Stalin's Russia: autocratic, highly coercive, ideological and all-embracing.

Traditional legitimacy   Authority based on custom and an established way of doing things – for example the King has the right to govern because the King has always governed.

Transnational corporations (TNCs)   Also known as multinationals, TNCs are companies that operate in many different nations across the globe. The ideal-type TNC will have no single national emphasis; in practice, most major TNCs are US-based.

Unicameral   One chambered, usually of assemblies.

Unitary government   Where the powers and sovereignty of government are concentrated in central government. Local government is thus subject to the legal authority of the centre.

Voluntary participation   People can choose whether to get involved with politics or not (e.g. by voting or abstaining) and how to get involved (e.g. by joining a party or signing petitions). Voluntary participation is chiefly found in liberal democracies.

Welfare state   A state which takes a prime role in ensuring the provision of a minimum standard of life to all its citizens. The main aspects of 'welfare' are medical care, education, income maintenance, personal social services and housing.

Index

Numbers in **bold** refer to the pages on which a term is defined.